# Studying the Social Worlds of Children

# Studying the Social Worlds of Children: Sociological Readings

*Edited by*

Frances Chaput Waksler

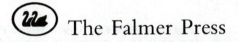 The Falmer Press

(A member of the Taylor & Francis Group)
London · New York · Philadelphia

UK      The Falmer Press, 4 John Street, London, WC1N 2ET
USA     The Falmer Press, Taylor & Francis Inc., 1900 Frost Road, Suite
        101, Bristol, PA 19007

---

First published 1991

**Library of Congress Cataloging-in-Publication Data**
Studying the social worlds of children: sociological readings/
   Frances Chaput Waksler, [editor].
       p.   cm.
     Includes index.
     ISBN 1–85000–910–4: ISBN 1–85000–911–2 (pbk.):
     1. Socialization.   I. Waksler, Frances Chaput.
   HQ783.S73   1991
   305.23'1—dc20                                    90–46268
                                                        CIP

**British Library Cataloguing in Publication Data**
Studying the social worlds of children: sociological
   readings
   1. Children. Social development
   I. Waksler, Frances Chaput
   305.23

   ISBN 1–85000–911–2

Jacket design by Caroline Archer

Typeset in 10/11 pt Bembo by
Graphicraft Typesetters Ltd., Hong Kong

*Printed in Great Britain by Burgess Science Press, Basingstoke
on paper which has a specified pH value on final paper
manufacture of not less than 7.5 and is therefore 'acid free'.*

# Contents

Contents

# Preface

What is a child? How do children differ from adults? How are they similar? What do children know? What do they do? How do they view the world? Are children merely incomplete adults or do they have their own identity and their own culture? Do they have their own rules, both for themselves and for adults? When adults are rearing, caring for, teaching, disciplining, and otherwise acting towards children, what are those children doing and thinking? Are children simply objects in the social world or are they actors as well? All these questions and more emerge as the social worlds of children are explored.

There are many reasons for seeking to understand children and the social worlds they inhabit. Those responsible for child care, teaching, and a range of other child-related activities constantly look for answers to the everyday questions that arise. An extensive body of common-sense knowledge has been developed to guide practical activities involving children. Scientific knowledge has also been developed in answer to practical needs as well as in response to scientific curiosity. Biology has devoted many resources to the study of childhood in a range of life forms. The study of children holds a central place in psychology. Anthropology has considered childhood all over the world. History has studied childhood through time.

The status of the *sociological* study of children, however, is curious. The process of socialization, whereby children become members of adult society, is central to sociological theory. Studies have been done and theories constructed that provide extensive evidence of this process. Children, however, commonly appear as *objects* of this process rather than as *actors* in it. Until recently, socialization has been almost exclusively studied from the perspectives of adults, with little recognition of the possibility that children themselves may have their own — and quite different — perspectives.

When I was asked to develop a sociology course for students preparing for careers working with children, I sought materials that would acquaint students with the kinds of insights about children that can be provided by sociology. Books and articles on the topic of socialization were readily available but those that focused on children and their experiences from any other sociological perspective were far less common and widely scattered. Thus originated the idea for this book. I began to gather sociological materials that would be both insightful and enjoyable and that would provide an understanding of children not available elsewhere. Through the years, I have added and deleted articles, provided commentary to make materials more accessible to those new to sociology, and, intrigued by the many ideas that have arisen in class discussions and written assignments, have written some papers myself.

I have learned a great deal from my students. I have also reinforced my long-standing commitment to the idea that although a legitimate distinction can be made between theory and action, well-constructed and clearly presented theory can be used as a practical guide to everyday action. I have come to see that the study of children is a far more diverse sphere than I had initially thought and that such study can make valuable contributions to understanding adult behavior as well that of children. An examination of children in adults' worlds and in children's worlds provides insights into the social world as a whole.

## Design of the Book

This book was designed for use by those new to sociology. For those familiar with sociology, the articles themselves have much to offer and judicious skimming of introductory materials is recommended. Teachers, teachers of teachers, parents, and those simply interested in the social worlds of children, regardless of sociological background, should find the materials both useful and accessible.

The papers in Part I: Studying Children provide an account of socialization as it is commonly conceived of by sociologists, offer criticisms of socialization as a concept, and detail the wide range of ideas and data that come to light when investigators move beyond socialization to other ways of looking at children. One pariticularly important idea that emerges is that adult views of children and children's views of themselves differ. The recognition of these different perspectives and the sociological suspension of belief that any one perspective is necessarily superior make it possible to see children as inhabiting two worlds: that of adults and that of children.

The papers in Parts II and III grow out of the criticisms and embody the insights of Part I. These papers expand understanding of children's social worlds and exemplify the contributions that are claimed in Part I to emerge from moving 'beyond socialization'. Part II: Children in an Adult World consists of papers that display a range of adult perspectives on children. Rather than criticizing these papers for adopting adult perspectives and neglecting those of children, I recommend reading them as portrayals of adult perspectives while recognizing that other perspectives are possible. Read in this way, they provide rich data about the social worlds that children inhabit, worlds not of their making. A similar approach can be taken towards any article that takes an adult perspective, i.e. it can be read not as the truth but as *one* perspective. This approach makes it possible to learn from works conducted from points of view other than the ones espoused here, accepting their insights without being impeded by their limits. The papers in Part III: Children in a Child's World bring into clear view the richness of the worlds of children and the extensive work that children do to create and sustain their worlds. Read in conjunction with the articles in Part II, they show that adults' views of children and the actual social worlds that children inhabit are quite different. Neither is right or wrong. Both exist.

Appendix I provides a brief introduction to the sociological perspective that guided my selection of articles and that informs my own work. Those new to the field may find it useful to read before proceeding to the book proper. Those familiar with the field may find it a useful articulation of one sociological perspective. Suggestions for exercises to accompany the chapters are provided in Appendix II.

## A Note on Editing and Style

I have always been frustrated by edited materials because they left me wondering what had been left out and why. I have therefore edited as little as possible the materials included here. I have been guided by student responses, shortening articles students found too long and removing materials that were repetitive or were not directly relevant to the task at hand of understanding children in social worlds.

Only two articles were significantly shortened. In its original form, Chapter 1, Becoming a Member of Society — Socialization, contained a number of examples which, while interesting, extended a consideration of socialization beyond what seems necessary for a basic grasp of the concept. Chapter 10, The Culture of Children, is drawn from a detailed compilation of children's games, primarily from Britain. I eliminated a number of the examples and substituted, where possible, examples drawn from the US. For two other articles, Chapter 8, Dancing When the Music is Over, and Chapter 11, Kids, Culture and Innocents, I removed the introductory theoretical material since the general ideas are already presented in Part I. Lastly, for Chapter 12, Children's Negotiation of Meaning, I omitted the Introduction, which provided a review of the literature that is available in the References.

Authors and publishers of the materials included in this book have followed the different stylistic conventions of the United States, Canada, and Britain. Readers will thus find, depending on their own customary usage, a superfluity or dearth of 'u's' (behaviour/behavior) and other apparent oddities (programme/program); US readers will note different conventions for the use of quotation marks. To adopt exclusively the standard of any one country, however, would violate the relativistic spirit within which the book has been written and thus some of these stylistic differences have been retained.

## Acknowledgments

This book is the product of the work of a multitude of students — those who initially suggested that I teach a sociology course about children and those who have enrolled in the course in the years since its development. I cannot name them all individually but recognize the important part each has played in teaching me about children and in making this book possible. I would, however, like to name four students in particular: Erica Cavin, who showed me the kinds of empirical work to which my theoretical ideas could lead; Trisha Brown, whose use of ideas from these materials demonstrated their practical applicability in work with children; Michele Rennie, whose writings disclosed aspects of children's worlds of which I had not been aware; and Laura Kesten, whose enthusiasm encouraged me. I also want to thank all the contributors, not only for their generosity in making their papers available to me but also for their insightful work that led me to select their papers in the first place.

And, lastly, I want to thank all the children whose experiences are chronicled on the pages of this book.

Frances Chaput Waksler
November, 1990

# Studying Children

The five papers in Part I address various ways that children have been and can be studied sociologically. Chapter 1, from Peter and Brigitte Berger's introductory sociology book, presents in clear and thoughtful fashion the sociological concept of *socialization*. This concept has served as the fundamental orienting idea for the sociological study of children. Studies of socialization are certainly worthy of serious attention by anyone interested in understanding the social worlds that children inhabit. Socialization is a particularly useful topic to explore when one's concern is with what adults do when their goal is to prepare children for life in the social worlds of which adults are a part. Whenever adults and children are together or when children are with other children, however, a great deal is going on that is not socialization. An exclusive focus on socialization obscures from view these other activities and processes in which children are involved.

In Chapter 2, I demonstrate some of the limits of the notion of socialization, ways that it distorts lived experiences in the social world and blinds us to other aspects of the social lives of both adults and children. Chapter 3, by Robert Mackay, continues the critique of socialization, providing ample evidence of how much children know that has not been explicitly taught to them by adults. Chapters 4 and 5 provide suggestions for the study of children that respond to the criticisms of socialization as a concept and an exclusive framework within which to study children.

As a whole, Part I establishes socialization as but one process in which children are engaged. It is to other processes, those far less frequently investigated but equally important in understanding the social worlds of children, that the remainder of this book is addressed. In order to understand those other processes, however, it is important to grasp the strengths and limits of the concept of socialization. With this knowledge, reading of the papers in Part II can become a critical endeavor and adult views can be examined as data rather than accepted as necessarily true; adult views and sociological insights are not the same thing. Similarly, the papers in Part III can only exist if the concept of socialization is suspended. The papers in Part I thus require careful attention, for they provide a perspective for reading Part II and make possible the kind of sociological studies chronicled in Part III.

F.C.W.

*Chapter 1*

# Becoming a Member of Society — Socialization

## Peter L. Berger and Brigitte Berger

### Commentary

In their presentation, the Bergers provide a well-balanced description of socialization, a concept that has provided the major framework within which sociologists have studied children. Their treatment of the topic is sufficiently clear to require little introduction. Here I simply highlight some key features of the concept and suggest spheres of possible criticism.

Socialization can be conceived of as a fundamental social process through which 1) individuals becomes social members, i.e. members of specific social groups and of society as a whole, and 2) an individual develops a self. A person can be said to be *socialized* — and thus socialization can be said to most effectively support the status quo — when the self thinks and acts in consonance with what is deemed right by the social group of which it is a part. If, for example, murder is abhorrent to someone who belongs to a group that forbids murder, that person can be said to be well socialized to that group in that respect. If, however, someone craves meat who is a member of a vegetarian group, that person is not well socialized to that group in that respect — even if the person avoids eating meat for fear of punishment.

The socialization process rests on the idea that the self is a social product. People develop selves in interaction with others, creating selves as they simultaneously learn about others. As they learn language and the categories that make up language, they develop ways of viewing the social world that are similar to the ways of others with whom they share that social world. They learn the rules that exist in their social worlds, taking some for granted, questioning others, following some, learning how to break others. Some rules become so much a part of the self that they are unquestionably accepted as true; other rules are followed through fear of punishment; yet other rules are broken, with varying consequences for all those involved.

From *Sociology: A Biographical Approach*, Second, Expanded Edition, by Peter L. Berger and Brigitte Berger. © 1972, 1975 by Peter and Brigitte Berger. Reprinted by permission of Basic Books, Inc., Publishers.

The process of socialization can thus be used to explain how it is possible for people to come to display the kinds of patterned social behavior that they do. In some ways the socialization process is different for every person, and every person emerges from the process different in some respects from every other person. Without denying this difference, sociologists focus on the commonalities, on the ways that all people are alike and the ways that members of a category or group are more like one another than like members of other categories or groups. The concept of socialization is thus used to explain how individuals come to resemble members of their own categories and groups and to differ from others.

Certainly socialization is an important social process and the Bergers' article shows the many ways that it can aid in understanding children's behavior (and adults' behavior as well). Indeed sociologists have learned a great deal about children as they have conducted studies of socialization. For that reason Part I begins with an article on that topic. As will be seen in the remainder of Part I, however, criticisms can be directed to the whole notion of socialization and children can be studied in other frameworks as well.

Readers are advised to approach the Bergers' chapter critically. To facilitate this process, ideas that will be further discussed in Chapter 2 will be set in **bold face type**. The following questions can be raised about the concept of socialization — questions that are addressed in the remainder of Part I:

— Are mothers necessarily the only or major people to socialize children?
— What are children doing when adults are socializing them?
— What power do children, even infants, have in the socialization process?
— What effects do children have on adults? Do children socialize adults?
— What are the criteria for deciding that socialization has/has not taken place?

F.C.W.

## Being an Infant: Non-Social and Social Components

For better or worse, all of us begin by being born. The first condition we experience is the condition of being an infant. When we begin to analyze what this condition entails, we obviously come up against a number of things that have nothing to do with society. First of all, being an infant entails a certain relationship to one's own body. One experiences hunger, pleasure, physical comfort or discomfort and so forth. In the condition of being an infant one is assaulted in numerous ways by the physical environment. One experiences light and darkness, heat and cold; objects of all sorts impinge upon one's attention. One is warmed by the rays of the sun, one is intrigued by the smoothness of a surface or, if one is unlucky, one may be rained upon or bitten by a flea. Being born means to enter into a world with a seemingly infinite richness of experience. A good deal of this experience is not social. Needless to say, an infant at the time does not make such distinctions. It is only in retrospect that it is possible to differentiate the social and the non-social components of his experience. Having made this distinction, however, it is possible to say that the experience of society also begins at birth. The world of the infant is populated by other people. Very soon he is able to distinguish between them, and some of them become of overwhelming significance for him. From the beginning, the infant not only interacts with his own body and with his physical environment, but with other human beings. The biography of the individual, from the moment of birth, is the story of his relations with others.

More than that, the non-social components of the infant's experience are mediated and modified by others, that is, by his social experience. The sensation of hunger in his stomach can only be assuaged by the actions of others. Most of the time, physical comfort or discomfort is brought about by the actions or omissions of others. The object with the pleasurably smooth surface was probably placed within the infant's grasp by somebody. And very likely, if he is rained upon, it is because somebody left him outside without cover. In this way, social experience, while it can be distinguished from other elements in the infant's experience, is not in an isolated category. Almost every aspect of the infant's world involves other human beings. His experience of others is crucial for *all* experience. It is others who create the patterns through which the world is experienced. It is only through these patterns that the organism is able to establish a stable relationship with the outside world — not only the social world but the world of physical environment as well. But these same patterns also penetrate the organism; that is, they interfere with the way it functions. Thus it is others who set the patterns by which the infant's craving for food is satisfied. But in doing so, these others also interfere with the infant's organism itself. The most obvious illustration of this is the timetable of feedings. If the child is fed at certain times, and at certain times only, the organism is forced to adjust to this pattern. In making this adjustment, its functioning changes. What happens in the end is not only that the infant is fed at certain times but that he is hungry at those times. Graphically, society not only imposes its patterns upon the infant's behavior but reaches inside him to organize the functions of his stomach. The same observation pertains to elimination, to sleeping and to other physiological processes that are endemic to the organism. . . .

### Socialization: Relative Patterns Experienced as Absolute

The process through which an individual learns to be a member of society is called *socialization*. . . . [S]ocialization is the imposition of social patterns on behavior. And, as we have tried to show, these patterns even interfere with the physiological processes of the organism. It follows that, in the biography of every individual, socialization, and especially early socialization, is a tremendously powerful and important fact. From the point of view of the outside observer, the patterns that are imposed in socialization are highly relative. . . . They depend not only upon the individual peculiarities of the adults who are in charge of the child but also upon the various social groupings to which these adults belong. Thus, the patterns of a child's behavior depend not only upon whether he is a Gusii [of Kenya] or an

American but also whether he is a middle-class or working-class American. **From the point of view of the child, however, these same patterns are experienced in a very absolute way. Indeed, there are reasons to think that if this were not so, the child would become disturbed and socialization could not proceed.**

The absoluteness with which societies' patterns confront the child is based on two very simple facts — the great power of the adults in the situation, and the ignorance of the child of alternative patterns. Psychologists differ in their view as to whether the child experiences the adults at this stage of life as being very much under his control (because they are generally so responsive to his needs) or whether he feels continually threatened by them (because he is so dependent upon them). However this may be, there can be no question that, objectively speaking, adults have overwhelming power in the situation. **The child can, of course, resist them, but the probable outcome of any conflict is a victory on the part of the adults.** It is they who control most of the rewards that he craves and most of the sanctions that he fears. **Indeed, the simple fact that most children are eventually socialized affords simple proof of this proposition.** At the same time, it is obvious that the small child is ignorant of any alternatives to the patterns that are being imposed upon him. The adults confront him with a world — for him, it is *the* world. It is only much later that he discovers that there are alternatives to this particular world, that his parents' world is relative in space and time, and that quite different patterns are possible. Only then does the individual become aware of the relativity of social patterns and of social worlds — in the extreme case, he might even follow up this insight by becoming a sociologist.

### Initiating a Child: The World Becomes His World

There is, thus, a way of looking at socialization from what one might call the 'policeman's point of view'; that is, socialization can be viewed primarily as the imposition of controls from without, supported by some system of rewards and punishments. There is another, if you will, more benign way of looking at the same phenomenon, namely, one can look upon socialization as a process of initiation in which the child is permitted to develop and expand into a world available to him. In this aspect, socialization is an essential part of the process of becoming fully human and realizing the full potential of the individual. Socialization is a process of initiation into a social world, its forms of interaction and its many meanings. The social world of his parents first confronts the child as an external, vastly powerful and mysterious reality. In the course of socialization, that world becomes comprehensible. The child enters it, becomes capable of participating in it. It becomes *his* world.

### Language, Thinking, Reflection and Talking Back

The primary vehicle of socialization, especially in this second aspect, is language.... [We want to] stress how essential language is for socialization and, indeed, for any continuing participation in a society. It is in acquiring language that a child learns to convey and retain socially recognized meaning. He begins to be able to think abstractly, which means that his mind becomes able to move beyond the immediate situation. It is also through the acquisition of language that the child becomes capable of reflection. Past experience is reflected upon and integrated into a growing, coherent view of reality. Present experience is ongoingly interpreted in terms of this view, and future experience can not only be imagined but planned for. It is through this growing reflection that the child becomes conscious of himself as a self — in the literal sense of re-flection, that is, of the child's attention turning back *from the outside world to himself.*

It is very easy, and, of course, up to a point correct, to think of socialization as a shaping or molding process. Indeed, the child is shaped by society, molded in such a way that he can be a recognized and participant member of it. But it is also important not to see this as a one-sided process. The child, even the very young infant, is not a passive victim of socialization. He resists it, participates in it, collaborates with it in varying degrees. Socialization is a reciprocal process in the sense that not only the socialized but the socializers are affected by it. This can be observed fairly easily in everyday life. **Usually parents succeed to a greater or lesser degree in shaping their children in accordance with the overall patterns established by society and desired by themselves. But the parents also are changed by the experience.** The child's capacity for reciprocity, that is, his capacity to act on his own upon the world and other people inhabiting it increases in direct relation to his capacity to use language. Quite literally, the child then starts to *talk back* to the adults.

In the same vein, it is important to recognize that there are limits to socialization. These limits are given in the child's organism. Given an average intelligence, it is possible to take an infant from any part of the world and socialize him into becoming a member of American society. Any normal child can learn English. Any normal child can learn the values and patterns for living that are attached to the English language in America. Probably every normal child could also learn a system of musical notation. But clearly every normal child could *not* be developed into a musical genius. Unless the potential for this were already given in the organism, any efforts at socialization in this direction would come up against hard and impregnable resistance. The present state of scientific knowledge (especially in the area of human biology) does not permit us to describe the precise limits of socialization. All the same, it is very important to be aware that these limits exist....

### Internalization, Conscience and Self-Discovery

... [O]ne of the terms used to describe socialization, and sometimes used almost interchangeably with it, is that of *internalization.* What is meant by this is that the social world, with its multitude of meanings, becomes internalized in the child's own consciousness. What previously was experienced as something outside himself can now become experienced within himself as well. In a complicated process of reciprocity and reflection, a certain symmetry is established between the inner world of the individual and the outer social world within which he is being socialized. The phenomenon we usually call conscience illustrates this most clearly. Conscience, after all, is essentially the internalization (or, rather, the internalized presence) of moral commands and prohibitions that previously came from the outside. It all began when somewhere in the course of socialization a significant other said, 'Do this', 'Don't do that'. As socialization proceeded, the child identified with these statements of morality. In identifying with them, he internalized them. Somewhere along the line, he said to himself, 'Do this', or 'Don't do that', — probably in much the same manner that his mother or some other significant person first said them to him. Then these statements became silently absorbed into his own mind. The voices have become inner voices. And finally it is the individual's own conscience that is speaking to him.

Once more it is possible to look upon this in different ways. One can look at internalization from what we previously called the 'policeman's point of view', and it will be correct to do so. As the example of conscience clearly illustrates, internalization has something to do with controlling the individual's conduct. It makes it possible for such controls to be continuous and economical. It would be terribly expensive for society, and probably impossible, to constantly surround the individual with other people who will say, 'Do this', and 'don't do that'. When these injunctions have become internalized within the individual's own consciousness, only occasional reinforcements from the outside are necessary. Most of the time, most individuals will control themselves. But this is only one way of looking at the phenomenon. Internalization not only controls the individual but opens up the world for him. Internalization not only allows the individual to participate in the outside social world but it also enables him to have a rich inner life of his own. *Only by internalizing the voices of others can we speak to ourselves. If no one had significantly addressed us from the outside, there would be silence within ourselves as well. It is only through others that we can come to discover ourselves.* Even more specifically it is only through significant others that we can develop a significant relationship to ourselves. This, among other reasons, is why it is so important to choose one's parents with some care.

### 'He's Only a Child' — Biological Growth and Biographical Stages

**There is, of course, a certain parallelism between the biological processes of growth and socialization. If nothing else, the growth of the organism sets limits to socialization.** Thus, it would be futile if a society wanted to teach language to a child one month old or calculus to a child aged two years. However, it would be a great mistake to think that the biographical stages of life, as defined by society, are directly based on the stages of biological growth. This is so with regard to all stages of biography, from birth to death, but it is also true of childhood. There are many different ways of structuring childhood not only in terms of its duration but in terms of its characteristics. It is no doubt possible for the biologist to provide a definition of childhood in terms of the degree of development of the organism; and the psychologist can give a corresponding definition in terms of the development of the mind. Within these biological and psychological limits, however, the sociologist must insist that childhood itself is a matter of social construction. This means that society has great leeway in deciding what childhood is to be.

Childhood, as we understand and know it today, is a creation of the modern world, especially of the bourgeoisie.[1] It is only very recently in Western history that childhood has come to be conceived of as a special and highly protected age. This modern structure of childhood is not only expressed in innumerable beliefs and values regarding children (for example, the notion that children are somehow 'innocent') but also in our legislation. Thus, it is today a just about universal assumption in modern societies that children are not subject to the ordinary provisions of criminal law. It was not so very long ago that children were simply looked upon as little adults. This was very clearly expressed by the manner in which they were dressed. As recently as the eighteenth century, as we can see by looking at paintings from this period, children walked around with their parents dressed in identical fashion — except, of course, in smaller sizes. As childhood came to be understood and organized as a very special phase of life, distinct from adulthood, children began to be dressed in special ways.

A case in point is the modern belief in the 'innocence of children', that is, the belief that children ought to be protected from certain aspects of life. For fascinating comparative reading, we may look at the diary kept by the royal physician during the childhood of Louis XIII of France at the beginning of the seventeenth century.[2] His nanny played with his penis when Louis was less than one year old. Everyone thought that this was great fun. Soon afterward, the little prince made a point of always exhibiting his penis amid general merriment. He also asked everyone to kiss it. This ribald attention to the child's genital parts continued for several years and involved not only frivolous maids and the like but also his mother, the Queen. At the age of four the Prince was taken to his mother's bed by a lady of the court and told, 'Monsieur, this is where you were made.' Only after he reached about seven years of age did the notion arise that he ought to have a certain degree of modesty about this part of his body. One may add that Louis XIII was married at the age of fourteen, by which time, as one commentator remarks wryly, he had nothing left to learn....

### Appropriating an Identity: Being Assigned or Subscribing

The socialized part of the self is commonly called *identity*.[3] Every society may be viewed as holding a repertoire of identities — little boy, little girl, father, mother, policeman, professor, thief, archbishop, general and so forth. By a kind of invisible lottery, these identities are assigned to different individuals. Some of them are assigned from birth, such as little boy or little girl. Others are assigned later in life, such as clever little boy or pretty little girl (or, conversely, stupid little boy or ugly little girl). Other identities are put up, as it were, for subscription, and individuals may obtain them by deliberate effort, such as policeman or archbishop. But whether an identity is assigned or achieved, in each case it is appropriated by the individual through a process of interaction with others. It is others who identify him in a specific way. Only if an identity is confirmed by others is it possible for that identity to be real to the individual holding it. In other words, identity is the product of an interplay of identification and self-identification. This is even true of identities that are deliberately constructed by an individual.

For example, there are individuals in our society who are identified as male who would prefer to be female. They may do any number of things, all the way to surgery, in order to reconstruct themselves in terms of the desired new identity. The essential goal which they must achieve, however, is to get at least some others to accept that new identity, that is, to identify them in these terms. It is impossible to be anything or anybody for very long all by oneself. Others have to tell us who we are, others have to confirm our identity. There are, indeed, cases where individuals hold on to an identity that no one else in the world recognizes as real. We call such individuals psychotics. They are marginal cases of great interest, but their analysis cannot concern us here. . . .

## Secondary Socialization: Entering New Worlds

In talking about education, we have already implied that socialization does not come to an end at the point where an individual child becomes a full participant in society. Indeed, one may say that socialization never comes to an end. In a normal biography, what happens simply is that the intensity and scope of socialization diminish after early childhood. Sociologists distinguish between *primary* and *secondary* socialization. By primary socialization is meant the original process by which a child becomes a participant member of a society. By secondary socialization are meant all later processes by which an individual is inducted into a specific social world. For example, every training in an occupation involves processes of secondary socialization. In some cases, these processes are relatively superficial. For example, no profound changes in the identity of an individual are required to train him to be a certified public accountant. This is not the case, however, if an individual is to be trained to be a priest or to be a professional revolutionary. There are instances of secondary socialization of this kind that resemble in intensity what goes on in the socialization of early childhood. Secondary socialization is also involved in such widely different experiences as improving one's general social position, changing one's place of residence, adapting to a chronic illness or being accepted by a new circle of friends.

## Relations to Individuals and the Social Universe

All processes of socialization take place in face-to-face interaction with other people. In other words, socialization always involves changes in the micro-world* of the individual. At the same time, most processes of socialization, both primary and secondary, relate the individual to complex structures of the macro-world. The attitudes which the individual learns in socialization usually refer to broad systems of meaning and of values that extend far beyond his immediate situation. For example, habits of neatness and cleanliness are not only eccentric notions of a particular set of parents but are values of great importance in a broad middle-class world. Similarly, roles learned in socialization refer to vast institutions that may not be readily visible within the individual's micro-world. Thus, learning the role of being a brave little boy is not only conducive to approval by one's parents and playmates but will have significance to the individual as he makes his career in a much broader world of institutions, ranging from the college football field to the military. Socialization links micro-world and macro-world. First, socialization enables the individual to relate to specific individual others; subsequently, it enables him to relate to an entire social universe. For better or for worse, being human entails having such a relationship on a lifelong basis.

## Notes

1  Philippe Aries, *Centuries of Childhood* (New York, Knopf, 1962).
2  Aries, *ibid.*, pp. 100ff.
3  It is not quite clear who first used the concept of identity in this sense. Its popularity in recent years is largely due to the work of Erik Erikson, who may be described as a sociologically inclined psychoanalyst. See his *Childhood and Society* (New York, Norton, 1950).

---

* The term *micro-world* refers to that part of the social world within an individual's immediate grasp — that world which is directly available to the senses. It includes friends, neighbors, and acquaintances, living situations, household arrangements, and other immediate features of the social world. The term *macro-world* refers to that part of the social world that seems to lie outside of the individual and may be perceived as existing 'out there', beyond an individual's control or influence. It includes laws, governments, religion, and other aspects of the social world that appear massive and beyond one's grasp. It is important to note, however, that the macro-world is itself composed of micro-worlds — laws are hammered out through social interactions among individuals, government officials meet together face to face, and religious experiences take place on the individual level. (Waksler)

## Chapter 2

# Beyond Socialization

*Frances Chaput Waksler*

### Introduction

The purpose of this chapter is to set forth some major criticisms that can be made of the concept of socialization as it is formulated and used by sociologists. To identify problems is not necessarily to provide resolutions, but clearly it is a fundamental step in that process.

The Bergers' description of socialization was chosen for inclusion as Chapter 1 and for criticism in this chapter because theirs is a particularly sophisticated introductory treatment. While they avoid the pitfalls inherent in overly simplified presentations, the very clarity of their work sets in relief problematic aspects of the concept of socialization. Such problems characterize virtually all introductory treatments (see, for example, Robertson, 1989 and Vander Zanden, 1990). In this chapter, the specific criticisms to be put forth center around two general features of socialization: the concept itself and its range.

#### The Concept Itself

Is socialization the name for an identifiable and documentable process whose existence is subject to proof or refutation, or is it rather the name for an assumption made to organize a wide range of activities? Either can prove useful to understanding but they are in no sense interchangeable. What follows is not dependent upon either answer to the question posed, though the ideas presented lead towards the conclusion that the concept of socialization names an assumption rather than an empirically verifiable process. (In Chapter 3, Mackay argues that the concept as it is currently constituted is not a sociological concept at all but merely an everyday adult view of children.)

#### The Range of the Concept

In the sociological literature, studies of socialization have focused extensively on children and the study of children has been conducted primarily in terms of socialization. As a consequence, socialization of children and of adults have been conceived of as different rather than similar processes, as evidenced, for example, in the distinction between initial and secondary socialization. Children's activities unrelated to socialization have been, until quite recently, minimally investigated by sociologists. The range of the concept of socialization can thus be said to be both too narrow (when it focuses only on children) and too broad (when it serves as the major way to understand children).

In what follows I first discuss an important distinction sociologists make between initial and secondary socialization, a topic touched upon in the previous chapter. This distinction assumes the existence of clear differences between adults and children and obscures similarities. Next I consider Dennis Wrong's classic criticism of socialization. Then I provide some further criticisms of the concept and locate the source of many of the problems in adult taken-for-granted assumptions. Lastly, I suggest some ways that the concept of socialization might be modified and the advantages to be gained from moving beyond the concept altogether.

## Initial and Secondary Socialization

Face-to-face interaction is the fundamental setting for socialization. When individuals are together, sharing time and space, able to see and hear and feel the actions of each as responses to the actions of the other, a very special situation occurs for learning about others, one's self, and one's impact on the world. Socialization can take place in a variety of settings, but face-to-face interaction, as the prototypical social experience (Berger and Luckmann, 1966), is the key one.

Sociologists identify two different kinds of socialization: initial (or primary) and secondary. Initial socialization refers to those processes that take place *first* — learning one's first language, discovering one's first 'others', encountering one's first rules. Two characteristics of initial socialization are particularly crucial for the unfolding of the process: 1) The agent of socialization (the person carrying out the process) has power over the person being socialized. In the extreme, this power can be that over life and death. Although this claim may sound a bit strong, in fact adults have such power over infants, as the extensive evidence on child abuse makes clear. That adults do not routinely make full use of their power does not eliminate it; social limits on that power can be overcome. Exactly how children perceive the power of adults is unknown but there is no reason for assuming that they are unaware of it. 2) The person being socialized has no prior experience of that being inculcated. Compare the difference between learning one's first language and learning a second. In learning a second, one can translate into terms of the first, use the first as a basis, etc. One's first language is learned in a sense through faith — faith that what others are teaching has meaning, is worth trying, and/or somehow works.

Secondary socialization differs in one very basic respect from initial socialization: it comes *after* initial socialization. Those undergoing secondary socialization have already been socialized and thus may be either more receptive or more defensive towards the new ideas and actions to which they are being socialized. To be born into a religion and practice it throughout one's life is very different from converting from one religion to another; in the latter process, one has both more choice (e.g. the very choice of converting or abandoning the endeavor) and more limits (e.g. the difficulty or even impossibility of coming to believe something that one had previously thought unbelievable). Secondary socialization is most successful in bringing about fundamental changes in people when the conditions under which it occurs most closely approximate those of childhood, i.e. when the one being socialized is dependent on the agents of socialization, has significantly less power than they, and has little access to outsiders. To illustrate secondary socialization when it adopts some of the fundamental features of initial socialization, sociologists commonly offer the examples of the novitiate/ seminary and of basic training in the military sphere. Typically, however, secondary socialization is less extensive and more congruent with earlier socialization.

Sociological studies of children tend to focus on initial (primary) socialization, routinely assuming that children come into the world 'empty', to be filled with the social ideas of the groups into which they are born. Even those who articulate objections to such an assumption may implicitly use it nonetheless. Sociological studies have explored both of the earlier-mentioned aspects of socialization — becoming a group member and developing a self — by focusing on who gets socialized by whom to what with what outcomes. What is neglected in such an approach, by being assumed as non-problematic, is *what the one being socialized is doing at the time* — both with reference to the socialization process and to other projects that person has in mind. By slapping a child when that child tries to touch a hot stove, one may indeed *socialize* that child to keep away from that stove and even stoves in general, but 1) the child may not have planned to touch the stove but simply see how close one could get, already 'knowing' not to touch it and 2) the child's activities, whatever they are, are aborted.

Two fundamental criticisms can be addressed to the concept of socialization at this point. First, the concept of initial socialization in particular assumes that children are 'empty buckets' who readily contain whatever is poured into them. If, however, there is something already in the bucket (e.g. children's own experiences), the resulting contents are of necessity different from that which was poured in. In such cases, what has been studied as initial socialization may in fact be an outcome of secondary socialization. Second, the concept assumes the existence of an agent of socialization and an object of socialization and thus a one-way process that neglects the reciprocity that is the very heart of sociology's subject matter. (Indeed the Bergers do refer to this reciprocity, but nonetheless they focus on the child and offer no examples of children affecting adults.)

## 'The Oversocialized Conception of Man'

Dennis H. Wrong, in an article entitled 'The Oversocialized Conception of Man in Modern Sociology' (1961), provides what has come to be viewed as a classic critique of the concept of socialization. Even though his objections have been widely accepted, they have not led to sufficient modification of the concept to render his criticisms obsolete.

In his article Wrong argues that overuse and overextension of the concept of socialization has obscured that which it has claimed to study. He begins by considering one of the central questions of sociological inquiry: How is it possible that people follow social rules? One common sociological answer is: Because they are socialized to do so. Wrong finds this answer unsatisfactory, for it suggests that rule-following automatically follows socialization, that once socialized one has no choice but to follow those rules to which one was socialized, and thus that the question itself is trivial. If, as Wrong argues, the question is an important one, then any answer that trivializes it is suspect. In everyday conversation, it is not uncommon to explain why one has done something by claiming: 'That is how I learned to do it' or 'That is how I was brought up.' The insufficiency of such explanations can be demonstrated by posing the questions: Do you do everything as you learned to do it? Do you do everything that you were brought up to do? More accurate and fruitful as an empirical questions is: Of those things one has learned to do/been brought up to do, which does one adopt and which does one not? This question keeps alive the question: How is it possible that humans follow social rules? for it keeps it a question in search of an answer rather than setting it as a question with the automatic answer, socialization.

Wrong claims that the very significance of this and other fundamental questions in sociology is that they may never be answered definitively and for all times because of their complexity, but, nonetheless, their very existence serves as a basis for continued exploration and thought. New sociological studies continually make possible reconsideration of answers to these central questions, but any facile and definitive answers are suspect, for they obscure the essentially problematic nature of the questions themselves.

Although he does not criticize the concept of socialization in itself, Wrong does fault the way it has been used by sociologists. Without denying that human beings are socialized or that they internalize social norms, he argues that socialization cannot explain all human behavior, or even all rule-following behavior. He offers objections to the 'empty bucket' theory of human nature, the idea that people are born without any social or personal ideas and that through the socialization process this empty bucket is filled with the ideas of the social groups in which socialization takes place. The view he criticizes is called *social determinism*, for it claims that individual behavior is determined by the social world. In everyday talk it is exemplified in the statement made to explain one's behavior: 'Society made me do it.' Such a view in its extreme form rejects the possibility of independent human action and choice.

In everyday life it may be common to see the behavior of others as socially determined, but seldom does one apply such a notion to one's own behavior, except perhaps as a justification to others. When one seeks explanation for one's own behavior, the idea that something lying outside made one act in a particular way is more likely to be viewed as an attempt to avoid responsibility for one's acts. If indeed it is true that social determinism is found wanting when applied to one's own behavior and only plausible when applied to the behavior of others, then the theory itself should be viewed with suspicion, for it fails to explain one's own experiences, those with which one is most familiar. If any theory fails to explain one's own experiences, it may be that it explains nobody's experiences. Any theory that creates a division beween the theorist and those theorized about and that can only explain the latter contains some basic flaw.

Wrong argues that the process of internalization is not nearly as inevitable or as unproblematic as some sociologists take it to be. Indeed social ideas do become a part of the individual through internalization, but such a process is always incomplete and tentative. A focus on internalization also ignores other forces in the social world that encourage rule-following behavior. People certainly do follow rules they have internalized, but they are not compelled to do so for one indeed may violate rules in which one believes. And people also follow rules they have not internalized, as when they engage in or forgo behavior in order to avoid punishment. In studies of social control, sociologists certainly recognize that the existence of punishment can inhibit occurrences of behavior in which people might otherwise engage, but discussions of socialization customarily minimize this aspect of rule-following.

While recognizing the two different aspects of socialization — creation of group members and creation of the self — Wrong emphasizes that these two processes are not identical and in any given instance may be *either* antithetical or sympathetic. Sociologists have focused on the sympathetic dimension of this process — what's good for the group is good for the individual; Freud (see especially *Civilization and Its Discontents*, 1930) focused on the antithetical dimension, the sacrifices the group requires of the self. Wrong urges a more balanced view which, while more ambiguous and complex, is more reflective of the social worlds in which we live and act.

## Further Criticisms

Against the background of the concepts of initial and secondary socialization and Wrong's criticisms, we can now consider specific objections that can be made to the concept of socialization. The Bergers' presentation in the foregoing chapter is by no means the naive approach to the topic Wrong faults; indeed it displays many insights. Nonetheless, their rendition of the socialization process includes a number of commonly made claims that can be viewed as problematic. The objections that can be made to their presentation are even more applicable to less clear and sophisticated formulations.

The Bergers* retain the notions of children as 'empty buckets' and the agents of socialization as routinely successful in their endeavors. They claim that children *as a matter of course* accept the patterns that surround them as the

---

* In this discussion, particular attention is focused on those passages in the Bergers's article that were printed in bold type.

only possible patterns, for those patterns 'are experienced in a very absolute way' (Berger and Berger, p. 6). Although examples can be offered in abundance to show that children do experience their own ways in absolute terms, as *the only ways* — the author was reprimanded by a 3-year-old for making a peanut butter and jelly sandwich 'the wrong way', putting the peanut butter on one slice of bread and the jelly on another rather than putting the jelly *on* the peanut butter — the issue to be raised here is not: Can children experience the world in absolute terms? for indeed they can, but: Must they do so? Over-dependence on the notion of socialization impedes the very asking of such a question.

Evidence also exists, however, that children do experience at least some aspects of their world in their own terms and in contrast to others' views, providing children with at least the possibility of relativism. Food preferences may serve as one example, for the youngest of children may display likes and dislikes that defy adult efforts at modification and that those children maintain into adulthood, when they have more power to carry through on their own preferences. One might argue that food preferences can be biologically based; other examples, however, can be offered. Children who 'always wanted a pet' may resist all adult efforts to eradicate the idea and may find in adulthood that they both enjoy having a pet and feel they would have done so in childhood. Children's conceptions of the aesthetic and practical qualities of insects can be quite at odds with the views of those with whom they associate; where then do their ideas come from? (To suggest that ideas come from peers simply pushes the problem back a step. Where did peers get their ideas?) In a more general sense, children may perceive a diffuse sense of a gap or a 'wrong' in their lives. That they do not have the power to implement their alternative views and that adults can deny that there is any gap or 'wrong' does not mean that children accept the world around them in absolute terms; it only means that they appear to do so.

The assumption that agents of socialization are routinely successful in their endeavors is captured in the Bergers' statement that 'the probable outcome of any conflict [between child and adult] is a victory on the part of the adults' (Berger and Berger, p. 6). Rather than making assumptions about the results of any such conflicts, it would be more scientific to take such outcomes as problematic. What constitutes victory, what defeat? For whom is a midnight feeding a victory? When the outcome of adult/child conflicts is viewed as problematic, it becomes possible to consider, for instance, the power resources that children have available to them, resources that may make it possible for them to achieve victories. Children's resources may differ from those available to adults but they are not thereby either negligible or ineffective. Adult power over children ultimately rests on the fact that they have control over children's life and death; conversely, children have the power to die — power that failure-to-thrive children might be said to display. The results of attempts to bottle-feed a child accustomed to the breast are not so certain as the Bergers' claim would suggest.

What are the criteria for judging the success of socialization? One such criterion might be parental claims of their own success: 'My children turned out just the way I wanted them to.' Such claims are so rare that they can hardly be put forward as self-evident proof that socialization is routinely successful. In the absence of criteria for judging the success of socialization, any such claims appear more a matter of faith than evidence. Empirical study of the success and failure of various socialization endeavors would seem necessary before any scientific claims could be made.

Although it might seem that knowledge drawn from the natural sciences could inform the notion of socialization, rendering it more scientific, in fact the natural sciences themselves are not immune to the social context in which they develop. Medical statements, to all appearances scientific, are made about children's 'needs'. Such apparently absolute claims, however, routinely embody, albeit implicitly, conditional claims: these needs must be fulfilled *if one is to emerge a human being of the kind recognizable in the biologist's society* and *if one is to avoid certain outcomes judged as negative in that society.* Children need three balanced meals a day only *if they are to have access to the health advantages deemed important in a given society.* But not all societies structure food consumption around three meals — some have fewer, some more — and what is viewed as an avoidable nutritional or medical problem in one society can be viewed, in another society, as unavoidable or even 'normal'. In the not too distant past in the US, it was normal for a woman to lose at least some of the children she bore to childhood diseases — so normal that the answer to the question 'How many children do you have?' could routinely be 'Seven living'.

Statements drawn from the natural sciences about children's abilities and inabilities may well serve as blinders, preventing the recognition of what children can do, especially those children who do that which science tends to assume they cannot. Child prodigies — 6-year-old mathematicians and virtuoso violinists — are taken to be exceptional. Would there be more child prodigies if they were seen as normal? There are societies where 3-, 4-, and 5-year-olds live almost entirely without adult supervision, where 13-year-old females routinely bear and rear children, and where young children themselves have the care and responsibility of those younger. Whether or not such practices are desirable is a moral issue that has no relevance for whether or not the practices are possible, as indeed they are. That people in the US do not socialize children to be mothers at age 13 obviously does not mean that they cannot *be* mothers. To see negative implications of such practices and to choose to avoid them does not drive them out of existence as possibilities.

Many of the criticisms that can be directed to the concept of socialization have in common their source in sociologists' failures to explore their taken-for-granted assumptions about their own social worlds and in particular about children in those social worlds. In Chapter 5 I describe some of the assumptions that adults make about children that, when made by sociologists, can distort the data they collect. In the next section I detail three notable and consequential assumptions that are embedded in socialization as it is used conceptually by sociologists.

### Taken-for-granted Assumptions

The sociological literature on socialization embodies two assumptions, seldom investigated or even recognized, that are embodied in the following two renditions of the same sentence:

*Parents* routinely socialize their children.
Parents routinely *socialize* their children.

With respect to the first formulation, indeed it does happen throughout the world that the biological parents of children rear those children. And it also happens that children are reared primarily by others: step-parents, adoptive parents, foster parents, one parent (and the usage of the term *parent* in all these terms should not delude us into thinking those to whom the term is applied are interchangeable and the same), siblings, other relatives, friends, affiliates of social service and charitable agencies, nannies and nursemaids, day care workers, and so on. The assumption in the sociological literature, however, is that parents or those acting like parents (whatever that might entail) are the primary agents of socialization. (See both Robertson, 1989 and Vander Zanden, 1990 for discussions of the family as the major agent of initial socialization.) Support for the assumption that sociologists have made about the primacy of parents, however, is provided far more by the ideological status of the family in the US and in the West in general than by the data. A fresh look at arrangements throughout the world and a genuine asking of the question 'Who socializes children?' would seem to be in order.

The claim that parents routinely socialize their children can be read in a second way, emphasizing not *parents* but the term *socialize*. Such a reading brings to light a second unexamined assumption, namely that parents routinely socialize their children. The first issue to raise here is: How is 'socializing children' to be distinguished from the other activities that adults direct towards children? Could one, for example, reasonably ask on a questionnaire: How much time per day do you spend socializing your children? If socialization is viewed as an intentional activity engaged in by an agent of socialization, perhaps the questionnaire question could be answered. If, on the other hand, socialization is viewed as the outcome of myriad activities, intentional and unintentional, successful and unsuccessful, measured only by manifestations in adult behavior, and if socialization is so inextricably linked to child-rearing in general, how can it be studied sociologically as an independent phenomenon?

Although it is certainly the case in the US, for instance, that the task of socializing children is ideologically and legally assigned to the parents of those children, it does not follow that those parents always and necessarily do socialize their children. Indeed such an inference is contradicted by ample evidence of parents who neglect their children (in the sense of ignoring them), whose acts towards children are directed largely to controlling them (in the sense of preventing them from being a disruption to adult activities), or whose notion of socializing children departs radically from the social norms (as can been seen in the regularly appearing stories in sensational newspapers of children caged, chained, etc. 'for their own good'). That children learn from their experiences is indisputable, but the application of the term socialization to the above examples appears to be a distortion of either the concept or the experiences or both. Can children who have the kinds of experiences described in this paragraph be said to be socialized? If so, by whom? And to what?

In descriptions of socialization, adults are likely to appear as deity-like figures, solely concerned with the welfare of their charges and subsuming their own needs to those of children. Adults appear as kindly, loving, both motivated to socialize children to the broader society and equal to that task. Such a glowing picture has far more in common with an ideological than a scientific formulation. Interestingly enough, when examples are provided of children who have been isolated from human contact, caged, chained, etc., attention centers on what can be learned about the importance of socialization for children. Such examples can also be, though seldom are, read as challenges to the view that all adults actively and competently socialize their children.

Yet a third taken-for-granted assumption underlying socialization is that there is only one available social group — commonly termed 'society' — to which one can be socialized. While the sociological literature on deviance does address the issue of groups competing to socialize individuals, e.g. the family and the gang, such competition is not routinely addressed in theoretical presentations of the concept of socialization. When it is addressed, it tends to be as an explanation of some particular discrepancy — a 'good' child from a 'bad' home, a 'bad' child from a 'good' home — rather than as a general feature of the socialization process. An assumption of social homogeneity obscures consideration of the groups that might compete for individuals, but once such competition is recognized as a possibility, it can be sought in such situations as disagreements in child-rearing between spouses, between parents and teachers (see, for example, Goode with Waksler, 1990), between church and state, and between and among any competing groups which in some sense have access to the same individual.

Taken-for-granted assumptions embodied in the idea that parents socialize children obscure from view the many situations where socialization is done by others and where parents' activities directed towards children are either occasionally or primarily oriented to goals other than socialization. The assumption that there is only one group — society — to which one is socialized obscures from view alternative groups, groups that may well vie with one another for members/followers.

## Socialization and Beyond

In the foregoing I have presented some fundamental criticisms of the notion of socialization. Pervading the presentation is the idea that socialization as it is generally employed by sociologists obscures from view significant aspects of children's and adults' social behavior. Refinement of the concept by setting as problematic aspects heretofore taken for granted as true could make some of these aspects available for study. In reconceptualizing socialization I would recommend directing particular attention to the following kinds of questions:

1   Is socialization the name for an identifiable and documentable process or is it the name for an assumption made to organize a wide range of activities?
2   In what respects are the socialization of children and adults (both initial and secondary) different processes and in what respects are they similar?
3   When socialization is taking place, what is the one being socialized doing at the time — both with reference to the socialization process and to other projects that person has in mind?
4   Are children empty buckets who readily contain what is poured into them? If not, and I suspect that there is general sociological agreement that they are not, what do they contain and what are the implications of these contents for socialization?
5   Is socialization best understood as a one-way process between an agent of socialization and an object of socialization or is it better conceived of as a reciprocal relationship with each influencing the other?
6   Are agents of socialization routinely successful in their endeavors? What are the criteria for judging the success of socialization? Setting as problematic the outcomes of socialization would seem to be a more scientific approach than making assumptions about those outcomes.
7   *Who* routinely socializes children? How, specifically, do they go about it? Taking these to be empirical questions rather than rhetorical ones would seem fruitful.
8   Of the many activities that adults and children participate in together, which ones can be identified as socialization? Which ones cannot?
9   Is there only one group (society) to which children are socialized or are there alternative groups, groups which may well vie with one another for members/followers? If there is competition and conflict, documentation would seem to be in order.
10  How can socialization best be studied to preserve the integrity of the fundamental sociological questions (e.g. those identified by Wrong)?

Even if the concept of socialization were modified to take into account the questions posed above, it could never encompass the entirety of children's experiences, for children do more than 'get socialized'. To expect any single concept to have such range and such explanatory power is in all likelihood unreasonable. Just as the concept of *family* does not explain all of the experiences of family members, and just as the concept of *deviance* omits the non-deviant aspects of those labeled deviant, the concept of socialization omits aspects of children's behavior (and of adults' behavior as well). In particular it leaves out both what children are doing when others are socializing them, and when others are not. It neglects the worlds that children design by themselves for themselves. It fails to examine children's ideas and activities as their ways of being in the world. Furthermore, these omissions are not shortcomings of the concept itself and cannot be rectified by modifying the concept; they are a necessary consequence of the fact that socialization is only one way of looking at children.

Thus I recommend moving *beyond socialization* to consider other ways of looking at children's lives. No systematic theoretical guidelines are readily available in the sociological literature, but some guidelines are explicit in the work of a number of sociologists. Two major approachers can be inferred from that work: 1) to consider studies conducted from an adult perspective not as findings about children but as data on how adults can view children and thus on the adult worlds in which children live (a perspective I have labeled 'children in an adult world') and 2) to conduct studies from children's perspectives (a perspective I refer to as 'children in a child's world'). The selections in Parts II and III of this book provide examples of both of these perspectives and thus of what can be learned about children by going beyond socialization.

### Endnote

In this chapter I have raised criticisms about the ways that sociologists have studied children and indicated alternative approaches. Before considering data from those alternative perspectives, however, it will be helpful to learn what other sociological critics have to recommend. In Chapter 3 Mackay, drawing on data gathered in a classroom setting, shows the complexity and subtlety of the knowledge children need to possess simply to carry out classroom tasks, features that are obscured when one limits oneself to an adult perspective. In Chapter 4 Mandell shows some of the practical problems that arose when, studying children in a day care center, she focused on their perspectives and took them seriously as actors in social worlds. In Chapter 5 I detail some of the taken-for-granted assumptions that adults make about children, assumptions that impede understanding children in their own terms. Although the three remaining chapters in Part I raise a number of theoretical issues, they also provide abundant data about children's worlds and lives so that as readers gain theoretical insights, they can apply those insights to data as well as to the experiences and examples they are able to generate themselves.

*Chapter 3*

# Conceptions of Children and Models of Socialization

*Robert W. Mackay*

**Commentary**

In this article Mackay provides a new perspective for looking at children, based on recognition of an adult perspective as one way rather than the only way to do so. He begins by offering fundamental criticism of the concept of socialization, casting doubt on its very validity. He suggests that 'socialization' is an adult formulation or creation based on the taken-for-granted assumption that adults are knowledgeable and competent actors in the social world while children are incomplete, incompetent, and lack knowledge. He argues that by focusing on socialization, researchers and theorists have failed to notice the rich and varied interactions that take place between adults and children as equally social beings. Similar criticisms might also be directed to the more psychological formulations of child development, which tend to embody an implicit notion of adult superiority.

Mackay's article is intellectually very radical, with some perhaps disturbing practical implications. He is suggesting that children can be viewed as fully social beings, capable of acting in the social world and of creating and sustaining their own culture (a point that is documented by Iona and Peter Opie in Chapter 10). He does not suggest that children must be viewed only in their own terms. He does, however, provide an option to the common-sense assumption, embodied seemingly without investigation into sociological and social science thought, that children are only 'incomplete' adults and that adulthood is the goal of childhood. This new option is exemplified in the set of readings provided in this book, Part II considering children from an adult perspective while Part III takes the perspective of children themselves.

The previously published version of this article included an Appendix in which is presented a conversation between a teacher and a student about the story of 'Chicken Little'. I have set this conversation at the beginning of the article so that readers can compare their initial impressions of it — perhaps

From H.P. Dreitzel (ed.), (1973) *Recent Sociology*, No. 5, Macmillan, pp. 27–43 and revised by the author for R. Turner (Ed.), (1974) *Ethnomethodology*, Penguin, pp. 180–193. Reprinted by permission of the author.

that it is just 'ordinary talk', 'nothing special', etc. — with those they have after they have the benefit of Mackay's insights. Those unaccustomed to reading transcriptions of talk may be surprised at just how ungrammatical it can be. Each utterance is numbered — for example, Teacher 5, Tom 7 — for easier reference.

F.C.W.

### Transcript of Interview (from Appendix)

During the interview the teacher is seated at her desk looking sideways into the camera, the boy is standing beside her between her and the camera. The sentences to be sequenced are in front of him on her desk.

| | |
|---|---|
| Teacher 1 | Pick out the ones that should come first. Which one would come first in the story? Why did you choose that? |
| Tom 1 | Because that's the first one. |
| Teacher 2 | Why is it the first one? |
| Tom 2 | Whack something fell on Chicken Little's ... head I guess. |
| Teacher 3 | Umhum. When you read the story in the book was that the very first sentence? Was it exactly like that in the book? |
| Tom 3 | No. |
| Teacher 4 | No but this does tell what happened first. Find the sentence which would tell what happens next. |
| Teacher 5 | Why did you choose that one? |
| Tom 4 | Because I guess that's was what happened (next). |
| Teacher 6 | What, who was the first animal in the story? |
| Tom 5 | Chicken Little. |
| Teacher 7 | And the next? |
| Tom 6 | Henny Penny. |
| Teacher 8 | And who came next? |
| Tom 7 | Goosey Loosey. |
| Teacher 9 | No, not quite, somebody else came after Henny Penny, some |
| Tom 8 | Cocky Locky. |
| Teacher 10 | Cocky Locky. And then? |
| Tom 9 | Henny. |
| Teacher 11 | Goosey Poosey. And then, then what? |
| Tom 10 | Turkey Lurkey. |
| Teacher 12 | Ya in the flannel board who came story who came last? |
| Tom 11 | Foxy Loxy. |
| Teacher 13 | Who was not in the book that was in the flannel board story? |
| Tom 12 | Foxy Loxy. |
| Teacher 14 | Alright, good, alright see if you can find the sentence |

|  | then that tells best what happened after Henny Penny went with Chicken Little. |
|---|---|
| Teacher 15 | Why didn't you choose this one it's got Henny Penny and Chicken Little in it. |
| Tom 13 | Ah. Umm. Henny Penny. Cocky Locky and Chicken Little. Cocky Locky and Goosey Poosey he he isn't here yet. |
| Teacher 16 | That's right. |
| Tom 14 | Here Goosey Poosey, here boy. |
| Teacher 17 | That's fine Tom, just tell me quietly please you don't have to act it out right now. There are times for acting but this is not one of them, 'k. |
| Tom 15 | They all met Goosey Poosey. |
| Teacher 18 | Alright. Why did you choose that 'Four animals met Turkey Lurkey' next? |
| Tom 16 | Because he's the last one they ( ) met. |
| Teacher 19 | How do you know he's ... all the other animals like Henny Penny and Cocky Locky are there it doesn't give their names? |
| Tom 17 | Because ... |
| Teacher 20 | What does it say? |
| Tom 18 | 'The four animals met Turkey Lurkey.' There wasn't four animals. |
| Teacher 21 | Weren't there? |
| Tom 19 | One. |
| Teacher 22 | Right. |
| Tom 20 | Right. |
| Teacher 23 | Henny Penny is. |
| Tom 21 | One. |
| Teacher 24 | Cocky Locky ⎰is |
| Tom 22 | ⎱two |
| Teacher 25 | Two. |
| Tom 23 | Three ... four. |
| Teacher 26 | See there you are forgetting about Chicken Little he has met three people but Chicken Little's there too so that makes an extra one ( ). Alright what comes next? The animals have seen Turkey Lurkey what would come next? |
| Teacher 27 | Craig would you please take your seat. |
| Teacher 28 | Why did you choose that. Will you read it to me please. |
| Tom 24 | Turkey Lurkey saw a nut under a big tree. |
| Teacher 29 | Why did you choose that ⎰instead of |
| Tom 25 | ⎱because |
| Teacher 30 | That one. |
| Tom 26 | Because the the sky is not falling. He can't say it because he doesn't know it yet. |
| Teacher 31 | Umm. Did Turkey Lurkey know all the time that it |

|  | was a nut that fell on his head — that fell on ah Chicken Little's tail?* |
|---|---|
| Tom 27 | I guess so, I don't know. |
| Teacher 32 | Humm this is interesting. What did it say in the story that Chicken Little ah where the nut fell on Chicken Little? |
| Tom 28 | At the tree. |
| Teacher 33 | Umhum what part of his body did it land on did it say? |
| Tom 29 | Tail. |
| Teacher 34 | Read the first sentence. |
| Tom 30 | Whunk. |
| Teacher 35 | Whack. |
| Tom 31 | Whack something fell on Chicken Little's head ( ) |
| Teacher 36 | Did you notice that when you were putting the sentences together? |
| Tom 32 | Ya, but I always thought. |
| Teacher 37 | In some stories it does fall on his head so it didn't bother you did it that it said head? |
| Teacher 38 | Have you ever heard a story where it fell on Chicken Little's head ... instead of his tail. |
| Tom 33 | Ya. |
| Teacher 39 | Umhum, so you understood the story and it didn't matter about that word did it because the idea was that it fell on Chicken Little and it was really a nut instead of ah a piece of the sky. Thank you very much Tom. |

### Note on Mackay's Introduction

Those new to sociology might find Mackay's Introduction somewhat difficult. Trying to talk about that which is customarily taken for granted may require somewhat awkward and convoluted language if the taken-for-granted is to be brought to light. In the following paragraphs I provide elaboration of the key terms he uses in his Introduction.

*Norms* are expectations for behavior; *normative rules* prescribe how to act. Cicourel, to whom Mackay refers, identifies two kinds of rules that guide social behavior: *normative* and *basic*. Basic rules underlie normative ones and are customarily taken for granted. The distinction between normative and basic rules is complex and clarification would lead us too far astray here. The point Mackay is making is that traditionally sociology has been normative, only recognizing those rules that lie on the surface of social behavior and neglecting the basic or underlying rules that make normative behavior possible. He urges the investigation of basic rules.

Mackay is arguing that the term *socialization* covers a wide variety of

---

* This statement is consequential for what follows because the confusion between 'head' and 'tail', was introduced by the teacher, not by Tom. (Waksler)

activities that sociologists do not specify but simply assume to be a part of that process. The term socialization *glosses* or slides over all these taken-for-granted ideas. If we avoid using the term socialization, we have to be much more specific about the activities we are considering; without the term we cannot simply label them socialization and be done with them.

Individuals can be viewed as subjects and their perspective on their experiences as their *subjectivity*. *Intersubjectivity* refers to the shared experiences of individuals acting together and is evident in face-to-face interaction where people share time, space, ideas, and activities.

Mackay's discussion relies heavily on the idea of *competence*, which can be understood in its everyday meaning of possessing capacities to engage in and carry out whatever activities in which one is competent. *Interpretive competence* is the ability to make sense out of activities and normative rules by grasping their underlying structure (basic rules). Mackay argues that adults customarily deny that children have interpretive competence while at the same time involving them in activities that require such competence — a competence that children indeed display.

F.C.W.

## Introduction*

In sociological writings characterized as *normative*[1] the term socialization[2] *glosses* the phenomenon of change from the birth of a child to maturing or old age.[3] To observe that changes take place after birth is trivial, but the quasi-scientific use of the term socialization masks this triviality. In fact, the study of these changes as socialization is an expression of the sociologists' common-sense position in the world, i.e. as adults.[4] The notion of socialization leads to theoretical formulations mirroring the adult view that children are incomplete beings. Investigators have consequently been distracted from the important area of study which is adult-child interaction and the underlying theoretically important problem of *intersubjectivity* implied in such interaction. Writing about the process of socialization, then, has become for me an occasion for exploring the interaction between adults and children.

In this paper I first examine what the *normative* sociological study of socialization implies both for the study of adult-child interaction and the development of sociological theory. I then examine the interpretive approach demonstrating that all interaction is based upon underlying *interpretive competence*. The competence is not acknowledged within the normative approach because the study of socialization takes the views of the dominant culture (adult) and proposes them as scientific findings. It ignores the interactional nature of adult-child relationships. Finally through the analysis of adult-child interaction I show the interpretive competence of the child and the paradoxical nature of interaction between adults and children where competence is simultaneously assumed and interactionally denied.

---

* Terms described in the note on pages 26–27 appear in this section in italic. (Waksler)

## To Be — Is To Be Socialized: The Normative Perspective

Children are incomplete — immature, irrational, incompetent, asocial, acultural depending on whether you are a teacher, sociologist, anthropologist or psychologist. Adults, on the other hand, are complete — mature, rational, competent, social, and autonomous unless they are 'acting-like-children'.[5] Introductory texts (e.g. Broom and Selznick, 1968; Horton and Hunt, 1968) in the social sciences suggest that without language and culture new born infants are not human because 'language creates minds and selves' (Broom and Selznick, 1968, p. 96). An implication is that children who are profoundly retarded or severely brain damaged are never human.

For the sociologist, to be human is to be socialized. To be socialized is to acquire roles (see, e.g. Brim, 1968; Clausen, 1968; Elkin and Handel, 1960; Inkeles, 1966; Parsons and Bales, 1955). To be (human) is transformed by sociologists into, to be (roles). But such theorizing is not an indifferent practice. As I have suggested in the Introduction and note 4, it is the formulation of the writer's own view of the world (i.e. his self). Considered thus, to conceive of being human as being roles is to conceive an eviscerated view of life. The consequence of this is that, under the auspices of current formulations of socialization, the conception of children as essentially deficient *vis-à-vis* adults has, in practice, led to no research into children *qua* children and it has served to, scientifically, warrant common-sense conceptions of children as incomplete. When adult-child interaction is formulated as the process of socialization, children as a phenomenon disappear and sociologists reveal themselves as parents writing slightly abstract versions of their own or other children.

Socialization is a gloss (see note 2) which precludes the explication of the phenomenon it glosses, i.e. the interaction between adults and children. This glossing is characteristic of normative sociology's reliance on the common-sense world as both topic and resource.[6] As Zimmerman and Pollner (1970, p. 82) indicate,

> Sociology's acceptance of the lay member's formulation of the formal and substantive features of sociology's topical concerns makes sociology an integral feature of the very order it seeks to describe. It makes sociology into an eminently *folk discipline* deprived of any prospect or hope of making fundamental structures of folk activity a phenomenon.

This confounding is illustrated in the following quotation.

> In other words both the *practice and study* of child socialization are 'forward looking'. It seems obvious, furthermore, that of the various, later stages which socialization looks forward to, it is the personally relatively enduring and *socially important adult* stage which is the *critical one* to consider. Therefore, a central task of the study of socialization is to enquire into the effects which the experience of the child has on the shaping of the adult. (Inkeles, 1968, pp. 76–7; emphasis added)

The terms adults and children are borrowed from the common-sense world by sociologists, but if they are viewed as theoretical formulations, then a very serious problem emerges. That is, to suggest theoretically that there are adults and children is to imply that to pass from one stage to the other is to pass from one ontological order to another.[7] The passage from one ontological order to another is also suggested in the formulation of the world as static[8] and as constituted by successive discrete stages — childhood and adulthood, incompleteness and completeness, lack of agreement and shared agreement (see note 1). If each of these ontological orders implies, on the level of social life, different communicative competencies, then the traditional formulations of socialization make communication between adults and children impossible, since they are assumed not to share common interpretive abilities.

I am suggesting that in the socialization literature the confounding of the common-sense world as topic and resource has resulted in the unavailability for sociologists of interaction between adults and children as a phenomenon of study. The phenomenon of study is adult-child interaction and how it is accomplished.

## The Interpretive Perspective

> For two days I watched some sixty children between the ages of three and six joyfully writing stories of their own, making up poems, exploring the typewriter keyboard and reading paragraphs based on their own conversations. They did this as spontaneously as young children ask questions. I realized then that I had stumbled onto something more important than the mechanical ability to read a few words. Evidently tiny youngsters could reason, invent and acquire knowledge far better than most adults suspected. If they could learn this much through exposure to the talking typewriter for only half an hour a day, the potentialities of preschool children were almost limitless. (Pines, 1966, p. ix)

I take this quotation to represent what might be sociologists' similar surprise at the ability of children to 'reason, invent and acquire knowledge', that is, at their interpretive competencies. In contrast to the study of socialization suggested by normative sociology (discussed in the previous section) work in interpretive sociology (see, e.g. Cicourel, 1970b; Garfinkel, 1967; Holt, 1969, Labov, 1972; Neill, 1960; Schutz, 1962) restores the interaction between adults and children based on interpretive competencies as the phenomenon of study.[9] Without reviewing the literature in this area (see especially Cicourel, 1970, 1972; Garfinkel, 1967), the interpretive perspective posits interpretive and surface rules,[10] the reflexive articulation of which enables people to assign meaning to the world, The complexity of the world and its orderliness is seen to rest on persons' (adults and children[11]) interpretive competencies. The focus of investigation is *how* persons display the meaningfulness of the world.

A demonstration of children's interpretive competencies can be found in research conducted in a grade one classroom.[12] After completing a statewide reading test designed to measure reading and inference skills, children were asked by researchers how they had decided on answers. The children often linked the stimulus sentence and the answer in ways which the test constructor had not 'meant' but which demonstrated their inference/interpretive skills in providing reasonable accounts of the world. For example, the stimulus sentence of one test item was about an animal that had been out in the rain. The 'correct answer' was a picture of a room with dotted wallpaper walls and a floor imprinted with a trail of animal tracks. When the child was asked what the picture was about, she replied, 'It's snowing.' When questioned about the design on the wallpaper — 'Do you know what these are?' — she replied, 'sprinkles'. The child had perceived the picture to be the exterior of a house with snow falling rather than the interior of a house covered with dotted wallpaper. Because of this 'misperception' she had chosen an answer which while it was reasonable within the frame of reference was the wrong answer. While the child demonstrated the inference/interpretive skills that were claimed to be 'measured by the test', no credit was given for this item. This research[13] makes clear that children possess interpretive competencies undiscerned in standard research. The interpretive perspective makes available, then, children as beings who interpret the world as adults do. By revealing the child's competencies, it transforms a theory of deficiency into a theory of competency.

In addition to suggesting that children are competent interpreters in the world, I want to suggest that they are also in possession of their own culture or succession of cultures. Although the evidence for this is only fragmentary, the Opies have presented the most convincing case for the existence of separate cultures.[14] [See Chapter 10 of this book.] Aries (1965) also points to the possibility of separate children's cultures and their changing particularity over time (see also Plump, 1971).

If the two claims are correct, that children are competent interpreters of the social world and that they possess a separate culture(s), then the study of adult–child interaction (formerly socialization) becomes substantively the study of cultural assimilation, and theoretically the study of meaningful social interaction.

## Adult–Child Interaction

I have suggested that adult–child interaction is problematic because of cultural differences. Hall (1959) has documented that problems arising out of poor cultural translation can have serious practical outcomes (i.e. misunderstandings, breaches). Teachers and other adults remain cultural strangers to the world of children and their interaction with children often results in the generic type of misunderstandings that Hall describes.[16] I have argued on two fronts, first that understanding between two separate cultures requires adequate translation and second the *all* human interaction rests on the participants' interpretive abilities. On a theoretical level, however, there is no difference between these two.[17]

I turn now to an analysis of a specific occasion of interaction between an adult and a child which indicates how understanding based on interpretive abilities is built up through the course of the interaction. The teacher treats the child as a cultural stranger while relying on his 'adult' competencies to understand the lesson and review. The following excerpts[18] are from a written transcript of the audio portion of a video taped interview between a grade one teacher and one child in her class [provided at the beginning of this chapter]. In the interview, which took place at the end of the lunch hour, the teacher is asking the child about the assignment distributed earlier in the morning. This assignment was to sequence a series of dittoed sentences which were either taken verbatim or paraphrased from the story read before lunch. In the lesson and assignment the teacher had been concerned with introducing the concept of sequencing to the children. The interview was carried out at the request of the researchers to find out how the child would describe his understanding of the lesson and assignment.

### Instruction: Understanding as the Location of the 'Correct' Answer

Given the working assumption that children are *tabula rasa** beings on which to etch programmes, teachers and other adults ignore the fact that understanding rests upon ongoing reflexive, constructed, convergence of schemata of interpretation (see Garfinkel, 1967; Schutz, 1962). In the transcript it can be seen that the teacher acts as though the world is a static (i.e. not dialectical) place in which she can move the child cognitively from point A to point B while ignoring the child's contributions. In the lesson and review her concern was with moving him from a state of not knowing the concept of sequencing to a state of knowing the concept of sequencing. The teacher thus treats the child as empty of knowledge (i.e. correct answers) and moves him from this state of emptiness to a state of fullness (i.e. knowledge), a process she accomplishes by asking questions and reformulating them until the child gives the 'correct' answer. In some instance the teacher not only asks the questions but also finally *gives* the 'correct' answers (see Teacher 39, page 26). Instruction is the occasion for adults to exercise their preference for a certain meaning of the world for the child. The child as more or less passive in the situation is involved only is so far as he is conceived to be an organism capable of memory.[19] The child can/must *remember* the instructions (i.e. in this case the lesson).

### Children's Interpretive Competence

I am using interpretive competence in an analytic sense to refer to the ability to use interpretive procedures to assign meaning to the world (Cicourel,

---

* *Tabula rasa* is the Latin for 'blank slate' and suggests the idea that I presented in Chapter 2 as the 'empty bucket' theory. (Waksler)

1970b, esp. pp. 147–57; Garfinkel, 1967, esp. ch. 1).* I demonstrate in the following sections that children possess the same interpretive abilities as adults do.

### Competence as the Teacher's Assumption

The teacher assumes the child's interpretive competence in doing lessons and reviews. One example of this assumption of interpretive competence in the transcript is when the teacher (Teacher 14) asks Tom '... see if you can find the sentence that tells best ...' where 'best' implies the careful evaluation of the total situation, i.e. the exercise of those abilities she herself uses to decide which is 'best'. This assumption by adults of children's interpretive competence can be found even in situations where children are considered unlikely ever to be competent. For example, in one research study (Mayer, 1967) with mentally retarded children (measured IQ between 50 and 75) the researcher administered a measure which consisted of a list of twenty-two personality traits. The children were to rank themselves on a five point scale for each item. The format was:

> I am happy, clean, lazy, etc. / not at all / not very often / some of the time / most of the time / all of the time

The researcher assumes that these children have interpretive competence if he assumes that they are able to reflect upon their personalities-as-traits and then rate them on a five-point scale. After the measurement is completed it is assumed that the aggregated measure of self-concept is of persons unable to reason well — they are, after all, mentally retarded.

The teacher assumes the child's interpretive competencies at every point. In the transcript this is especially clear in the segments following.

> Teacher 39   Umhum, so you understood the story and it didn't make any difference about that word did it because the idea was that it fell on Chicken Little and it was really a nut instead of ah a piece of the sky. Thank you very much Tom.

The above segment was uttered at about 1:05 p.m. The segment below was said by the teacher about 10:45 a.m. the same morning in reference to the story of Chicken Little she was about to tell them.

---

* Cicourel and Garfinkel make the point that knowing surface (normative) rules is not enough to enable people to follow them. People must also understand basic rules that tell them *how to follow* the surface rules. I may know that it is wrong to steal but interpretive rules allow me to decide in any particular situation whether or not an act is indeed stealing. Mackay is arguing that children use interpretive rules even when they use these rules to arrive at answers different from those of adults. (Waksler)

Teacher   My story might be a little bit different from the way you
          heard it, the names might be different but the ideas are the
          same.

In both segments she is assuming that what she is saying is obvious, i.e. she
does not elaborate, ask if it is clear, etc. She is asserting that ideas subsume
many different words and names and in doing so eliminates what appears to
be a difference. It is important to note that this is a more complex notion to
grasp than the one that she makes the topic of the lesson — a concretized
presentation of sequencing. What I am proposing is that she is assuming in
an analytic sense the interpretive procedures which define competence. The
following describes one aspect of interpretive competence and it is clear in the
above segments that the teacher assumes this ability of the child.

> A corollary of this property (reciprocity of perspectives) is that
> members assume, and assume others assume of them, that their
> descriptive accounts or utterances will be intelligible and recogniz-
> able features of the world known in common and taken for granted.
> (Cicourel, 1970b, p. 147)

When the two segments are considered together it can be seen that she is also
assuming that the child can remember the earlier utterance and find the
principle of consistency in the lesson, assuming that her use of the word
'idea' in the later utterance is a tacit reference back to the earlier utterance as a
way of finding the mistake to be irrelevant to the sense of the lesson. (The
'mistake' is discussed more fully below.) Here the teacher has assumed
further interpretive competence, viz. the ability to search retrospectively
(Cicourel, 1970b, p. 149) for the sense of the present utterance.
    I offer the following segment as a final example of the child's interpre-
tive competence.

Teacher 32   Humm this is interesting. What did it say in the story
             that Chicken Little ah where the nut fell on Chicken
             Little.
Tom 28       At the tree.
Teacher 33   Umhum what part of his body did it land on did it say?

Tom has formulated the correct answer to the question 'where was Chicken
Little when the nut fell?' i.e. the location of Chicken Little was the scheme of
interpretation. While this is a correct interpretation of her question the
teacher treats it as 'incorrect' by invoking her own scheme of interpretation
'Where on the body of Chicken Little did the nut fall?' While interpretive
ability is demonstrated by Tom in that he articulates the particular words of
the teacher with a frame of reference which allows a reasonable answer to the
question, what is also demonstrated is that adults can pre-empt the interaction with children for their own purposes without explanation. For example,
the teacher might have said to another adult 'Oh no, what I meant was where
on Chicken Little's body.' The teacher not only has the power to ignore

reasonable answers but also assumes more competence of the child than of an adult, i.e. that he can figure out both that and why his answer was wrong and the other answer correct.


### Understanding as Evidenceable

The paradigmatic example of verifying a child's understanding is found in Socrates' encounter with the boy in *The Meno* (see Plato, 1956, pp. 48–9):

| | |
|---|---|
| Socrates | Very well. How many times the small one is the whole space. |
| Boy | Four times. |
| Socrates | But we wanted a double space, don't you remember? |
| Boy | Oh, yes I remember. |
| Socrates | Then here is a line running from corner to corner, cutting each of the spaces in two parts. |
| Boy | Yes. |
| Socrates | Are not these four lines equal and don't they contain this space within them? |
| Boy | Yes that is right. |

The verification of the boy's understanding is in the answer 'yes'. *The Meno* can be read as a monologue and the 'yes' answer by the boy as Socrates' own production. A similar example is found in the transcript, beginning with Teacher 32 and ending at dismissal of Tom. The segment begins with the teacher's recognition that she has made a mistake, 'Humm this is interesting.' She has incorrectly written the sentence on the assignment sheet to read that the nut fell on Chicken Little's head while in the story it fell on his tail. The rest of the segment is the teacher's attempt to find out if the error made any difference in Tom's understanding of the lesson. What is important, however, is that beginning at Tom 32 it is absolutely clear that Tom no longer has any part in the interaction (i.e. it becomes a monologue); perhaps he no longer even knows what is going on although at the end the teacher seems convinced that Tom understood.

| | |
|---|---|
| Tom 32 | Ya but I always thought. |
| Teacher 37 | In some stories it does fall on his head so it didn't bother you that it said head? |
| Teacher 38 | Have you ever heard a story where it falls on Chicken Little's head ... instead of his tail? |
| Tom 33 | Ya. |
| Teacher 39 | Umhum, so you understood the story and it didn't matter about that word did it because the idea was that it fell on Chicken Little and it was really a nut instead of ah a piece of the sky. Thank you very much Tom. |

A viewing of the videotape[20] reveals that Tom's sentence 'Ya but I always thought' did not end unfinished because the teacher interrupted but was a complete utterance. What is evident from the tape is that Tom turns his eyes from looking at the teacher down to the desk in front of him when he concludes the utterance. He continues to look down in this manner until the end of the interview. When he utters 'Ya' (Tom 33) it is softly and he does not look up. This is in marked contrast to the rest of the interview where he meets the eyes of the teacher whenever her gives an answer. The teacher, however, continues to find his understanding even though he is no longer a participant. The teacher appropriates the interaction and asserts the child's understanding. In doing this she provides for both speakers and suspends the possibility of the child's use of his interpretive competencies in the interaction, i.e. the child is treated as incompetent. The teacher asserts that Tom has understood '... you understood ...' and points out why '... because the idea ...', not the word, was what mattered. The assertions imply the teacher's assumption of the child's interpretive competence to figure out the sense, i.e. understand.

Thus, throughout the interview, the teacher guides the child to the correct answers and finds in the answers the sense of the lesson which constitutes the evidence of its success, i.e. that the child understood. What is equally important is that the teacher finds both her own competence *qua* teacher and the child's understanding in the pre-constituted structure of the lesson, i.e. there are no surprises.[21]

### The Paradox

The analysis has revealed the paradoxical[22] nature of adult–child interaction. On the one hand, the teacher relies on the child's interpretive competencies to understand the lesson but, on the other, treats him throughout as incompetent (i.e. she creates or gives the 'correct' answers). The child is treated as deficient as he is under the normative sociological view of children. The sociological view and the teacher's view are characterized by the fact that they are eminently common-sensical. As such, sociological writings on adult–child interaction are not theoretical but part of the very order that was intended for description (Garfinkel, 1967, ch. 1). Seeing the child's interpretive competencies implies that the interpretive theory applies to both adult–adult and adult–child interaction. Differences between the two types of interaction are not theoretical but substantive. Substantively, the phenomena of study are (a) the ways in which adults attribute incompetence to children and create situations for its manifestation, and (b) the structure of children's culture. Theoretically, the phenomenon of study is the interpretive basis of intersubjectivity.

### Notes

1 Here I follow the formulations of normative found in Cicourel (1970a) and Wilson (1970).

2  I use the concept gloss throughout this paper in opposition to the concept explicate. I follow the usage found in Garfinkel (1967, p. 33).

3  Persons concerned with adult socialization see all of life as a process of socialization. For instance see Brim (1968).

4  What I am suggesting here is the same as Alan Blum has elegantly formulated, that 'Through theorizing the theorist searches for his self, and his achievement in theorizing is a recovery of this self' (Blum, 1970, p. 304).

5  The problem with children is that they don't think like adults or so it seems in the vast literature on socialization, child rearing and its popular, and usually more empirical, variants in Spock, Ginst, etc. But then not thinking like adults could be applied to other large segments of the world — the people next door, this or that group. There is an extensive literature on how to *train* children, I suppose because they are smaller and less powerful. A similar argument could be applied to the poor, mental patients and prisoners, a similar literature supports this view. Incomplete socialization, deviance, etc. are particular sociological ways of indicating this.

6  An excellent paper which makes this distinction clear is Zimmerman and Pollner (1970).

7  This formulation is based upon a footnote to be found in Merleau-Ponty (1964).

8  Both theory and measurement in sociology formulate the world as *static*. For example, ideal types and questionnaires take a moment in time and freeze it. If the world was not *dynamic* this would be adequate but since change is constant the models of the world and their concomitant measurement systems are inadequate. Often what passes for theory in sociology are only high level abstractions from which anything can be deduced through the application of anyone's common-sense knowledge of the world. Measurement systems are misconceived in any event because they do not measure but constitute the phenomenon. Consequently measurement is by fiat and the world remains to be described.

9  This perspective implies a notion of liberation and as such offers the intellectual possibility of freeing children as political prisoners. See especially the writings of Holt, Labov, and Neill.

10  This formulation is particularly Cicourel's based on his critique of Chomsky.

11  Particularly important to the discussion of children is Cicourel's article mentioned above (Cicourel, 1970b).

12  For a fuller report of the work referred to see Mackay (1974).

13  For further demonstration of children's competencies see Mehan (1971), Roth (1972) and a related work by Labov (1969).

14  Opie and Opie (1959). The idea of separate children's culture was suggested by Harvey Sacks in a lecture at a conference on 'Language, society and the child,' Berkeley, 1968. Also see Spier (n.d.).

15  The data reported here is part of a larger study that was supported by a Ford Foundation Grant, Aaron V. Cicourel Principal Investigator. Although this research was conceived in part to study children's communicative competencies, the videotapes which were taken focus on the teacher's face with the result that often the children have their backs to the camera. In the segment reported on in this paper the teacher's face is clear but when the child looks at the teacher his back is to the camera. This is in part, I would suggest, because of the ubiquity of the adult view of the world mirrored in the organization of the classroom which makes shooting videotapes towards the children almost impossible.

16  Hall (1959, pp. 9–13). It should also be noted here that culturally different persons who are serious about understanding each other spend long periods of time working out the translation problems. A good example is an anthropologist doing field work. I can think of no similar attempts on the part of teachers and other adults to understand children.

17  Cultural differences may add an element of practical difficulty created by the problems of doing adequate translation but this is not a principled difference. I am following Cicourel's formulation of interpretive abilities as invariant. Under this formulation culture differences are surface rules. See Cicourel (1970b).

18  The reader is asked to consult the full transcript presented in the appendix in order to locate the excerpts in the larger context of the interview.

19  A persistent feature of the common-sense world seems to be a 'trust in memory'.

20  For a discussion of the methodological consequences of the use of videotape, see Cicourel (1972).

21  This observation has strong implications for the educational system. Learning for the teacher is to find evidence of its accomplishment *now* (during the lesson and review). When later on (i.e. grade 5) the child demonstrates the ability covered in the grade one lesson it is assumed that the genesis of the ability was in the lesson and not in his ability to learn it *somewhere*. By referring to somewhere, I mean to point out that the child has competencies to figure out the world in a variety of different ways and in a variety of settings. The assumption of the importance of the lesson provides the *raison d'etre* for formal instruction to be located in organizations called schools. If the focus in schools is on the practical organizational activities *here* and *now*, how can these activities produce children committed to the pursuit of knowledge in a larger and more temporally extensive sense? Practically, how is it possible under these circumstances to get children to see that the material 'learned' in schools applies beyond its walls?

22  A major assumption of this paper is that phenomena maintain a transparency of being more than one thing at once. Although the phenomenon is unitary the various parts seem sequential when talked or written about. For some phenomenologists (Merleau-Ponty, 1962) this is regarded as the perspectival nature of experience and for the Zen monk the unity of experience. One of the most dramatic examples of a phenomenon being two things at once is Carlos Castaneda's experiences using 'smoke' (reported in Castaneda, 1971).

## Chapter 4

# The Least–Adult Role in Studying Children

*Nancy Mandell*

### Commentary

In this article Mandell describes some of the practical problems that she encountered in her sociological study of children. By adopting the kind of perspective described in the preceding two chapters (Waksler and Mackay), she achieved new insights into what she calls 'children's ways', but to achieve those insights she had to recognize and resolve problems that can be attributed to the stringent demands of the perspective she chose.

The method she used to conduct her study, *participant observation*, involves observation of those studied by directly participating in their actions with them. Participant observation seems to be most readily undertaken when the sociological observer can blend in with those being studied, engaging in actions with them in such a way that the sociologist's presence as other is not intrusive. As Mandell clearly demonstrates, an adult engaging in participant observation of children, especially of young children, is open to questioning both by children and by other adults. A first response to her choice of method might well be: 'That's impossible. An adult cannot pass for a child.' Indeed that may be the case, but one can, as Mandell demonstrates, be accepted by children as part of their ongoing activities in many of the ways that children would accept another child. (A similar issue arose for Elliot Liebow (1967), a white sociologist studying black streetcorner men. Liebow did not pass for black, but he was sufficiently accepted by the men to study their actions by participating with them.)

It should be noted that Mandell is describing processes involved in studying children, not necessarily in working with or teaching them. The understanding that she provides is clearly of use to those working with children but the strategy she uses of least–adult is a researcher's role; its use as a teacher's role is both questionable and undocumented.

From *Journal of Contemporary Ethnography*, Vol. 16 No. 4, January 1988 pp. 433–467, copyright 1988 by Sage Publications, Inc. Reprinted by permission of Sage Publications, Inc. and the author.

The difficulty of the task Mandell set herself of studying children through participant observation, the insights necessary both to recognize and to undertake such a task, and the resulting accommodations she made to the exigencies of the research situation all emerge clearly in this article. In addition to the ample data she provides in this chapter, examples of the results of her approach can be found in Part III, Chapter 12, of this book.

F.C.W.

## The Least-Adult Role in Studying Children

Few qualitative studies of children's social worlds exist. Yet all of those works agree that the central methodological problem facing an adult participant observer of children concerns the membership role (Adler and Adler, 1987b) adopted by the researcher. Some (Coenen, 1986; Damon, 1977) argue that the worlds of adults and children are so socially, intellectually, and culturally distinct that adults can only assume a detached oberver role. Others (Fine, 1987; Corsaro, 1985) suggest that age and authority separate children from adults, preventing the researcher from taking on a complete participant role. Instead the researcher assumes a friendly, nonauthoritative, marginal role. Still others (Waksler, 1986; Goode, 1986 [both of which articles appear in this volume]) insist that all aspects of adult superiority except physical differences can be cast aside, allowing the researcher entree to the children's world as an active, fully participating member.

All three of these roles — a detached observer role, a marginal semi-participatory role, and a complete involvement role — are based on certain epistemological assumptions about adults and children as social members. After exploring these assumptions in the rest of this article, I will discuss the completely involved membership role, one I label the 'least-adult' role.

### Research Roles with Children

Researchers advocating the detached observer role argue that our hierarchical structure of age roles and adult ethnocentrism preclude a complete participant role (Fine, 1987). Children are conceptualized as socially incompetent, intellectually immature, and culturally ignorant. Relative to adult researchers, who view themselves as developmentally complete, children are viewed as striving to achieve adult representations of behavior. According to this perspective,[1] the worlds of children and adults are so separate, so dichotomous, that adults can only research children from an objective, impersonal stance. The majority of deterministic studies of children, particularly those in psychology, subscribe to this view.

In contrast, advocates of the semiparticipatory role focus on the similarities, rather than the differences, between adults and children. Fine and Glassner (1979) and Fine (1987) suggest four possible roles, including supervisor, leader, observer, and friend. While they advocate the friend role, all four types recognize some dimension of age and authority as separating children from adults. These researchers suggest what while adults were physically unable to 'pass unnoticed in the society of children' (Fine, 1987: 222), they can take on a nonauthoritative, helpful role of adult-as-friend. The goal of this membership adoption is not to achieve an equal-peer status with children since researchers agree that according to age, cognitive development and physical maturity, adults are superior to children. Rather, the goal is to minimize these differences by assuming the less-threatening role of non-interfering companion.

The third membership role, that of an involved participant observer, assumes that adult-child differences are more ideological than previously acknowledged. The active involvement of the researcher in the daily lives of children is accepted as a tenable possibility. While acknowledging adult-child differences, the researcher suspends all adult-like characteristics except physical size. By suspending the ontological terms of 'child' and 'adult' and by participating in the children's social world as a child, the central methodo-logical problem rests on essentially a technical question of the extent to which physical superiority prevents adults researchers from participating in the role of child.

### The Least-Adult Role

In this article I advocate the third, complete involvement, research role, that of least-adult, in studying young children. I argue that even physical differ-ences can be so minimized when participating with children as to be inconse-quential in interaction. In particular, three methodological principles that arise from George Herbert Mead's (1938) philosophy of action guide my conceptualization of this membership position and help abolish adult-child differences.

In the first instance, Meadian field workers accept their research subjects as they come to them. Status differentials generated by age, race, class, and gender are endemic in adult-adult studies. Chicago field workers (Becker *et al.*, 1961; Geer, 1967; Strauss, 1978; R. Wax, 1979) have developed a long tradition of strategies and techniques for minimizing social distance. In adult-child studies, once the assumption of adult superiority based on age and cognitive maturity is cast aside, researchers can build on these previously tested techniques and use them to gain entry into the child's world. For example, strategies for dealing with issues of informed consent, rapport, confidentiality, and adult supervision are applicable in studies of young children.

Second, having decided to apply adult-adult research strategies to adult-child studies, researchers are forced to suspend their judgments on children's immaturities and focus on how children fit together lines of action. As Waksler (1987 [Chapter 8 in this volume]) has noted, suspending the notion of children and viewing them simply as social members allows us to reveal how much children must know in order to act like children. Gaining know-ledge of children's views and of the ways in which children accept and challenge adult perspectives means taking young children seriously (Joffe, 1973). Yet 'to take children's ideas, beliefs, activities and experiences serious-ly as real, and as embodying *knowledge*, is to risk being taken for a fool'

(Waksler, 1986: 71). Adult and professional sociological notions of children as contaminated data sources seriously constrain adult researchers who question these assumptions.

Third, in order to gain entry into the children's world adult researchers must engage in joint action with the children, thus creating mutual understanding. One of Mead's (1938) absorbing philosophical questions, the origin and meaning of joint action, is exemplified in the context of adults and children exchanging meaning. According to Mead meaning, or mutual understanding, is a social product, a joint creation that emerges in and through the defining interactions of selves (adult researchers) and others (children) around social objects. Mead was perplexed about the process by which people, from quite different perspectives, created or exchanged meaning with others. In short, Mead asked if perspectives, people's ordinary way of thinking, feeling, and acting in situations (Becker *et al.*, 1961), so separate and distinguish groups of people, how can different groups ever accomplish any joint actions?*

Mead's answer has profound methodological implications for adult researchers studying children. Mead suggest that while perspectives may separate people, shared objects specifically unite.[2] People with quite different perspectives on an object can act together and in the same way with the object thus reaching immediate, shared understandings. As I discuss later, sand for the children and sand for me constituted quite different social objects. Since perspectives are relative in time and space, children are unlikely to share an adult researcher's larger perspective of sand, for example. Yet, by seeing and acting on children's social objects as they themselves do, adults and children can coordinate their acts and reach enough meaning, sufficiently understood, to facilitate joint action. The Meadian premise that people act on the basis of the meaning of their objects suggest that achieving a close involvement with the children on shared social objects is the basis on which adult researchers fit into the children's world.

## Methods and Sources of Data

My data are drawn from participant observations with preschool children in two day-care center playgrounds, classrooms, hallways, bathrooms, and lunchrooms. Between 1976 and 1978 I conducted observations for a period of fifteen months at a private, parent-cooperative day-care center in Boston, Massachusetts. During 1978–79 I conducted field work in Hamilton, Ontario for ten months in a day-care center that was publicly sponsored by an established Canadian non-profit organization.

Both centers had about sixty children of mixed sexes and races between the ages of 2 and 5. My observations focused on the 2–4 year olds in both sites. Throughout my field work I tried to observe children in situations where they actively participated in building social exchanges with others.

---

* The issue discussed in this paragraph is what Mackay in Chapter 3 referred to as *intersubjectivity*. (Waksler)

This meant that most of my experiences and observations as least-adult focused on peer episodes in which children were less likely to be under adult supervision and direction. When children participated in highly adult structured environments, including circle time, nap time, lunchtime, and teacher-directed activity time, I often remained detached from these episodes, merely observing. However, during semi-child-structured and entirely child-structured activities I engaged actively with the children as least-adult. These episodes occurred during free play periods indoors and outdoors, in sandboxes, climbing areas, home centers, building block areas, gymnastic centers, and grassy areas. Low-structure areas are ones in which tasks are undifferentiated, and thus peers engage in the process of 'creating' structure: constructing rules, routines, and ritualistic interactional procedures (Mandell, 1986). Within these semistructured and free play settings, I assumed an active observational role, following the children as they pursued their interests, doing whatever they were doing, and, when invited, interacting with them as an older playmate might.

My role as least-adult included undertaking a responsive, interactive, fully involved participant observer role with the children in as least an adult manner as possible. This entailed neither directing nor correcting children's actions. While my size dictated that I could never physically pass for a child, I endeavored to put aside ordinary forms of adult status and interaction — authority, verbal competency, cognitive and social mastery — in order to follow their ways closely.

Since I initially had little understanding of children's interactional entry patterns, I assumed the role of learner, and allowed the children to teach me their ways. As a neophyte, I either attached myself to small groups of children or I placed myself strategically in activity areas. In both instances I stayed close physically, watched carefully, said very little, and closely followed their behavior. Once admitted to their social exchanges, I interacted freely with the children, making full use of the physical space and equipment provided by the centers. As a member of the children's social world, I both observed and participated in rule stretching and breaking.

Corsaro's (1981) recommendation of the peripheral role as a way to enter the child's world is close to my conceptualization of the least-adult role enactment in its early stage. Corsaro cast himself in the role of eager participant, someone who tried to become part of the activities without affecting the nature or flow of peer episodes. He followed his own guidelines: he never attempted to 1) initiate or terminate an episode, 2) repair disrupted activities, 3) settle disputes, or 4) coordinate or direct activity. As a peripheral participant, Corsaro 'placed myself in the ecological area, moved when necessary, responded when addressed and occasionally offered contributions when appropriate' (1981: 133).

Unlike Corsaro, however, over time I became an active participant, not merely a peripheral, passive, or reactive observer. This means I closely followed children's ways, initially observing and imitating their words, actions, and responses, and gradually fitting my line of action into theirs. As an active participant I committed many mistakes by acting in nonchildlike ways that the children either did not comprehend or mistook for adult responses. These interactional errors, or what Mead (1938) has called perspectival problems, disrupted my engagement with the children and forced me to forge new lines of action more appropriate to the children.

This ongoing trial-and-error interaction with the children characterized my early enactment of the least-adult role. Yet encountering problematic social objects and being forced to accept the children's definition of action in order to participate had positive results. In the first place, learning to become least-adult helped diminish my adult status with the children and render negligible the effect of my physical size. Second, in the process of actively role-taking with the children, I came to grasp their meaningful social objects. Since many young children cannot articulate clearly and many others cannot act with adults in an adult perspective on objects, it is pointless to ask young children what it is like to be a child and what is important to them. It is only by engaging them in action that these questions are answered.

As an adult attempting to pass as a child, my gender, age, and experience may well have affected my ability to take on this role. As a mother of young children, I was accustomed to playing with, directing, and chasing 2–year-olds. Moving from the role of adult supervisor to least-adult companion represented a small step along a continuum of adult-child participatory roles. I found it easy to understand and contribute to children's building of social exchanges, since the skill and complexity of children's negotiations had long been my private fascination. It may well be that adults less engrossed in child raising might well have found the movement from director to peer more significant.

## Dilemmas of Being Least–Adult

In my ideal conception of the role of 'least-adult', conceived previous to site entry, I imagined that I would play with the children and merely observe the teachers at work. I had loosely decided to follow a few guidelines with both the teachers and the children, namely that I would say very little on the site, proffer little personal information, and engage in much informational questioning of all activities and participants. During the course of field work I not only violated every guideline, but also I quickly discovered that the children's interactional patterns were more complex than I had imagined. By committing mistakes and allowing the children to correct me, I came to see their interactional rules. Having been a child, I assumed I knew how children behaved. Yet when forced to construct joint acts with them, I realized the extent to which I had underestimated the skill and negotiation required of children to assemble intricate interaction.

My early interactions with the children represented an elaborate process of guesswork. Throughout this trial-and-error stage, the field worker's major challenge is to adopt techniques for repairing social exchanges while simultaneously analyzing interactional errors.

### Who Are You?

So often it is assumed that if supervisors of children admit adult researchers into sites to observe children, then gatekeeping problems are resolved. This misconception stems from adult assumptions that children themselves are not a gatekeeping group, and that the usual unobtrusive role of adult researchers does not necessitate research bargaining with children. The least-adult role demands entry into children's perspectives, and thus necessitates negotiating an acceptable participant-observer role with children. As in any research bargain, the children wanted to know what I was doing on their turf and what they stood to gain by cooperating with me (Wax, 1971).

As other researchers of children have indicated (Fine and Glassner 1979; Corsaro, 1981), actions are the central ways in which the children learn the researcher's intentions. I wanted to indicate to the children that I did not want to be treated as a directive or judgmental adult or worse, a teacher. Repeatedly, in both centers, the children asked 'Who are you?' meaning not what is your name, but what is your role.

10/10/78N Sam asks me, 'Will you read my book now?' I replied, 'I'm not a teacher. You'll have to ask Sarah, she's a teacher.' Sam replied, 'Who are you?' I answered 'I just come here to watch and play with you.'

The least-adult role demanded that I demonstrate to children the boundaries of my role. Since I did not want to be treated as a teacher, I had to show children that I could not be called on to perform adult tasks such as tying shoes, pushing them on the swings, holding them in my lap, or changing diapers. Children's requests for these types of activities I rebuffed by stating, 'I'm not a teacher. You'll have to ask a teacher to do that.' As I discovered, in the beginning, the children protested my refusals.

13/10/77E Mac, David, and Daniel were lifting plastic and metal boxes up. Mac was giving the orders to lift the cartons. The others were complying and talking about it. Mac says to me, 'Nancy can you lift these up?' I replied, 'They are heavy.' Mac said, 'You can lift them up, you're a teacher.' I responded, 'No, I'm not a teacher.' Mac says nothing but looks puzzled. I go on 'I just watch here, I'm not a teacher. Teachers come here every day, and I don't.' Mac listens carefully and then asks, 'Well, can you lift these up?' I respond 'sure' and hand him the boxes.

The main reason children have difficulty in accepting an adult as nondirective stems from their lack of experience of adults as participatory, enjoyable, and nonjudgmental. Adult observers of children rarely enter children's space and time. Adults, for example, are almost never found in children's activity areas, including sandboxes, swings, climbers, or playhouses, For the most part, adults, in the role of parents and teachers, watch, stand over, and peer down at children (Corsaro, 1981). When adult-child contact occurs, it is usually in age- and status-appropriate situations. Teachers, for example, direct and monitor children's play, help in times of trouble, and tell children what they can and cannot do (Corsaro, 1981). Since being least-adult is such an unusual role for adults to perform, the role requires behavioral demonstration in order to reveal its character.

Having reiterated that I was not a teacher, this left the children and me in this curious scenario of uncovering just who I was. Just as my adult ideological conceptions had not anticipated the children's ability to discern the situational demands on my role and hence evolve their own criterion of acceptable least-adult behavior, I was also unprepared for the degree of role negotiation in which the children were prepared to engage. Until I demonstrated what I had to offer the children in exchange for being accepted into peer exchanges, I constituted one more uninteresting adult observer.

I took to demonstrating to the children, and to the suspiciously watchful teachers, just who I was by swinging on their swings, following them into the sandbox, or hiding with them underneath the porch and in the concrete pipes. At first the children giggled hilariously and the teachers followed me and stared, as if they 'knew' that adults didn't do things unless they were being 'silly', out of role. A typical child's response is indicated by the following comment.

> 28/4/77E I went outside and swung on the rubber tires. Some of the older children came up to swing with me. The others who were watching giggled as if they knew adults didn't do those things.

By perching on the edge of a sandbox, swinging beside children, or sitting on the climbers, I was invading the children's territory. This seemed different from children's regular experience of adults within those centers, but within the realm of normal adult behavior. But by making myself continually available to the children for interaction (Cook-Gumperz and Corsaro, 1977) and by actually participating in the children's activities in childlike ways, I clearly distinguished myself from marginal or reactive observers. Children's initial responses to being taken as serious and worthy playmates were ones of joy and incredulity.

### Identification with Adults

Not only did the children find my research role unusual, but the teachers were also suspicious. They wanted to know what I was 'really doing' with the children. Was I in fact responsible enough and morally correct enough to be left alone with their charges? Did I exhibit evidence that I knew how to get along with children? What sorts of things was I saying to them while I sat in the sandbox and swung on their swings? In the early days, the teachers followed me as often as the children did. If I wandered out of vision, the teachers would casually stroll over to where I was, listen with an indifferent stance, smile their approval and leave. No doubt my involvement with the children appeared ridiculous to the teachers, as evidenced by their arched eyebrows, quizzical glances, and teasing comments such as 'enjoying the sand today?' and 'Nancy, what is it you're trying to do with the children?'

Initially I was uncomfortable and embarrassed, since I wanted to be taken seriously as a researcher. Yet, the teachers' initial reactions are data on adult conceptions of childhood interaction as being immature, sometimes cute, but not worthy of this kind of constant attention.

My research role as least-adult is not as rigidly prescribed as some methodological accounts suggest (Gold, 1969). Rather, I experienced this role as one spontaneously invented and constructed by the combined efforts of my respondents and myself (Wax, 1971). For example, as the children grew to trust me, my involvement with them during their free play periods increased and so alleviated the teachers from some of their supervisory burdens. My relationship with the teachers thus evolved into an agreeable compromise as we continually reshaped the research bargain.

In bargaining initially with the teachers as gatekeepers, I presented my observer role as an attempt to be an unobtrusive visitor who observes and plays with the children. I was never directly asked what contribution I would make to the center in exchange for being allowed access. Nor did I raise the reciprocity issue. However, it was clear from the beginning that the teachers saw me as fulfilling a range of possible adult relationships including confidante, friend, and helper. In particular, teachers wanted an extra pair of hands to change diapers, wipe noses, tie shoes, and comfort the distressed. Even though my initial bargaining with the gatekeeping supervisors had left my role open, the teachers assumed they would derive concrete benefits from my presence.

The role of least-adult thus placed me in the tenuous and unexpected position of middle manager. Each group, teachers and children, had cerain requests with which they considered I had to comply in order to allow me continued access. These requests were, I felt, contradictory. Acquiescing to the teachers' demands compromised my role as a nonauthoritarian visitor. Over identification with the children left the teachers feeling exploited.

Teachers viewed my presence as beneficial only as long as I was willing to help out. As the days wore on it became obvious in both centers that hectic was the norm. Teachers were often short staffed and fragmented by multiple demands. Having an extra person to assume the menial and non-skilled jobs of cleaning up and changing diapers freed teachers to complete the more skilled tasks of instructing, nurturing, and monitoring. Only in exceptional circumstances was I called on to assume a more senior 'teacher's' role. During these situations it was untenable to maintain a neutral observer role. In the following extreme example, a supply teacher found her circle time overwhelming and begged me to intervene.

> 28/4/77 Margaret's (a supply teacher) meeting time had disintegrated into chaos. The eight children are all bouncing, running, and throwing themselves down on the floor. Having abandoned her attempts to read them a story since the children were not listening, Margaret puts a record on and announces 'Now, it's movement time.' The children, already moving, pay no attention, the shouts and squeals of delight are getting louder. Margaret turns to me and begs me to do something. Up until then, I had been passively sitting on the floor watching.

While this proved to be an extreme example, there were numerous incidents, especially in the early days, when my assistance enabled the teachers to respond to multiple demands. In Boston, my first research site, I interpreted any teacher requests on my time as threatening my least-adult status with the children. I was afraid that the children would never learn to stop making adult requests if I complied with the teachers' requests and helped them out. Once I learned that my presence during the dirty-work times would prompt requests for help, I learned to avoid those scenes. In retrospect, this fear of personal disclosure was based on a traditional, non-reciprocal image of the researcher-subject relationship as being somehow inviolable and contaminated by subjectivity unless distance was maintained. In the second research site in Hamilton, Ontario, having had some experience, I was more open to assisting the teachers, having learned that the children and the teachers would eventually accept the situationally variable dimensions of my role.

During child-structured periods (free play) the children learned that I was accessible and open to participation. During the teacher-structured periods (circle time, nap time, eating time, dressing time), I could be approached to tie shoes, wipe noses, or comfort a beleaguered child. In fact, by not approaching the child with comforting or nurturing tasks and by responding unenthusiastically on the few occasions when I was approached, the children rarely solicited my adult-like behavior. It may be that their dominant impression of me was of someone who played with them. Nurturing and restitution of arguments was better left to those who rarely engaged with them in this manner, namely the teachers.

The teachers also developed a multifaceted view of my role. During free play periods, they learned that I could be found in one of the various children's sites (the sandbox, doll center, paint table) engaged with the children in conversation or play. During circle or music time, I sat on the floor with the children and responded with the appropriate gestures or songs when the other children were queried. However, during field trips, walks outdoors, lunch time, nap time, or going-home time, I was a responsible adult presence who could be relied on to dress, feed, bathroom, or comfort a child. In Boston I simply tried to avoid adult scenes. In Hamilton I rarely offered to help but neither refused when asked nor avoided these situations. The research relationship is reciprocal, and offering help and disclosing personal feelings and experiences as a mother, worker, and student did not compromise my least-adult role with the children, nor did it bias my relationship with the teachers. In fact, it established that I was an okay person with everyday concerns.

### Following Children's Ways

The early stage of least-adult enactment was difficult, since I experienced methodological problems in following children's ways. In particular, the children's patterns of movement and their language presented obstacles.

These dilemmas were masked in the first few days by my preoccupation with grasping the basic elements of the social order (Geer, 1967). I concentrated on general observation of the situation, including such introductory tasks as getting names, describing setting and dress, and grasping the calendar of daily events. The field worker assumes the stance of a detached outsider, sitting on the fringes, mentally recording as many patterns of activity as possible. While this scanning phase allows the observer to plan appropriate entry and sampling procedures (Corsaro, 1981), this phase is exhausting. After my first day of observing in Boston, I noted in my observer's comments[3] that, ·

> 21/4/77E O.C. I was struck by how difficult it is to observe every-thing, how tiring it is, how hard it is to assume the observer's role with both the children and the teachers. Seems very confusing ... don't feel at ease in the situation and the others feel tense with me. Will need to spend the next few sessions sorting out the action.

The novelty of the situation, the trying on of a comfortable research role, and the difficulty of becoming familiar with the children were compounded with the issues of following the children.

I quickly discovered that the pattern of children was one of scatter. To me, this constituted chaos. My adult conception of an orderly entry and passage from one activity to the next was of no use in guiding or ordering my attention. The following comment from my second day illustrates my difficulty in grasping this pattern of roaming,

> 28/4/77E It is too difficult to keep track of what happened to whom because the group disintegrated. The children flit from one activity to another so quickly that it is difficult and confusing to find a pattern.

This limiting strategy provided me with time to focus on a few children, discern their entry and exit patterns and concentrate on understanding their verbal and nonverbal language.

### Understanding Children's Language

Not only following the children but also grasping their language proved difficult. Many of the 2- and 3-year-olds did not enunciate in a clear, adult-like fashion. Frequently I asked the children to repeat themselves. While this is a common adult communication technique, it is a completely inappropriate least-adult access tactic. Adult clarification requests ('What did you say?' 'Pardon', 'Say that again') communicate adult ignorance and impatience and disturb the flow of interaction sufficiently to end encounters.

After repeated failures, I adopted the least-adult technique of relying less on precise verbal explications and concentrating more on nonverbal cues. Verbal and nonverbal gestures are linked in children's communication, creating a language of their own. Babbling, or not speaking English as adults understand the language (deVilliers and deVilliers, 1977), is central to children's own language. Unintelligible noise is both part of children's involvement with each other and a device to exclude adults from their play. Children often do not understand others' precise meanings. They require less detail and specification to create acts. Yet, when pressed to present an intelligible-to-adults explanation of their behavior, children construct acceptable accounts. In this early example, I demonstrate the inadequacy of an adult participant role with children.

> 21/11/78N Brock has been watching my interactions with Amy in the doll center. He has been hanging over the front end of the stove and follows us to the table. Brock starts to look at me and talk and I can't understand. I ask, 'Say it again. Pardon? Pardon Brock.' Finally in exasperation I look at Jenny, who has been standing and watching, and I ask 'What is he saying?' Jenny says something I don't understand and turns to Brock and says it questioningly, Brock gestures towards the box with dolls. I ask, 'Jenny, what does he want?' Jenny replies 'I'll look.' She starts pulling items out of the box until she holds up a small, wooden blue block, hands it to Brock and says 'This?' Brock shakes his head, Jenny throws it back, takes out a Big Jim doll and hands it to him saying 'Here it is.' Brock takes it without expression and moves on.

Children demonstrate Mead's (1938) adage that shared meanings, perhaps only roughly understood, are sufficient grounds on which to build public involvements.


### Screening Out Noise

Another aspect of learning children's language involves screening out extraneous noise and concentrating on immediate activities. As a newcomer I found both centers noisy, confusing, tiring, and incomprehensible. Upon my return to one center after a two-week Christmas break, I was sharply reminded of how loud and chaotic children's behavior appears:

> 9/1/78N I had been absent for so long — two weeks — that the morning seemed very confusing and noisy to me. Had difficulty seeing patterns of behavior. They looked like a bunch of screaming, unhappy children who couldn't get along with one another. What is interesting about this feeling, particularly given the amount of time I have spent there, is that this must be the impression of any newcomer to this center, so in fact, anyone who didn't spend a considerable length of time getting to know the patterns of activity would no doubt come out with an entirely different view of the children from what I have.

As least-adult, I had, like the children, to become accustomed once again to the daily noise level.

Intense involvement in action becomes the means for filtering out irrelevant sound. One of the skills children acquire is distinguishing adult sound from immediate action sound. As members of a larger social group, children learn to expect and listen for teacher announcements interrupting their ongoing activities. It was not until I violated this implicit rule that I became aware of children's ability to monitor and anticipate adult intrusions. Once, on an elaborate pretend fishing trip with four children, I became so immersed in my noninterfering least-adult role that I calmly watched one boy cut open another boy's head with the shovel, ignoring an observing teacher's warnings to intervene and avert the blow. The teacher classified my inattention as negligence. Yet, interestingly, despite her astonishment, she accepted my apologies and seemed considerably warmed to me. Perhaps my error made visible the serious responsibilities of caretakers and validated the nonparticipatory supervisory role of teachers. In contrast, the participating children seemed neither surprised nor upset by my lack of interference.

### Role Testing

Both the children and the teachers subjected me to a number of tests of my commitment to the role of least-adult. My neutral stance was tested by the children's violation of center rules in my presence. I witnessed children hiding in forbidden areas, urinating outside, laughing when asked to be quiet, nor responding to teacher requests, and taking teacher-designated materials.

I also encountered many incidents of rule stretching (Strauss, 1978). Children routinely violated the adult norm of sharing by struggling over involvement objects. They shattered the norm of discursive arbitration by resolving disputes with screaming and shouting. Children strained the norm of rationality with their boisterous aggression. These violations were so frequent that adults customarily intervened only when children demanded arbitration.

In both the explicit and negotiable transgressions I declined to judge. In order to avoid confrontations with the teachers, I usually left an explicit rule-breaking and rule-stretching scene.

For example, in one center urinating in the yard was a forbidden but regular event for a small group of children. The teachers never caught any children in the act, and I avoided being implicated for irresponsibility.

> 22/6/77E Outside in the yard, Nicole comes running up to me and says 'I can go pee-pee outside you know. Do you want me to do it?' I shrug my shoulders (and look around to see where the teachers are!) Nicole runs under the porch, pulls down her pants and urinates. Daniel, David, Saskia, Jenny, and Amber are watching. Jenny pulls her pants down and urinates. Then Saskia and David do the same. I leave, since I feel I could not account for this. Amber then runs and tells the teacher about the incident.

Rule-stretching scenes were more likely to result in teacher intervention. In this typical case, for example, the child Kyle was unable to stop the violator, Crystal. Since he was committed to his act, it was imperative that she be stopped. Hence his demands for immediate restitution.

14/11/78N Crystal is dressed up in black shoes and is carrying a purse. She wanders into the lunchroom, drops her purse and puts on a plastic apron for painting. She starts to paint all over Kyle's painting and on the actual paint board. Kyle turns to me and says, 'She's painting my picture.' I shrugged and replied 'Tell Pam (the teacher) if you want her to stop. I can't stop her. I'm not a teacher.' Kyle repeated his request. I repeated my reply. Finally he went and got Pam.

While it took time, the children eventually used me as a nonauthoritarian participant. In cases in which I did not leave a rule-stretching scene before the children's cries demanded teacher intervention, the teachers were almost always annoyed with my neutral stance. Since I was present, the teachers requested my judgment in assigning blame. I avoided collusion with the teachers by responding that I had not witnessed or could not assess the exchange.

Field work accounts with older children (Fine, 1987; Fine and Glassner, 1979; Thorne, 1986) report similar incidents of stealing, lying, and cheating with outsiders. Clearly my rule-breaking encounters did not approximate the illegality of many adolescent pranks. Yet witnessing infractions of any type represents a form of role testing. The host community judges researchers by their complicity, and all researchers acknowledge the personal tension generated by their silent acceptance.

This tension is perhaps exacerbated in studies of young children who, by virtue of their immaturity, are constantly monitored. Physically and culturally, children have little privacy and secrecy. A least-adult researcher actively involved with children is similarly publicly scrutinized. The researcher must be sensitive to the teachers' dual and contradictory perspectives on the researcher as peer and least-adult.

### Rapport

Trust or rapport is often touted as a solution to the problems of reactivity (Emerson, 1981: 365). Adult researchers of children (Corsaro, 1981; Fine, 1987; Fine and Glassner, 1979) have assumed that rapport with their subjects provides access to information hidden from outsiders. The similarity of my data with that of others (Corsaro, 1979a, 1979b, and 1981) suggests that this is the case. Yet rapport also leads to unexpected demands.

With the teachers, as mentioned earlier, I exchanged my help with the dirty work and playing with the children for continued access. Similarly, the children allowed me to join in their action in exchange for correctly following their ways. With both groups, being trusted meant that I was no longer seen as a threat but as someone they wanted to include in all their activities.

With the teachers, indications of acceptance took the form of routinely setting me a place for lunch, opening friendly conversations, and quizzing me on my absences. 'Where were you?' or 'You should have been here yesterday' became familiar preludes to accounts of missed activities. They wanted me to see 'everything'. Although the teachers trusted me as someone who could be left with the children, I obtained only situated access. My status as a temporary teacher's aide, in their eyes, excluded me from many of the routinized disagreements they engaged in with one another. In Boston, during interviews and through overhearing conversations openly carried out in my presence, I heard accounts of intrastaff and staff–parent conflicts. In fact, most of the toddler staff were in open disagreement with each other within and between the morning and afternoon programs. In Hamilton the center was chronically underfunded and as a result, short staffed. Because of insufficient financial support from their parent corporation the center eventually closed. The uncertainty generated job anxiety and intrastaff competition and merit ranking. Since I was primarily interested in adult–children and peer interaction, I noticed these events to the extent that they affected programming.

With the children, the clearest indication of my acceptance was their immediate inclusion of me in their involvements and their concurrent refusal to use me as a substitute nurturer or disciplinarian. The adult ideological bias underestimates the extent to which children contextualize adult behavior. This entails more than simply forming personality preferences for certain teachers. It suggests that the hosts, the children, judged me by patient observation and by learning how I could be helpful (Wax, 1980: 275). By the focusing stage when I had acquired their access strategies my arrival in a group of children elicited only mild indifference.

Other acts both tested and provided validity of my understanding of the children's ways (Bruyn, 1966: 180–185). The children's acceptance of my least-adult role was made all the more evident in Hamilton when, after six weeks of observation, I arrived one day armed, for the first time, with paper and pencil. I concentrated on recording action passively. My refusal to participate prompted a barrage of inquiries as to who I was.[4] In the following example, Mark continued to use me as a participant as he had come to expect me to behave in spite of my attempts to record:

> 14/11/78N I walked into the little room with paper and pencil and Mark came running up immediately saying, 'You're the bad pirate. Come with me.' He threw beads at me. I followed him to the corner where he covered me with a blanket and told me to 'be quiet'. I was still carrying my paper and pencil and feeling rather foolish.

I had firmly established with the children that I would learn their ways in situ. When I temporarily abandoned this approach, they were confused. After an hour of rebuffing access attempts and trying to sample systematically, I relinquished the paper.

Categorical acceptance (Denzin 1970b: 192) by the children created unanticipated dilemmas. As a visitor who followed and focused, I was expected by the children to be everywhere with them. But this presented problems. I could not physically do what they did, such as perch on the top of a climber, rock in the wooden boat, or chase them on their riding toys. The children apparently forgot about my size limitations and were annoyed when I didn't come when called.

The other dilemma centered around the escalating demands on my time.[5] Once I had mastered the access strategies, my role as a participant became both more prescribed and limitless. It was limitless in that being able to enter situations quickly, the children and I could then negotiate lengthy and more complex encounters than I had been able to accomplish in the early days. The role also became more prescribed in that, as an integrated least-adult, the children became intolerant of my interactional mistakes and less willing to allow me reflection time in the form of self-involvement. In retrospect, having achieved this degree of acceptance, this would have been the opportune period to withdraw and videotape sampled incidents.

### Learning Children's Access Rituals

Becoming least-adult with the children is a gradual role-enactment process that occurs in two ways: naturally, in the course of interaction and reflectively, as a result of encountering problematic situations. Unproblematic inter-action, or what Mead (1938) called habitual action, refers to interchanges in which self-other dialogue flows spontaneously. Enough meaning is sufficiently understood and exchanged for acts to continue unabated. Much of my later experience with the children fell into this category. We engaged in elaborate fantasy enactments and remained self-absorbed alongside others for lengthy periods (Mandell, 1984 [Chapter 12 in this volume]). However, my earliest attempts to engage in action were problematic, demonstrating my ignorance of their interactional rules. In the rest of this article I will concentrate on elucidating common access strategies children use. My eventual mastery of these techniques enabled my further integration into the children's world.

Goffman (1971) considers access rituals to consist of common greetings and farewells employed by adults to mark the beginning and end of most interactions. Children's access strategies refer to frequent techniques children use to open peer exchanges. Children must understand and master these behaviors in order to produce joint acts. Access rituals thus provide a structure for the acquisition and maintenance of peer interaction (Corsaro, 1979). They represent the patterned ways in which children enter into interactional dialogue.

In the *Philosophy of the Act*, Mead (1938) reveals three stages through which all interactions proceed. In the selection stage, self-others choose social objects with which to become involved. For example, children typically select the involvement of others with toys, puzzles, or painting as their object of attention (focus). In the second stage, children jointly manipulate their involvement objects. They physically or mentally do something with the object. Pictures are painted, blocks are piled high, or firemen-children put out pretend fires. The third stage is labelled evaluation or consummation. Here children bring their acts to completion, finishing art work, terminating fantasy productions, or putting away their toys.

Peer interactions begin with the children's selection of objects and end with their evaluation. Interactional episodes vary widely in terms of duration, content, and the degree to which shared meaning is achieved. To some extent, these variables are correlated with the type of access-ritual employed. Yet, common to all peer episodes is their initial structuring through the children's employment of access behavior. Engagement with children reveals four common access strategies: monitoring, action reproduction, object involvement openers, and supplications. In the course of uncovering and mastering these techniques, problems of following children's activity patterns, absorbing children's noise levels, and comprehending their language and gestures were encountered.

### Monitoring

Children cannot engage in peer interaction unless they learn how to join groups on their own. Successful interactants, including both neophytes and experienced children, are those who interpretively observe the behavior of others before they attempt to join in. This monitoring takes two forms: staring, by strategically placing oneself in a position to scan the behavior of others, and physically following others around while cautiously maintaining social distance.

Monitoring is a common access ritual which enables children to remain peripheral to the acts of others and to absorb information on how others build social exchanges. Children unobtrusively observe others' manipulation of social objects, neither contributing to nor disrupting their involvement, as is evident in this example:

> 14/6/77E Ana, Marissa and Candice were in the sandbox, each holding a container and a shovel. Ana was singing to herself. They were all putting sand in the containers, walking to the climber and dumping it out. Josh arrives with a small wheelbarrow and runs it into the box. The children start putting their containers into the wheelbarrow. The extent of the conversation was Josh saying 'Fill it up. Fill it up.'

Here the children monitored and then joined by doing what the others were doing. Throughout the exchanges, gestures prevailed.

Other researchers have noted that monitoring represents one of the central ways children come to understand others' situational use of objects. Garvey and Berndt (1975) regard procedural or preparatory behaviors as necessary for setting the stage for children's communication of pretend play. Corsaro (1979), in his study of nursery school behavior, concluded that over 80 per cent of children's access attempts involved the strategy of nonverbal entry. In both my settings, monitoring was a technique employed over 90 per cent of the time in which successful entry into sustained peer involvement was obtained.

Once familiar with others' patterns, interpretive observation takes place almost instantaneously. With a glance, children could assess the action and judge correct entry patterns. The more exaggerated staring and following noted above were indicative of newcomers.

As a newcomer to the day care scene, I too invoked the monitoring strategy to discern patterns in children's movements. The tenuous and fragile nature of peer episodes gave them a hasty, chaotic feeling. Not only did access and withdrawal patterns seem random, but the accelerated pace of children's movements contributed to the impression of chaos. The fieldwork technique of focusing my observations on a few children enabled me to grasp access behaviors. Interpretive observation aided my discernment, and it emerged as the child's primary access technique.

The conceptual opposite of monitoring was the act of crowding. Defined as invasion of interactional space, crowding included pushing or shoving into physical proximity with other children who were engaged in action, stealing their interactional props, and verbal ('You fucky', 'You asshole') or physical (punching, kicking, slapping) abuse. Unlike monitoring, which preceded successful building of peer interactions, crowding was an access ritual which inevitably destroyed peer exchanges.

### Action Reproduction

One of the children's most acceptable access strategies was to physically place themselves near other children and do what the others were doing. Monitoring was a precursor of action reproduction. Repeatedly a typical pattern emerged. The child attempting access first scanned and assessed the action. Having selected this social object, the child then made evident his or her desire to join by manipulating objects in the same manner as the others. This parallel manipulation represented an efficient way to signal intent. In the following example, Mark joined in with Tim's activity by utilizing this access strategy.

> 19/12/78N Tim is busy putting some blocks together. Mark has walked over to these blocks with a wooden truck. He is running his truck up and down Tim's ramp making car noises. Tim allows him to do this and joins Mark in assembling the ramp.

Similarly, Symie allows Elise and Debbie to participate with her in pouring water from one container to the next.

> 05/12/78N Symie is at the water table. She is pouring water into the containers and smiling. Elise and Debbie try to pour some water into Symie's container and she allows them to do this until they have over-flowed the water in the container.

In both these cases, nonverbal dialogue prevailed. Through action reproduction newcomers mapped their behavior onto that of others. This was not a passive but rather an active repetition which allowed entry into the others' social environment. As Garvey (1977) has explained, repetition and repetition with variation are essential ways in which children synchronize behavior and thus establish a framework for continued interaction. Action reproduction signaled the arriving child's desire to join. It provided an open and non-threatening channel for further elaboration of the social act. Others then had the opportunity to respond by incorporating newcomers into the act or by rebuffing their attempts. As a least-adult observer, action reproduction was the first technique I learned. By carefully and patiently doing what the others were doing, I provided the children an opportunity to observe and react to me.

> 4/10/79N I went to the sandbox. Stephanie, Kristin, Brock, Lindsey, and I were making cakes. I sat down and filtered sand through my fingers. Lindsey looks over and offers me some sand. I take it, silently, and put it on her pile. We continue building this way for a few minutes. Eventually Lindsey holds out her hand and says 'Cake'.

Most often, action reproduction results in successful group entry, eventual acceptance into an ongoing episode (Corsaro, 1979). When combined with the technique of monitoring, these two nonverbal strategies proved highly successful. Their success as access rituals is explained by the type of interactional possibilities they opened up for the participants.

For most of the younger children, action reproduction involved the physical manipulation of objects. Sand was patted, water was poured, and playdough was stretched. Shared objects provided a link between children, an avenue for the creation of a joint social act. With young children's physical manipulation of objects we see clearly how crucial sharing objects is to social interchange. Through joint manipulation, children experience others' attitudes toward and use of objects. This is what Mead (1938) called experiencing the 'inside of an object'. Children become aware of others' differing reactions to objects. So objects now appear stubborn, resistant, and less easily controlled. By experiencing others' responses to a physical thing, children get 'outside of themselves' and take the role of the other child toward their own use of this item. This role taking occurs through a silent conversation of gestures in which children exchange and adjust their use of objects. Physical objects become a vehicle for symbolic interaction. By sharing objects, children create joint meanings. Mutual manipulation becomes a social structure in which children negotiate further lines of action. As children grow older and more experienced, they can mentally reproduce actions others are seen as performing (Garvey, 1977). Presumably this emerging capacity to construct cognitive representations of actions and events has its initial beginnings in joint physical action reproduction.

As a least-adult participant, I monitored and reproduced children's behavior. Yet I experienced this continual mapping as frustrating. Exchanges of sand food, a particular favorite at both centers, often persisted for twenty minutes. Moreover, children's initiation of further activities and their turn-taking lapses seemed longer than adult sequences. Often I longed to speed up the action and fill up the empty conversational space. Even when the acts themselves expanded to include five children, a common feature of repetitive frames (Mandell, 1986), the pace and content of these exchanges felt confining. I had to remind myself that both monitoring and action reproduction represent the beginning phases of the process in which children actively gathered and created social information. As such, they could not be hurried into an adult tempo.


### Object Involvement Openers

Access rituals represented initial ways children structured joint acts. In both centers, children needed to understand both nonverbal and verbal strategies in order to build peer episodes. Verbal access rituals included object involvement openers and supplications. Older children were more likely to rely on explicit verbal messages than were the younger 2- and 3-year-olds.

Object involvement opener represented the linguistic equivalents to action reproductions. Children verbally identified their action plans using declaratives ('*I'm* a fireman!'), commands ('*You* be a fireman!'), and direct questions ('*Are* you a fireman?'). Since all three types addressed the core of social exchanges, peers promptly replied. Objects constituted the center of children's social behavior. Object involvement rituals thus announced action plans and displayed children's willingness to be joined by others in creating novel actions around these objects.

Declaratives can be either primarily gestural in nature or used in conjunction with verbal explanations. In this example, the child declared her open script using monster gestures and sounds:

> 28/11/78N Abby comes up to me screaming and gesturing like a monster. I scream, monster style, back. She screeches again at me and leaves.

In his analysis of declaratives, Corsaro (1979b) analyzed baby animal talk separately and discovered that these forms refer to phonetic strings often produced with high pitch confined primarily to the subordinate position in role play. In this example, Abby merely indicated an open script which I had the option of picking up on. Other cases used gestures alone as scripts.

In contrast to nonverbal invitations to join, the majority of declaratives were centered around verbal exclamations. Linguistic gestures often evoked meaningful responses in children who used and understood similar messages. As Mead (1938) has explained, children use language gestures to initiate social acts. Language provokes linguistic responses from interactants which leads to joint manipulation of common objects. Language thus facilitates the process of interactional adjustment in a way not found with nonverbal gestures. Peer episodes based on verbal exchanges stimulate more complex action plots. The active role taking which emerges from this type of communication allows children more opportunity to reflect and respond to their own and others' behavior with more elaborate lines of action.

Commands also represent object-involvement openers in a manner similar to declaratives. Imperatives are another way children begin to construct scripts around social objects. In these typical examples, children explicitly announced their action plans and signaled a participant's role:

22/6/77E Saskia rides her big wheels into me. She says 'You are hurt' (declarative). 'Get on the ambulance' (command). 'We are going to the hospital' (declarative).

29/11/78N Elsie comes up to me in the gym, takes my hand and leads me back to the gym mats, saying 'Go to the fire station.'

Commands are an access strategy used to facilitate engagement in public alignments. Corsaro (1979) has suggested that their main function is to control the behavior of other interactants by acknowledging a specific-topic, activity or role as constituting the focus of involvement. Children issued many commands to me, thus validating my role as an acceptable, least-adult participant.

Less successful than declaratives and imperatives as access rituals were direct questions. Children verbally requested others' engagement (Do you want to play?) and gesturally labeled the involvement object. In the following example, the request was denied.

15/05/79N In the puzzle corner, Debbie, Brad and Rod were each putting their own puzzles together. Brad turns to Rod and says, 'Want to play with me?' Rod replies, 'You play.'

### Supplications

Similarly unpopular were supplications in the form of pleading, begging, and negotiated queries. 'Please let me play' and 'I'll be your friend if you let me play' were infrequently used even though they usually resulted in successful entry. This type of formal, direct entry procedure appears contextually vague and reminiscent of ritualistic adult approaches. Teachers often employ pleading when they are soliciting cooperation ('Please, let's sit down now, okay?'). It may be that children associate other children's supplications with nonnegotiable adult commands disguised as bargaining entreaties. Children's greater reliance on object involvement openers attests to the centrality of social objects as mediating the actions of children and peers.

Both direct questioning and supplications are familiar adult access rituals in interacting with children. In my initial interactions with the children I mistakenly employed these traditional adult openers. By rebuffing these rituals, the children forced me to adopt their access techniques. As an adult participant I initially relied too heavily on verbal communication and neglected the children's reliance on gestural explanations.

## Conclusion

In this account I have presented a completely involved research role, that of least-adult, as an example for pursuing participant observation with young children. I conceptualize being least-adult as a membership role which suspends adult notions of cognitive, social, and intellectual superiority and minimizes physical differences by advocating that adult researchers closely follow children's ways and interact with children within their perspective. Achieving a close involvement with small children is accomplished by sharing social objects. Through joint manipulation of objects, children and the least-adult researcher take each other into account and create social meaning. By acting with children in their perspective, adults gain an understanding of children's actions.

This account outlines some of the dimensions of the least-adult role and chronicles dilemmas of role enactment. I have discussed challenges of following children, understanding their language, distinguishing noise, identifying with adult supervisors of children, enduring role tests, establishing rapport with children and adopting children's access rituals. While field workers are loathe to relate mistakes, such acknowledgment enables future studies to avoid these errors and advance methodological pursuits. Research into the worlds of children reveals the complex, rich, and situated details of their day-to-day accomplishments. By trying on different participant observational roles with children, field workers gain insights into children's patterns of behavior. The research challenge is to capture the dynamics of children's interactions and to fit into children's interpretative acts without disturbing the flow. Least-adult suggests a potential means of achieving these goals.

Author's note: I wish to thank Blanche Geer for her encouragement and creative feedback on earlier versions of this article.

## Notes

1  Speier (1976) calls this the adult ideological bias in studying children.
2  I am grateful to Blanche Geer for suggesting I stress the significance of shared objects in adult-child interaction (Personal communication, 1985).
3  Becker *et al.* (1961) first originated this use of recording data and the time of observation as a validity check. The abbreviation 'O.C.' refers to the term 'observer's comments', which are the researcher's way to record personal reflections and examine accumulating biases. [The designations 'E' and 'N' refer to two research settings, Eastern and Northern.] As Johnson (1975) notes though, personal accounts of field work mistakes and unease are usually presented in a doctored fashion for publication purposes.
4  Corsaro (1981) noted the same increase in interest when he introduced video taping.
5  The teachers also made increasing demands on my time. During a period in Hamilton when the staff was particularly shorthanded, my rapport with the supervisor was such that she counted on my daily presence.

## Chapter 5

# Studying Children: Phenomenological Insights

*Frances Chaput Waksler*

### Commentary

In this article I detail some of the fundamental biases that adults have towards children. By favoring one interpretation of children's behavior over others without empirical grounds for doing so, these biases impede sociological understanding. The articles in Part II, Children in an Adult World, provide data to document the existence of these biases; the articles in Part III, Children in a Child's World, exemplify the kinds of insights that can emerge when these biases are set aside.

The first bias I describe involves, among other things, taking socialization as a fact rather than as merely one way of thinking about children and their activities. The criticisms of socialization offered in Chapter 2 serve as a background for the somewhat more detailed ones offered here. The second bias refers to what children are said to know and not know. (In philosophical terminology, this concern with knowledge is called *epistemology*.)

As was noted in the introduction to Chapter 4, it is important to distinguish between *understanding children* and *working with children*. The former is a scientific undertaking, the latter an activity in the world of everyday life. In science our concern is with truth; in everyday life our concerns are likely to focus on practicality, truth at times being less relevant than what works. Adult biases towards children have certain advantages in the world of everyday life, advantages that may account for the existence, use, and tenacity of these biases. That biases have advantages, however, does not mean that they are valid but only that they can be useful. Thus there may be practical, *political* reasons for maintaining these biases when working with children even if these biases are questionable or incorrect.

Since initially it may seem odd to claim that in everyday life fiction may prove more useful than truth, I will provide an example of how a bias with questionable validity can be of practical use. As a teacher trying to gear my teaching to the intellectual abilities of my students, I could seek what is taken

From *Human Studies* 91: 71–82 (1986). © Martinus Nijhoff Publishers, Dordrecht. Printed in the Netherlands. Reprinted by permission of Kluwer Academic Publishers.

to be objective evidence about those abilities — SAT scores, grades, and the like. In my own teaching, however, I have found it practically useful not to seek such evidence but instead to adopt the bias that my students are intellec-tually capable and to teach accordingly. Whether or not my bias is valid, I find that it seems to work, e.g. I have been told that my students are brighter than those in other classes and that even the same student is brighter in my classes than in others. My bias may well guide my behavior so that by treating students as bright I aid them in responding accordingly (a process sociologists refer to as *self-fulfilling prophecy*). Whatever the process by which the outcome is achieved, however, I find it of practical use maintain my bias.

In reading this article, it may be useful to consider the practical implica-tions of the insights provided. Where those implications are such that it seems advisable in working with children to maintain rather that eliminate a particular bias, it will still be useful to know that one is doing so. Biases can facilitate action in the world of everyday life, but recognizing biases as such provides a flexibility that is not available when those biases are taken as truth.

F.C.W.

## Introduction

The ideas to be presented in this paper emerge from a phenomenological approach to the sociological enterprise. [*Phenomenology* is a philosophical perspective that some sociologists, including many of those whose work appears in this volume, use as the foundation upon which to construct their specific theories of how the social world works.] In particular they derive from Husserl's directive to respect 'the originary right of all data'. Such respect entails setting aside belief and doubt in ontological and epistemologic-al matters [i.e. belief and doubt in what is real (*ontology*) and what is known (*epistemology*)]. There are some important advantages to be gained from adopting such a stance towards children and there is a serious practical problem.

First, the advantages: Seeing children as nothing special but simply as actors in the social world makes it possible to draw on social science re-sources not usually applied to children. Routinely, in seeking to understand children, traditional sociology has either turned to psychological theorists (especially Freud, Erikson, and Piaget) or elaborated on sociological theories of socialization. As a consequence, the sociological study of children has neither benefited from nor contributed to sociological understanding in general but has for the most part been an independent sphere of study. I contend that taking children seriously as sociological subjects encourages the application of a wide range of sociological concepts and theories to children's activities and experiences (see, for example, my study of *deviance* in a kinder-garten classroom, 1987, [Chapter 8 in this volume] and Ardener's idea of *muted voices*, 1977) and the application of concepts developed in studying children to adult activities (consider, for example, adult instances of the Opies' notion of *half-belief*, 1959 [Chapter 10 of this volume]). In this way sociological knowledge about children and sociological understanding in general can be enhanced.

Second, the disadvantage: To take children's ideas, beliefs, activities, and experiences seriously, as real and as embodying knowledge, is to risk being taken for a fool [a point that was eloquently evidenced by Mandell in the previous chapter]. When I as a sociologist take seriously that which in everyday life is not, when I question what all adults know, when I entertain childish ideas and immature formulations, my standing both as an adult and as a sociologist comes into question. The criticism of Laud Humphreys for his studies of sex in public bathrooms (1970), criticisms which in a variety of ways amounted to labeling him a 'dirty old man', still allowed him his adult status. To put one's adult status in question is a serious matter indeed.

Perhaps adulthood is at heart a tenuous achievement, being adult a continuous accomplishment, and the serious questioning of adult understandings thus a challenge to a fragile view of the world. Children constantly threaten adults: their knowledge, the very achievement of adulthood itself, and adult accommodations to issues from childhood that were never resolved but simply overridden with adult conceptions. Much of adult knowledge is based on faith — faith in the correctness of what people were taught as children. Detailed sociological examination of children's creation and sustenance of world views and the ways in which children do and do not adopt adult world views can provide the data for an examination of the nature of adult conceptions and the differing degrees of certainty which accompany them.

What seems clear at the present time is that adults, including sociologists, display a clear reluctance to take children's ideas seriously and even express actual hostility. An anonymous reviewer of Mandell's work (Mandell, 1984a), in a rather vituperative set of comments, saw her claims of children's competence as *self-evidently* erroneous and as *evidence* of *her* incompetence. The reviewer asserted, without substantiation, that 'children *are* cognitively immature' and 'do *not* yet possess the social skills appropriate for independent social living'. Indeed this reviewer accused her of 'anthropomorphizing' children. That a sociologist could reject proposals of children's competence out of hand suggests the professional constraints on such study.

Nonetheless, in what follows I claim that taking children seriously as sociological subjects is a legitimate, though difficult, undertaking. I will detail some of the major problems and suggest the kinds of insights that emerge from the approach I am suggesting.

## Identification and Suspension of Adult Beliefs

Children occupy an unusual place among data, for in everyday life adults routinely set themselves up as the understanders, interpreters, and translators of children's behavior. Adult common-sense explanations have been generally adopted by sociologists studying children and thus the sociological literature is full of studies of common-sense explanations of children's behavior. The absence of children's explanations is rarely missed because its very existence is not recognized.

Some sociologists have indeed addressed the topic of the current limits and future possibilities of studying children sociologically and critiques, theories, and data exist (see, for example, the works of Mackay, 1973; Skolnick, 1976; Denzin, 1979; Mandell, 1984a, 1984b; and Goode, 1983, 1984, and 1986). I want to move forward with those ideas as a basis and to demonstrate the kinds of biases that have hampered the sociological study of children and its general acceptance by sociologists. I will do this by identifying and exploring two fundamental adult biases that particularly distort children's worlds and that I judge to be fruitful candidates for suspension in the research enterprise. I urge the consideration of both these biases and these *kinds* of biases. An examination of them suggests the many kinds of topics that reveal themselves when these biases are suspended.

### *Bias No. 1: Children are unfinished, in process, not anywhere yet*

This bias is central to the notion of socialization but, more importantly, pervades adult common-sense views of children. Indeed in everyday life it has the status of a truism. Children are viewed as in their very nature not grown up and thus *not something* rather than *something*.[1]

In sociological study, and psychological work as well, less evaluative terms may be used to describe children, but such terms preserve rather than suspend the bias. Developmental theory is most overt in this regard, for those who have not achieved adulthood are viewed as in some sense under-developed. To be precognitive is to be defined in terms of one's lacks. There is an assumption that no one wants to be precognitive; it is not an achievement. The notion of children as immature is a similar negative category. To speak of children as lacking language ability is again to focus on what they don't possess. Terms applied to children and even claimed to be objective or neutral may be, when applied to adults, terms of criticism or contempt; the very label of childish is negative.

In everyday life we adults take for granted that children *as a category* know *less* than adults, have *less* experience, are *less* serious, and are less important than adults in the ongoing work of everyday life. I suggest that for the word *less* we as sociologists try substituting the word *different* and consider the theoretical and methodological implications. What is children's knowledge and in what ways is it like and unlike adults' knowledge? The distinction between adult and child may become irrelevant as we come to focus simply on varieties of knowledge. To say that children have different experiences from adults focuses on a researchable topic, whereas the designations *more/less* clearly ground study in judgment. The very idea that experiences are cumulative might be set as problematic, for when are experiences constructed on those that go before and when are they new productions? To see children as less serious than adults is again to judge; to ask how children display seriousness is to set a research problem. To examine children's part in day-to-day life is to ask questions not only about their nature but about their political position in the social world — what can they do and what are they allowed to do? If children were by nature non-participants in the world of work, child labor laws would seem unnecessary. The central suggestion here is to see the bias of defining children in terms of what they cannot do and to recommend consideration of what they do do.

The sociological concept of socialization embodies the bias under consideration here, for children are viewed as the objects, the raw material of socialization. Existent criticisms of the 'oversocialized' view of children (Wrong, 1961) and of socialization as an adult perspective (Mackay, 1973 [see Chapter 3 in this volume]) serve as the background for my setting the entire notion of socialization as problematic.

Socialization takes for granted the adult common-sense assumption that children need to be brought up. I want to claim that the statement *children need to be reared, raised, etc.* is but part of a conditional statement of the form *children need to be reared, raised, etc. if they are to become adults just like us, if they are to support the world we've made, if they are to 'outgrow' or 'get over' their childish behavior,* etc. Children as children disrupt and challenge the adult taken-for-granted world and for that reason are a political problem: their knowledge contradicts what adults claim is obvious and known to everybody. What is presented in much of the sociological literature as children's needs may well be more accurately understood as adults' needs. Fictional accounts of 'unsocialized' children, e.g. Golding's *Lord of the Flies* (1955) and Hughes' *A High Wind in Jamaica* (1928), indicate a challenge to common-sense views that children cannot manage on their own; indeed they seem to manage, but in ways that adults find abhorrent. The very fact that they manage at all may be more abhorrent to adults, for it gives lie to the claim the children need adults in some absolute sense.

If children are by nature social and capable of acting in their own terms (and the Ik studied by Turnbull, 1972, provide anthropological support for such a claim), then adults' claims that they cannot takes on the status of an ideological position rather than a scientific fact and can be seen as political moves to control children and turn them into adults, whatever adult turns out to be. Adults' abilities to sustain their common-sense views in the face of children's challenges is certainly a political advantage as well as a reflection of that advantage. As an adult I am permitted to override a child's view merely because I am an adult. To refuse to do so as a sociologist studying children is to show the possibility that children have competing world views.

What I find a particularly intriguing idea is the possibility that what is called socialization is a far less certain and fundamental process than is commonly imagined. If it is a fully interactive process, with participants engaged in a struggle rather than in a one-sided helping, leading, nurturing, rearing relationship, what emerges is the strong likelihood that it may appear to work far more than it indeed does. Consider that the process of socialization entails not children becoming adults but learning to act like adults. We might ask: are children truly socialized or do they simply learn to translate their experiences into adult common-sense terms? Many of the adult ideas we claim to possess we may not fully accept but only talk as if we did. The unsettling aspect of this consideration is, of course, that there are no adults, only adult actors — a sociologically plausible but common-sensically disorienting idea.

Piaget's study of children's learning the principle of conservation (1952) serves as a useful illustration. Children fail to see, for example, that two equal-sized balls of clay remain the same size even if one is shaped into a pancake; they claim that the pancake shape is larger. Their recognition of the error of their ways is taken as an indication of maturity. Do adults in fact learn this principle or simply learn to utter the principle but continue to act on an earlier intuitive sense? If you ask me which of two items is larger — and the very asking suggests to me some kind of a trick — then I invoke the principle so I can give the right answer. When however, at a party, the hors d'oeuvres tray is passed, I tend to take the one that looks like the biggest and somehow this look matters to me.

Not only can socialization be demonstrated to be political, but it can be shown to be carried out in such a way in everyday life that its inevitablity and success are assumed whenever possible. One common technique in socialization is to respond to children as if they were already socialized in a particular sphere. The interpretation of children's behavior in adult terms thus serves as a mode of socialization rather than of understanding. To say to a child enjoying a repast of mudpies, 'You don't want to do that. They taste awful!' is not a statement of fact, of a reality to which adults are privy but which holds for all; it is a way of translating children's experiences into adult terms so children will learn those terms. In this process, children's experiences go unrecognized by adults and their continued existence for children is hampered by adult constraints on children's justifying their experiences. In elementary school a number of us developed a taste for library paste and adults responded in ways that made clear not only that we ought not to eat the paste but that it wasn't good. My adult tastes do not include library paste, but I want to preserve my childhood experience that it was good — that it was to be sought out, enjoyed, and, further, concealed from adults whose judgments prohibited such use and, less successfully, such enjoyment.

I have argued that socialization can be conceived of as a political activity engaged in by adults and as a claim made by those directing the process as part of the way of bringing it about. If so, then research would seem to require an investigation of these processes as topics themselves; a setting of the whole idea of socialization as problematic rather than as a taken-for-granted assumption; and a realization that the process itself has very different appearances depending on where one is placed in the process. Much that is available in the sociological literature is not sociological analysis but a documentation of adult perspectives, valuable as data but not as theory. What we don't have in any substantial way is data on children's perspectives on socialization, a perspective that only becomes accessible if we suspend belief in children as unfinished, in process, not anywhere yet and if we suspend a second fundamental bias, namely

*Bias No. 2: Children are routinely wrong, in error, and don't understand*

In disputes between adults and children, like those between psychiatrists and patients, the former is assumed to be right, at least, in Garfinkel's terms, 'until further notice' (Garfinkel, 1967). Justification for this assumption may be made in terms of children's immaturity, etc., but such justification may not be asked for because adults' rightness *vis-à-vis* children is itself a taken-for-granted assumption. The inequality of power between adults and children further reinforces this situation, making it possible for adults to decide arguments with children by pulling rank. Argument-stoppers such as 'because I say so', 'because I'm your mother', 'stop arguing and just do it', suggest that on numerous occasions adults do not need to explain the superiority of their judgment or understand children's points of view. One might notice a certain circularity here, for children are wrong because they are immature and the evidence for their immaturity is their error. Nonetheless, children's views are routinely discounted when they challenge adult views. To take children's views seriously is to allow them to contend with adult views on an equal basis, with the winner not predetermined.

A consideration of children's 'errors' in playing formal games, i.e. those with rules written by adults, will suggest some of the limits to understanding imposed by this bias. Children are often said to play such games wrong, for they do not — some say thus cannot — follow *the* rules. What is not generally considered is whether children indeed accept such rules, intend to follow such rules, and fail; or if instead they make up their own rules in their own ways for their own purposes. That they violate adult standards is not at question; that they fail to follow such standards is. That children can take adult-created items, e.g. a pack of cards, with or without adult instruction or observation of adult use, and fashion a workable game — strange to adults but followable by other children — is denied existence as an accomplishment and set aside as error. Adult correction may, however, destroy the game for children whose own rules were working and acceptable in the context in which they were being used. If adult rules are viewed as foreign and imposed on children without their consent, children's practices and their responses to adult intervention begin to become clear.

A common practice of children, changing the rules as you go along, may be offered as evidence of children's violation of adult rules for making rules; or, the violation may lie in children's doing openly what adults see as legitimate only when done covertly. Children change rules to their own advantage and other children accept such action; it is adult participants who get bent out of shape by such self-serving practices, though clearly in card games adults seek their own advantage, though secretly or indirectly, as in bluffing.

Another instance of children's 'error' is their use of language in ways different from adults, a practice that also leads to the presumption of their inadequacy as describers of their own experiences. When adults cannot understand children's talk, the talk is faulted, That children can understand one another is not taken as contradictory evidence. Similar to Goode's findings about interactions between social workers and the retarded (1983), adults can ask children to explain what another child has said and then judge the latter as unable to speak or communicate. In the face of such contradictory data, sociologists might expect that power issues rather than issues of ability and competence are at the fore.

In many important respects children's views are different from adults'. That adults in charge of children, like colonists in charge of natives, see their charges as wrong is an important social fact, but that those in power are in some absolute sense correct is a shaky foundation on which to construct sociological insights.

And so we come to the question: can adults study children? I say no, *not as adults*. Adults and children have separate versions of childhood. Adulthood is a perspective, a way of being in the world, that embodies a particular stance towards children, a stance that allows adults to deal with children in everyday life but that limits sociological understanding. To ask adults (even in the guise of sociologists) what children are like is on a par with asking jailers what prisoners are like or asking dog trainers what dogs are like. They are like what those doing the defining need to see them as like if they are to engage in the kind of activities that involve those others.

Sociologists, however, can study children. If adult and child are seen not as given in the nature of things but as social roles, then sociologists can suspend their adult role much as they suspend other partisan roles as they carry out research. What is necessary is that they see such a role as suspendable. To study children sociologically involves asking what children are like in the social role of child and in other roles as well. That adults treat child as a 'master status' (Hughes, 1945) is not to say that children do not play other roles invisible to adults but available to sociologists who look.

## Implications of Suspending Adult Beliefs

I am arguing that by suspending adult beliefs about children, sociologists can claim children as full-fledged subjects of sociological understanding. The particular strength of the view being espoused here is that it makes available for wider application insights derived from such study and allows more general sociological concepts, theories, and ideas to be applied to an understanding of children. I have suggested in passing a number of fruitful areas of research on children, areas that emerge when adult biases are suspended. I now want to articulate some of those areas a bit more fully.

First, one can examine things that children can do and adults cannot or will not. Only by suspending the assumption of adult superiority, however, can such a research topic emerge. Then it becomes possible to look for things that children can and do do better than or easier than adults. My first glimmer of this idea came when my husband was learning to jump rope as part of an exercise program, experiencing the difficulties one encounters in learning a new adult activity. Looking out the window of the room where he was practicing to the street below, I saw some 7- and 8-year-old girls jumping rope in the complex and athletically sophisticated ways common to playgrounds. Young children, were doing effortlessly what adults can find a difficult accomplishment. A second example comes to mind, an old one in my experience but now more significant: The tale is of a 3-year-old English-speaking child whose Danish-speaking paternal grandmother came to visit for the first time. Within a week this child was translating between his grandmother and his English-speaking mother. How is this possible? How could he learn so apparently effortlessly what his mother could not or did not? Once this topic is posed, a multitude of examples emerge that might tell us a great deal about children and adults and learning.

Second, one can explore the role of child *as a role*, for child and adult require each other to play their roles. Indeed, adults recalling childhood experiences[2] can tell of altering their behavior in order to make it conform to adult expectations of children. They can also remember adults altering the adult role in interactions with children, as when adults run slower than they are able so children will win races; what intrigues me is the fact that children know that this is going on and may even work to sustain the fiction that the race is a fair one. If we take seriously that child is a role, the following kinds of questions become possible: How do children reconcile the conflicting expectations of adults and peers? How do they deal with role strain and role conflict? Where do they find *backstage*? What do they reveal to and conceal from adults? How do they resolve the problem of engaging in what adults define as *age-appropriate* activities when they are deemed inappropriate by those who are expected to engage in them? What parts of the child role does one give up on the road to adulthood, what parts does one keep openly, what parts does one keep but conceal? Are there adults who still sleep with the lights on?

To recognize that child is a role is to suspend the assumption that childhood has some absolute, real, transcendent existence beyond the social, an assumption that embodies the very topic it could endeavor to study. Alternatively, we could study the category of child as a social category, focusing as Becker (1963) might on those who are labeled children, investigating how one comes to be so labeled, considering the social characteristics of those so labeled, their responses to that label, and so on. If the very facticity of children is set as problematic, a host of sociological questions become available for study. If we can see childhood as an achievement, we can see how childhood is achieved and pursue the topic of adulthood and its achievement as a related and significant question.

Third, if we see children as actors in the social world, we can ask how their actions constrain, facilitate, encourage, and in myriad ways have implications for others, adults in particular. Adults are known to make children eat their vegetables if those adults are to claim they are being good models, but less noticeable is that children make adults eat *their* vegetables. Can we say that children make adults watch their language, follow rules more carefully, bring their talk and action into closer consistency? 'Make' may be a trifle strong, but something is going on here. How do adults alter their behavior in the presence of children? Do children in some sense have power over adults and, if so, what kind of power is it and how does it operate? That children can learn at rather young ages how to play adults against one another, can know whom to ask first for the necessary permissions, can test adults to see what limits exist, suggest a certain use of power that is not routinely acknowledged as such in everyday life — these children's strategies are known to adults but their implications for children's competence seem to be submerged in the general assumptions about children's *in*abilities.

Fourth, perhaps the most fruitful line of investigation phenomenologically is of the *praxis* or lived experience of childhood. What issues arise in being a child? I offer the following partial list:

a. sustaining their own views in the face of others' challenges;
b. defining their experiences in others' terms, terms not necessarily designed for that purpose;

   c.    reconciling the world as given in experience with others' interpretations of that world;

   d.    finding and playing roles other than those provided by the social world;

   e.    adapting to a world not of their making, in many ways designed for those with other resources and abilities;

   f.    gaining power/adapting to lack of power;

   g.    meeting the expectations of others in ways that leave one's sense of self intact and that support or at least do not violate one's own experiences and sense of reality.

It is worth noting that none of these issues, phrased as they are, turn out to be unique to children's experiences.

If this paper has achieved its purpose, readers should now be able to continue on their own.

## Notes

1  The study of children brings to light the idea of negative categories, i.e. categories constructed on the *absence* of one or more characteristics, e.g. pre-cognitive, non-verbal, immature, developmentally delayed. Such categories are akin to the fault-finding process that Goode (1983) finds implicit in social work practice, a process based on the identification of what one cannot do rather than on one's abilities. I am claiming 1) that children may indeed be doing what we claim that they cannot (e.g. talking, even though adults may not understand), 2) that not doing is not necessarily an act or a perceived lack, and 3) that children are doing other things, things that go unnoticed by adults.

2  I have elicited some very promising data by asking adults to recall their childhood experiences with adults. I have used such questions as: What kinds of things did adults do that bothered you? How did adults treat you? What did it feel like to be a child? I think the limits of such retrospective data may be counterbalanced by the fact that adults have the power to speak of that which as children it was politically wise for them to conceal. Based on responses to these questions, I have casually asked children about these experiences and have reason to believe that this would be a fruitful line for further research. [Since I wrote this article, I have undertaken such research. Some of the findings are presented in Chapter 15 of this volume.]

*Part II*

---

# Children in an Adult World

---

The four papers in Part II bring forward for attention aspects of the adult worlds in which children live and the views about children that are a part of those adult worlds. They all serve as a basis of contrast to the articles in Part III, which describe children in worlds of their own making. The articles in Part II were not written explicitly to describe adult worlds, but all contribute to an understanding of worlds through examples: a humorous account of pets discussing their role as child substitutes; a report of a study of children using marijuana with the guidance of or approval of parents; a description of teachers' taken-for-granted rules for kindergarten students; and a description of the ways that adults look at children.

None of these papers claims that the adult perspective is the only one or the correct one. By documenting the existence of an adult perspective, however, each serves as a basis for raising important questions about the implications of such a perspective for understanding children and for engaging in interaction with them. The power that adults have over children — not only over their physical beings but also over their ideas, beliefs, world views, and activities — emerges clearly and sometimes starkly.

Throughout Part I of this book sociology has been faulted for assuming an adult perspective rather than seeing that perspective as a suitable topic for sociological study and as an important feature in the social worlds of children. If this criticism is accepted, then the many studies of children that have been conducted from a taken-for-granted adult perspective cannot be used sociologically as studies of children; they can, however, be used as *data*, as studies of adult perspectives. Having read the papers in Part II, readers should then be able to read the abundant available studies conducted from a taken-for-granted adult perspective as studies not of *the* world but of the *adult* world and to benefit from the authors' insights without being restricted by their limits. Reading studies in this way can provide new insights into the ways that adults construct children's social worlds, ways that are often incompatible with children's constructions.

F.C.W.

*Chapter 6*

# Once Upon a Time

*Norman Waksler*

### Commentary

This light little essay on pets as child substitutes is included here as a way of bringing forth for examination certain taken-for-granted ideas about what, in adult terms, children are 'for'. The sociological significance of this essay should not be exaggerated. Waksler is a fiction writer, not a scientist, and his work can be read as an entertainment. For our purposes here, however, his essay also enables us to raise a number of significant issues.

The very idea that children are 'for' something challenges taken-for-granted beliefs. To ask adults why they want children can be viewed as posing a foolish question, for it is commonly assumed that people indeed *do* want children and that those who do not want to have children are somehow either deprived or peculiar. The extensive medical energies devoted to making the infertile fertile testifies to the cultural support for the desire for children. If called upon to account for their desire for children, adults are able to draw on the culture of which they are a part, providing such common-sense answers as 'because I love children', 'to be fulfilled', 'to carry on the family name'. Those who do not want children have no such readily available accounts. Waksler challenges the view that having children is normal and having pets is some kind of displacement or weak substitute. In presenting such an idea, he reformulates the notion of what a pet is and is for and makes it possible to rethink the notion of what a child is and is for.

The truthfulness of Waksler's picture of pets is clearly not at issue here. What his portrayal can do is direct us to questions about the idealized view of children — a view that pervades not only the popular but also the social science literature. What family functions do children in fact serve? What do they do? What are they good for? What is the role of parental expectations? Do such expectations benefit children? adults? both? neither? If people can be said to have children in the same way that they are said to have pets, to whom do children belong? Do they indeed belong to their parents?

---

This essay originally appeared in *The Cambridge Express*, Cambridge, Massachusetts, May 7, 1983. Daniel D. Savage, Editor and Publisher.

The pets' discussion of affection can lead us to ask: how in fact is affection displayed towards children? Are some kinds of children more likely recipients than others? Children deemed flawed or ugly might well find themselves in the position of the turtle, but without the turtle's psychological resources for finding such a state of affairs normal. The turtle's unsentimental view of the entire matter also reminds us of just how often discussions about children are characterized by sentimentality. An unsentimental view of human behavior can disclose taken-for-granted assumptions worthy of sociological analysis. Furthermore, as the turtle says, 'The child substitute types just fail to grant us the breadth and potential of our characters.' By freeing our analysis of both sentimentality and taken-for-granted assumptions, we are able to address ourselves to actual adult-child interactions in everyday life and to children's characters as *themselves*.

Waksler's essay can lead us to a recognition of assumptions *as assumptions*, open to question and to study. Taken-for-granted assumptions can be difficult to discover, especially when they are related to that which is highly valued. Sociologists concerned with unearthing taken-for-granted assumptions are constantly alert for methods of doing so. Humorous, even irreverent, presentations are one source of such insights. Waksler's essay can perhaps be best appreciated if it is read for fun but with attention to the common-sense ideas about adults and children that it challenges.

F.C.W.

## Once Upon a Time

Once upon a time, there were four pets sitting around the living room of an evening while their childless owners were out. 'Did you see Victor Burg's article in the *Express*,' asked one, a small black dog, remarkably fuzzy, who'd once been described as 'unnervingly cute' by a friend of the owners.

'Which?' said the cheerful teal blue parakeet.

'The one where he claimed that having pets is a way of having children,' said the fuzzy black dog.

'I saw that,' said the lean brown dog with a whitening muzzle and a perpetual expression of curiosity. 'A most unfortunate conclusion on his part. Master and mistress were steamed.'

'And well they might be,' said the *scripta elegans*, i.e. a dime-store turtle 16–years-old who was the size of half a grapefruit. 'And so was I. I hardly consider myself a child substitute. Coldblooded creatures don't inspire warmblooded responses after all, and I can't very well imagine being considered the replacement for some Billy or Mary who never was.'

'True enough for you,' said the parakeet. 'But people do have the habit of talking baby talk to their budgies.'

'Just a manner of speaking,' said the brown dog with the white muzzle, 'but they hardly have the expectations of a parakeet that they'd have of a child.'

'That's right,' chipped in the cute fuzzy dog. 'They're hardly going to expect you to grow up morally straight, go to college, and avoid espousing causes of which they disapprove. They'd be happy if you just wouldn't eat their plants. They'd be happy if we all didn't eat their plants for that matter.'

'Besides,' said the turtle, 'How *do* you speak to a parakeet? In *basso profundo*? Anyway, they don't have the expectations of birds that they do of dogs, that's for certain.'

'But that hardly makes us child substitutes,' pointed out the brown dog.

'Well, they do lavish all that affection on us,' said the black dog, 'and if they had children, mightn't they lavish it there instead?'

'Oh sure, and if they had children and pets, wouldn't they lavish it in both places?' said the parakeet. 'I suspect that affectionate people who have children and/or pets are affectionate to them, and unaffectionate people who have children and/or pets are unaffectionate to them.'

'Speaking as one who is neither fluffy nor fuzzy,' said the turtle, 'I think that people who claim that pets are a way of having children are just thinking of the equation of a fuzzy, warm puppy or kitten with a chubby, warm human baby, and then extrapolating without considering the implications. People do get similarly gooey over all three.'

'Indeed,' said the brown dog. 'But like children, we once-fuzzy, chubby things grow up, and I hardly imagine that I'm now playing the part of a surrogate for the adolescent daughter master and mistress could never have. They've never even asked who's taking me to the prom!' she added, rolling over on her back and kicking her four legs in the air in mock despair.

'Well then, how do you explain all that affection?' asked the black dog, after an irrepressible, but good-natured nip at the brown one's ear.

'Maybe they just like us,' said the parakeet.

'Maybe we're just likable,' said the brown dog.

'Now there's a point,' said the fuzzy black dog, her button eyes aglint as she considered. 'We animals do have some fairly charming characteristics of our own, don't we? After all, why assume that anything amiable about pets is amiable only because it's actually an attribute of children?'

'You're right,' said the turtle. 'We pets have our particular species charms — I my ancient floating turtle wisdom; parakeet his bounding budgie bravura; black dog her terrier alertness, and brown dog her intelligent greyhound drive — and we have endearing personality characteristics like friendliness, curiosity, senses of humor, slyness, and a good number of other emotional and behavioral capacities, some of which are especially brought out in contact with people. The child substitute types just fail to grant us the breadth and potential of our characters.'

'Not to mention,' said the parakeet, 'that if you don't think of us as a mere child substitute, you have to start seeing that we're all kinds of things — acquaintances, friends in one degree or another, housemates, useful dependents, honored guests, retainers, entertainers, you name it. Interspecial relations are much more interesting than the parent/child paradigm allows — don't you all think so?'

'Well,' said the brown dog with a toothy grin. 'You know what mistress has always said'.

'What?' asked the parakeet, who hadn't been in the family as long as the brown dog.

'Mistress says that having children is the way the people compensate for their inability to raise pets.'

'Right on!' chorused the others, who, it must be admitted, were a little out of date in their jargon. But this kind of thing is to be expected of talking animals.

Chapter 7

# Tinydopers: A Case Study of Deviant Socialization

*Patricia A. Adler and Peter Adler*

## Commentary

The Adlers' article introduces a subject that some may never have considered a possibility, namely marijuana smoking by children from ages 0 to 8. In their presentation four issues arise to which it is useful to direct attention: 1) morality and the sociological enterprise; 2) diversity in adult perspectives; 3) concealment; and 4) social change as a continuous process.

### Morality and the Sociological Enterprise

Readers may find themselves with varied moral responses to the data. It is important to note, however, that the authors themselves neither recommend nor encourage any particular response, for their concern is merely with presenting their findings. Some may want to judge the authors' silence on the subject of morality and the absence of condemnation as tacit approval for the activities they studied, but such a judgment seems to me unwarranted. The authors simply do not see their sociological task as requiring their moral judgment but rather as requiring presentation of data as it appears to those actually engaging in the activities under study.

This article can serve as a useful vehicle for considering one's own values and the often ambiguous and contradictory forms they can take. Thus those who are morally opposed to any drug use may judge harshly the parents described in the article, perhaps even labeling them child abusers, while those who themselves smoke marijuana or approve of its use by others may nonetheless object to marijuana smoking by children. (Note, however, that some readers may themselves be labeled by adults as children, and, on this basis, those adults may see them as 'too young' to smoke marijuana.) Some readers may also find that in their own responses they sound more like their

From *Symbolic Interaction*, Spring 1978, Vol. 1 No. 2, pp. 90–104. Reprinted by permission of JAI Press Inc., Greenwich, Connecticut.

own parents than like themselves, thereby gaining insight into that adult perspective.

### Diversity in Adult Perspectives

Although the Adlers studied both adults and children, their analytic perspective is implicitly adult and does not provide significant data about children's perspectives *in children's own terms*. (When this issue arises in their article, I have provided a footnote to call it to attention.) The theorists they cite — in particular Piaget, Mead, and Erikson — take for granted children's inabilities and incompetencies. The Adlers do, however, provide extremely useful data to document the existence of quite different adult worlds in which children might live. The adult perspective held by the parents described by the Adlers is clearly different from the adult perspectives held by those who do not use marijuana, by those who see it as an adults-only substance, and by those who condemn its use at all.

This description of children engaged in marijuana smoking shows that activity both as possible and, in terms of the perspective of the adults studied, as justifiable. Those adults defined marijuana smoking as an activity that adults and children can reasonably share. Rather than concealing their activities from children, they urged them to participate, in their terms opting for openness rather than hypocrisy. Certainly the situation can be defined otherwise, but it is sociologically important to recognize the definitions applied by those engaged in the activity itself.

### Concealment

What activities are acceptable for adults but 'ought to be' concealed from children? What does such a distinction imply about the nature, capabilities, and opportunities of children? Under what circumstances and for what reasons do adults modify or conceal activities in the presence of children? Articulation of one's own views can serve as a useful basis for examining taken-for-granted assumptions. The resulting personal answers are *not* sociological answers, but they can serve as useful sociological data.

### Social Change as a Continuous Process

This study predates the 'War on Drugs' and the increasing condemnation of drug use. At the time of the study, drug use, and marijuana use in particular, was viewed in some circles as a rather routine form of recreation. The claims the authors make about the increasing normality of marijuana, such as their statement that 'Marijuana use ... may soon take its place with alcohol, its "prohibition" a thing of the past,' certainly sound odd in the 1990s, and there is no way of knowing how it will sound in 2000. Any model of social change is likely to need revision when the postulated future becomes the present.

The authors' claims should be seen as providing a description of the times in which they were writing and the historical setting for the actions they describe. To judge drug users of the 1960s and 1970s by moral standards of the 1990s is to distort the data and the understandings to which it can lead.

F.C.W.

## Tinydopers: A Case Study of Deviant Socialization

Marijuana smoking is now filtering down to our youngest generation; a number of children from 0–8 years old are participating in this practice under the influence and supervision of their parents. This phenomenon, *tinydoping*, raises interesting questions about changes in societal mores and patterns of socialization. We are not concerned here with the desirability or morality of the activity. Instead, we will discuss the phenomenon, elucidating the diverse range of attitudes, stratagems and procedures held and exercised by parents and children.

An examination of the history and cultural evolution of marijuana over the last several decades illuminates the atmosphere in which tinydoping arises. Marijuana use, first located chiefly among jazz musicians and ghetto communities, eventually expanded to 'the highly alienated young in flight from families, schools and conventional communities' (Simon and Gagnon, 1968: 60. See also Goode, 1970; Carey, 1968; Kaplan, 1971; and Grinspoon, 1971). Blossoming in the mid-1960s, this youth scene formed an estranged and deviant subculture offsetting the dominant culture's work ethic and instrumental success orientation. Society reacted as an angry parent, enforcing legal, social and moral penalties against its rebellious children. Today, however, the pothead subculture has eroded and the population of smokers has broadened to include large numbers of middle class and establishment-oriented people.

Marijuana, then, may soon take its place with alcohol, its 'prohibition' a thing of the past. These two changes can be considered movements of moral passage:

> *Movements to redefine behavior may eventuate in a moral passage, a transition of the behavior from one moral status to another ... What is attacked as criminal today may be seen as sick next year and fought over as possibly legitimate by the next generation.*
>
> *(Gusfield, 1967: 187. See also Matza, 1969; Kitsuse, 1962; Douglas, 1970; and Becker, 1963 for further discussions of the social creation of deviance.)*

Profound metamorphoses testify to this redefinition: frequency and severity of arrest is proportionately down from a decade ago; the stigma of a marijuana-related arrest is no longer as personally and occupationally ostracizing; and the fear that using grass will press the individual into close contact with hardened criminals and cause him to adopt a deviant self-identity or take up criminal ways has also largely passed.

The transformation in marijuana's social and legal status is not intrinsic

79

to its own characteristics or those of mood-altering drugs in general. Rather, it illustrates a process of becoming socially accepted many deviant activities or substances may go through. This research suggests a more generic model of social change, a sequential development characteristic of the diffusion and legitimation of a formerly unconventional practice. Five stages identify the spread of such activities from small isolated outgroups, through increasing levels of mainstream society, and finally to such sacred groups as children.[1] Often, however, as with the case of pornography, the appearance of this quasi-sanctioned conduct among juveniles elicits moral outrage and a social backlash designed to prevent such behavior in the sacred population, while leaving it more open to the remainder of society.

Most treatments of pot smoking in the sociological literature have been historically and sub-culturally specific (see Carey, 1968; Goode, 1970; Grupp, 1971; Hochman, 1972; Kaplan, 1971; and Simon and Gagnon, 1968), swiftly dated by our rapidly changing society. Only Becker's (1953) work is comparable to our research since it offers a generic sequential model of the process for becoming a marijuana user.

The data in this paper show an alternate route to marijuana smoking. Two developments necessitate a modification of Becker's conceptualization. First, there have been many changes in norms, traditions and patterns of use since the time he wrote. Second, the age of this new category of smokers is cause for reformulation. Theories of child development proposed by Mead (1934), Erikson (1968) and Piaget (1948) agree that prior to a certain age children are unable to comprehend subtle transformations and perceptions. As we will see, the full effects and symbolic meanings of marijuana are partially lost to them due to their inability to differentiate between altered states of consciousness and to connect this with the smoking experience. Yet this does not preclude their becoming avid pot users and joining in the smoking group as accepted members.

Socialization practices are the final concern of this research. The existence of tinydoping both illustrates and contradicts several established norms of traditional childrearing. Imitative behavior (see Piaget, 1962), for instance, is integral to tinydoping since the children's desire to copy the actions of parents and other adults is a primary motivation. Boundary maintenance also arises as a consideration: as soon as their offspring can communicate, parents must instruct them in the perception of social borders and the need for guarding group activities as secret. In contrast, refutations of convention include the introduction of mood-altering drugs into the sacred childhood period and, even more unusual, parents and children get high together. This bridges, often to the point of eradication, the inter-generational gap firmly entrenched in most societies. Thus, although parents view their actions as normal, tinydoping must presently be considered as deviant socialization.

## Methods

Collected over the course of eighteen months, our data include observations of two dozen youngsters between the ages of birth and 8, and a similar number of parents, aged 21 to 32, all in middle-class households. To obtain a complete image of this practice we talked with parents, kids and other involved observers (the *multiperspectival* approach, Douglas, 1976). Many of our conversations with adults were taped but our discussions with the children took the form of informal, extemporaneous dialogue, since the tape recorder distracts and diverts their attention. Finally, our study is exploratory and suggestive; we make no claims to all-inclusiveness in the cases or categories below.

## The Kids

### Big Ed: The Diaperdoper

Big Ed derives his name from his miniature size. Born three months prematurely, now 3 years old, he resembles a toy human being. Beneath his near-white wispy hair and toddling diapered bottom, he packs a punch of childish energy. Big Ed's mother and older siblings take care of him although he often sees his father who lives in a neighboring California town. Laxity and permissiveness characterize his upbringing, as he freely roams the neighborhood under his own and other children's supervision. Exposure to marijuana has prevailed since birth and in the last year he advanced from passive inhalation (smoke blown in his direction) to active puffing on joints. Still in the learning stage, most of his power is expended blowing air into the reefer instead of inhaling. He prefers to suck on a *bong* (a specially designed waterpipe), delighting on the gurgling sound the water makes. A breast fed baby, he will go to the bong for oral satisfaction, whether it is filled or not. He does not actively seek joints, but Big Ed never refuses one when offered. After a few puffs, however, he usually winds up with smoke in his eyes and tearfully retreats to a glass of water. Actual marijuana inhalation is minimal; his size renders it potent. Big Ed has not absorbed any social restrictions related to pot use or any awareness of its illegality, but is still too young to make a blooper as his speech is limited.

### Stephanie: The Social Smoker

Stephie is a dreamy 4-year-old with quite good manners, calm assurance, sweet disposition and a ladylike personality and appearance. Although her brothers are rough and tumble, Stephanie can play with the boys or amuse herself sedately alone or in the company of adults. Attendance at a progressive school for the last two years has developed her natural curiosity and intelligence. Stephanie's mother and father both work, but still find enough recreational time to raise their children with love and care and to engage in frequent marijuana smoking. Accordingly, Stephanie has seen grass since infancy and accepted it as a natural part of life. Unlike the diaperdoper, she has mastered the art of inhalation and can breathe the smoke out through her nose. Never grasping or grubbing for pot, she has advanced from a preference for bongs or pipes and now enjoys joints when offered. She revels in being part of a crowd of smokers and passes the reefer immediately after each puff, never holding it for an unsociable amount of time. Her treasure box contains a handful of roaches (marijuana butts) and seeds (she delights in munching them as snacks) that she keeps as mementos of social occasions with (adult) 'friends'. After smoking, Stephanie becomes more bubbly and outgoing. Dancing to records, she turns in circles as she jogs from one foot to the other, releasing her body to the rhythm. She then eats everything in sight and falls asleep — roughly the same cycle as adults, but faster.

When interviewed, Stephanie clearly recognized the difference between a cigarette and a joint (both parents use tobacco), defining the effects of the latter as good but still being unsure of what the former did and how the contents of each varied. She also responded with some confusion about social boundaries separating pot users from non-users, speculating that perhaps her grandmother did smoke it but her grandfather certainly did not (neither do). In the words of her father: 'She knows not to tell people about it but she just probably wouldn't anyway.'

### Josh: The Self-gratifier

Everyone in the neighborhood knows Josh. Vociferous and outgoing, at age 5 he has a decidedly Dennis-the-Menace quality in both looks and personality. Neither timid nor reserved, he boasts to total strangers of his fantastic exploits and talents. Yet behind his bravado swagger lies a seeming insecurity and need for acceptance, coupled with a difficulty in accepting authority, which has led him into squabbles with peers, teachers, siblings and parents.

Josh's home shows the traditional division of labor. His mother stays home to cook and care for the children while his father works long hours. The mother is always calm and tolerant about her youngster's smart-alec ways, but his escapades may provoke an explosive tirade from the father. Yet this male parent is clearly the dominating force in Josh's life. Singling Josh out from his younger sister and brother, the father has chosen him as his successor in the male tradition. The parent had himself begun drinking and smoking cigarettes in his early formative years, commencing pot use as a teenager, and now has a favorable attitude toward the early use of stimulants which he is actively passing on to Josh.

According to his parents, his smoking has had several beneficial effects. Considering Josh a *hyper* child, they claim that it calms him down to a more normal speed, often permitting him to engage in activities which would otherwise be too difficult for his powers of concentration. He also appears to become more sedate and less prone to temper tantrums, sleeping longer and more deeply. But Josh's smoking patterns differ significantly from our last two subjects. He does not enjoy social smoking, preferring for his father to roll him *pinners* (thin joints) to smoke by himself. Unlike many other tiny-dopers, Josh frequently refuses the offer of a joint saying, 'Oh that! I gave up smoking that stuff.' At age 5 he claims to have already quit and gone back several times. His mother backs this assertion as valid; his father brushes it off as merely a ploy to shock and gain attention. Here, the especially close male parent recognizes the behavior as imitative and accepts it as normal. To others, however, it appears strange and suggests surprising sophistication.

Josh's perception of social boundaries is also mature. Only a year older than Stephanie, Josh has made some mistakes but his awareness of the necessity for secrecy is complete; he differentiates those people with whom he may and may not discuss the subject by the experience of actually smoking with them. He knows individuals but cannot yet socially categorize the boundaries. Josh also realizes the contrast between joints and cigarettes down to the marijuana and tobacco they contain. Interestingly, he is aggressively opposed to tobacco while favoring pot use (this may be the result of anti-tobacco cancer propaganda from kindergarten).

*Kyra: The Bohemian*

A worldly but curiously childlike girl is 7-year-old Kyra. Her wavy brown hair falls to her shoulders and her sun-tanned body testifies to many hours at the beach in winter and summer. Of average height for her age, she dresses with a maturity beyond her years. Friendly and sociable, she has few reservations about what she says to people. Kyra lives with her youthful mother and whatever boyfriend her mother fancies at the moment. Their basic family unit consists of two (mother and daughter), and they have travelled together living a free life all along the West Coast and Hawaii. While Josh's family was male-dominated, this is clearly female-centered, all of Kyra's close relatives being women. They are a bohemian group. generation after generation following a hip, up-to-the-moment, unshackled lifestyle. The house is often filled with people, but when the visitors clear out, a youthful, thrillseeking mother remains, who raises this daughter by treating her like a sister or friend. This demand on Kyra to behave as an adult may produce some internal strain, but she seems to have grown accustomed to it. Placed in situations others might find awkward, she handles them with precocity. Like her mother, she is being reared for a life of independence and freedom.

Pot smoking is an integral part of this picture. To Kyra it is another symbol of her adulthood; she enjoys it and wants to do it a lot. At 7 she is an accomplished smoker; her challenge right now lies in the mastery of rolling joints. Of our four examples, social boundaries are clearest to Kyra. Not only is she aware of the necessary secrecy surrounding pot use, but she is able to socially categorize types of people into marijuana smokers and straights. She may err in her judgment occasionally, but no more so than any adult.

## Stages of Development

These four and other cases suggest a continuum of reactions to marijuana that is loosely followed by most tinydopers.

From birth to around 18 months a child's involvement is passive. Most parents keep their infants nearby at all times and if pot is smoked the room becomes filled with potent clouds. At this age just a little marijuana smoke can be very powerful and these infants, the youngest diaperdopers, manifest noticeable effects. The drug usually has a calming influence, putting the infant into a less cranky mood and extending the depth and duration of sleep.

After the first one and a half years, the children are more attuned to what is going on around them: they begin to desire participation in a 'monkey see, monkey do' fashion. During the second year, a fascination with paraphernalia generally develops, as they play with it and try to figure it out. Eager to smoke with the adults and older children, they are soon discouraged after a toke (puff) or two. They find smoking difficult and painful (particularly to the eyes and throat) — after all it is not easy to inhale burning hot air and hold it in your lungs.

But continual practice eventually produces results, and inhalation seems to be achieved somewhere during the third or fourth year. This brings considerable pride and makes the kids feel they have attained semi-adult status. Now they can put the paraphernalia to work. Most tinydopers of this age are wild about *roachclips*, itching to put their joints into them as soon as possible after lighting.

Ages 4 and 5 bring the first social sense of the nature of pot and who should know about it. This begins as a vague idea, becoming further refined with age and sophistication. Finally, by age 7 or 8 kids have a clear concept of where the lines can be drawn between those who are and aren't 'cool', and can make these distinctions on their own. No child we interviewed, however, could verbalize about any specific effects felt after smoking marijuana. Ironically, although they participate in smoking and actually manifest clear physical symptoms of the effects, tinydopers are rationally and intellectually unaware of how the drug is acting upon them. They are too young to notice a change in their behavior or to make the symbolic leap and associate this transformation with having smoked pot previously. The effects of marijuana must be socially and consensually delineated from non-high sensations for the user to fully appreciate the often subtle perceptual and physiological changes that have occurred. To the youngster the benefits of pot smoking are not at all subtle: he is permitted to imitate his elders by engaging in a social ritual they view as pleasurable and important; the status of adulthood is partially conferred on him by allowing this act, and his desire for acceptance is fulfilled through inclusion in his parents' peer group. This constitutes the major difference in appreciation between the child and adult smoker.*

## Parents' Strategies

The youth of the 60s made some forceful statements through their actions about how they evaluated the Establishment and the conventional American

---

* As the Adlers themselves state, their data is merely suggestive. Given the small number of children they studied, the stages of development exemplified may not be representative of children in general. As an adult construct, *stages of development* may better reflect adult expectations than the range of children's abilities. Further study is clearly indicated, with particular concern directed to understanding children's perspectives in children's terms. An assumption of clear-cut age differences seems premature and involves the danger of forestalling investigation into similarities between adults and children. [Waksler]

lifestyle. While their political activism has faded, many former members of this group still feel a strong commitment to smoking pot and attach a measure of symbolic significance to it. When they had children the question then arose of how to handle the drug *vis-à-vis* their offspring. The continuum of responses they developed ranges from total openness and permissiveness to various measures of secrecy.

### Smoking Regularly Permitted

Some parents give their children marijuana whenever it is requested. They may wait until the child reaches a certain age, but most parents in this category started their kids on pot from infancy. These parents may be 'worried' or 'unconcerned'.

*Worried* — Ken and Deedy are moderate pot smokers, getting high a few times a week. Both had been regular users for several years prior to having children. When Deedy was pregnant she absolutely refused to continue her smoking pattern.

> I didn't know what effect it could have on the unborn child. I tried to read and find out, but there's very little written on that. But in the Playboy Advisor there was an article: they said we advise you to stay away from all drugs when you're pregnant. That was sort of my proof. I figured they don't bullshit about these types of things. I sort of said now at least somebody stands behind me because people were saying, 'You can get high, it's not going to hurt the baby.'

This abstinence satisfied them and once the child was born they resumed getting high as before. Frequently smoking in the same room as the baby, they began to worry about the possible harmful effects this exposure might have on his physical, psychological and mental development. After some dicussion, they consulted the family pediatrician, a prominent doctor in the city.

> I was really embarrassed, but I said, 'Doctor, we get high, we smoke pot, and sometimes the kid's in the room. If he's in the room can this hurt him? I don't want him to be mentally retarded.' He said, 'Don't worry about it, they're going to be legalizing it any day now — this was three years ago — it's harmless and a great sedative.'*

---

* The contrast between this statement by a medical doctor and present-day claims of the dangers of all drug use demonstrate a dramatic change in what is taken to be knowledge. Rather than viewing those in the past as wrong and we in the present as right, it is more useful sociologically to recognize that what is known changes in time. There is a tendency to view any present answer as the definitive one but experience suggests that it too will be superseded. [Waksler]

This reassured them on two counts: they no longer were fearful in their own minds, and they had a legitimate answer when questioned by their friends.[2]

Ken and Deedy were particularly sensitive about peer reactions:

> Some people say, 'You let your children get high?!' They really react with disgust. Or they'll say, 'Oh you let your kids get high,' and then they kind of look at you like, 'That's neat, I think.' And its just nice to be able to back it up.

Ken and Deedy were further nonplussed about the problem of teaching their children boundary maintenance. Recognizing the need to prevent their offspring from saying things to the wrong people, they were unsure how to approach this subject properly.

> How can you tell a kid, how can you go up to him and say, 'Well you want to get high, but don't tell anybody you're doing it'? You can't. We didn't really know how to tell them. You don't want to bring the attention, you don't want to tell your children not to say anything about it because that's a sure way to get them to do it. We just never said anything about it.

They hope this philosophy of openness and permissiveness will forestall the need to limit their children's marijuana consumption. Limits, for them, resemble prohibitions and interdictions against discussing grass: they make transgressions attractive. Both parents believe strongly in presenting marijuana as an everyday occurrence, definitely not as an undercover affair. When asked how they thought this upbringing might affect their kids, Deedy offered a fearful but doubtful speculation that her children might one day reject the drug.

> I don't imagine they'd try to abuse it. Maybe they won't even smoke pot when they get older. That's a big possibility. I doubt it, but hopefully they won't be that way. They've got potheads for parents.

*Unconcerned* — Alan and Anna make use of a variety of stimulants — pot, alcohol, cocaine — to enrich their lives. Considered heavy users, they consume marijuana and alcohol daily. Alan became acquainted with drugs, particularly alcohol, at a very early age and Anna first tried them in her teens. When they decided to have children the question of whether they would permit the youngsters to partake in their mood-altering experiences never arose. Anna didn't curtail her drug intake during pregnancy; her offspring were conceived, formed and weaned on this steady diet. When queried about their motivations, Alan volunteered:

> What the hell! It grows in the ground, it's a weed. I can't see anything wrong with doing anything, inducing any part of it into your body any way that you possibly could eat it, smoke it, intravenously, or whatever, that it would ever harm you because it grows in the ground. It's a natural thing. It's one of God's treats.

All of their children have been surrounded by marijuana's aromatic vapor since the day they returned from the hospital. Alan and Anna were pleased with the effect pot had on their infants; the relaxed, sleepy and happy qualities achieved after inhaling pot smoke made child-rearing an easier task. As the little ones grew older, they naturally wanted to share in their parents' activities. Alan viewed this as the children's desire to imitate rather than true enjoyment of any effects:

> Emily used to drink Jack Daniels straight and like it. I don't think it was taste, I think it was more of an acceptance thing because that's what I was drinking. She was also puffing on joints at six months.

This mimicking, coupled with a craving for acceptance, although recognized by Alan in his kids, was not repeated in his own feelings toward friends or relatives. At no time during the course of our interview or acquaintance did he show any concern with what others thought of his behavior; rather, his convictions dominated, and his wife passively followed his lead.

In contrast to the last couple, Alan was not reluctant to address the problem of boundary maintenance. A situation arose when Emily was 3, where she was forced to learn rapidly:

> One time we were stopped by the police while driving drunk. I said to Emily — we haven't been smoking marijuana. We all acted quiet and Emily realized there was something going on and she delved into it. I explained that some people are stupid and they'll harm you very badly if you smoke marijuana. To this day I haven't heard her mention it to anyone she hasn't smoked with.

As each new child came along, Alan saw to it that they learned the essential facts of life.

Neither Alan nor Anna saw any moral distinction between marijuana smoking and other, more accepted pastimes. They heartily endorsed marijuana as something to indulge in like 'tobacco, alcohol, sex, breathing or anything else that brings pleasure to the senses'. Alan and Anna hope their children will continue to smoke grass in their later lives. It has had beneficial effects for them and they believe it can do the same for their kids:

> I smoked marijuana for a long time, stopped, and developed two ulcers; and smoked again and the two ulcers went away. It has great medicinal value.

### Smoking Occasionally Permitted

In contrast to uninterrupted permissiveness, other parents restrict marijuana use among their children to specific occasions. A plethora of reasons and rationalizations lie behind this behavior, some openly avowed by parents and others not. Several people believe it is okay to let the kids get high as long as it isn't done too often. Many other people do not have any carefully thought-out notion of what they want, tending to make spur-of-the-moment decisions. As a result, they allow occasional but largely undefined smoking in a sporadic and irregular manner. Particular reasons for this inconsistency can be illustrated by three examples from our research:

1 Conflicts between parents can confuse the situation. While Stella had always planned to bring her children up with pot, Burt did not like the idea. Consequently, the household rule on this matter varied according to the unpredictable moods of the adults and which parent was in the house.
2 Mike and Gwen had trouble making up their minds. At one time they thought it probably couldn't harm the child, only to decide the next day they shouldn't take chances and rescind that decision.
3 Lois and David didn't waver hourly but had changing ideas over time. At first they were against it, but then met a group of friends who liked to party and approved of tinydoping. After a few years they moved to a new neighborhood and changed their lifestyle, again prohibiting pot smoking for the kids.

These are just a few of the many situations in which parents allow children an occasional opportunity to smoke grass. They use various criteria to decide when those permissible instances ought to be, most families subscribing to several of the following patterns:

*Reward* — The child receives pot as a bonus for good behavior in the past, present or future. This may serve as an incentive: 'If you're a good boy today, Johnny, I may let you smoke with us tonight,' or to celebrate an achievement already completed like 'going potty' or reciting the alphabet.

*Guilt* — Marijuana can be another way of compensating children for what they aren't getting. Historically, parents have tried to buy their kids off or make themselves loved through gifts of money or toys but pot can also be suitable here. This is utilized both by couples with busy schedules who don't have time for the children ('We're going out again tonight so we'll give you this special treat to make it up to you') and by separated parents who are trying to compete with the former spouse for the child's love ('I know Mommy doesn't let you do this but you can do special things when you're with me').

*Cuteness* — To please themselves parents may occasionally let the child smoke pot because it's cute. Younger children look especially funny because they cannot inhale, yet in their eagerness to be like Mommy and Daddy they make a hilarious effort and still have a good time themselves. Often this will originate as amusement for the parents and then spread to include cuteness in front of friends. Carrying this trend further, friends may roll joints for the little ones or turn them on when the parents are away. This still precludes regular use.

*Purposive* — Giving marijuana to kids often carries a specific anticipated goal for the parents. They know effects of pot are occasionally desired and actively sought. They may want to calm the child down because of the necessities of a special setting or company. Sleep is another pursued end, as in 'Thank you for taking Billy for the night; if he gives you any trouble just let him smoke this and he'll go right to bed.' They may also give it to the child medicinally. Users believe marijuana soothes the upset stomach and alleviates the symptoms of the common cold better than any other drug. As a mood elevator, many parents have given pot to alleviate the crankiness young children develop from a general illness, specific pain or injury. One couple used it experimentally as a treatment for hyperactivity (see Josh).

### Abstention

Our last category of marijuana smoking parents contains those who do not permit their children any direct involvement with illegal drugs. This leaves several possible ways to treat the topic of the adults' own involvement with drugs and how open they are about it. Do they let the kids know they smoke pot? Moreover, do they do it in the children's presence?

*Overt* — The great majority of our subjects openly smoked in front of their children, defining marijuana as an accepted and natural pastime. Even parents who withhold it from their young children hope that the kids will someday grow up to be like themselves. Thus, they smoke pot overtly. These marijuana smokers are divided on the use of other drugs, such as pills and cocaine:

    a. *permissive* — One group considers it acceptable to use any drug in front of the children. Either they believe in what they are doing and consider it right for the kids to observe their actions, or they don't worry about it and just do it.

    b. *pragmatic* — A larger, practically oriented group differentiated between 'smokable' drugs (pot and hashish) and the others (cocaine and pills), finding it acceptable to let children view consumption of the former group, but not the latter. Rationales varied for this, ranging from safety to morality:

> Well, we have smoked hashish around them but we absolutely *never ever* do coke in front of them because it's a white powder and if they saw us snorting a white powder there goes the drain cleaner, there goes the baby powder. Anything white, they'll try it; and that goes for pills too. The only thing they have free rein of is popping vitamins.

Fred expressed his concern over problems this might engender in the preservation of his children's moral fibre:

> If he sees me snorting coke, how is he going to differentiate that from heroin? He gets all of this anti-drug education from school and they tell him that heroin is bad. How can I explain to him that doing

coke is okay and it's fun and doesn't hurt you but heroin is something else, so different and bad? How could I teach him right from wrong?

c. *capricious* — A third group is irregular in its handling of multiple drug viewing and their offspring. Jon and Linda, for instance, claim that they don't mind smoking before their child but absolutely won't permit other drugs to be used in his presence. Yet in fact they often use almost any intoxicant in front of him, depending on their mood and how high they have already become.

In our observations we have never seen any parent give a child in the tinydoper range any kind of illegal drug other than marijuana and, extremely rarely, hashish. Moreover, the treatment of pot has been above all direct and open: even those parents who don't permit their children to join have rejected the clandestine secrecy of the behind-closed-doors approach. Ironically, however, they must often adopt this strategy toward the outside world; those parents who let it be known that they permit tinydoping frequently take on an extra social and legal stigma. Their motivation for doing so stems from a desire to avoid having the children view pot and their smoking it as evil or unnatural. Thus, to de-stigmatize marijuana they stigmatize themselves in the face of society.

## Conclusions

Tinydoping, with its combined aspects of understandably innovative social development and surprising challenges to convention, is a fruitful subject for sociological analysis. A review of historical and cultural forces leading to the present offers insight into how and why this phenomenon came to arise. Essentially, we are witnessing the moral passage of marijuana, its transformation from an isolated and taboo drug surrounded by connotations of fear and danger, into an increasingly accepted form of social relaxation, similar to alcohol.* The continuing destigmatization of pot fosters an atmosphere in which parents are willing to let their children smoke.

Marijuana's social transition is not an isolated occurrence, however. Many formerly deviant activities have gradually become accepted forms of behavior. Table 7.1 presents a general model of social change which outlines the sequential development and spread of a conduct undergoing legitimization.

---

* Now, in the 1990s, we are witnessing another moral passage of marijuana with its transformation back into 'an isolated and taboo drug surrounded by connotations of fear and danger'. There is no reason to believe that this transformation will be the last. Although the Adlers refer in what follows to five stages in the legitimization of marijuana and take the fifth stage to be the final one, present circumstances suggest the need to identify further stages to account for the movement towards increasing delegitimization. [Waksler]

Table 7.1   *Sequential model of social change: the diffusion and legitimization of marijuana*

| Stage | | Carriers | Marijuana |
|---|---|---|---|
| I | 1940s | Stigmatized outgroup | Blacks |
| II | 1950s | Ingroup deviants who identify with stigmatized outgroup | Jazz Musicians |
| III | 1960s | Avant garde ingroup members | College Students and Counter-culture |
| IV | 1970s | Normal ingroup members | Middle Class |
| V | 1975+ | Sacred group | Children |

Particular behaviors which first occur only among relatively small and stigmatized outgroups are frequently picked up by ingroup deviants who identify with the stigmatized outgroup. In an attempt to be cool and *avant garde*, larger clusters of ingroup members adopt this deviant practice, often for the sake of non-conformity as well as its own merits. By this time the deviant activity is gaining exposure as well as momentum and may spread to normal ingroup members. The final step is its eventual introduction to sacred groups in the society, such as children.

Becker's (1953) research and theory are pertinent to historical stages I and II. More recently, Carey (1968) and Goode (1970) have depicted stage III. To date, sociologists have not described stage IV and we are the first to portray stage V.

The general value of this model can be further illustrated by showing its application to another deviant activity which has followed a similar progression: pornography. Initially a highly stigmatized practice engaged in by people largely hidden from public view, it slowly became incorporated into a wider cross-section of the population. With the advent of *Playboy*, mainstream media entered the scene, resulting in the present proliferation of sexually-oriented magazines and tabloids. Recently, however, this practice passed into stage V; a violent societal reaction ensued, with moralist groups crusading to hold the sacred period of childhood free from such deviant intrusions.

Tinydoping has not become broadly publicly recognized but, as with pornography, the widespread (collective) softening of attitudes has not extended to youngsters. Rather, a backlash effect stemming from conventional morality condemns such 'instrusions and violations of childhood' as repulsive. Thus, the spread of deviance to Group V prompts social revulsion and renewed effort to ban the behavior by children while allowing it to adults.

These data also recommend a re-examination of sociological theories about marijuana use. Becker's (1953) theory is in some ways timeless, illuminating a model of the actor which encompasses a dynamic processual development. It proposes an initiation process that precedes bona fide membership in a pot smoking milieu. Minimally, this includes: learning the proper techniques to ensure adequate consumption; perception of the drug's unique effects; association of these effects with the smoking experience, and the conceptualization of these effects as pleasurable. Symbolic *meaning* is crucial to this schema: through a 'sequence of social experiences' the individual continually reformulates his attitudes, eventually learning to view marijuana smoking as desirable. The formation of this conception is the key to understanding the motivations and actions of users.

Accepting this mode for the adult initiate, the present research has explored an historically novel group (tinydopers), describing a new route to becoming a marijuana user taken by these children. As has been shown, tinydopers are unable to recognize the psychological and physiological effects of pot or to connect them with having smoked. This effectively precludes their following Becker's model which accords full user status to the individual only after he has successfully perceived the effects of the drug and marked them as pleasurable. Our research into child perception relied mostly on observation and inference since, as Piaget (1948) noted, it is nearly impossible to discover this from children; the conceptual categories are too sophisticated for their grasp. That the marijuana affects them is certain: giddy, they laugh, dance and run to the refrigerator, talking excitedly and happily until they suddenly fall asleep. But through observations and conversations before, during and after the intoxicated periods, tinydopers were found to be unaware of any changes in themselves.*

Their incomplete development, perceptually, cognitively and interactionally, is the cause of this ignorance. According to the socialization theories of Mead (1934), Erikson (1968), and Piaget (1948), children of 8 and under are still psychologically forming, gradually learning to function. Piaget particularly notes definitive cognitive stages, asserting that conservation, transformation and classification are all too advanced for the tinydoper age bracket. According to Mead (see also Adler and Adler, 1979), the essence lies in their lack of mature selves, without which they cannot fully act and interact competently.** The ages 8–9 seem to be a decisive turning point as youngsters change in internal psychological composition and become capable of *reflecting* on themselves, both through their own eyes and those of the other. (Mead argues that this is possible only after the child has completed the play, game and generalized other stages and can competently engage in roletaking.) Hence, before that time they cannot genuinely recognize their normal selves or differentiate them from their high selves. Without this perception, the effects of marijuana are held to those created by the parents, who frame the experience with their own intentional and unintentional definitions of the situation. Thus, tinydopers become marijuana users almost uncon-

---

* Readers are advised to read critically the statements concerning children's *inabilities* that appear in this paragraph and the next, keeping in mind the ideas presented in Chapters 2 through 5. The authors cited here by the Adlers adopt the adult perspective criticized in Part I and thus have in many ways assumed children's abilities and inabilities rather than subjecting them to empirical study. Further empirical research from children's perspectives seems indicated before it is possible to assert with confidence what young children do and do not experience. (Waksler)
** See in particular Mackay's earlier discussion of interpretive competence (in Chapter 3) for a critique of this claim. (Waksler)

sciously, based on a decision made by others. Moreover, the social meanings they associate with its use are very different than those experienced by adult initiates.

How does this new practice correspond to conventional modes of child-rearing? One traditional procedure we see re-affirmed is imitative behavior (see Piaget, 1962), through which the child learns and matures by copying the actions of significant adult models. Several of the illustrative cases chosen show particularly how directly the youngsters are influenced by their desire to behave and be like older family members and friends. They have two aspirations: wanting to be accorded quasi-adult status and longing for accept-ance as members of the social group. Parents have corresponding and natural positive feelings about inculcating meaningful beliefs and values into their offspring. Teaching boundary maintenance is also a necessary adjunct to allowing tinydoping. Marijuana's continued illegality and social unacceptabil-ity for juveniles necessitates parents ensuring that information about pot smoking is neither intentionally nor accidentally revealed by youngsters. Children must learn early to differentiate between members of various social groups and to judge who are and are not appropriate to be told. This is difficult because it involves mixing positive and negative connotations of the drug in a complex manner. Valuable parallels for this contradictory socializa-tion can be found in child use of alcohol and tobacco, as well as to families of persecuted religious groups (i.e. Marrano Jews in fifteenth century Spain, covert Jews in Nazi Germany and possibly Mormons in the nineteenth century). Members of these enclaves believed that what they were teaching their offspring was fundamentally honorable, but still had to communicate to the younger generation their social ostracization and the need to maintain some barriers of secrecy.

Juxtaposed to those aspects which reproduce regular features of socializa-tion are the contradictory procedures. One such departure is the introduction of mood-altering intoxicants into the sacred childhood period. Tinydoping violates the barriers created by most societies to reserve various types of responsibilities, dangers and special pleasures (such as drugs and sex) for adults only. Yet perhaps the most unusual and unprecedented facet of tiny-doping socialization observed is the inter-generational bridging that occurs between parent and child. By introducing youngsters into the adult social group and having them participate as peers, parents permit generational boundaries to become extremely vague, often to the point of nonexistence. Several cases show how children have come to look at parents and other adults as friends. This embodies extreme variance from cultures and situa-tions where parents love and treasure their children yet still treat them unequally.

How then can tinydoping be compared to traditional childrearing prac-tices and habits? Existing indicators suggest both similarity and divergence. The parents in this study consider marijuana a substance they overwhelm-ingly feel comfortable with, regard as something natural (i.e. Alan and Anna), and would like their progeny to be exposed to in a favorable light. To them, tinydoping represents a form of normal socialization within the con-text of their subcultural value system. From the greater society's perspective, however, the illegality of the behavior, aberration from conventional child-rearing norms and uncertain implications for futurity combine to define tinydoping as deviant socialization.

The authors wish to thank Fred Davis, Murray Davis, Jack Douglas, Virginia Forrest and Richard Travisano for various comments and inspirations on earlier drafts of this paper.

## Notes

1  The period of childhood has traditionally been a special time in which developing adults were given special treatment to ensure their growing up to be capable and responsible members of society. Throughout history and in most cultures children have been kept apart from adults and sheltered in protective isolation from certain knowledge and practices (see Aries, 1965).

2  Particularly relevant to these 'justification' is Lyman and Scott's (1968) analysis of accounts, as statements made to relieve one of culpability. Specifically, they can be seen as 'denial of injury' (Sykes and Matza, 1957) as they assert the innocuousness of giving marijuana to their child. An excuse is further employed, scapegoating the doctor as the one really responsible for this aberration. Also, the appeal to science has been made.

*Chapter 8*

---

# Dancing When the Music is Over: A Study of Deviance in a Kindergarten Classroom

---

*Frances Chaput Waksler*

## Commentary

Although the purpose of this article is simply to describe certain kinds of activities in a kindergarten classroom, it suggests the useful practical information that can emerge from sociological research. Teachers, for example, might find it very useful — though not necessarily pleasant — to have such a study done of their own classrooms, for in this way they might be able to identify many of the taken-for-granted assumptions that underlie their behavior and see their activities in the stark terms in which research presents them. Some behavior might be reconsidered, other kinds discontinued, yet other kinds reaffirmed; results of such a study would provide a particularly fruitful basis for making such choices.

As in the foregoing article by the Adlers, readers may find the issue of right/wrong and good/bad arising and will find that that issue is not addressed. Rather, the findings are presented in a way that allows readers with different moral positions to gain knowledge. Is the teacher described here a *good* teacher? Answers will differ according to different moral positions, different conceptions of the goal of teaching, whether or not one has had experience teaching, and so forth. The article itself does not provide an answer but does present evidence for those who wish to develop such an answer.

Seldom if ever, in its detailed daily manifestations, does behavior fit the public image that exists of it. Whether that image is positive or negative, elements of the opposite moral cast are also routinely present. Thus good teachers can be judged as doing bad things, bad teachers as doing good things. Practical activities are constructed as ways of acting in very specific situations

---

From Patricia and Peter Adler, Eds, *Sociological Studies of Child Development, Vol. 2*. Greenwich, Connecticut: JAI Press, 1987. Reprinted by permission of JAI Press Inc. A version of this paper was presented at the meetings of the American Sociological Association, New York City, August, 1986.

while public images are designed to present a view for public consumption. Detailed scrutiny of everyday behavior almost always reveals elements that even those engaged in the behavior might want to disclaim or at least explain as being undesirable but required by the situation. Readers might find it instructive to consider what would be revealed by a detailed examination of their own daily activities — work habits, housekeeping, study methods, etc.

The rules identified in this article — and note that they are *adults'* rules, not children's — are for the most part taken-for-granted; when they are set forth formally they may sound a trifle odd. Their oddness, however, does not disqualify them as rules. As long as they set forth guidelines for behavior and as long as breaking them is in some sense viewed as problematic, they are indeed rules. Identification of such rules is an important method for understanding the taken-for-granted dimension of everyday social behavior.

F.C.W.

## Introduction

This paper addresses the issue of children as topics of sociological analysis. In an earlier article (see Waksler, 1986, [in this volume, Chapter 5]) I have argued that although there have been many sociological studies of children *qua* chidlren, these studies almost exclusively focus on the 'childrenness' of children; few consider children as ordinary social beings, as members of the social world, as social actors. Clearly there are ways in which children and adults differ; my argument is simply that there are also respects in which they are alike. That children are labeled 'children' obviously has implications for them and for others in everyday life, but I see that label as a social one rather than as one with any particular ontological primacy. I want to suspend the notion of children and explore the sociological implications of so doing . . .

I claim that it is possible to apply to children sociological concepts that have been applied almost exclusively to adults. If children are seen as mere social members, rather than as special and as excused from ordinary sociological analysis because they are children, then the concepts that sociologists have developed and used in studying adults are applicable to children as well.

In this paper I will make use of the adult notion of deviance, particularly as it has been developed by Becker (1963). In the extensive sociological literature on deviance, that term is seldom applied to children and even less often applied to children who have not been judged mentally ill, abused, neglected, or those in some other social category that labels them different. Perhaps the term 'deviance' is seen as too harsh to apply to children; perhaps the notion of intentionality still hangs over the notion of deviance, and children are seen as too young to mean to be deviant. Or perhaps the term seems too strong for the kinds of activities that I have called deviance in this paper. In what follows I will argue and demonstrate that deviance can be fruitfully used as a concept to make sense out of children's behavior and out of adults' behavior towards children and that in the process, the notion of deviance is enriched.

## Methodology

The data for this study was gathered, analyzed, and originally written in 1965. I then set the paper aside. When a few years ago I became interested in children as a topic for sociological analysis, I unearthed the paper and was struck by the implications I saw in it. In what follows I will present the data and analysis in essentially the same form in which they appeared in my initial paper, foregoing the often felt but seldom acknowledged temptation to change one or both in the service of new ideas. The introductory materials and conclusion have been newly written to point out the ideas I now see in this data.

The school I studied was selected for me by the local school department when I requested permission to carry out observations; their criteria for selection were not disclosed to me. I was granted permission subject to the following conditions: I could not do a critique of the school; I could not take up the teacher's time; I could observe only for eight weeks (I was later granted a three week extension), once a week, two hours at a time; and I would not interfere with the classes. I observed during morning sessions — ten weeks in Kindergarten A and one week in Kindergarten B. I arrived during the free play period and left with the children.

The role of non-participant observer existed prior to my arrival, filled customarily by students from local teachers' colleges. On the first day of my observations, the teacher put a chair beside her desk for me and I sat in this position thereafter, except when I was following activities that took place elsewhere. The teacher asked no further explanation from me once she was told that I was an observer. No explanation of my presence was given to the children while I was there. Few children initiated conversation with me. When the teacher left the room, the children initially seemed to be curious about what I might do in response to their behavior but my failure to do anything seemed to establish my role as non-participant. Throughout my observations I took notes frequently, fully, and openly.

Most of my findings derive from my observations though some of my material comes from informal conversations with the teacher. During certain of the class activities the teacher was not actively involved with the children; if she was not occupied with preparing other activities, she would often talk casually with me. She answered the questions I asked about the children and volunteered information about their behavior, their families, and her attitudes towards them. During recess the teacher usually talked to the first grade teacher, who was outside at the same time, and I was generally included in the conversation as a listener. This conversation was often about the children. I occasionally asked questions during this time.

When I began this study, my interest was in observing children in kindergarten simply to see what I could see. I gathered varied kinds of data but quite early in the study became interested in those children's activities towards which teachers seemed to show disapproval. I focused my observations on such activities, working towards an identification of disapproved activities (those that were in some sense punished) and the rules, both explicit and implicit, that existed and were broken.

I worked with a rather diffuse notion of deviance. Rather than asking teachers what their rules were, I was interested in inferring these rules from instances of their violation. My particular interest in taken-for-granted rules made this course seem advisable since it seemed unlikely that teachers would be able to state those rules of which they were not aware and would be unwilling to state those that, when articulated, seemed in some sense objectionable. Instead of working from rule to violation to punishment, I worked in the opposite direction and was able to identify a number of rules and a number of instances of rule-use that have implications for the sociological notion of deviance.

## Theoretical Aspects of Deviance

The application of notions of deviance to children has been impeded by the assumption that adults' rules for children are in some sense *necessarily* right or at least 'righter' than those created by children and that children need rules in general and some specific set of rules in particular. From this point of view, children's rule breaking has been viewed as distinct from considerations of deviance, since the wide variety and range of reasons that adults can provide for their rule-breaking is denied children, whose reasons are routinely dismissed as wrong simply because they are children's reasons.

For the purposes of the following discussion I will define deviance as 'any thought, feeling, or action that members of a social group judge to be a violation of their values or rules' (Douglas and Waksler, 1982: 10). This definition was developed to be as inclusive as possible of the range of activities that get labeled 'deviant'. Although it has, to my knowledge, been applied only to adults, I see it as suitable for understanding the deviance of children.

Kindergarten deviance, during the course of my study, clearly emerged as that which the kindergarten teacher judged to be a violation of values or rules. Whose values or rules? Tentatively I will suggest three different sources of rules: 1) societal/cultural rules that the teacher imparted as part of preparing children for life in broader society; 2) classroom rules that the teacher viewed as useful for the conduct of classroom behavior; and 3) the teacher's own personal or subcultural rules that were taken for granted and simply transmitted as 'the way to do things'. Problems arise in distinguishing among these three sources of rules *in situ* since two or three sources may combine in a rule and since the first and second source, but not the third, are commonly accepted as legitimate reasons to give for rules, regardless of the proximate reason for their invocation.

Less clear in my data was kindergarteners labeling one another deviant, though where I do have data in this regard, I have included it. Further research would be required to distinguish between children's use of the teacher's rules and children's creation and use of their own rules.

I assume, on the reader's part, a certain familiarity with Becker's (1963) notion of deviance and will here, as a reminder, quote just a few of his ideas — ones that I found of particular significance in understanding kindergarten deviance:

— the questions of what rules are to be enforced, what behavior regarded as deviant, and which people labeled as outsiders must also be
regarded as political (p. 7);

— whether a given act is deviant or not depends in part on the nature of
the act (that is, whether or not it violates some rule) and in part on
what other people do about it (p. 14);

— deviance is not a quality that lies in behavior itself but in the interaction between the person who commits an act and those who respond
to it (p. 14);

— Who can, in fact, force others to accept their rules and what are the
causes of their success? This is, of course, a question of political and
economic power (p. 17).

All of these aspects of deviance inform my understanding of kindergarten
deviance.

In the data that follows, I will describe a variety of ways that adults label
children. What underlies this process, though it is a taken-for-granted process
embedded in everyday life and seldom, if ever, articulated, is that the term
'children' is itself a label, with all the attendant consequences of any label.
The common-sense notion that adults discover in children characteristics that
are there customarily obscures this labeling process. Analysis of the process
of labeling some social actors 'children' awaits future study. Here my concern is with what might be called *secondary labeling*, for labeling children
'deviant' would seem, at least on some occasions, to presuppose their primary labeling as 'children'. What gets labeled as deviant behavior of children
appears from my data to be at least in some respects different from what
constitutes deviant behavior in adults. Am *I* deviant if I spill my milk? Set
my chair crooked in relation to others? Not, it would seem, in the same way
as when I was a child. Getting labeled 'child' seems to have consequences for
which of one's actions get labeled deviant.

## The Setting

The public school I studied was located in a large urban area; students were
drawn from the local community. At the time of my study (1965), the school
was about ten years old and referred to by school personnel as new. In the
school were two kindergarten classrooms, each presided over by a teacher.
Four classes a day were offered: two in the morning from 8:30 a.m. to 11:15
a.m. for the younger kindergarteners (those who would be five years old by
1 April of the coming year) and two from 11:45 a.m. to 2:00 p.m. for the
older kindergarteners. The schedule of morning activities provided to me by
the Kindergarten A teacher, and followed pretty closely when I observed,
was as follows:

| | |
|---|---|
| 8:15–9:00 | Free play |
| 9:00–9:30 | Singing and/or listening to records |
| 9:30–10:00 | Individual projects |

| 10:00–10:30 | Kindergarten A goes to recess; |
| | Kindergarten B continues with projects and has milk break |
| 10:30–11:00 | Kindergarten B goes to recess; |
| | Kindergarten A resumes projects and has milk break |
| 11:00–11:15 | Stories and/or games |
| 11:15 | Children leave |

There were twenty-seven children in Kindergarten A's morning program and initially twenty-five in Kindergarten B's but this latter number changed to twenty-eight during the course of my study.

## A Caveat

In what follows, readers might be tempted to criticize the teacher's activities, policies, etc. I want to emphasize that the kind of close observation in which I engaged necessarily brings to light those features of everyday activity which are commonly concealed, ignored, covered up, explained away, etc. If *every* piece of my everyday life were brought forth for public scrutiny, behaviors would be disclosed that I myself might well deny or want to deny. Explication of the taken-for-granted routinely brings to light that which might well have been quite appropriately left at the taken-for-granted level for the purposes of conducting everyday life. The teacher I present here is not a storybook teacher but rather a real teacher engaging in the multiplicity of actions characteristic of living in the world of everyday life. To call the teacher either good or bad is to obscure the nature of her actions as actions.

## Procedure

In collecting data about deviance, I began by looking for instances of *discipline*, i.e. actions that in an everyday-life mode I identified as indicating that children, according to someone, were doing something wrong. I focused initially on the teacher as disciplinarian, but also collected some data on children engaging in disciplinary activities. I identified varieties of deviance by drawing inferences from the data; none of my informants articulated any of these methods of discipline. Having identified varieties of discipline, I observed the behaviors to which they were applied, primarily by the teacher since she was the most actively involved in the process, and I articulated the taken-for-granted rules that seemed to have been violated. I thus moved from discipline to rule-breaking to rule through an inferential process. The rules I was able to articulate through this process turned out to be rather complex and sophisticated, especially when they were applied to kindergarteners whose knowledge was, in the everyday life view of adults, neither complex nor sophisticated. Having identified rules, I then returned to observations of discipline and found that rule-breaking did not inevitably bring discipline. Finally, I developed a set of criteria that seemed to operate in the enforcement of rules.

*Varieties of Discipline*

I classified the discipline I observed into two types: verbal and physical. Verbal discipline involved only words. Physical discipline involved some form of control of or access to the child's body. I further subdivided these two types as follows:

*Verbal discipline*

command — telling a child not to do what that child is doing.

statement — describing what the child is doing or what people in general do, e.g. 'You're being awfully noisy this morning,' 'When someone spills his milk, he cleans it up.'

sarcasm — 'insulting' the child, e.g. 'For someone as bright as you are, you sure are sloppy,' 'Poor Ann doesn't want to play the game. Isn't that a shame?' (the latter said in a mocking tone).

threat — threatening either deprivation or the use of outside authorities such as parents or teacher.

*Physical discipline*

deprivation — preventing the child's joining activities with the rest of the class, e.g. having a child sit at a table rather than with the rest of the class during a story, sending a child inside during recess.

mild physical punishment — physically constraining or coercing the child, e.g. pulling the child by the arm, holding the child's chin while giving commands, statements, etc.

I observed the teacher using all of these methods and I used these instances as indicators that some rule had been broken. (After I had identified the rules, I was able to observe instances where those rules were broken and were not met with any noticeable method of discipline, a point to which I will return in a later section.) Of these methods of discipline, perhaps the clearest was the command, for it said what it meant and as long as the referent was clear (i.e. what of the many things one is doing one is supposed to stop), the child's expected response was relatively unambiguous. As Mackay (1974) would certainly point out, all the other modes of discipline required extensive knowledge and work on the part of the child if the intention of the discipliner was to become clear. That a descriptive statement can be a punishment, that a public announcement of one's action can be heard as a command to desist, that in a statement of what people in general do can be heard a criticism of one's own and differing action, implies sophisticated hearers, ones who are able to make complex inferences and thereby modify their action. Sarcasm seems even more complex and subtle, for it involves hearing a statement not only as a description of one's self but as an identification of something that one can and ought to change. It requires that one hear not literally but indeed the opposite of what one hears. Threats, when they occur alone rather than combined with commands, are similarly subtle, for they require one to assess all of one's behavior in order to identify that behavior which is at issue. 'I'll tell your mother' is mute as to *what* the mother is to be told. Similarly, physical discipline did not necessarily embody that which it disciplined. In the absence of commands (and even in the presence of commands of the form 'Stop *that,*'), children were likely to be aware that a rule had been broken but certainly did not necessarily know what rule had been broken.

At the time of my observations I was able to make common-sense inferences about the rules being violated — though my inferences may not have matched those the teacher would make — but it is significant that a task I found complex and ambiguous was assumed to be able to be carried out by kindergarteners in the course of their ongoing activities and without instruction. Furthermore, there is ample evidence that the children I observed indeed carried out this task in ways that satisfied the teacher.

Although my data on children disciplining other children is scant, I did see instances of children using disciplinary procedures. It would seem that all the teacher's methods were theoretically available to children — and fuller observations might well disclose all of them; I only observed 'commands' and 'mild physical punishment', the latter involving pushing and pulling, as well as a particular form of 'threats', namely, telling the teacher. I observed instances of this threat as well as its realization, i.e. a child telling the teacher. The realization, however, I see not as a form of discipline but as a step between two types of discipline: threat and whatever disciplinary method the teacher chose to use. Thus a child might as a form of discipline say to another child, 'Give me back the ball or I'll tell the teacher.' One response to this might be a return of the ball (and I would identify a taken-for-granted rule about possession of balls).

To actually tell the teacher, however, was an ambiguous and even risky step to take, and thus not necessarily a form of discipline in and of itself. In actual observed practice, telling the teacher could, and did, bring any one of four responses. The teacher might:

1    deal with the rule-breaker and ignore the teller;
2    deal with the rule-breaker and discipline the teller;
3    ignore the rule-breaker and discipline the teller;
4    ignore the rule-breaker and ignore the teller.

Children who chose this course of action could not with any accuracy predict the results of the telling and might, instead of bringing punishment on the head of another, call it down on their own.

I observed children's use of discipline most frequently during game playing. The teacher gave tacit approval to this use and seldom intervened though she too engaged in disciplinary activities related to games.

On the basis of observed instances of discipline, I inferred the existence of a variety of taken-for-granted rules, to which I turn now.

*Taken-for-granted Rules*

The rules presented in this section should be considered in the light of my earlier comments concerning rules that apply particularly to children and rules that apply to people in general. Some of the rules which follow can be considered in the light of social rules for social members in general, while others seem particularly child-oriented.

*Rule 1: Do not talk at 'inappropriate' times.* Although I did not hear any articulation of the notion of 'inappropriate', I observed a number of instances where children were disciplined for talking. I found this an ambiguous category and the data suggests the children did too. I saw children disciplined for infractions of this rule more than for any other. My observations suggest that this rule was violated if any one of the following criteria were met:

a.  if the child's voice was audible above the sound of the group as a whole;
b.  if the child talked 'frequently' during the course of a class;
c.  if the child talked when the teacher was talking or was preparing to talk;
d.  if the child's talking seemed to be causing slow behavior or poor work.

Understanding these criteria requires rather sophisticated discriminations on the part of those attempting to follow them. The first criterion presupposes an awareness of and attention to the volume of one's own voice in relation to those of others. The second calls for a kind of tally-keeping of one's occasions of talking and an assessment of what is *enough* and what *too much*. The third requires the subtle perception of the state *preparing to talk*. The fourth necessitates understanding a causal relationship between talk and action, a relation that may well differ among people.

Certainly this rule can be viewed as applicable to adults if for *teacher* one simply substitutes *other*. Adults also encounter difficulty in meeting the criteria for appropriateness, for adults can be loud, talk too much, interrupt or butt in, and allow talk to interfere with work. An examination of the disciplining of adults in such circumstances might provide useful comparative data. That adults encounter difficulties with this rule suggests that children's violations are not surprising either.

*Rule 2: Follow directions.* The violation of this rule was relatively easy to see, for it involved a child's failing to follow directions which were explicitly given. Disciplinary measures suggested that directions were non-negotiable, understandable, followable, and executable. I gathered no data to suggest that children were provided with an alternative to following directions. Again it would seem that in some situations adults may come in for negative sanctions for failing to follow directions where in other situations they may choose not to without prejudice. The adult experience that comes to my mind, one I certainly don't understand, is that of getting lost, driving into a gas station for directions, and not listening to or following the directions offered. I myself can feel clearly how my eyes glaze over and I fail to pay attention. Although I can't say why I do this, I can get away with it, paying only the penalty of staying lost. Arguments over directions among adults might provide useful data to compare with children's experiences (see Psathas, 1976).

*Rule 3: Follow explicit rules for games, toys, and singing.* Although I never heard these rules stated except when they were violated, their statement on those occasions suggested that they had been given to the children earlier and children were expected to remember and follow them. Rule 2 is based on the assumption that children will follow directions at the time they are given; Rule 3 suggests that children will remember and follow directions given some time in the past.

*Rule 4: Follow classroom rules.* Whether or not these rules were ever stated prior to any rule violation, they brought on discipline accompanied by the assumption or statement that children knew these rules and that rule-violation was thus in some sense intentional. I saw these rules as specific to the classroom, i.e. as not necessarily applicable elsewhere but required in the classroom. The specific negative sanctions I observed applied to the following violations:

    a. Not being able to put on outside clothing (jackets, hats, etc.) unaided;
    b. Not wiping up spilled milk;
    c. Not paying attention; not listening;
    d. Fighting;
    e. Running in the classroom;
    f. Throwing dirt;
    g. Going outside without permission;
    h. Not cleaning up after projects;
    i. Not sitting in one's own seat;
    j. Leaving milk in the carton;
    k Not carrying one's chair 'correctly';
    l. Not completing work during assigned time.

Disciplinary responses to these actions were accompanied with the statement or assumption that one knew better than to do that. As an adult, I can personally call to mind adult occasions when I have broken all of these rules, except fighting and throwing dirt, and perhaps my memory is simply faulty with respect to those two. I of course, as an adult, would argue that I had *good* reasons for my violations or that I did not accept the rules forbidding what I did. Children in the classroom I observed did not seem to have these alternatives.

*Rule 5. Act like a 'normal' person.* Violations of these rules were met with comments such as 'people don't do that'. The teacher's commands to stop behavior that violated this rule seemed to be the first classroom articulations of the specific rule. That a child would need to be told any one of these rules was taken by the teacher as an indication of the child's limits. Disciplinary action was taken in the face of the following violations:

a. Banging the eraser with one's hand;
b. Pouting;
c. Following the teacher around the room;
d. Being too quiet;
e. Rolling on the floor;
f. Being overzealous;
g. Blocking the slide at recess;
h. Ripping one's book;
i. Dancing when the music was over.

I remember this final violation clearly: The teacher had put on a record for the children to dance to. When the record stopped, all the children save one stopped dancing. He seemed to me to be having such fun — fun which abruptly stopped when the teacher told him to stop dancing because the music was over.

I have little difficulty in understanding why the teacher might find these behaviors disruptive, but I am intrigued with what the children themselves had in mind in engaging in these behaviors, an issue that was not addressed during my observations, either by the teacher or by me. To respond to these actions as rule-violations rather than as innovations, experiments, learning experiences, etc. is to submerge their meanings under the label of deviance.

If a child set a goal of avoiding discipline, successful attainment would require that a child remember all rules spoken by the teacher; understand, remember, and follow all directions given; listen to the reprimands directed towards others; and use 'common sense' as that is defined by the teacher. Those who seem to choose to draw disciplinary actions to themselves may well have been choosing that which they seem unable to avoid anyway. If one chooses to get into trouble, it is indeed a choice; if one gets into trouble unintentionally, choice is absent.

It should be obvious at this point that being a rule-abiding kindergartener is no mean accomplishment; it involves extensive, sophisticated knowledge and the grasp of a wide array of subtleties and nuances of words and action. Were every rule-breaking act to be followed by discipline, however, there would be far more discipline than I was seeing. Certainly the teacher simply missed some, but only when I turned my attention to violations of the rules cited above did I see the ways in which at least some of this missing was intentional on the teacher's part.

### Selective Discipline

Indeed every instance of rule-breaking did not result in discipline. Once I articulated the rules I saw operating, I noticed patterns in kinds of children who did or did not get disciplined. I constructed categories on the basis of the teacher's informal talk about the children. The teacher's assignment of children to categories seemed to have important consequences for the frequency with which they were disciplined and the acts that brought discipline. Some children whose behavior seemed very similar to me and who were disciplined quite differently turned out to be in different teacher categories.

Through the teacher's talk about children, I was able to identify the following categories. The categories are thus my creation, but the labels for them are direct quotes from the teacher.

*The independent and promising.* These children were characterized by the teacher as 'inventive', 'a character', 'everyone likes him', 'bright', 'nice', or 'cute'. These children seemed to be allowed to break the rules without negative consequences. I observed instances where the teacher seemed aware of the rule-breaking and did not discipline the child.

*The promising but in need of supervision.* These children were said by the teacher to possess some of the characteristics of the foregoing category but were also termed 'fresh', 'lazy', 'a talker', or 'a leader'. Rules were applied most rigorously to these children.

*Those for whom, with supervision, there is some hope.* These children were said to possess some negative characteristics which might or might not be overcome. Descriptions of these children included the terms 'strange', 'slow like the mother', 'like a wild animal', 'sour-faced like the mother', and 'a wise guy'. These children were allowed some leeway in rule-breaking, being disciplined more than the first category, less than the second.

*The too young.* These children were said by the teacher to be unlikely to be promoted from kindergarten. They came in for a moderate amount of discipline.

*Those for whom there is little or no hope.* This category included children whom the teacher said had serious problems. One was said to have an I.Q. of 68, another to be 'crazy like the mother', a third to 'make unconnected remarks like the mother'. These children were disciplined only moderately.

*The ignored.* This final category included children whom the teacher disciplined infrequently but the reasons did not emerge clearly in her conversations. One of these children spoke no English, only German; another was said to 'never talk'; others simply seemed to be infrequently disciplined.

Although I do not have observations to substantiate my claim, it is my impression that the teacher established categories early in the school year and did not frequently change a child's assignment from one category to another. My evidence does, however, suggest that children were disciplined with reference to their category membership rather than to the nature of the rule broken. Further work could usefully be done on the teacher's creation of categories. I found these categories not through observations but through teacher's talk, though after such talk I was able to observe instances of category use. The basis of the teacher's categorization was not always available through observation. Although some children were categorized on the basis of their observable behavior, others were categorized on the basis of what the teacher knew from other sources. Thus in one instance the teacher explained to me that although one child seemed to have little promise (a potential member of the category 'those for whom there is little or no hope') the teacher categorized that child as having some promise (a member of the category 'those for whom, with supervision, there is some hope') because the teacher had previous experience with the child's siblings, who were 'just like him' and eventually 'managed' in later grades.

In light of the teacher's categorizations, it is clear that not all children are equally disciplinable. Labeled deviance occurred in this kindergarten classroom when a rule was broken *and* the child who broke the rule was viewed by the teacher as a disciplinable child. Indeed I may have missed some rule-violations if they were committed only by children who were in non-disciplinable categories. To be disciplined, a child had to both *act* (break a rule) and *be* (the kind of child who is disciplinable).

### How to Make It in Kindergarten

If kindergarteners in the class I studied wanted to make it through the day both 1) avoiding any discipline and 2) engaging in all possible activities, including those prohibited by the rules, those children could follow the descriptive pattern which I will now present. The kind of child to be described would be able to avoid discipline and thus avoid being defined as a rule-breaker or deviant. From the teacher's point of view, such children would be typical, non-deviant, not rule-breakers. Such children are not necessarily ideal, good, in the process of learning, having fun, or bright; such children merely avoid discipline with the minimal possible sacrifice of activities.

These children may be of either sex and either white or black. They will arrive at school after 8:15 a.m. but enough before 8:30 a.m. to be ready to begin class at that time. When they arrive at school, they will remove coats, hats, mittens, leggings, and boots unaided and will put them in the proper place in a compartment provided for them. If they have brought in books or records, they will either leave them in their compartments or on the teacher's desk; in either case, they will tell the teacher about it.

They will then play or talk until school begins. When talking, they will not let their voices rise above the level set by the children as a group, i.e. their voices will not be individually distinguishable in the group.

When the *Star Spangled Banner* begins to play over the loudspeaker, they will immediately cease activities and face the flag. Under the teacher's direction they will salute the flag. They will then stand quietly while the teacher calls the roll, answering 'here' when she calls their names. If they know that a child is absent, they may tell the teacher so when she calls that name.

After all names have been called, they may resume playing. Again, they may talk or sing as long as no one voice is distinguishable. They may play with any of the toys (with the possible exception of the blocks, which may require the teacher's permission) and may play either alone or with other children.

Around 9:00 a.m., when the teacher instructs the class to clean up, they will put away the toys they have been playing with — completing puzzles they have been using (it is interesting to note that doing a puzzle is considered a game until game time is over, after which the same activity becomes cleaning up, and indeed may be done quickly even if it had presented apparent problems as a game), putting all else back where they found it — and under the teacher's direction and with the consent of any child involved, they may help to put away other toys that they haven't been playing with.

Either before or when the teacher indicates, they will stand behind any unoccupied chairs and will assume this to be their place for the day unless the teacher instructs otherwise. Whenever the children are told to return to the tables, they will return to their place. When the teacher calls the number of the table where they are sitting, they will carry their chairs — with seats facing towards them, hands on either side — to the circle and after placing the back legs of the chairs on the dotted line on the floor and the left side of the chair against the chair beside it, they will sit down some time before all others are seated. (The formulation of this rule makes the 'last' child a rule-breaker by definition. There is always one potential deviant in this activity, though such deviance may not be disciplined.) They may talk until all others are seated, at which time they will be quiet.

If the teacher addresses questions to the class they may call out their answer but will probably raise their hands. They will certainly do the latter if the teacher instructs it. When called upon by the teacher, they will answer immediately, briefly, and pertinently. They will remain sitting. When singing, they will sing loudly but without shouting. The teacher should be just barely able to distinguish each voice. They will know the words to the older songs and will pay close attention to the newer songs and learn the words. They will clap to the songs if the teacher suggests it or they may clap a bit on their own.

After the singing, when the teacher is giving instructions for the day's project, they will sit quietly, listen, and may volunteer brief information, especially if they have not done so before today. They will not speak with other children at this time. When the teacher tells the children to return to their tables, they will take their chairs and return to their place. They may speak until all children are seated but then will be quiet and listen for further instructions.

They will follow all instructions. When told to do so, they will line up for necessary supplies. If it is absolutely necessary, they may ask the teacher for help. They will work steadily on their project. If they are ahead of most of the other children, they may talk quietly a little. If the teacher has given such instructions, they will bring their finished projects to her as soon as they are done. They will be able to do all projects adequately or better. As long as they are working steadily, they may finish any time before the last child does. They will put away their supplies.

If the children are called together to have a story read, they will sit within the area from which they can see the book but not too close to the teacher. They will sit on the floor — not kneel — and will neither talk nor move while the story is being read. If responses are called for during the story, they will respond as soon as they know the answer.

During a game, they may raise their hands to be called on but will not ask to be chosen. They may talk with other children a bit. They will not give answers to the child who is 'it' and will not tell the teacher if another child does this. They may help those children who don't know the rules by telling them or indicating to them what is to be done.

During rest period they will put their heads down on their arms and be quiet. They may talk quietly when the teacher leaves the room but will be quiet when she returns. They will not swing their feet or tap on the table. When it is time to line up for milk and crackers, they will not push in line and will watch their milk as they are carrying it so that it won't spill. They may spill it once, but if they do so they will wipe it up with a paper towel. They will either finish their milk completely or spill the last of it into the sink. When the teacher is in the room they will return their carton to the wooden box, having first thrown the straw in the wastebasket. If they finish their milk when the teacher is out of the room, they will await her return before leaving their desks.

They will always walk inside the room. When it is time to go out to recess and the teacher instructs the children to get ready, they will walk up to their compartments, get completely ready unaided, and line up by the door, where they will wait until the teacher tells the children to go outside. They may talk during this period.

Once outside, they will not hang around the teacher but will play with the other children or alone. They will not get covered with dirt. They may yell, scream, or run. They will not throw dirt, nor will they climb on the fence or obstruct the slide. They may otherwise play with relative freedom. When the teacher calls the children to come inside, they will stand in line at the door, not pushing, and will wait until the children are told to go inside.

They will hang up their coats in their compartments unless the teacher instructs the class to hang them on the backs of their chairs, in which case they will do so and perhaps check to be sure any projects they are taking home are in front of their chairs on the table. They may talk during this time but will be attentive to any instructions the teacher gives.

If a record is going to be played, they will sit down on the floor near the record player and may talk a bit but will be quiet when the teacher approaches the record player.

At the teacher's instruction, they will put on their outside clothing and sit in their compartments until an adult arrives to take them home. They will remember to take their projects home though they may ask the teacher if she wants to keep them. They may run out of the building to meet the adult who has come for them and will leave the school at a little before 11:15 a.m.

It should be clear that 'making it' in kindergarten, i.e. avoiding discipline, requires extensive and complex knowledge. If the above description were to be elaborated in terms of the knowledge it presupposes, the result would suggest an impressive array that is assumed to be within the grasp of those who are also assumed to be 'immature', 'lacking in experience', and 'too young' for many adult activities. Here I simply will note two such spheres of knowledge that strike me as of singular subtlety.

These kindergarteners were expected to be able to see themselves in terms of others and make comparisons to guide their own behavior. They were expected to keep their voices at or below the level of others, regardless of what that level was or how it was achieved. They could talk if they were ahead of others in projects but not if they were in step with others or behind. They could talk until everyone was seated but not after. No one was supposed to be last (and thus, except in the case of ties, every activity could generate a deviant).

Kindergarteners were also expected to make judgments without clear guidelines, based primarily on experiences, by self or others, of negative responses to 'wrong' judgments. They were, for instance, not to sit too close to the teacher, but criteria for 'too close' were vague at best. They were expected to be 'normal', again an apparently criteria-less condition. And they were expected to talk enough but not too much.

There is an external constraint on kindergarteners using the above model to 'make it' in kindergarten: the model does not, because it cannot, embody the teacher's categorizations of children, for such categorizations seem to lie largely outside of children's sphere of influence. Or do they? Do kindergarteners seek to influence teacher's perceptions of them? As an adult, acting in everyday life, I might have said they don't, they can't, they're too young, they don't know enough, but as a sociologist suspending adult everyday conceptions about children, now I'm not so sure. I'm inclined to ask how they might go about this and to direct research to the topic.

## Conclusion

A consideration of kindergarteners' deviance reveals insights into some aspects of deviance that heretofore were less clear. By taking a sociological rather than an adult perspective, one can gain knowledge about children that would otherwise be hidden.

The link between deviance and difference emerges clearly from my data. To stand out in relation to others — by being louder, quieter, faster, slower, etc. — can in itself be sufficient to draw the label of 'deviant'. The road to non-deviance seems to follow the path of unnoticeability. To be like others — whatever those others are like — is to achieve a kind of anonymity and a safety from discipline. The issue here is not to conceal what one does but to do it unnoticeably. When adults are found to be different or find others different, a variety of rhetorics emerge to justify, rationalize, and explain why such difference is good/bad, acceptable/unacceptable, etc. Such rhetoric may conceal what is disclosed in the study of children — the implicit deviance in merely being different.

By suspending an adult view and thus the taken-for-granted assumptions that the teacher's rules are right and for the children's own good, I found myself puzzling over the origins and functions of the teacher's rules. Where do they come from? What do they do? My data does not allow me to answer these questions but does allow me to pose them. Further, my data suggests that the answers will be found not in the needs of children but in the social world which teacher and children inhabit.

It certainly is no surprise to any sociologist that rules are differentially applied, but I found it noteworthy that the teacher could explicate so clearly reasons for this differential application. My data on selective discipline suggests that the teacher was doing something when she was disciplining and when she was not disciplining that was in some sense independent of the violated rule itself. Furthermore, what she was doing was related to previously formulated notions about children's membership in categories and to strategies for acting in terms of members of different categories. In this view, the rule seems less important than the nature of the rule-breaker.

Certainly there are many ways that one can learn rules. One method that emerged from my study — a method that might have emerged in a study of adults but that caught me by surprise as so obvious when I was looking at children — was learning a rule by being punished (or seeing someone else punished) for its breaking. The rule that one should be 'normal' displays this method most clearly: one learns to stop dancing when the music is over by dancing when the music is over and getting disciplined. Folk wisdom calls this 'learning the hard way'. Adult experiences of this kind of rule-learning would seem to be a promising source of data. The risk, of course, in this kind of learning, is that one may get labeled deviant through one such experience and retain the label even though the behavior itself is forsworn.

Although one could certainly make the argument that children's deviance is different from adults' deviance, I am impressed with the many similarities that emerge when children's deviance is taken seriously. One characteristic of children that is of particular significance in understanding their deviance is their relative powerlessness in terms of rule-making, enforcement, and breaking, given the adult world they inhabit for so much of their everyday lives. Further comparison of children's deviance with that of other relatively powerless groups would seem particularly promising.

Another potential source of data that emerges from consideration of children's deviance lies in the reasons for their rule violations. Everyday life adult views suggest that children violate rules because they don't know any better, because the haven't learned the rules yet, because they are 'too young', etc., but suspending such views allows us to ask children themselves for explanations of their behavior. Why was one child rolling on the floor? Why was another banging the eraser? Why dance when the music is over? Posing these questions serves as both an insight from this research and a stimulus to further research.

By applying the concept of deviance to children, one can bring into view aspects of deviant behavior less obvious in the deviant behavior of adults. Studying children can thus serve sociologists as a way of bringing to light that which is hidden to them from an adult perspective. Applying to the study of children a whole range of sociological concepts customarily reserved for the analysis of adult behavior is thus a fruitful way to clarify and enrich those concepts.

Taking children seriously as subjects of sociological study — not as children but as members of the social world — not only promises conceptual insights but also brings to light a whole range of previously hidden data: what children do and think and see and mean in their own terms and how they live their lives with others, both adults and children. Viewing children as social actors in social worlds makes it possible to pose questions about what they are doing; such questions can only be asked, however, if one begins by considering the possibility that children *are* doing something and have reasons for what they are doing. I have found that by suspending my adult assumptions about children and looking at them as I look at other social actors, I find far more that children are doing than my everyday life attitude as an adult could have ever led me to expect.

I would like to thank the following people, who read various versions of this paper and offered helpful suggestions: Julius A. Roth, Norman H. Waksler, Erica Cavin, Nancy Mandell, and Peter and Patricia Adler.

Chapter 9

# Watching People Watching Babies

*Mary Constantine Joyce*

### Commentary

This study was conducted by a college student for a course entitled Sociology of Everyday Life. Joyce provides useful material for considering what interactions between adults and children can be like, shows the kinds of insights within the grasp of a neophyte sociologist, and suggests the difficulties of seeing sociological significance in 'what everybody knows'.

The major insight of the paper is Joyce's identification and documentation of what she calls simply The Look — a facial arrangement that she first notes on adults looking at babies. That such a look exists is certainly not an astounding finding, but recognition of it as a sociological phenomenon allows for its investigation in a systematic fashion. When is it used? By whom? With what implications? Joyce provides a preliminary exploration of the first two questions. She does not deal with the implications of The Look; at the conclusion of her article I suggest a few ideas in this regard.

As a study, Joyce's work is avowedly suggestive rather than definitive. Implicit in it are a variety of lines for further systematic study. It invites the reader's participation in identifying other instances and in following through on the interactional implications of The Look. It takes the perspective of the adults involved and does not explore the children's perspective — a perspective deserving of a study in its own right. It documents, however, a feature of the adult world that has important implications for children's social worlds.

F.C.W.

### Watching People Watching Babies

When thinking about a topic for a sociological study, I thought of how I found it interesting to watch the ways people act when they are around small children. I narrowed down my topic to: watching people watching babies.

Used by permission of the author. Editorial revision by F.C.W.

My information was gathered through observations at maternity wards in hospitals, in a local day care center, and in public parks by simply watching and recording the different types of behavior displayed by people watching babies.

As I proceeded with the gathering of my data, I began to get quite nervous because I was finding very much what I expected to find. People were acting in just the ways I knew they would act before I began this study: they would smile continuously at small children, raise their voices to a higher pitch, and bend over or kneel down to the child's level. At this point I wanted to change my topic and probably would have done so if it hadn't been too late in the semester to start something new. I continued, but felt I wouldn't learn anything new or interesting from doing it. The first phase of my study was thus a set of observations with no surprises.

## Phase One: Adults Watching Babies

I obtained my initial data through observations in the maternity wards of three local hospitals. I began by just walking around each maternity ward, then standing in corners taking notes, trying to be as inconspicuous as possible. My invisibility was quite easy to achieve; people were so busy watching the babies that not once did anyone question or even acknowledge my presence.

After gathering a modest amount of data in three maternity wards, I identified four areas of behavior that seemed to take on specific features when adults were watching babies: 1) tone of voice, 2) form and content of verbal statements, 3) facial expressions (The Look), and 4) posture. In all of my observations, my findings were quite similar.

### Tone of Voice

A frequent observation was that the tone of voice used by adults was noticeably higher than that used in ordinary adult conversation. There were some exceptions to this finding but the higher tone appeared to be both typical and unnoticeable to those using it. The sight of a baby seemed to elicit this tone.

### Form and Content of Verbal Statements

Some adults engaged in what I would call 'baby talk', i.e. talk used *by* adults when addressing babies (not the goo-goo-ga-ga that is sometimes called baby talk, i.e. talk *by* babies, though few babies seem to use it). Examples include 'Hi, honey', dragging out the 'y' when pronouncing the word 'honey', and 'You're such a pretty baby', dragging out the 'y' in 'baby' so that it sounds like 'baybeeeeee'. Another frequent occurrence was the repetition of a simple statement coupled with a high-pitched voice and The Look on their faces:

'You're gonna be such a big boy, yeah, you're gonna be a big boy.' To an outside observer both form and content can sound ridiculous but those engaged in the activity proceeded as if their behavior were quite ordinary. They seemed not to be listening to what they were saying but just went on and on.*

## Facial Expressions: The Look

This category was particularly enjoyable to observe and became the central feature of my study. I observed a definite facial change in all those I observed who were watching babies. People certainly didn't all look alike — they didn't all have the exact same facial expression — yet I could definitely say I saw a certain identical look on their faces when they were looking at babies. The Look can be impressionistically characterized as a constant, whole-hearted, everlasting smile accompanied by sparkling eyes fixed with fascination upon the child. People looked like they were dazed, yet happily dazed. The smiles did not leave their faces the entire time they were talking to or watching the child. The Look seemed so obviously one of pleasure, happiness, and contentment. The Look is very difficult to describe verbally but I found it immediately recognizable when I saw it.

## Posture

Since all my observations at the maternity ward took place where people were standing in front of a glass looking through to the babies, I did not notice anything of significance in this category. It is included here because it seems to me that the physical structure of the hospital might have prevented behavior that would occur in other settings. Indeed, my later observations demonstrate a posture that is typical of adults watching babies when they are tactilely available to each other.

After collecting and organizing my data from the maternity wards, I reached the point described earlier where I just was not happy with what I had. I had findings but my response was 'so what?' and 'who cares?' This drawback, however, worked into an advantage because my dissatisfaction led me to search elsewhere for The Look and I was somewhat surprised at where and when I found it. My further investigations led me to day care centers, where I observed adults interacting with young children (older than infants) and to pet stores, where I continued to see The Look.

---

* Further study might be devoted to the use of verbalizations that are designed for something other than communication. Is the infant expected to understand statements like those described? What indeed are such statements designed to do? [Waksler]

## Phase Two: Adults Watching Children and Children Watching Babies*

I went to a local family day care center located in a private home, where I sat in a corner and observed what was going on. The children here were older than the infants in the maternity wards, ranging in age from 22 months to 4 years. All of the children were able to walk around.

My observations here had many similarities with those made in the maternity wards. Again I observed adults talking to children in high pitched voices. When they watched the children, the adults here too had that same Look. In contrast to the maternity wards, I recorded far more 'baby talk'. I also had the chance to observe the posture of people watching children. When adults were talking to children, they typically adopted a kneeling or bending position that brought them to the child's level.

Although I did overhear adults talking to children without using it, 'baby talk' was clearly an ordinary event. Since I was able to gather more instances of 'baby talk', I was able to characterize this kind of talk more fully. 'Baby talk' as uttered by adults can be said to differ from adult talk in its distinctly higher pitch, wide fluctuations in intonation (from a low to a high range), a simple vocabulary, and shorter sentences. I heard a lot of repeated syllables (ma-ma, da-da) and the regular use of words ending in a 'y' sound (tummy, beddy). I recorded sentences such as 'Mama is coming to take you bye-bye now' and 'Do you want your ba-ba now?' ('ba-ba' referring to 'bottle'). When I heard this latter question being asked by the mother of the child, I asked why she used the word 'ba-ba' and she told me that her child could not say 'bottle' and said 'ba-ba' instead. The mother thus communicated with her child using the child's language.

The facial expression I have termed The Look was clearly in evidence at the day care center and seemed almost identical to its form in the maternity wards. The Look was not always used, however, but seemed to alternate with a modification characterized by a more ordinary adult expression combined with a special sparkle in the eyes. The eyes seemed in fact to be physically larger, opened very wide, alive and shining.

A surprising finding of my day care observations was the presence of The Look on the faces of children observing children younger than they. On a number of occasions when adults came to the center with younger children, I observed children displaying The Look when looking at 'the baby'. I observed children running over and saying 'Look! A little baby!' (Note that the speakers were no older than 4 themselves.) Next they would hunch over or bend down on their knees and all of a sudden that same look would appear

---

* The dividing line between the categories of 'babies' and 'children' is not clear and is drawn in different ways by different people for different purposes. The author does not provide criteria for her assignment of members to these two categories but does provide evidence that criteria vary according to who is making the assignments. Clearly this topic would be a fruitful one for study in its own right. [Waksler]

on their little faces. The constant smile, the glowing eyes, everything was the same as that displayed by adults.

Since the facial expression used by the children was similar to that of the adults observed here and in the maternity wards, I sought for instances of such similarities in 'baby talk' as well. I really wondered if I could identify children's 'baby talk' since those using it were to my mind little more than babies themselves, with what I thought would be a somewhat precarious grasp of their own language abilities. I was surprised to find that I could very easily identify their 'baby talk'. The children used a higher pitched voice than their normal one and simpler sentences and words than they customarily used.

One example is provided by Lauren, age 3, who was speaking to her brother Logan, 13 months. She said, 'Hi, Logan. I miss you today', extending the 'y' in the word today. Then she tried to pick up her brother but stopped when he started to cry. She continued talking, saying 'Come on, Logan, we go bye-bye now'. Taking his hand, she said, 'We have to go home and eat mum-mum now'. These kinds of observations were not uncommon when children were talking to 'babies', suggesting both that they identify babies and that they can treat them like babies.

### Phase Three: Informal Observations of Other Instances of The Look

My concern with The Look led me to notice its occurrence as I went about my everyday life. Here I note two settings worthy of more systematic study.

I dropped into a pet store simply to look at the puppies but as I moved from watching the puppies to watching the puppy-watchers, I noticed The Look. I must have been in dozens of pet stores in my life but it was only after working on this study that I saw what I must have had many opportunities to see before. The Look was unmistakable, just like the one used by both adults and children watching babies. I also heard people talking in 'baby talk' to the puppies: 'Hi, doggie. You're a pretty doggie'. Once again there was the extended 'y' sound and the repetition.* When one of the puppies was let out in the shop to run around, almost all of those in the crowd that gathered had The Look on their faces. My observations here are certainly not extensive or systematic but they do suggest fruitful lines for further research.

### The Look Between Adults

When I was telling a friend of mine about my study, she began to laugh and offered an example that suggests yet another area where The Look might be

---

* Those interested in experiencing the strength of this taken-for-granted rule to use 'baby talk' with kittens should try to say 'Hi, kitty' just once, without repetition, and in a deep voice. [Waksler]

found. She explained that whenever her boyfriend wanted her to do something, he would adopt a 'baby look' and she, struck by his resemblance to a baby, found that 'something came over her' and made her smile and 'kind of get hypnotized' and do what he wanted. The look she described herself adopting sounded very much like The Look, used not towards a baby but towards someone intentionally looking like a baby.

My study is clearly preliminary and requires further documentation. There do appear to be a number of places that The Look can be sought. Certainly The Look is not restricted to adults watching babies, but I have only identified the possibility that there is a broad range of situations where it occurs and have only begun to identify some of these sources. I have found, however, that merely recognizing the existence of The Look allows me to identify it in places where I had never noticed it before.

## Concluding Note

Having established that The Look exists, what are the implications of its existence? If we set aside the idea of socialization and focus our attention on adult-child interactions, we can see The Look as an important constituent of such interactions. It need not occur, but when it does it seems to add a noteworthy feature. It both creates and reflects an adult perspective in which children seem to be viewed as *highly-valued objects*. Clearly The Look is appreciative, but at the same time those to whom The Look is directed are defined as 'to be looked at,' i.e. as objects, rather than as interactional partners.

As Joyce demonstrates, The Look can be accompanied by 'a voice', a particular way of talking that reinforces the idea that the one looked at has some special quality. It can also be accompanied by a 'posture' that, while enabling the two participants to be on the same level, may also indicate that the one comes down to the level of the other. Neither look nor voice nor posture allows for ordinary interaction, for one of the partners is set aside as in some sense different and even extraordinary.

The Look indicates both that the object is special and that others to whom The Look is not directed are, by implication, not special. Further observations of adults, newborns, and their older siblings would seem a particularly fruitful source of observation, for The Look can be put on for the newborn and taken off for the sibling, perhaps unknowingly by adults but perhaps all too apparently to the sibling.

The role of The Look, 'the voice,' and 'the posture' in adult/child interactions would appear to be a fruitful topic for further study.

F.C.W.

*Part III*

---

# Children in a Child's World

---

The articles in Part III contribute to an understanding of children's social worlds from the perspectives of the children who inhabit those worlds. The authors have taken children seriously — watching them and listening to them as sociologists would any adults being studied. Unlike some of the adults described throughout this book, the authors here do not present children as 'unfinished', 'undeveloped', or 'merely emergent' or as objects to be socialized or in other ways acted upon, nor do they look at children with The Look described by Joyce. Rather they take children to be fully human actors, both constructing social worlds of their own and acting in worlds not of their making.

Readers are urged to suspend judgment on the reality, truth, or correctness of children's views and to resist the urge to view children's ideas and actions as 'simply a stage in development' or as something they will outgrow. In everyday life, adult biases towards children are both strongly pronounced and taken for granted. Vigilance is necessary if one is to avoid such biases and come to an understanding of children *as children,* in their own terms. To aid this process, readers might recall their own experiences as children, and in particular their own frustration and anger at adult interference and redefinition of activities. Those who remember being interrupted by adults because they were 'just playing' or being told 'you're wrong and you'll understand when you grow up' will find such memories a useful prod to taking seriously the children's experiences described in Part III.

F.C.W.

Chapter 10

# The Culture of Children

*Iona and Peter Opie*

## Commentary

The Opies have devoted enormous effort to extensive collecting of children's lore — sayings, rhymes, cautionary slogans, games, etc. — much of which is neither created by nor taught by adults. Origin *and* transmission rest with children, and transmission can occur, sometimes quite rapidly, both within and among countries. The Opies' concern is not with how this happens — clearly an exceedingly complex, intriguing, but separate concern — but with the surprising fact that it occurs at all.

The material that follows, excerpted from two chapters of the Opies' book, provides a wide variety of examples of children's lore. The existence of such material clearly suggests that children are more than receivers of adult culture and of ideas developed by adults; children are in fact active creators of the social worlds in which they live. For this reason the Opies speak of children's *culture*, i.e. what anthropologists refer to as a 'design for living'. All of the Opies' material suggests the existence of a culture or cultures of childhood independent of adults, created, sustained, and destroyed by children *for their own purposes,* whatever those purposes might be.

Children's accomplishments are quite clearly beyond what could be achieved by mere 'reacting objects' or 'empty buckets' but *are* within the capacities of those called children. The children who produce the kind of data gathered by the Opies possess knowledge, wit, a sense of the possibilities of language, and detailed ideas about the worlds they inhabit. That children are capable of such productions suggests that in other ways as well their capacities may well transcend adult expectations.

The data presented by the Opies is largely British in origin. Some will nonetheless be familiar to members of other cultures, thus reinforcing the

Opies' claim that such 'knowledge' can be shared by children worldwide. Other examples may not be familiar in their specifics but examples of the same kind can be found. I have provided [in brackets] some US examples; readers will in all likelihood be able to supplement the Opies' examples and mine with ones drawn from their own childhood.

In analyzing children's lore, the Opies introduce, though they don't really analytically develop, the intriguing concept of 'half-belief' to refer to those beliefs both held and denied, simultaneously believed and not believed. Any adult who knocks on wood or avoids walking under a ladder, not out of conviction but rather 'just to be on the safe side', knows the meaning of half-belief. The Opies also use the word 'superstition', but the negative connotations of that word — the idea of a belief without any foundation — biases what could otherwise be viewed in value-neutral terms. 'Half-belief' suggests an idea that is simultaneously questioned and used. This 'of two minds' quality of the concept strikes me as its core, a fundamental ambiguity that is lost in the idea of 'superstition'.

The Opies' presentation of the concept of half-belief embodies a somewhat condescending, 'adult' approach to this topic. If, however, the concept is not restricted to children and the 'childish' but instead is seen as referring to a human possibility, it can provide insights into children's 'knowledge', particularly where it differs in detail from adult 'knowledge', and into children's particular concerns. It can also be entertained as a possible sociological concept applicable to adults as well as children. (Indeed Roth's 1957 article, 'Ritual and Magic in the Control of Contagion', would seem an excellent example of a half-belief in germs held by medical professionals.)

Readers may find as they make their way through this selection that many of the beliefs and practices cited sound silly, peculiar, or obviously false until they encounter a belief they themselves hold; that belief or practice somehow seems to be far less peculiar and more sensible. Readers might find it useful to identify some of their own half-beliefs, both from childhood and in use in adulthood, e.g. those associated with the taking of examinations or the attainment of love. Recognition of such half-beliefs of one's own may prove useful in taking seriously those held by children.

F.C.W.

# The Culture of Children 1: Introductory

The scraps of lore which children learn from each other are at once more real, more immediately serviceable, and more vastly entertaining to them than anything which they learn from grown-ups. To a child it can be a 'known fact' that the Lord's Prayer said backwards raises the devil, that a small knife-wound between the thumb and forefinger gives a person lock-jaw, that a hair from the head placed on the palm will split the master's cane. It can be a useful piece of knowledge that the reply to 'A pinch and a punch for the first of the month' is 'A pinch and a kick for being so quick'. And a verse a child hears the others saying,

> Mister Fatty Belly, how is your wife?
> Very ill, very ill, up all night,
> Can't eat a bit of fish
> Nor a bit of liquorice.
> O-U-T spells out and out you must go
> With a jolly good clout upon your ear hole spout,

may seem the most exciting piece of poetry in the language. [Compare with the two US rhymes,

> Fatty, fatty two-by-four
> Couldn't get through the bathroom door
> So he did it on the floor.
>
> One potato, two potato, three potato, four,
> Five potato, six potato, seven potato more.
> Out goes Y-O-U.]

Such a verse, recited by 8-year-olds in Birmingham, can be as traditional and as well known to children as a nursery rhyme; yet no one would mistake it for one of Mother Goose's compositions. It is not merely that there is a difference in cadence and subject-matter, the manner of its transmission is different. While a nursery rhyme passes from a mother or other adult to the small child on her knee, the school rhyme circulates simply from child to child, usually outside the home, and beyond the influence of the family circle. By its nature a nursery rhyme is a jingle preserved and propagated not by children but by adults, and in this sense it is an 'adult' rhyme. It is a rhyme which is adult approved. The schoolchild's verses are not intended for adult ears. In fact part of their fun is the thought, usually correct, that adults know nothing about them. Grown-ups have outgrown the schoolchild's lore. If made aware of it they tend to deride it; and they actively seek to suppress its livelier manifestations. Certainly they do nothing to encourage it. And the folklorist and anthropologist can, without travelling a mile from his door, examine a thriving unselfconscious culture (the word 'culture' is used here deliberately) which is unnoticed by the sophisticated world, and quite as little affected by it, as is the culture of some dwindling aboriginal tribe living out its helpless existence in the hinterland of a native reserve. Perhaps, indeed, the subject is worthy of a more formidable study than is accorded it here. As Douglas Newton has pointed out: 'The world-wide fraternity of children is the greatest of savage tribes, and the only one which shows no sign of dying out.'

### Continuity

No matter how uncouth schoolchildren may outwardly appear, they remain tradition's warmest friends. Like the savage, they are respecters, even venerators, of custom; and in their self-contained community their basic lore and language seems scarcely to alter from generation to generation. Boys continue to crack jokes that Swift collected from his friends in Queen Anne's time; they play tricks which lads used to play on each other in the heyday of Beau Brummel; they ask riddles which were posed when Henry VIII was a boy . . .

The same continuity obtains in their games and play songs. When the Birmingham 8-year-olds chant about 'Mister Fatty Belly' they are perpetuating a verse with a lineage going back to schooldays under the Regency, for P.H. Gosse (the father of Sir Edmund) recorded that when he was at school, 1818–23: 'One boy meeting another would address him with these queries, the other giving the replies:

> Doctor! Doctor! how's your wife?
> Very bad, upon my life.
> Can she eat a bit of pie?
> Yes, she can, as well as I.[1]

Today, sets of these responses, usually repeated for counting-out [i.e. selecting one member from a group, as in choosing who will be 'it' for tag or hide and seek] or skipping, have been collected from schoolchildren in Aberdeen, Bath, Manchester, Market Rasen, Scarborough, Spennymoor, Tunstall, and York City; and some of the versions are all but identical with the rhyme as it was known more than 130 years ago. Thus a 12-year-old Spennymoor girl reports:

When I get home from school there is usually some little girls out of the infants school playing in the street, and their special little rhyme is:

> Little fatty doctor, how's your wife?
> Very well, thank you, she's alright.
> Can she eat a twopenny pie?
> Yes sir, yes sir, and so can I.

The older girls think that rhyme is silly for them, so they play faster games.

### Apparent Uniformity of the Lore

The fact that schoolchild lore continues to thrive in a natural manner amongst unselfconscious adherents, and that we have been able to watch it functioning in a number of widely separated communities, has allowed us to carry our study a step further than we thought possible at the outset; it has enabled us to obtain a picture of the state of traditional lore over the country as a whole. Thus it has shown that traditional lore exists everywhere; that as many, if not more, traditional games are known to city children as to country children; and that children with homes and backgrounds as different from each other as mining community and garden suburb share jokes, rhymes, and songs which are basically identical.[2] Conscious as we were of the economy of human invention, and the tenacity of oral tradition (the two elements without which there would be no folklore), we were not prepared for quite the identity of ritual and phraseology which has been revealed throughout the land in children's everyday witticisms, and in the newer of their self-organized amusements.

The faithfulness with which one child after another sticks to the same formulas even of the most trivial nature is remarkable. A meaningless counting-out phrase such as 'Pig snout, walk out', sometimes adapted to 'Boy Scout, walk out', or a tag for two-balls like 'Shirley Temple is a star, S-T-A-R', is apparently in use throughout England, Scotland, and Wales. If, in the vicinity of Westminster, a visitor hears for the first time children skipping to the simple chant,

> Big Ben strikes one,
> Big Ben strikes two,
> Big Ben strikes three,

he may well suppose that the words are the just-for-the-minute invention of a particularly unimaginative local child. Yet this formula is repeated all over London, down side-streets behind the Victorian mansions of Kensington, in the bustle of Hackney, in Manor Park, and outside London in Croydon, Enfield, and Welwyn. Travelling farther afield it will be found in use at Scunthorpe in Lincolnshire, at Cwmbran in Monmouthshire, in Edinburgh, in Glasgow, and, in fact, apparently everywhere. Nor is it a passing fad of the juvenile fancy, for it will be found that Norman Douglas quotes it in *London Street Games* (p. 49); and the fact has to be faced that since 1916 some

30 million children have dashed through the nation's playgrounds, respecters neither of persons nor property, yet preserving the silly chant as carefully as if it was a magic incantation. Similarly 'Pig snout, walk out' is known to have been current in the Island of Bute in 1911.[3] And although 'Shirley Temple is a star' cannot be so old, children have carried it to Australia and Canada and have planted it in those countries, or, perhaps, have brought it here from across the sea . . .

### Speed of Oral Transmission

Since, through our collaborators, it has been possible to keep an eye on several widely separated places simultaneously, we have, on occasion, been afforded glimpses of oral transmission in actual operation. The speed with which a newly made-up rhyme can travel the length and breadth of the country by the schoolchild grapevine seems to be little short of miraculous. Some idea of the efficiency of oral transmission can be obtained by the following verses which are topical, or which are parodies of newly published songs, and can consequently be dated, although for test purposes it is, unfortunately, best to study specimens which are of a scurrilous or indelicate nature for with these there is, in general, less likelihood of dissemination by means other than word-of-mouth.

A notorious instance of the transmission of scurrilous verses occurred in 1936 at the time of the Abdication [of King Edward VII, Duke of Windsor, to marry American divorcee Wallace Simpson]. The word-of-mouth rhymes which then gained currency were of a kind which could not possibly, at that time, have been printed, broadcast, or even repeated in the music halls. One verse, in particular, made up one can only wonder by whom,

> Hark the Herald Angels sing,
> Mrs. Simpson's pinched our king,

was on juvenile lips not only in London, but as far away as Chichester in the south, and Liverpool and Oldham in the north. News that there was a constitutional crisis did not become public property until around 25 November that year, and the king abdicated on 10 December. Yet at a school Christmas party in Swansea given before the end of the term, Christmas 1936, when the tune played happened to be 'Hark the Herald Angels Sing', a mistress found herself having to restrain her small children from singing this lyric, known to all of them, which cannot have been composed much more than three weeks previously. Many an advertising executive with a six-figure budget at his disposal might envy such crowd penetration. Similarly, the ultra juvenile verse,

> Temptation, temptation, temptation.
> Dick Barton went down to the station,
> Blondie was there
> All naked and bare,
> Temptation, temptation, temptation

wherever it may have originated, was reported to us in quick succession as rife among children in Kirkcaldy in January 1952, as known to children in Swansea in January 1952, and it reached children in Alton in February 1952. These three places are up to 400 miles apart; yet an instance of even more distant transmission can be cited. At the beginning of 1956 'The Ballad of Davy Crockett' was launched on the radio. It was especially intended to appeal to children, and quickly reached the top of the adult hit parade. But the official words of the ballad, beginning

> Born on a mountain top in Tennessee,
> Greenest state in the Land of the Free,

were very small beer compared with the word-of-mouth stanzas which rapidly won approval in juvenile society. One composition, beginning 'The Yellow Rose of Texas', was collected in Perth in April 1956, in Alton, Battersea, Great Bookham, Reading, and Scarborough in July 1956, in Kent in August 1956, and in Swansea in September 1956. Another parody sung by schoolgirls in Swansea in September 1956, appeared to have local associations:

> Born on a table top in Joe's Cafe,
> Dirtiest place in the USA
> Polished off his father when he was only three,
> Polished off his mother with DDT.
> > Davy, Davy Crockett,
> > King of the Wild Frontier.

The teacher who sent this verse remarked that Joe's Cafe was a popular Swansea establishment near the beach. Subsequently, however, we had news of the verse being current in Brentwood, Hornchurch, Reading, Upminster, and Woolwich, all naming 'Joe's Cafe'. But unknown to any of our home observers, and before the official Davy Crockett song had reached Britain, an Australian correspondent, writing 3 January 1956, had reported that the following ditty was 'sweeping the schools' in Sydney:

> Reared on a paddle, pop in Joe's cafe,
> The dirtiest dump in the USA,
> Poisoned his mother with DDT
> And shot his father with a .303
> > Davy, Davy Crockett,
> > The man who is no good.

It seems that the schoolchild underground also employs trans-world couriers.

*Wear and Repair During Transmission*

The previous section has shown how quickly a rhyme passes from one schoolchild to the next, and illustrates a further difference between school lore and nursery lore. In nursery lore a verse or tradition, learnt in early childhood, is not usually passed on again until the little listener has grown up, and has children of his own, or even grandchildren. The period between learning a nursery rhyme and transmitting it may be anything from twenty to seventy years. With the playground lore, however, a rhyme may be excitedly passed on within the very hour it is learnt; and, in general, it passes between children who are the same age, or nearly so, since it is uncommon for the difference in age between playmates to be more than five years. If, therefore, a playground rhyme can be shown to have been current for a hundred years, or even just for fifty, it follows that it has been retransmitted over and over again; very possibly it has passed along a chain of two or three hundred young hearers and tellers, and the wonder is that it remains alive after so much handling, let alone that it bears resemblance to the original wording.

In most schools there is a wholly new generation of children every six years; and when a rhyme such as 'Little fatty doctor, how's your wife/' can be shown to be more than 130 years old it may be seen that it has passed through the keeping of not less than twenty successive generations of schoolchildren, and been exposed to the same stresses that nursery lore would meet only after 500 years of oral conveyance. This, in itself, makes schoolchild lore of peculiar value to the student of oral communication, for the behavior and defects of oral transmission can be seen in operation during a relatively short period, much as if the phenomenon had been placed in a mechanical stresser to speed up the wear and tear.

Thus we find that variations, even apparently creative ones, occur more often by accident than by design. Usually they come about through mishearing or misunderstanding, as in the well-know hymnal misapprehension:

Can a woman's tender care
Fail towards the child she-bear?

[I remember being taught as a child a song called *Playmate* with the line 'slide down my rain barrel'. I have recently overheard children singing the song with the transformation 'slide down my rainbow'. Variations heard in recitations of the Pledge of Allegiance further exemplify the process the Opies are describing here.] A line in the song 'I'm a knock-kneed sparrow' quickly becomes 'I'm a cockney sparrow'. 'Calico breeches', no longer familiar to youth today, become 'comical breeches'. 'Elecampane' becames 'elegant-pain'. 'Green gravel, green gravel' becomes by association 'Greengages, greengages'. And the unmeaning 'Alligoshee, alligoshee', in the marching game, is rationalized to 'Adam and Eve went out to tea'. At one school the pledges 'Die on oath', 'Dianothe', and 'Diamond oath' were all found to be current at the same time. The common tendency to speed up a ritual or abridge a formula also produces surprising results. At a Surrey school the pledge 'Cub's honour' became, by jest, 'Cub's-on-a-car', which was presently abridged, so that the standard pledge became 'Car'. Indeed the corruptive influence of the pun on language and custom is more considerable than might be supposed. When a child, as a sign of derision, expels air through his compressed lips, the stock retort is 'We have them with custard'. The chain here is that breaking wind was, at one time, by the process of rhyming slang, known as a 'raspberry tart', hence 'raspberry'. Subsequently this became the name for the imitative noise made with the mouth; and this term is still retained, although it has disappeared as a name for the original exhalation.

Again, a fool is very generally called a 'blockhead', his head being likened to the denseness of wood. Consequently, as a joke, when somebody says 'touch wood' he is liable on occasion to touch the head of a notorious dunce, or of a child whom he wishes to make out to be a dunce, or, in self-deprecation, his own head. This joke has in fact become so common-place that many children are already forgetting that touching the head is a joke, and state seriously: 'If you say that something nice is going to happen you must either touch wood or your head', or, without qualification, 'To avert ill-luck it is the custom to touch your head'. So it is that the time is upon us when, in a prefabricated classroom with desks and fittings manufactured entirely out of plastic and chromium, it will not be possible for children to touch wood, only their heads; and when these children grow up it may become normal with the adult population, too, to put a finger to their brow as a superstitious act of self-protection.

Thus, it may be seen, oral lore is subject to a continual process of wear and repair, for folklore, like everything else in nature, must adapt itself to new conditions if it is to survive ...

### Sources of the Rhymes

The children themselves often have a touching faith in the novelty of their oral acquisitions. Of the rhyme,

> House to let, apply within,
> Lady turned out for drinking gin,

which we have collected from twenty-four places in the British Isles, also from South Africa, Australia, and the United States, and which was recorded as traditional in 1892 (G.F. Northall, *English Folk-Rhymes,* p. 306) an Alton girl remarked: 'Here's one you won't know because it's only just been made up.' Of the couplet,

> Mrs. Mason broke a basin.
> How much did it cost?

lines which are the recollection of a counting–out formula recorded in 1883 (G.F. Jackson, *Shropshire Folk-lore,* p. 573), a Birmingham child vouched the newness because it was 'named after a teacher's wife'. Children are, in fact, prone to claim the authorship of a verse when they have done no more than alter a word in it, for instance substitute a familiar name for a name unknown to them; and they tend to be passionately loyal to the presumed genius of a classmate, or of a child who has just left their school, who is credited with the invention of each newly heard composition. [A similar process takes place with jokes; children will offer the oldest jokes as new inventions.] The unromantic truth, however, is that children do not 'go on inventing games out of their heads all the time' as Norman Douglas believed; for the type of person who is a preserver is rarely also creative, and the street child is every bit as conservative as was George VI with his lifelong preference for the hymns he sang in the choir at Dartmouth. The nearest the normal child gets to creativeness is when he stumbles on a rhyme, as we have overheard: an 8-year-old, playing in some mud, suddenly chanted 'Stuck in the muck, stuck in the muck', whereupon his playmates took up the refrain, 'Stuck in the muck, stuck in the muck'. A 10-year-old added:

> It's a duck, it's a duck,
> Stuck in the muck, stuck in the muck,

and the group echoed this too, and went on chanting it, spasmodically, with apparent satisfaction, for above an hour, so that it seemed certain that we were in at the birth of a new oral rhyme. But when we asked them about it a week later they did not know what we were talking about. The fact is that even a nonsense verse must have some art and rhythm in it if it is to obtain a hold on a child's mind, although exactly what the quality is which gives some verses immortality is difficult to discover.

Where, then, do the rhymes come from? The origins of only a few can be traced, but these few may be indicative. The popular verse,

> Sam, Sam, the dirty man,
> Washed his face in a frying pan;
> He combed his hair with a donkey's tail,
> And scratched his belly with a big toe nail,

known throughout Britain in a multitude of versions (this one is from a 13-year-old Boy in Pontefract) is a relic of a once famous song 'Old Dan Tucker' composed by the black-faced minstrel Daniel Decatur Emmett, of 'Dixie' fame, and printed in 1843.... [A] further 'Ethiopian' legacy is the little tongue-tripping verse,

> I saw Esau sawing wood,
> And Esau saw I saw him;
> Though Esau saw I saw him saw
> Still Esau went on sawing,

sometimes sung by children when skipping (this version from an 8-year-old Alton girl) which is descended from the lyric 'I saw Esau kissing Kate' written by Harry Hunter for the Mohawk Minstrels sometime about 1875 . . .

This process of children adopting or adapting popular songs for use in their games continues, of course, in the present day. Such songs as 'The more we are together', 'Show me the way to go home', 'Horsie, horsie don't you stop', and 'The Lambeth Walk' (now sometimes 'Lambert's Walk') have a playground existence today far removed from their dance-band origins.

More recently, the American song 'Music! Music! Music!' ('Put another nickel in') written by Stephan Weiss and Bernie Baum, and published in 1950, seems assured of immortality, for both the original lyric, and juvenile extemporizations of it extolling film stars or denigrating teachers, can still frequently be heard in the playground, seven years and a whole school-generation after its original publication. [My remembrance here of a US example is of 'Lady of Spain.'] It is, perhaps, only to be expected that the most memorable verses should turn out to be the work of professional humorists and song-writers.

### Regional Variation

If the uniformity of schoolchild lore, to which we have so far been witness, was the whole story it would of course only be necessary to study one locality to know what goes on in every locality; and no matter how comprehensive and virile the lore was found to be, if it was the same everywhere, it would confirm the apprehensions of those who suppose that standardized education, mass entertainment, and national periodical literature have already subverted local traditions and characteristics. Happily our tale is not yet complete. Two distinct streams of oral lore flow into the unending river of schoolchild chant and chatter, and these two streams are as different from each other as slang and dialect. The slangy superficial lore of comic songs, jokes, catch phrases, fashionable adjectives, slick nicknames, and crazes, in short that noise which is usually the first that is encountered in playground and street, spreads everywhere but, generally speaking, is transitory. The dialectal lore flows more quietly but deeper; it is the language of the children's darker doings: playing truant, giving warning, sneaking, swearing, snivelling, tormenting, and fighting. It belongs to all time, but is limited in locality. It is so timeworn indeed that it cannot be dated, and words of which Shakespeare would have known the meaning, as 'cog', 'lag', and 'miching', are, in their particular districts, still common parlance; while the language which children use to regulate their relationships with each other, such as their terms for claiming, securing precedence, and making a truce, vary from one part of the country to another, and can in some instances be shown to have belonged to their present localities not merely for the past two or three generations, but for centuries.

Conflicting as are the characteristics of these two types of lore, the one rapidly spreading from place to place and having a brief existence, the other having a prolonged existence but rarely spreading, it is not impossible to see how they subsist together. When a child newly arrives in a district any slang expression he knows, any jokes or tricks, or any new skipping or 'dipping' rhymes he brings with him, are eagerly listened to, and if found amusing, are added to the local repertoire, and may eventually supplant similar pieces of lore already known. But the local children, while willing to enlarge their store of jokes and rhymes, will not consciously brook any alteration to what they already know. The new child must learn, and very quickly does so, the 'legislative' language of new playmates. He must learn the local names for the playground games, and the expressions used while playing them. Unless he does this, he will not merely be though peculiar, he will not be understood. A child who moves from Lincoln and cries 'Screams' for mercy in Leicester will find that he receives no sympathy, since the accepted truce term in Leicester is 'Croggies'. Similarly a 12-year-old Spennymoor girl who says,

> When the rope is turning away from the nobby-ender it is lupey-dyke. When the nobby-ender is out he takes the laggy-ender's place and the laggy-ender takes the foggy-ender's place so that the foggy-ender becomes the nobby-ender.

will be thought out of her mind if she says this in the hearing of a Spitalfields girl, although both children in fact adhere to this practice while skipping, and both may skip to the same rhymes. [US terminology includes, for jumping rope: steady swingers, hot peppers, and double Dutch; and, for other games, terms for calling in players at end of a game or part of a game — 'allie, allie infree'; and, for claiming safety — 'my gools, 1-2-3; for starting hide and seek, after counting saying 'Anyone around my gools shall be it'.]

This regional variation in the children's dialectal lore has been as unexpected as the slavish uniformity of their slang lore; and when the children's customs and superstitious practices are examined, in particular their calendar customs, the regional differences are remarkable. While some children roll eggs at Easter, or nettle the legs of classmates on the twenty-ninth of May, or leave little gifts on people's doorsteps on St. Valentine's Day, or act under the delusion that they are above the law on the night of 4 November, other children, sometimes living only the other side of a hill, will have no knowledge of these activities. It is not perhaps of much consequence that in different parts of England children have different ritual ways of disposing of their milk [baby] teeth, that there are more than sixty names for the illegal pursuit of knocking at doors and running away, that in some places walking under a ladder can be lucky and seeing a black cat can be unlucky, and that some children makes fools on the first of May with more zeal than on the first of April; but the children's loyalty to local customs and forms of speech is at least evidence that the young in Britain do not take as their authority only what they hear and see on the wireless and television and at the cinema.

[It may be helpful at this point to review briefly the somewhat complex processes the Opies have described in this excerpt. They distinguish between *nursery rhymes*, part of the *literary* culture of childhood, transmitted by adults to children; and *school rhymes*, part of the *oral* culture of childhood, transmitted by and to children. The Opies' concern is with the latter. They claim that children possess a culture, characterized by its:

1 transmission through generations in much the same form though with some wear and tear
2 transmission of *new* lore within and between societies, a process that is often rapid but also transitory
3 uniformity within and between children's culture of different societies as well as local variations that endure, do not spread to other localities, but may be translatable in terms of one another.]

# The Culture of Children 2: Half-Belief

Outwardly the children in the back streets and around the housing estate appear to belong to the twentieth century, but ancient apprehensions, even if only half believed in, continue to infiltrate their minds; warning them that moonlight shining on a person's face when he is asleep will make him go mad, that vinegar stops a person growing no matter how young he is, that a bleeding wart never stops bleeding and the person will bleed to death. They confide to each other that a stone-chip picked up off a grave brings a curse upon him who takes it; that a nose which is too long may be shortened by rubbing it with wet grass on the night of a new moon; and that if a photograph in a frame is dropped and the glass breaks, a painful accident will befall the subject of the photograph. 'I shudder if I break a mirror, fearing seven years' bad luck', says a 14-year-old Yorkshire girl; and a Radnorshire lad affirms, 'If you break a mirror they say seven years' bad luck to you. This is true in my family.' With simple faith they accept beliefs which have not changed since Shakespeare's day: that if a dog howls outside a house or scratches at the floor someone is going to die in that house; that if owls screech at night it is a sign of death; that if a person hears of two deaths he will assuredly hear of a third; and in evening places where children meet the telling of each dark precept is supported with gruesome instances. [Mark Twain's *Tom Sawyer* comes to mind here.] They begin to share the awe felt by Mole in *The Wind in the Willows* when Ratty warned him of the hundred things an animal had first to understand before entering the Wild Wood:

> Passwords, and signs, and sayings which have power and effect, and plants you carry in your pocket, and verses you repeat, and dodges and tricks you practise; all simple enough when you know them, but they've got to be known if you're small, or you'll find yourself in trouble.

It is such dark thoughts which cause children at Brierley Hill in south Staffordshire to hide their little fingers when an ambulance goes by for fear that their finger-nails will drop out; which induce children in the Gower Peninsula to spit when they see a dead animal and cry:

Fever, fever, stay away
Don't come in my bed today;

and which lead children in Scotland when they see a large black slug or snail to spit on it, declaring, 'It's no ma Dye, an' its no ma Grannie' (reported from Ballingry, Cowdenbeath, and Gartcosh, near Glasgow). And one wonders how many bishops are aware of the jockeying for places which goes on beforehand among the candidates for confirmation when word gets about that to be confirmed with the bishop's right hand is lucky, but to be confirmed with his left hand means bad luck.


### Juvenile Attitude to Folklore

The beliefs with which we are concerned here are those which children absorb through going about with each other, and consequently mostly involve happenings out-of-doors; people met in the street, objects found in the road, and mascots carried with them to school. We find, what is understandable, that the younger schoolchildren treat the beliefs and rites of their companions more seriously than those practised by their parents and grandparents; although it is noticeable that later (14-years-old onwards) the child-to-child superstitions tend to be discarded, along with the rest of the lore, and even forgotten, while the more domestic traditions, which are passed down in the family, are mentioned with increasing frequency.

When asked how much they believe in their superstitions most children will say (as they feel they are expected to say?) that all superstitions are silly. But it may, in passing, be observed that few people, adult or juvenile, are above doing what is silly. As a 10-year-old Nottinghamshire girl candidly confesses, 'If I want to have good luck I do very funny things', and she goes on to say:

First of all I close my eyes and wave my arms about ten times.

Secondly I always wear my vest [undershirt] inside out and my jumper [sweater] back to front. I did that in the selection examination and that brought good luck. When I heard the results that I had passed, as soon as I got home I changed everything round; if I had not done it would have brought bad luck.

If I am going in for a competition I do not do that, I put a glove on my left hand and suck my other hand at night. I did that once in a Competition and I won first prize — a bike.

Further it may be remarked that when a practice or omen is termed a 'superstition' it is generally one which is not believed in by the person so referring to it. When collecting this lore from children we have not asked for 'superstitions' as such, but have inquired after the 'magic practices' they knew, or asked for their 'ways of obtaining luck or averting ill-luck'.

Many charms and rites are of course practised by children 'just for fun', because everybody else practises them, and it is the fashion. Other charms, although recognized as being 'probably silly', are repeated because they also feel that there 'may be something in it'. Others, again, are practised because it is in the nature of children to be attracted by the mysterious; they appear to have an innate awareness that there is more to the ordering of fate than appears on the surface. And yet other practices and beliefs are undoubtedly so taken for granted that it is not appreciated that the custom or belief is in fact superstitious. . . .

The children's beliefs do not, as may first appear, consist of a miscellany of unrelated scraps. Looked at all together they are seen to fall into a definite pattern, and the dominant motives which emerge in the things that they feel bring good luck or evil, e.g. dislike of seeing the backs of objects (ambulances, mail vans, hay wains; also blind men, men with wooden legs, and nuns); reluctance to anticipate events, for instance not putting water in a jar before the first tiddler [tiny fish] has been caught; and love of safeguards as shown in their addiction to lucky charms, scapegoats, and finger-crossing, probably satisfy psychological impulses as well as following the path of tradition.

### Ambulances

An understandable instance of a custom attaching itself to an inanimate object is the hospital ambulance fetish. Amongst children throughout England the sight of an ambulance passing in the street instantly evokes a self-protective charm. 'I was bringing a bunch of orphans to a party in my car yesterday', reports a Manchester teacher (1953), 'when one of them saw an ambulance. "Touch your collar and look for a four-footed animal", she commanded the rest'; and this practice appears to be commonplace, the rite very often being decreed in rhyme. . .

### Omens on the Way to School

. . . Superstitious regard for some objects, such as beetles, bridges, cats, hay carts, ladders, falling leaves, lumps of coal, and cracks in the pavement, seems to extend to every corner of Britain; and these beliefs, and the customs which accompany them, are far from being the 'fast perishing relics' they are sometimes assumed to be.

It must always be remembered that although to an adult a particular belief may seem like a coelacanthine survival from the past, to the schoolchild who learns it from his mate the belief is a novelty; it is something just learnt, and often excitingly full of possibility for his immediate welfare.

When a child steps out of his home to go to school, whether he lives in a remote hamlet or in one of the backstreets of a great city, he is on his own, and looking after himself. The day ahead looms large and endless in front of him, and his eyes are wide open for the prognostics which will tell him his fortune. . .

[At this point the Opies provide details about specific beliefs and practices that for the most part seem more typical of Britain, or perhaps of rural Britain, than of the US. They are related to beetles, birds, blind men, bridges, cats, chimney sweeps, cross-eyed women, crows, cuckoos, dogs, dung, funerals, hares, hats, hay carts, horses, ladders, lady drivers, ladybirds, leaves, magpies, mail vans, money-puzzle trees, nuns, oil patches, rabbits, and rain, the following two being perhaps more familiar to US readers:

> Rain, rain, go away,
> Come again another day
>
> It's raining, it's pouring
> The old man's snoring;
> He got into bed
> And bumped his head
> And couldn't get up in the morning.

as well as rainbows, sailors, snow, spiders, trains, and wooden legs. The beliefs and practices of children in many different societies could generate lists of 'omens on the way to school' that, while differing in particulars, would be the same *kind* of list.]

### Lines on Pavements

One of the inexplicables is the amount of lore which has become associated with flagstones, and apparently all children, when the fever is on them, are punctilious about the way they walk along an ordinary pavement. To step on a crack in the stone, or on the lines between the stones, is invariably taken to be unlucky, and the precise catastrophe which will follow is very often known to them, for instance: 'You will get your sums wrong' (Ipswich); 'Your hair will fall out' (Loughton); 'You will fall downstairs next day' (Manchester); 'You will break your spine' (Newcastle upon Tyne)[4]....

In Lancashire and adjacent parts of Cheshire and the West Riding, children have the quaint saying:

> If you tread on a nick
> You'll marry a brick (or a 'stick')
> And a beetle will come to your wedding.

Around Sheffield, they chant:

> If you stand on a line
> You'll marry a swine;
> If you stand on a square
> You'll marry a bear.

The fable that sillies who step on lines will be chased by bears when they reach the corner of the road, unforgettable in A.A. Milne's *When We Were*

*Very Young* (1924), is recounted throughout southern England where it is variously asserted: 'bears will bite you', 'they will squeeze you', 'they will eat you'. It is also exotically reported that snakes will chase you home (Norfolk), or that you will marry a snake (Manchester); that you'll drown in the sea (Loughton); that each time you tread on a line you kill a fairy (one boy, Peterborough) or that 'you walk on the old man's toes' (Oxford). Old Nick's perhaps?

Further sayings, apparently not peculiar to any locality, associate the lines with broken crockery. In Ballingry, Fife, if a person treads on the lines he is said to be 'breaking God's plates.' In Aberdeen if he walks on cracks (as distinct from lines) he is 'breaking the devil's dishes', or his 'mother's best china dishes', and the more cracks he walks on the more he breaks.... In parts of East Anglia, if a child steps on lines or cracks, or slips off the kerb, it is said he will break his mother's best teapot.

In Peterborough and Swansea the mother's attitude is reflected in the jingle:

Tread on lines your mother's kind;
Tread on squares your mother swears.

And in Portsmouth it is reported that children also take notice of the water-courses across the pavement:

If you tread on a crack, or tread on a spout,
It's a sure thing your mother will turn you out.

In America pavement lore appears to be more uniform than in Britain. Recordings made in recent years in Illinois, Iowa, New Jersey, Louisiana, New York State, Ohio, and Texas, have all been similar. The child says 'Step on a crack', and continues 'You'll break your mother's back' or 'You'll break your grandmother's back', or 'Break the devil's back'.

### Finding Things

It is not usually considered enough merely to find a lucky object. If the finder is to benefit by his encounter he must go through prescribed actions with his find, step on it, threaten it, spit on it, implore of it, or, very often, throw it away. The only exception seems to be the four leaf clover, the discovery of which appears to be felt singular enough to be lucky in itself ...

[At this point the Opies provide a variety of British examples related to finding buttons, cigarette packets, and four leaf clovers, noting that Sir John Melton records an example of the latter in his *Astrologaster*, 1620, p. 46 (cited by Brand): 'If a man, walking the fields, finde any foure-leaved grasse, he shall, in a small while after, finde some good thing'; and of finding coal, coins, feathers, horseshoes, pins, rings, sticks, and stones. US examples include some of the above as well as *a penny* (finding it and picking it up will bring good luck; not picking it up will bring bad luck); and *an eyelash* (upon which one can wish and then blow it away).]

It will be noticed that to find any of the above objects is potentially beneficial. But there are three things which if found should never be picked up: a needle, a broken knife, and a flower dropped by somebody else. To meddle with these means ill luck, a quarrel, or even death. It is unlucky, too, to find a dead bird (a boy from Stock in Essex particularizes 'a dead pigeon'). A girl in Canobie, Dumfriesshire, says: 'When we see a dead bird lying on the road we spit on it so that we don't get it for our supper.'

### Luck in Examinations

Naturally the approach of an examination makes children doubly conscious of omens. They become watchful for anything held to be significant, and take notice not only of the everyday prognostics, but of some auguries specifically belonging to the occasion. Thus at Ecclesfield a boy says: 'If you have a dream about a horse before the exams you will have bad luck.' At Hampstead, and doubtless elsewhere, children believe that to have an argument before an examination is bad luck. And at Lydney, by the river Severn, they consider it unlucky if, when going into examinations, there are no seagulls flying around outside. In some places children even take note of whether, when they enter the examination room, the master is smiling (a propitious sign), or who it is they walk in behind (they like to walk near a prefect or an entrant of known ability). And they are as careful as possible about their choice of desk. (At one school, at least, when the desks are being set out number 13 is omitted, for no child would willingly sit at it.) [Compare with US adult beliefs about the number 13; do buildings taller than twelve stories have a thirteenth floor?]

More actively they bring a piece of magic with them: a pet small toy or mascot, a woolen, wooden, glass, brass, or china likeness of a pig, elephant, frog, dog, owl, black cat, white horse, or silver horseshoe, a Jack o' Lantern, Joan the Wad (popular in Wales), or other lucky image such as fancy gift shops regularly sell, but perhaps purchased on some special occasion with happy or mystic association, such as at a fair, or from a gipsy or Indian pedlar at the door. [A US college example is provided by Kate Miller: 'My exam-taking practices at Wellesley College (class of 1989) included wearing as many clothes with 'karma' as possible — borrowed clothes, gifts, and anything with a Wellesley insignia. A typical exam outfit might include a boyfriend's fraternity jersey, Wellesley sweatpants and class ring, earrings from a friend, jewelry from parents, scarf from brother and, to top it all off, a Wellesley sweatshirt. A sweatshirt without a hood could be worn inside-out so that the luck in the school logo would rub off on the wearer. I also slept with the most relevant book underneath my pillow the night before.'] The mascots are set up in front of them on their desks (and tactfully ignored by the examiners), or are worn as brooches or pendants. Sometimes they wear a sprig of white heather, or holly, or an ivy leaf, or have steel pins stuck into the lapel edge of their coat or a safety pin fastened in the hem of their dress. Or they bring — secreted in grubby pockets — talismans of personal but no intrinsic value: prized round stones, polished stones, white stones, stones with holes in them, champagne corks, mother of pearl shells, pieces of coal (very common), treasured lumps of wood, rabbits' paws (surprisingly often), and sharks' teeth. Also, very frequently, they have special coins: coins with holes in them, coins which have been much polished, halfpennies with ships on, farthings which are bent, and silver coins, particularly new ones.

> It is supposed to bring good luck during an examination to have in your pocket a piece of coal, a silver three penny bit, or something silver with the present year's date, e.g. 1952 if the examination was tried this year.
>
> Girl, 14, Aberdeen

> I think a silver sixpence is very lucky. If you were going in for an examination you might keep a silver sixpence in your pocket so that you might pass the exam, but some people say the sixpences should be very new sixpences, they should not have been used and they should have been new from a bank. Then people think you will have a good chance of passing.
>
> Girl, 12, Aberystwyth

They are particularly conscientious about bringing charms to the 11-plus examination, the 'scholarship' as they call it, which determines whether they shall go on to a grammar school [like a US college preparatory course] or to a secondary modern [like a vocational school]; and it may, perhaps, be reflected that the grammar school children (the children who were successful in the examination) are more likely to be superstitious than secondary modern school children, for children at grammar schools are children who have found that lucky charms work. [It is noteworthy that lucky charms are not simply accepted but are indeed in some sense tested in much the same way that common-sense, everyday beliefs generally are — not scientifically but pragmatically, in terms of what works. I used to carry a 'lucky' silver dollar, but once it was stolen I never replaced it, for who could believe in a lucky piece that couldn't even protect itself?]

> My mother has always treasured a little brass owl. On the day I went to sit the scholarship I took the little owl and wrapped it up in a handkerchief in my pocket for luck hoping it would bring me luck and when the results came I found it had proved its worth. I also wear other lucky charms such as a black and gold poodle or a lucky black cat.
>
> Girl, 11, about to go to a grammar school in the West Midlands

> A lot of boys around our school place most of their luck on wearing small things of a girl friend they know, articles such as silk scarves, small lace handkerchiefs, or a ring or a charm. On Thursday the 11th of April I was not wearing my friend's ring (in which I place my luck) and at school in the morning I broke the school's gramophone.
>
> Boy, 15, at a northern grammar school

I have a circular piece of red glass which I think is lucky because I take it to exams with me. I took it to the scholarship exam for the grammar school and I passed. I also took it to the A.T.C. exams and I have passed them all. I think it must be lucky although I found it in a stream.

Boy, 14, at a Yorkshire grammar school

Even during the examination some children are not happy unless they can entice the correct answers on to their papers by means beyond the ordinary power of nature. They put their faith in new pencils which have never written a mistake; they clasp their thumbs ('this is very lucky', says a Brixton boy); they cross their fingers or touch wood that an answer they have written down is correct (there is prolonged finger-crossing and wood-touching while they wait to hear the examination results); and a trick some of them have is to keep their legs crossed during the examination. A teacher at Portsmouth, who was having considerable trouble with collapsible desks during an examination, says that when she at last demanded of a girl why she would keep sitting in such discomfort with her knees bumping up under the flap, was told that the girl did not think she would pass the examination unless she maintained this position.

### Luck in Games

In their games, as in their work, it sometimes seems to children that it is more necessary to have luck than to have skill. Young marbles players, in particular, who on one occasion are able to hit their opponent out of the ring every shot, and on another, for no reason which is rational, cannot 'knock a shottie' however hard they try, easily become prey to strange thoughts. 'I started on Monday and had two days of good luck,' reports a 14-year-old, then 'on Wednesday I played with a green marble and it proved itself very unlucky because I never won a game. Now I never play with a green marble because I think they are unlucky.'

In some places marbles players are addicted to charms. At Stoke-on-Trent they call out:

One, two, three,
Lucky, lucky, lucky,
Four, five, six;

and in East Orange, New Jersey:

Roll, roll, tootsie roll,
Roll marble, in the hole.

Very frequently they practise what, in the old days, would have been called witchcraft, and today is known to the sophisticated as 'Gamesmanship';

If you are playing marbles and you want to win, you put a cross in front of the hole with red chalk and shout 'Bad luck!' and the person who is playing with you gets confused and misses the hole.

Boy, 10, Birmingham

In Nottinghamshire, 'when another boy is near our marble and it is his shot we draw a ring round it' (Boy, 10). In Dumfriesshire, 'if you make marks with your heel round your marble the person is said to miss' (Boy, 12). And in Swansea when a child is losing at marbles he cries the disconcerting supplication: 'Black cat follow me, not you.'

Casting spells is not, however, confined to marbles players. 'In any game in which a ball is used,' says an 11-year-old, 'when a person is shooting and we want him to miss we say: "Abracadabra, wall come up!" and somehow the ball seems to miss.' In Monmouthshire, when girls are playing hopscotch, if someone stands on a line of the scotch while another is hopping it brings her bad luck. In Swansea, when children reach the same point in a game as their rival, to bring themselves extra luck they say:

Tippet — Good luck to me — Bad luck to you — No back answers.

And if, in a game such as skipping, a girl is doing badly, to regain her luck she chants:

Touch wood, no good;
Touch iron, rely on.

In Essex, in similar pagan manner, if a boy has eventually achieved his object in a game, he spits on the ground, or on whatever has baulked him, in revenge for his past failures. In Essex, also, children spit behind an opponent's back as a method of bringing bad luck upon him.

In Newcastle to win a toss children call 'Lucky tails, never fails'. In Peterborough it is held that if a player counts his fagcards during a game he is bound to lose. At Knighton to bring luck in a race children customarily hold a piece of grass in their hand. And in Alton to obtain a three when dicing, or to bring luck when turning up a third playing card, one group of youngsters, well known to us, have taken to chanting, 'Lucky three, bring luck to me'.

Yet children's main efforts to affect a game by infernal means are concentrated on hockey and football. Mascot carrying is universal:

At a football match each side has a mascot. The mascot can be a doll, an animal, a midget, or a young boy. This mascot is regarded as it might bring good luck.

Boy, c. 13, Monk Fryston

If a football club has a lucky mascot and it is forgotten to be taken to a match I believe that they will lose, and I believe that the same thing will happen at school sports.

Girl, 14, Tunstall

I know of a footballer who earned the name of 'Corky' because he always carries a champagne cork in his pocket when playing.

Girl, 15, Forfar

Sometimes the charms are carried not only to ease the way to victory but for personal protection:

> When I go out to play football I always wear on my pants a little charm (an elephant). On my boots I put a piece of red cloth between my laces and I never get hurt.
>
> Boy, 13, Featherstone

And sometimes more than totemistic methods are employed. It appears to be not uncommon in the changing-rooms before an important match to hear a captain, when briefing his team and wishing them luck, direct them to wear their stockings inside out to make victory more probable. [Similar practices are common among members of US sports teams, both children and adults.]

It is also considered propitious to wear odd socks. A Pontefract boy states: 'Some boys when playing at football they sometimes wear two different-coloured socks. This, they say, brings them luck.'

The association of witches with ill-dressing is still maintained in France where a student informed one of our correspondents that any garment put on inside out was a sign that the person was afraid of witches.

### Courage

In nothing is sound psychology and ancient superstition more inextricably entangled than in their preparations for a daring deed. To give themselves guts when accepting a dare — tying-up door knockers, or standing on the parapet of a bridge as a train passes underneath — boys variously grit their teeth, clench their fists, kick themselves on the shins, put elastic bands around their wrists, or touch wood ('usually our heads'). Some boys recommend finger crossing. 'If you are going to do a daring act you cross your fingers for luck.' 'You cross your fingers,' says one boy, 'and cross them as much as possible.' [In the US crossing two fingers may be considered lucky whereas crossing more may be unlucky.]

Very commonly they spit on their hands; the practice being either to spit on the finger tips, or on the palms and then rub the hands together. 'Spitting on the hands seems to give an attitude to courage', observes a 12-year-old.

In Southwark they spit in ritual fashion three times on the ground.

In Barnsley, Yorkshire, 'To bring courage', says a 12-year-old boy, 'find a lucky stone and spit on it and throw it over your head and do not watch it land. If you see it land it will bring cowardice.'

'When performing something which takes courage', reports a 14-year-old boy from Romford, 'one makes the "Lucky Wall's Sign" by touching together your thumbs, and forming a big W with your thumbs and forefingers'.

A number of boys also recommend counting. 'You count up to ten, saying, "I am going to do it", and then on the last number you do it.' 'Close your eyes and count twenty.' 'Count twenty very slowly and stamp on left foot.' 'Count twenty very slowly and take two deep breaths.' 'Hold your breath and count twenty.'

One boy recommends giving somebody a cherished possession to hold 'which he can keep if you don't manage to do it.' Another recommends throwing a cap or coin over the wall first, so that it is essential to climb over to fetch it. A girl aged twelve says, 'Drink a glass of beer.'

Other boys, noticeably the more broadly educated, favour Coué principles, telling themselves: 'I've got to do it and I will do it,' 'If he can do it I can do it,' 'Come on old boy you must do it, think of your honour,' or they pretend to themselves that it is simple and not daring. 'This makes me succeed sometimes,' remarks a Brentwood boy.

One lad says, 'Trust to the Lord and He will get you there.'

And before embarking on the rash act they exclaim: 'Here goes', 'Wish me luck', 'Thumbs up', 'Let's get it over', 'Plucky-lucky', 'One can only die once', or 'I like dandelions on my grave'.

## Notes

1 'A Country Day-School Seventy Years Ago', *Longman's Magazine*, vol. xiii, 1889, p. 518.
2 The city child usually knows more games than the country child, for he has more time to play them. The real country child, living in a village or on a small-holding, is generally expected to do jobs around the home when he returns from school, and once he has passed the singing-game stage, his play tends to be limited to whatever free time there is at school. However, his knowledge of traditional wisdom — proverbs, dark sayings, and seasonal customs — is correspondingly greater.
3 *Miscellanea of the Rymour Club*, vol. ii, pt. ii, 1913, p. 69.
4 ... Dr. Fisher, Master of the Charterhouse, told Boswell [who wrote a biography of Samuel Johnson] that in the quadrangle of University College Johnson would not step on the juncture of the stones, but carefully on the centre; and according to Lord Elton, General Gordon when walking along a pavement would zigzag in order to avoid the cracks. [The Opies themselves thus provide data that half-beliefs are held by adults as well as children.]

## Concluding Note

The Opies suggest that half-beliefs are used by children to structure and make sense out of their daily experiences. Rather than seeking to disprove such half-beliefs, sociologists can fruitfully examine them for the functions they serve. Many of the half-beliefs cited by the Opies appear to have their source in situations where: 1) a course of action is contemplated that can be either successful or unsuccessful, 2) the outcome is important to participants, and 3) the strategies for achieving success are uncertain or ambiguous. Half-beliefs step in to provide guidance.

The subjects around which children's half-beliefs cluster suggest some of the concerns that children have. Some of these concerns are specific to childhood — e.g. examinations; some are shared by adults and children, but adults may have more resources available for explanation, e.g. safety, illness; and some concerns are shared by adults and children and both hold half-beliefs related to them, e.g. games of chance such as cards.

As with common-sense beliefs in general, half-beliefs are 'tested' in an informal, non-scientific fashion; those that 'work' are kept; those that 'fail' are abandoned. The non-scientific character of the process by which they are tested is evident in the limited data used as a basis for analysis (an object or practice that is associated with luck on one occasion may be taken as lucky-in-general). It is also evident in the role played by the desire for a belief to be true (or false), desire substituting for a weighing of evidence. Objects and practices are treated as lucky as long as their use is associated with luck, even when reason might suggest that such an association may be accidental. Along with magical beliefs and practices, people may engage in non-magical practices that are designed to bring about the desired result (as when one carries a good-luck charm to an exam for which one has studied) but success may still be attributed to the good-luck charm.

Despite the Opies' focus on children, it seems clear that half-beliefs are held by adults as well and in very much the same kinds of situations. The difference is that adults have a range of other resources for resolving ambiguity — e.g. science, religion, consultation with experts and professionals. The Opies' material provides a fruitful source for seeing the many commonalities as well as differences between adults and children.

F.C.W.

*Chapter 11*

# Kids, Culture and Innocents

*David A. Goode*

## Commentary

In this article Goode gives eloquent testimony to the existence of worlds inhabited by those children considered 'damaged' — the blind, the deaf, the alingual, the severely retarded. The oft-made assumption that children labeled 'severely handicapped' do not experience the world — that there is 'nothing going on' within them — has blinded *us* to their experiences. Goode brings those experiences to light.

As Goode describes the knowledge he has gained from studying 'damaged children', he raises issues that expand understanding of matters considered earlier in this book. Recall, for example, in Chapter 1, the Bergers' citation of Aries' claim that 'Childhood, as we understand and know it today, is a creation of the modern world ...' (p. 9). The Bergers could be said to be claiming that in past history it was routine for children to be denied childhood; it was not socially available, i.e. not a part of the culture of the times; but that nowadays, particularly in technologically complex societies, it is routine for childhood to be recognized as a distinct phase of life. Goode, however, demonstrates in this article that childhood is an experience still denied to some children. Such children may have no access at all to the channels of communication and thus the culture of children described by the Opies.

Just as some children are denied the experience of being a child, that experience can be available to some adults. In her role of *least adult*, Mandell in Chapter 4 could be said to have sought to 'enter the world of childhood'. Using research strategies similar in spirit to those of Mandell, Goode has studied *children* who have been denied that opportunity and has both documented that denial and discovered and described the worlds such children do inhabit.

Goode's discussion of the wild boy of Aveyron reintroduces the topic of

From *Human Studies*, 9 (1): 83–106 (1986). Copyright © Martinus Nijhoff Publishers, Dordrecht, The Netherlands. Reprinted by permission of Kluwer Academic Publishers.

the faultiness of the empty bucket (*tabula rasa*) assumption about children. He shows that although the worlds of 'damaged children' are in many respects vastly different from the worlds of adults and of normal children, such worlds indeed exist, can be described, and can be entered. Recognizing and studying those worlds can provide us with understanding not otherwise available.

In Chapter 5 I argued that 'one can explore the role of child *as a role*, for child and adult require each other to play their roles' (p. 67) and 'To recognize that "child" is a role is to suspend the assumption that childhood has some absolute, real, transcendent existence beyond the social ...' (p. 68). By suspending that assumption and considering 'child' and 'adult' as social roles, Goode has shown that those roles are available to only some of those who meet the age requirements. Although Goode does not detail how the status of 'child' is assigned, his comments suggest that members of certain professions, especially social work and teaching, may possess important social power to grant or withhold this label. By renouncing the view that 'child' is a biological category, ascribed to all who fall within a similar age range, Goode comes to see 'being in the world as a child' as a social fact and an *achievement*, granted to those who possess certain qualities and not granted to others.

F.C.W.

> My heart leaps up when I behold
>     A rainbow in the sky
> So it was when my life began;
> So it is now I am a man;
> So be it when I shall grow old,
>     Or let me die!
> The Child is father of the Man;
> And I wish my days to be
> Bound each to each by natural piety.
>                     William Wordsworth,
>                     26 March 1802

## Current Views About Children and Adults

... Reflecting upon written studies and my own observations of 'normal' children and of deaf-blind youngsters, seeing and doing things like a kid is not equivalent to a set of biological attributes, i.e. being chronologically young and physically small. It consists, instead, in socially organized ways of perceiving and acting upon one's world — ways which are social in origin and learned through participation with others. Participating in kids' culture is not guaranteed to all who are young. Nor is it barred to those who have accumulated experience, age and stature. Kids' culture is a way of doing the world which can be promoted, tolerated or repressed by adults. Likewise adultness (perceiving and acting upon the world as an adult) is not guaranteed by virtue of having matured biologically and is not something which is barred to children. Tuli Kupferberg portrayed this insight graphically in his

1983 pictorial essay 'Kiddie Porn' — a collection of photographs depicting children in various military and paramilitary situations (guerrilla warfare, shooting hand-guns, and so on). Certainly for the 8-year-old guerrilla in Nicaragua 'doing the world' as a child is at best an occasional affair if not an impossibility. In third world nations some 40,000 children die daily of malnutrition or disease (*Newsweek*, 27 Dec. 1982).

Although these are extreme cases of childhood deprivation, in America poverty also deprives the young of being kids. So for that matter do the whims and idiosyncrasies of some parents who, for a variety of reasons and employing a wide range of unkind techniques, are extreme in repressing childhood in their own progeny. Less extraordinary examples are also pertinent. In the middle classes child athletes are 'burned out' by the time they enter high school and 'gifted children' become 'imbeciles with high I.Q.'s' (to borrow a phrase from Laing) even earlier. Of course, there *are* liberated places, areas in our society where kids rule (notably playgrounds, street corners, recreational parks, and videogame establishments). But adult culture encroaches on childhood ubiquitously and insidiously. Big Brother is, after all, 'really' big father (or at least big adult).

The existence of these types of phenomena points to a variability of participation in kids' culture, a variability which is no less interesting in its less extreme forms. Partly, it is this variability in participation which is for each of us biographically ordered and which most of us face as we are hastened along the path to adult 'reality'. We are led to the goal sometimes gently and other times forcefully. We proceed at unique biographical rates and with unique qualitative experiences of both the losses and gains involved. We appear to share the belief that this process is 'growing up' but other than the physical analog, it is not at all clear that we understand to what we commit ourselves by using the term.

## Children Who Do Not Become Kids or Adults

For better and worse some persons are denied participation in both kids and adult cultures. The aetiologies of this denial vary and may involve fortuitous circumstance, willful or unplanned neglect, organic deficits or some combination of these. Many of these children are socially devalued and labeled deviant. They are children who are described as retarded, autistic, mentally ill, sensorily multihandicapped, chronically ill, social isolated and, in some very rare instances, feral. Each category collects youngsters who, apart from any organic insult or disorder they may have, have either experienced pathological forms of interaction with adults or children, or a persistent lack of human contact of any kind. Associated with many of their biographies is often a chronic undersocialization — an undersocialization resulting in 'pathological' behaviors which are often interpreted as organic in origin (see for a very recent example Lewis *et al.*, 1984 interpretation of stereotypy). This occurs almost always in the case of the retarded child who resides in an institution. Similarly, children diagnosed as autistic, mentally ill, multihandicapped and chronically ill, who experience pathological and/or limited contact with adults and with other children, or who act in ways which are socially unacceptable, are often interpreted to have *primarily* organically based deficits. That is, there is a materialistic and atomistic bias evident in dominant interpretations of behaviors of these children. Even children who are social isolates or feral are often interpreted as having physical pathologies which account for behaviors which are not resonant with dominant cultural posturings and expressions. I want to suggest an alternate interpretation which is descriptively more adequate to the phenomenon.

Because the attainment of being a kid is thoroughly dependent upon the individual's participation in kids' culture, it is possible to undergo the physical processes of growth and maturation which we associate with childhood without ever becoming a kid. This is what occurs with youngsters who are chronically environmentally deprived, although the process is somewhat convoluted since in the more severe cases the physical processes of maturation are also affected. When there is an organic component to the lack of participation, such as with the retarded or sensorily multihandicapped youngsters who are limited in their capacity to interact with other kids and are thereby denied full participation in kids' culture, there are often two levels to their predicament. The more severely afflicted children *often fail to become kids because of social deprivation which occurs for reasons extrinsic to their organic deficits per se*. That is, they are socially devalued, ostracized and until very recently were often incarcerated. In terms of the dominant materialistic bias in interpreting their behaviors, these types of children are likely to be seen as mentally retarded, neurologically damaged or, in current professional parlance, developmentally disabled. In my own experience these particular characterizations have primary relevance to a conception of life which is *adultcentric*.

It will be my intention in the remainder of this paper to describe how it is possible to come to less biased understandings of persons who fail to participate in kids' culture, and what these tell us about normal children and adults. I will offer two reinterpretations — one regarding the 'autistic' behaviors associated with prolonged exclusive contact between children and animals and the other of 'stereotypy' noted in children who are deaf-blind and retarded.

## The Wild Boy

One of the most interesting and revealing of encounters between youth and adulthood is that of Jean-Marc Gaspard Itard and Victoire, the Wild Boy of Aveyron (Itard, 1801; Mannoni, 1972; Malson, 1972; McNeil *et al.*, 1984). In a well-known and observationally meticulous series of notebooks Itard, an eighteenth century French pedagogist for the deaf, documented his attempts to habilitate *un enfant sauvage* — a wild boy — who had lived in the forests near Caune for many years as part of forest society.

Though there have been many reports of feral (wolf, forest, ape) children, few are in any sense genuine (Bettelheim, 1959). This is *not* the case with Victoire. His presence in the forests can be historically established, with reasonable certainty, through newspapers and other public documents substantiating multiple encounters, captures and escapes over a period of seven years. Itard's journals, which are rightly recognized as some of the most punctilious human observations in the history of human sciences, are, nonetheless, studies in pedagogical futility. When confronted with a child who had successfully adapted to a natural, non-humanly ordered environment, Itard seized the opportunity for his own professional advantage. He reasoned Victoire to be the classically ideal student; a blank slate upon which he would inscribe perfect knowledge through the perfect pedagogy. At least these were his hopes when he first heard about the child — hopes which, as we will see, lay the groundwork for both his and Victoire's fate.

In a bold and at the time noble experiment, Itard attempted to formulate scholastic teaching methods which would allow Victoire to learn the cultural knowledge he lacked. In these experiments, based upon the theories of his teacher Condillac, the founder of what we recognize today as 'classroom' learning, Itard attempted to teach Victoire speech, writing, arithmetic, and other academic skills, as well as social norms and proper behaviors. After many years of hard work on the parts of both teacher and student, none of these goals was achieved. Victoire failed to learn language and did not achieve what one might call a satisfactory adjustment of an adolescent to urban society. He died in his twenties substantially with the same 'developmental disabilities' he had when he first was captured and without having successfully acculturated, at least by the standards of eighteenth century French society, to fully human status.

The accounts of Itard's lessons, of his devoted, repetitive and sometimes violent attempts to provide Victoire with the culturally valued knowledge and practices he lacked, are quite moving. They have inspired a movie and over the years considerable commentary, not least of which concerns itself with why a fine educator such as Itard could have failed so miserably with the savage child. In a penetrating analysis by Mannoni (1972), Itard is accused of creating a narrow cultural image of Victoire and unreflexively employing completely adultcentered viewpoints in assessing his charge's competencies and deficits. Itard saw the child as the ignorant savage; that is, as *tabula rasa*, a slate clear from disuse, an empty vessel waiting to be filled up with knowledge. Despite the fact that this youngster may represent one of history's consummate survival artists, that he probably was of exceptional intellect and was reported by Itard to know a great deal about what we might call survival arts (such as the sound of different foods falling or, through smell, whether a dead bird was edible or not), his behaviors, when judged according to rather conventional standards of French society, were not considered evidence of human intelligence. In fact, Victoire's actions were decidedly maladaptive in humanly ordered social relationships. He was treated as a very stupid person; he was, in fact, considered to be retarded by medical authorities in Paris and was rescued by Itard from incarceration in an institution for imbeciles.

In the social construction of stupidity, words such as adaptive and maladaptive often conceal assumptions made about the relationship between an individual and his social context. If we were to suspend some of these usual assumptions with regard to Victoire, we can only wonder at the incredible tenacity, intelligence and strength which the child must have possessed in order to have survived in a forest community. Mannoni (1972) points out that with survival exercises being common today, *we* can easily imagine a scenario wherein Itard would find himself in a situation in which his knowledge would be inferior to that of Victoire. When judged by the criteria-employed-in-action by the society of forest animals, survival, Itard would be literally forced to become Victoire's student. Such a fantasy was unthinkable for Itard. And so,

> . . . Itard learned nothing from the savage . . . he made him into a blank screen on which he projected his own knowledge. If we learn something from reading him it is not really about the savage, nor about Itard, but about what is revealing . . . in their encounter. (Mannoni, 1972: 41)

In part what is demonstrated in the journals is the repeated insistence that Victoire conform to Itard's chronically adult ideas about knowledge, education, children and adults. Consistently, he ignored what the child knew, misconstruing Victoire's recreational walks through the forest as irrelevant to his pedagogy; calling them 'play' sessions. What was perhaps the central task, to have learned from Victoire about human competencies in a non-humanly ordered world, was assigned peripheral meaning through its designation as play. Victoire's skills were thereby euphemistically defined out of existence. No wonder Victoire remained resistant to Itard's experiment. Instead of using what was meaningful to the child as starting points for a tailor-made pedagogy, Itard remained faithful to adult edifices — the precepts of his teacher and scientific method. Because he could only see what he had been taught, and because the adult world was embraced passionately by Itard throughout his encounter with Victoire, what the child knew was specifically labeled as 'irrelevant'. The important question we must ask ourselves in considering the encounter between this man and this child is, irrelevant to whom and under that circumstances?

When judged by the standards of the adult French middle class, Itard's viewpoint seemed sensible — just as current medical views of organically retarded children seem today. In the long run it was precisely this narrow attitude about what was 'relevant' (or competent or human) which contributed to Itard's failure and Victoire's untimely end. In what must be regarded as a classic meeting between an adult and a developmentally disabled adolescent, we find no less than an exemplary instance of adultcentric thinking dominating the education of the young. In Itard's creation of an image of Victoire as deficient, ignorant and savage, we encounter evidence of the adult cultural narcissism so characteristic of current approaches to kids. One cannot help but be impressed with the practical cost of the lesson not learned by Itard. In many ways the incident previews current human service failures with children who are culturally ignorant.

### Deaf-Blind Retarded Children

For a number of years I worked on a state hospital ward for deaf-blind, retarded children. Although the 'feral' character of these children was evident from the outset, the application of Itard's failure with Victoire to my own work with the deaf-blind was not an obvious connection to make. I had been working in a research-volunteer capacity on ward for well over a year before the idea occurred (for details of this study see: Goode, 1979).

The children I observed had been diagnosed as having Rubella Syndrome. This meant that they were exposed to rubella virus *in utero* and suffered multiple congenital disease effects (sequelae) including: deafness, bilateral cataracts and other forms of blindness, central nervous system damage, microcephaly, skeletal and dental abnormalities, malformations of the vital organs, and numerous other pathologies. Concomitant with these organic insults, the residents displayed profound behavioral delays in all developmental areas: sensorimotor, cognitive, psychological and social. As an indication of the degree of damage and delay, *none* of the residents had expressive or receptive language of any kind. They did not speak, sign or spell, i.e. they were alingual. Few had self-help skills worthy of mention. Most were not toilet trained and could not eat or dress independently. They were regarded as the lowest functioning children on the hospital grounds. They regularly engaged in autostimulatory behaviors such as 'finger-flicking' and rocking. Their vocalizations consisted exclusively of animalistic gruntings and groanings. Similarly, their posturings resembled those of animals rather than children. They were sometimes described in animalistic terms by professionals and even parents. In addition, because of their sensory multi-handicaps, for the most part they acted in ways which were seemingly unresponsive to their surroundings.

These inmates of a state hospital also suffered the effects of social rejection and devaluation. Their presence in such an institution was evidence not only of severe organic insult but also indicated some biographically specific form of familial or societal rejection. They were persons who even in initial observations were evidently physically, psychologically and spiritually damaged. They were alone, unhappy and suffering to a degree which is, thankfully, uncommon in our society.

After six months on the ward I became convinced that, despite medical descriptions and staff testimony to the contrary, these children possessed a full range of human competencies. The fact that this went unnoticed had to do largely with the dominant adult authored representations of these young multihandicapped persons. These were exclusively pejorative since by *any* standards, commonsensical ones or those employed in human services for the retarded, the deaf-blind were about as helpless as persons come. When one examined their medical files one could see numerous references to incapacity and lack of skills *and* a complete absence of testimony about competencies. They received proportionately fewer of the hospital's resources than other populations; they were second class citizens in a second class society.

Because of this lack of regard for the children's viewpoints (more accurately, an incognizance that these children *had* valid viewpoints), the existing habilitative programs were completely indifferent to the residents' evaluations and experiences. That is, their 'training programs' (because they are not considered 'educable' their education was called training) were based upon a series of adultcentric judgments about what is desirable or undesirable in life and how these might be brought about, *in* developmental sequence, with particular children. These judgments evidenced the missionary-like stance described earlier, perhaps more extreme because many of the medical staff did not even believe these persons had experiences in the same sense as you or I. Through clinical assessments such as 'I.Q. 10 (untestable)' they were evaluated as *tabula rasa* — although, unlike Victoire, the deaf-blind retarded were without hope of ever being 'filled up'. The helping professions were so indifferent to the choices made by these children that under the inspection of their adult (worse, scientific) eyes, such choices were either invisible or insensible. Consequently, the education looked more like animal training than pedagogy. There was such an acute need for social recognition of these children as persons that the first article I wrote about deaf-blind children dealt with recognizing 'client choices and preference' in such persons and the implications of this recognition for their programming (Goode and Gaddy, 1976).

I became more convinced of the inappropriateness of the professional stance as my tenure on the ward grew longer. It occurred to me, oddly enough while preparing to teach introductory sociology, that these children were very much in the position of Victoire, and that the adults on the ward were much like Itard. After making observations of the residents for some time, I began to realize the degree to which adults had incorrectly understood these multihandicapped children. An even fuller appreciation of these children emerged as I befriended one of the children and made an attempt to empathize with her world view. Through unique research techniques (mimicking, remaining passively obedient during interaction, prolonged observation, video taping interaction and simulated deaf-blind experiences) I discovered that many of her seemingly pathological behaviors had a definite purposiveness and rationality. The more I 'saw' things from her point of view, the more I realized that because the staff and other professionals had operated with culturally dominant adultcentric conceptions of human competence, they incorrectly faulted these residents, just as Itard had incorrectly faulted Victoire.

There were many kinds of competencies which were ignored. For example, the staff seemed unaware of the fact that Christina, the child I worked with, and other residents were excellent hospital residents. They were 'institutionalized' which meant (for better or worse) that they understood something of the hospital's routines and rules. In the course of a day I would witness many scenes which would confirm this. One very common scenario involved 'pushing'. The children would typically wait to be taken from one activity to the next. They might be lying on the floor or lost in some autostimulatory behavior when a staff member would come up and fairly abruptly pick up a child and push her to her 'next' in the ward's routine. If it was 11:30 a.m. and lunch was approaching, a child would be picked up and pushed toward the bathroom (they were always taken to the bathroom before lunch). The typical reaction, and the child had a wide range of possible things she could do after being pushed, was to understand 'the push' (as I came to call it) as the communication it was intended to be. The child would wander to the bathroom, find a toilet, do her business, stick her hands in the running faucet after she was done, and walk to the (locked) door to the dining area.

To me these actions were clear indications of active intelligence at work.

They showed that these children understood the act of an adult pushing them to mean 'go this way now' — after all, they undoubtedly had been pushed this way all their lives. How else could one communicate 'go this way now' to a person without sight and language? The children assigned meaning to the interaction accordingly. Their action also showed that they were cognizant of the ward's layout and the temporal ordering of activities associated with a pre-lunch routine. While these are not terribly sophisticated skills, they are nonetheless skills; adaptations to an environment which are sensible. The point here is that a host of skills remained completely undetected because of the narrow categories with which staff judged competence.

Even stereotypy, rocking and repetitive actions without any apparent instrumental value, may be interpreted as institutionally adaptive behavior. One of the prolonged periods of observing Christina taught me this. During a thirty-six hour observation period during which I remained by her side, I tried to empathize with her lifestyle in the hospital. When I did so I realized just how much time she was left alone to her own devices to occupy her time. The *vast* majority of the day this was her situation and she did not have the external distractions of our culture such as television. She loved the radio (Chris had good sound reception but did not process the sound in a normal way) and whenever one was available she did her best to get close enough to it to listen. She loved to rock to the music and built some fantastic constructions from the available furniture to climb up to a small radio kept, for obvious reasons, on a high shelf away from the hands of the children. But in most places there was no radio and she was left alone to provide herself with amusement. She rocked, played with her sight and sound reception, masturbated and so on, *not* because of her organic deficits but because she was bored and these were things that she could do by herself and from which she received pleasure, reduction of anxiety or other gratification.

Chris lived life in a 'total institution'. Because of this the amount of waiting time during a typical day was far greater than we can imagine. She literally waited for everything and I developed a healthy respect for her abilities to entertain herself in solitary pursuits. In fact, the substantive similarities between Chris's inner voyages and those found in human behavior which has been culturally articulated are astounding. Repetitive rocking, recurrent vocalizations, enforced breathing, peak states of excitement — all aspects of her stereotypy — are found globally in socially organized pursuits of inner states of knowledge. This is particularly true of religious rituals of primitive cultures although it may also be found in advanced societies. Consider Reichian therapy, primal therapy, the Hare Krishna cults, LSD communes and so on, So similar are some of these culturally valued practices to achieve inner knowledge to those engaged in by Chris that I often wondered whether there was a bit of hypocrisy involved in the medical labeling and programmatic efforts to extinguish these behaviors in her. There was at least a distinct possibility that the basis difference between these was contextual and interpretive.[1] The Mahareeshee's followers make a living on street corners for doing much the same as Chris and perhaps for much the same motivation. People pay huge sums to Janovian therapists to engage in repetitive vocalizations and rocking. But in Chris's case we are so ready, so primed, to see her behaviors as evidence of her retardation, that we mask her skills as symptoms. Instead, they are ways for a deaf-blind child to occupy herself when she is alone, perhaps even to explore inner states of consciousness. They are without doubt activities of solitude of which we are generally ignorant and irrespectful.

There was yet another kind of bias against recognition of Christina's skills. These consisted of judgments which were seemingly obvious and unbiased in character and required no justification. They were matters of deep adult prejudice concerning generic relationships — for example, about the relationship between persons and objects, or about how a person should walk. A detailed illustration taken from notes made while viewing a videotape of a music lesson which I was giving Chris will make my meaning clear.

I am working with Chris sitting in front of the organ. Music is playing loudly in the background. The initial fifteen minutes I am trying a strategy from the deaf-blind curriculum of Perkins School. After an initial familiarization period, I show her how to use various percussion instruments — a tambourine, a triangle, maracas and a rattle. With each instrument there is a kind of ritual demonstration of its 'proper' use. For example, I would place a rattle in her hand, wrap my hand around hers and 'motor her through' a correct usage (i.e. shaking it to the beat of the music). Another way to say this would be that I am showing her the culture's recipe for the object's proper use. The arm is placed here, the hand thusly, the shaking is coordinated to the musical beat and so on.

During this part of the tape Chris appears decidedly bored. She does not appear to concentrate on the actions of our hands but stares off into the overhead fluorescent light and in various other directions around the room. All of a sudden my wife enters the room and announces that she has been hurt by one of the children. I go to her aid, dropping Chris's hand abruptly, and leave the room. The camera remains running while I am out of the room and the following occurs.

Chris brings the rattle — this particular instrument has a corrugated wooden handle, smooth spherical container and tiny metal cymbals — to her right eye (Chris can see with far more acuity in this eye). She has it close to her eye, perhaps two inches away, and is apparently inspecting its features. She begins to turn the rattle this way and that in order to reflect the fluorescent light overhead. She grasps all the different surfaces, tilting them and moving them closer and further from her eye, trying to see what she can visually produce with the rattle. After a minute of this she begins a whole series of usages in and around the mouth. Different parts of the rattle are used as tongue thumper, lip stimulator, teeth banger, and pushed against the cheek. The bumps of the handle are rubbed rapidly across the front teeth, the neck, then the breast. It appears to descend further to the genital area (I cannot be sure from the tape but I have seen her do this commonly when presented with new objects). After seven or eight minutes of investigating the immediate perceptual possibilities which the rattle presented her, Chris drops the instrument on the floor in a seemingly uncaring fashion without regard for its whereabouts or breakability. Out of sight, out of mind.

While viewing this segment of the tape with a group of physicians we counted more than twenty distinct uses to which Chris put the rattle during the eight minutes she was able to interact with it without my interference. While her activities were easily seen as 'wrong' and as requiring correction, an alternative and useful way to view the incident might be to ask, who is getting more out of their encounter with the rattle, Chris or us?

Christina's inability to use the rattle correctly — to grasp the intentional meanings behind the activities we associate with its appropriate employment — also credentializes her, providing her with a certain license in her relationships with objects. This is a license largely barred to those who use rattles singularly and in satisfaction of their intended and accepted mode of usage. Put in a positive way, Chris was 'an alternative object reader'; that is, a person who by virtue of not knowing objects' correct uses did things with them which were completely inaccessible to most persons. Instead of equating objects with their cultural recipes Chris grasped them with an openness unavailable to the average person. Since these behaviors were evaluated as retarded by the dominant standards, in our society it would appear that one basis for recognizing stupidity is the superordinate ranking of recipe uses of objects. The mode of employment which satisfies the use intended by the object's maker forms a kind of ground against which other uses appear as pejorative figures. This is what grounded the staff's conviction that Chris did not know how to use instruments 'correctly'.

This open-ended, 'horizontal' relationship to things was only pathological or abnormal by convention. From a more neutral vantage point it is possible to see these activities as perfectly reasonable adjustments to her sensory and cognitive handicaps. The mouthings of the rattle are particularly understandable. The sensitivity of the lips and tongue, the ability of the teeth to conduct vibrations, made Chris' mouth her primary perceptual organ. It seemed to be the receptor around which she could reliably, at least judging from the longevity of these activities, organize perceptual practices. While the naive observer or human services professional might equate Chris's actions with the mouthings of an infant, this would represent an improper faulting of these skills. Chris was well practiced in her oral perceptions. Her handicaps had made her an expert in the use of the mouth as the organ of perception and from this perspective it is possible to see her behaviors as an alternative set of perceptual practices — ones which are more differentiated and complex than our own oral perceptions. With respect to the oral exploration of our world, she was a gourmand of everyday objects, virtually unprejudiced in her inquiries, and would place almost anything she could get hold of in her mouth.

There were, thus, different levels of adultcentric thinking which surrounded these children. On a mundane level there was a lack of recognition of a host of adaptive interpersonal and institutional skills, On perhaps a deeper one, Chris's behaviors could be seen as expressions of powerful commitments and relationships which were inaccessible to normally seeing, hearing and thinking adults. These were actions which tapped into a reservoir which for most of us has been channeled and funneled into those forms of experience which we consensually agree is 'reality', but which for Christina existed relatively intact, untouched by society. This was why, I think, the custodians sometimes referred to these children as 'cosmic'.

There would appear to be a striking parallel between Chris' situation and that which existed between Itard and Victoire. Most of Chris' skills were ignored, or judged as irrelevant, by her custodians and teachers. These people, like the pedagogist-custodian of our feral child, examined Christina's behaviors through the conventional standards of their society as formalized and rationalized by their professions. Because such standards do not allow for relative definitions of skills and competence, the teaching systems based upon them did not recognize, and take advantage of, these particular children's abilities and interests. Most of the youngsters, like Victoire, showed almost no progress in accessing adult-defined skills, Many had behavior profiles, according to adult criteria, identical to those recorded in clinical reports ten years before I met them; so dismal was the success of habilitation efforts.

Through an appreciation of the Victoire-Itard affair we can understand why the children failed to progress and what one might do about it. Itard, and Christina's teachers, were not open to and could not passionately embrace diversity in human beings and human experience. This is an ability which is a *sine qua non* of valid human helping relationships. Because they lacked this sensitivity and orientation, they were unable, to use a term developed by Kielhofner (1983), to construct a 'relative' understanding of competence and intelligence. Though two hundred years and cultures apart, both were adultcentric in their actions with their respective children. Their helping efforts, instead of developing the innate human potentials of their students, revealed their devout attachment to the substantive beliefs and practices taught to them by their societies. The staff at the hospital learned nothing from Christina; just as Itard failed to ever understand Victoire. Their attempts at remediating the disabilities they perceived were equally unsuccessful.

Because of the phenomenological style of my own research, because of my cognizance of the dimensions of adult biases in judging these children, because I was able, through a variety of techniques, to remain relatively nonjudgmental about Christina's assessments about her world, I achieved better results from my efforts at habilitation. For the first six months of my relationship with her I was her 'super playmate', basically cooperating with any request she might make. I used a strategy of 'passive obedience' in which I physically allowed her to take the lead in structuring our interaction. This proved a most beneficial (though difficult to arrive at) stance. Once Chris knew that I was cooperative to this degree, she initiated a huge variety of activities and exchanges *in her terms*. She trusted me, perhaps loved me, and, I think, at some level understood how deeply I appreciated her demonstrations.

During this period I learned her feelings and reactions intimately and had clearly established a relationship with her in *her* terms. Using the Itard-Victoire analogy, I began my teaching of Christina 'in the woods'; at least as deep into them as I could travel. Since initially in our relationship I had virtually forgotten about the attempt to habilitate the child, preferring, in-stead, to allow her to show me the ways of her world, when the shoe was put on the other foot she was cooperative (at least by ward standards). For over a year, Christina had helped me to experience aspects of the human *Umwelt* (von Uexkull, 1934) which had been socially asphyxiated. She was unintentionally one of my most profound instructors. This is probably why I experienced some success at habilitation with her. I had become her student to become her teacher; that is a truth I learned from my relationship with her, that every good teacher is first his student's student.

To repay the debt I attempted to provide positive growing experiences which were both fair to Christina and to the adult-ordered hospital society in which she lived. This involved not so much extinguishing negative behaviors (such as rocking, etc.) as developing those choices she made which were culturally valued; for example, making and listening to music or doing gymnastics. By beginning pedagogy with what was valuable to her, Chris experienced a 'blossoming' which I could not have foreseen. In a short while she even began to cooperate with requests on my part which did *not* have an innate value or meaningfulness for her; for example, signing (in deaf sign language) her name. She began to act more acceptably, I hesitate to use the word normally. She was happier, I think because she knew inside that she was no longer invisible. It was her appreciation of my recognition of her which allowed for a more successful contact between the world of a seeing, hearing, and speaking adult and that of a deaf, blind and alingual youngster. That such success was short lived, ending with my departure from State Hospital, was an unhappiness for both Christina and me. The implications for her life were great. Without the benefit of her ally, she quickly regressed to a point where her behavior was indistinguishable from that of other residents (Gaddy, personal communication, 1982).

### Kids, Innocents and Their Intimates

What can be learned from these two encounters and from the observations of normal children interacting with adults? Can sociologists, teachers or, for that matter, parents ever hope to understand their kids, developmentally disabled or not?

Obviously the answer to this question varies historically, culturally and biographically. From my own experiences with disabled children and their families, from the recurrence of arguments such as those discussed earlier and their most recent expression in sociology, it would seem that there are currently reasons for hopefulness. In the case of the normal child who is participating in kids' culture, the possibility for genuine contact with adults rests upon two facts: that all adult members have participated in such a culture and were acculturated into adult belief-action systems; and that genuine cross-cultural communication is always a possible achievement between persons of even substantially differing cultures.

In the case of kids and adults in the same society, cultural differences may not be as substantial as those of persons who come from different societies. The participation of our youth leaves a permanent door to kids' culture. There is a Peter Pan in each of us (in the epigram, 'child is father to the man') which allows us to enter this door when we allow him life. Our self-cognizance about doing this may be overt or tacit; i.e. we may or may not be aware when we step into the world of kids. Sometimes we do so conspicuously and ingenuinely, for example, in a managed way when we 'act like children' in order to control their behavior. Other times, in activities which promote egalitarian contact, or in which we momentarily forget the adult we 'are', we become the kid we once were; not in the sense of playing *at* it, but actually *being* it. At these times we become the kid we were, not as a managed *presentation* of self but as a relatively spontaneous *expression* of self. The task for us adults is to recognize these occasions as opportunities for *mutual enrichment*, for effective teaching and learning, and to recapture how kids see and do things. Adult culture currently bears a largely unrecognized and unanalyzed relationship to that of kids. A firm conviction as a longtime student of kids' culture is that by studying it we stand to improve our educational attempts with children as well as our understanding of our own activities. In this way we can become more aware of adultcentrism and its negative influence on our pedagogy with the young. We can also begin to appreciate the ways adultcentric thinking victimizes those who participate in and promote it, regardless of age or size.

There are implications of these ideas which are important for the scientific community. Most importantly, the study of kids' culture deserves explicit recognition as a *bona fide* topic of research for the social sciences — and one with direct bearing upon our understanding of many of its traditional topicalities such as child development, the sociology of the family, socialization, sociolinguistics, the sociology of education and special education and others. Currently, the paradigms employed in our studies of these phenomena are largely uninformed by the existence of kids' culture and because this remains true these topics await rediscovery in a less adultcentric fashion. One cannot underestimate how significant such a recognition and exploration is to scientists studying groups and institutions involving children and adults. Those who are prepared to see and act upon these possibilities will be able to re-enter traditional areas of social scientific inquiry afresh and redefine domains of discourse. Thus the intellectual cognizance of kids' culture is as far reaching as one can imagine.

The study of kids' culture also holds out tremendous promise to practitioners in the helping professions who are concerned in a hands-on fashion with children and child-adult relationships. Whether it be teaching mathematics or understanding and remediating child abuse, an empirical grasp of kids' culture and its relationship to adult culture can only be of immense practical value to those negotiating particular change-oriented relationships. This is to say, I see tremendous utility for a science of kids' culture in human services of many types which involve children and child-adult groups. In some isolated instances, when adults have allowed kids' culture to concretely organize the learning experience, for example, we have already seen fruits of this approach.[2]

Politically, the commitment to the study of kids' culture is potentially to the formal recognition and empowerment of kids. It is important that those who engage in studies of kids with liberating motives consider their efforts within the overall history of children and their practices. Bearing such a history in mind it seems highly unlikely that the dialectic between children and adults will ever be resolved by *any* human efforts, intellectual or otherwise. But the character and form of our relationship with kids can be affected. Thus while it may never be possible to end the contradictions embedded in child-adult interaction, through an understanding of them which is 'fairer' to the subdominant perspective it will be possible for the scientific study of kids' culture to become part of an overall political process aiming at positive changes in the quality of life for kids. For example, formal studies of the inclusion and disinclusion mechanisms of kids' culture would have immediate relevance to current 'mainstreaming' efforts for mentally, physically and emotionally handicapped children. [In the next chapter Mandell reports on just such a study.] There are many immediately researchable and pragmatically beneficial issues whose exploration could have positive outcomes for all kids.

Regarding those youths who despite our best efforts fail to participate in kids' culture such as the multihandicapped, chronically ill or profoundly retarded, there is also reason for hope. I maintain this despite the fact that valid helping forms for such persons are blatantly absent in our society, and that we are witnessing a growing intolerance in human services for these types of children. There are even medical policies which legitimate their euthenasia (Wolfensberger, 1981). For those who live at home there is a usually a lack of appropriate services and available expertise. Yet, in spite of those developments, perhaps in part in an attempt to counteract them, it is possible to find a positive basis upon which adults might interact with such children. As kids provide us with opportunities to reenter kids culture, the acultural child presents an opportunity for the adult to appreciate his own aculturality. Mannoni (1972: 41) writes,

> Natural man; savage; ignorant; pupil newly purged with hellebore; what can they represent in their extreme destitution but *subject* separated from *knowledge that lies deep within each of us*, the internal ignoramus against which the autodidact and pedant wage arduous struggle in their different ways?

When I consider my own encounter with Christina, my studentship with her, it clearly was not kids' culture about which I was learning. I had always felt that Christina allowed me to reexperience my childhood, but it is not till relatively recently that I have come to understand exactly what that meant. Christina gave me a legitimate way to explore my own internal ignoramus, to recontact that part of myself which lies beyond reach of society, language or learning. She allowed me to recapture that part of me which, as George Konrad (1974) wrote, '. . . remains more faithful to the matter from which it came'. Through her I was able to find again that thoroughly human state in which all was possibility; an open ended, undefined, what-it-can-make-of-you, what-you-can-make-of-it world which was intoxicating and sustaining. It was a world in which there were no lasting achievements, no possessions and no competition. It was a world of mutually exploring whatever here-and-now possibilities presented themselves — music, toys, trampolines, dressing, eating — all again novel, open and without delineable horizons for interpretation. Lest I be misunderstood, a kind of magic existed between us, certainly for me. While I was helping Chris to learn some of the ways of adult society, I could not help but feeling that what she gave me in return far outweighed my efforts on her behalf. It was a life-long gift.

> If I were to wish for anything, I should not wish for wealth and power but for the passionate sense of the potential, for the eye which, ever ardent, sees the possible. Pleasure disappoints, possibility never. And what wine is so sparkling, what so fragrant, what so intoxicating, as possibility. (Søren Kierkegaard)

**Notes**

1  One reviewer commented that the text would appear to equate Chris' activities with those of socially organized groups who engage in the pursuit of inner knowledge. Because the procedures used to make sense of persons' behaviors are part of the very behaviors themselves, in the strictest sense I am not maintaining that Janovian therapy and Christina's actions were isomorphic. What I am maintaining is that they may be, and certainly I often felt from observing Christina that this was the case, grounded in the same human potentialities and differing *primarily* in the way that they are contexted and interpreted by others.

2  For an excellent example of a group doing precisely this, although without labeling it as such, the history of LOGO, as documented in Seymour Papert's book *Mindstorms*, suggests itself. Here, kids are allowed and prompted to solve problems on their own and in conjunction with other children. Astounding pragmatic results with normal and disabled learners are reported.

*Chapter 12*

# Children's Negotiation of Meaning

*Nancy Mandell*

## Commentary

In this article Mandell explores an aspect of children's worlds not dealt with in previous articles: the ways that children interact with one another when they are together. Her particular concern is with identifying and describing the ways that children *negotiate meaning*, i.e. work together to figure out what is going on, both from their own perspective and that of others. The negotiation of meaning involves taking account of others in the social worlds that they inhabit together.

I have deleted Mandell's introduction, which is a review of the literature relevant to her topic; references to these works are available in the bibliography. In footnotes that accompany this deleted material, however, she cites two important criticisms that have been addressed to previous studies of children: Markey's (1928: 151) assertion

> that Piaget's assumption that there is no real interchange of thought [among children] is gratuitous. The only basis for saying that there is no interchange is that the child's thinking is drawn from a common social process but there is certainly interchange in this process.

and Lewis and Rosenblum's (1975: 1) argument that

> psychoanalytic and Piagetian theories of human development have so dominated research that they have led to a suppression of active study of children's early social behaviour other than that directed toward the parents.

In contrast, Mandell describes children interacting in the social world *as they do it*. She takes children's perspectives seriously and displays the richness of

From *Symbolic Interaction*, Volume 7, Number 3, pages 191–211. Copyright © 1984 by JAI Press, Inc. Reprinted by permission of JAI Press, Inc., Greenwich, Connecticut.

children's efforts to understand and act in the social worlds in which they find themselves.

Since Mandell's work is based on that of George Herbert Mead (1863–1931), I here provide a few details about his idea of 'taking account' for those readers unfamiliar with his concept. Mead was concerned with 'taking the attitude of the other' and 'taking the role of the other', processes that are necessary for one person to align actions with those of another. Being able to put oneself in the place of others — literally (e.g. by standing where they were standing) or, more commonly, symbolically (e.g. by imagining what they would say or do) — is fundamental to being able to take account of others and predict how their actions will articulate with one's own. By establishing who the other is, what that person is up to, and how the other is likely to act in response to one's own acts, one can plan one's own strategies and actions. Mead saw the process of taking account as composed of three parts: 1) deciding what features of the other are important; 2) acting in terms of others on the basis of that decision; and 3) assessing or evaluating the outcome.

Since Mead saw 'taking account' as something that is learned, not something that one is born with, study might reasonably begin with those who are in the very process of learning how to take account of others. Mandell therefore chose to study young children's ways of taking one another into account in their activities. Rather than viewing children as 'incomplete' or as objects of socialization', she focuses on them as individuals engaged in activities. For this reason her paper is an appropriate example of children in a child's world.

'Given their [children's] limited interactional experience,' Mandell states, 'many situations are not yet conventionalized' (p. 175). How then do they go about figuring out what is going on, what others are doing, and what they are to do? Mandell answers this question by identifying four distinct ways of going about acting in the world of others, ways that she terms *involvement stances*. A preliminary introduction to these stances may prove helpful. In parentheses I include terms that Mandell used in an earlier version of this paper, terms that capture the stances in common-sense words:

1  *self-involvement* ('doing it'), observable when children are involved with physical objects and their own actions and responses. Two subdivisions of this stance can be identified, based on whether the involvement object or activity is chosen by the child or by an adult.
2  *interpretive observation and display* ('involvement from afar'), evident when children stand aside and observe others and their activities. This stance includes staring, public announcements, direct invitations to join an action, making initial overtures, and crowding.
3  *co-involvement* ('working agreements'), seen when children tentatively join others for common activities.
4  *reciprocal involvement* ('going the limit'), evident when children share definitions of the situation and common understandings.

All four of these involvement stances entail involvement with one's own self and with the world beyond, including the world of others, but the *kind* of involvement differs from type to type. Children are observed operating within each of these involvement modes; no one mode is necessarily better than or more advanced than another; each is appropriate to particular circumstances.

In her work Mandell has discovered a number of issues that are of concern to children — issues such as privacy and joining groups — that are sometimes viewed as applicable to adults but not to children. Her data makes clear the richness of children's interactions when they are taken seriously *in themselves* and not considered exclusively from an adult perspective. The sophistication and complexity of children's practices, documented so clearly by Mackay in Chapter 3, are, on the basis of very different data, as clearly evident in Mandell's work.

F.C.W.

## The Study

This study describes the processes by which children engage in what I call negotiating meaning with other children in their daily interactions in school settings. The essential Meadian question becomes one of documenting how little children move from private, hidden meanings to publicly shared understandings of involvement objects.[1]

My focus is on the process by which chidren take the line of action of the other. What is critical in the process is the basic self-other-object relationship which encompasses all forms of interaction.[2] Do the children understand other's situational use of objects? Can the children act on this understanding behaviourally (which is thus observable to a field worker) by picking up the other's act and working that line of conduct into one's on-going activity? How do the children recognize, articulate, build upon and negotiate these social objects in regulated ways? It is not role-taking *per se* which is at issue, but rather interactional awareness, and the ability and willingness to act on the actions of others.

How the children accomplish these interactional competencies provides four qualitatively distinct types of involvement.[3] Visualized as a continuum, these stances vary along two dimensions: the extent to which the act and its meaning are private or public, and the extent to which the interacting unit shares an understanding of the meaning of the act in which they are involved. There is no underlying hierarchy or progression of logic as one moves through these involvements. Rather these stances represent multiple levels of reflexivity and shifting degrees of interactional awareness. Knowledge of the act-object relationship is crucial for grasping the flow of the interaction. Each stance represents a situational and relational production in that it assumes varying levels of familiarity and understanding of the child with the acts of others.[4] Each social construction contains elements of time, duration, intensity, mood[5] and complexity which bear on its enactment. Regularities in production and presentation emerge then as characteristic stances of engrossment.

## The Setting and Methods*

This continuum of involvement is derived from participant observation research conducted over a two year period on children aged 2 to 4 years. The sample consists of sixty-two children from two different day care centres observed for a total of 106 hours. The study is not concerned with day care in any exhaustive sense. Day care centres represent convenient locations within which to find regularly assembled groups of children. Both centres observed serviced children aged 2 to 4. However, in most other physical and sociostructural characteristics, the two centres differed.

The American centre, named Eastern, was located in a large, metropolitan city in the Northeast. It was physically located in an old home, situated on a well equipped, fenced-in yard. As a parent cooperative, the relationship between the parents and teachers took on an adversary, rather than a complementary nature. Three teachers cared for the seventeen children in the 'toddler' section. In all, Eastern serviced fifty-five children in both its day care and after school program. A full-time director was employed to look after the administrative and funding operations.

In contrast, the Canadian centre, named Northern, was located in a medium-sized city in South Central Ontario. The centre was physically located in a one-story building belonging to the public agency with which it was affiliated. As a public, non-profit organization, the centre maintained an open, responsive relationship with its users while daily decision-making remained in the hands of the one supervisor and the two to three other teachers. The director of the agency ultimately oversaw the financial operation, the hiring and firing of staff and maintenance of the facility — all the tasks which the parents of Eastern controlled. Northern serviced thirty-seven children using four teachers.

In terms of the content of the scheduled activities, Northern varied from Eastern in only one important respect. The Northern teachers organized their weekly art and circle activities thematically. Parents were informed of the weekly theme (weather, snow, Christmas) by a sign on the door of the main activity room. In spite of this difference in planning activities, the qualitative distinctions of child-teacher interaction differed minimally between the two centres.

I gained entree to Eastern in the late spring of 1977. I presented the director and teachers of the 'toddler' section with a field work proposal stating that I wished to observe 2 to 4 year olds with the goal of gaining as complete an overview of their daily activities as possible. I explained that this entailed trying to see the centre through the eyes of the children with a view to understanding how the centre works on a day-to-day basis. I included a copy of Joffe (1973) and Denzin's (1973) work on children as examples of the kind of participant observation work which I intended to follow. A similar proposal and approach was used at Northern in 1978 with an equally positive and quick response.

My role as 'participant-as-observer' (Gold, 1969) included closely following the children, interviewing the teachers and the directors, both formal-

---

* For further details of Mandell's methods, see Chapter 4 in this book.

ly and informally, attending the parent meetings and 'helping' the teachers with routine tasks when they were overloaded.[6] By following the children's ways, by doing what they did, and by becoming involved with them on a daily basis, I was able to gain an understanding of their thoughts and actions. Specifically I focused on small (two to three) groups of children and literally followed them around their play space. If they sat in the sandbox making cakes, so did I. If they scrambled up the climbers, crawled under the porch or chased each other around the yard as 'Supermen', I followed. While I did not 'become a child', I nonetheless became as 'minimally adult' as possible. This required that I neither judge nor evaluate their actions, nor act as a nurturing nor authoritative teacher. I was a person who visited regularly and who was there to play with the children. When the children asked me who I was, I replied that I wasn't a teacher, just a visitor. While the children initially attempted to engage me in a teacher's role, with consistent refusal their demands subsided. They taught me their openers, rules for entry, procedure and exit from interaction and I, in turn, demonstrated who I was to be to them. Naturally the latter involved considerable testing of my neutrality, confidentiality and physical dexterity. However in time they either forgot I was there or engaged me fully in their activities.

The data accumulated comes from two different centres in two different countries. I analyzed the data separately and then, finding few negative cases (Geer, 1967), collapsed them into one analytic mode. What emerged is a depiction of role-taking as a processual and gradualistic ability displayed within a child's particular interaction with others.

### Stance One: Self-Involvement

The first stance, labeled self-involvement, includes self-reflective activity. Following Mead's triadic theory of meaning, the children are self-absorbed, completely engrossed with themselves and the object of their involvement to the exclusion of all others. This field work example captures the essence of self-reflective activity.

> Norm was sitting at one of the small tables. He had taken out the Fisher-Price toy phone, picking up one receiver and was talking into the phone and at the same time, moving the dials of the Fisher-Price clock. He kept repeating 'Hello clock, hello clock, are you moving?'

The children are busy exploring and manipulating objects and taking themselves and their relationship with objects into account. Private meanings prevail and the extent to which the child's self-other interaction with an object is meaningful for the child is indicated by the child's total absorption with his own activity.

Children absorb themselves in this stance with varying degrees of gusto and for varying lengths of time. They may be physically removed from a group of children or sitting side by side with others. They may be engaged in any degree of physical activity from sitting rather still, to walking around with a toy, to racing up and down the gym or yard with their bikes. They may be shouting, laughing, crying, or silent as they engage themselves. They may alter physical locale and cross several time-activity changes in the day care centre and still be self-involved. Changing space and time, use of physical or verbal motion, being separated or beside others — none of these superficial identifying characteristics are central to self-involvement. The essential element of this stance is the private self-other-object involvement within which the child becomes so engrossed that he is oblivious to other activity around him.[7]

Self-involvement can be subdivided into two categories including the private self-object exchange with self-chosen activities, or, the children's involvement in teacher directed activities. In each of these categories the children are still making their own objects, all of which have essentially a private meaning for the child. Yet the structure within which they manipulate objects and the actual physical material they use may have been provided by a teacher. Each way is equally as engrossing and shares the same elements as the other category. In fact, the lack of difference between these two ways indicates that the sociostructural organization of a day care setting is quite unlikely to prohibit this stance of involvement.

While I conceptually see no qualitative difference between these two forms of self-involvement, the teachers often do. A child who is self-absorbed with objects of his own choosing is often seen as egocentric. However, a child self-absorbed, involved with objects of a teacher's choosing is often labelled an active, cooperative child. Consider the two following examples.

> This whole time (meeting time) Roy is sitting on the floor outside the door of the toddler's meeting room playing with a spinning top, twirling it over and over again. He is not interested in listening to the others.

Now, compare this example with a second one from my data in which a child is self-involved using teacher designated objects.

> I sat down at the paint table; Adam, Tricia and Josh were painting. They were all concentrating on their painting judging by the lack of noise or conversation and their disinterest in my arrival and each other. Their motions were very slow and deliberate and they all seemed to be painting very slowly and with great caution. Their faces were all serious and involved in their work. They were not talking so I didn't talk either.

From an adult viewpoint, the latter group is seen as being more productive and constructive. They are doing something with their time. In the first example, the child is seen as being engaged in a relatively meaningless action.

There is a tendency in the literature (Smilansky, 1968) on children's play (Parten, 1932; Weininger, 1979) to differentiate between what is usually called solitary play (my first example) from what is called parallel play (my last example) on the basis of the extent to which the engaged child is in the actual presence of other children, and the extent to which the child is absorbed in some sort of meaningful play from an adult point of view. These categories fail to appreciate that from the child's point of view, active involvement with others is not being sought. Whether beside others or alone, the self-involved child is engaged in reflective activity. To assign a valuational assessment on this type of behaviour overlooks the amount of absorption, creativity and problem solving which engages the self-involved child.

Regardless of chronological age, becoming engrossed with ourselves in an activity seems characteristic of how we, as social role takers, develop. Acts become engaging for the children, repeated and also approached in different ways. Denzin (1977: 130–131) has described this type of activity as 'playing at a self' in which there occur dramatic encounters with the self that reside in the covert features of the act. The person converses with his alter ego while he is casting himself in a variety of different stances. The phrase 'playing at a self' conveys the message that there are many different selves children try on as they take account of themselves, others and their experiences through self-reflective activity.

A characteristic feature of self-involvement, especially as it increases in absorption, is the amount of repetition involved. In fact, the amount of repetition in this stance is so pervasive that it becomes one of the most trying features of observation. Repetition provides a framework for continued interaction (Garvey, 1977). When the involvement is no longer absorbing, the children move on and create new situations for themselves.

As the children become involved with themselves during the act, their verbal manipulation of their involvement objects becomes indicative of their absorption. The children adapt their speech to the objects which they are addressing. Denzin (1972: 292) has made the same point stating that it is consistent with an interactionist tradition to view language as a situated production which varies according to the definitions which people give objects, selves, others, time, place and the social relationship between speakers. Psychologists (Fein and Clarke-Stewart, 1973) have noted that children learn to use linguistic forms that are appropriate to particular occasions and settings. The children learn how to formulate diverse and subtle repertoires of information and intentions. They develop a theory of speaking and listening that deals with the appropriateness of language to their place and setting. Hence, I have examples of the children gooing like babies, hissing like bionic men and reading out loud like teachers.

The children also display long attention spans indicative of their engrossment in the act. In the following example, Abby spent longer than the twelve minutes I actually measured her acting, since she initially got my attention by being quietly absorbed for so long.

> Abby spent twelve minutes trying to place eight small wooden people upright on a school bus. She would knock them down with her arm as she set them up and start all over again. She would finish, run the bus, the people would fall over and she would start all over again.

In the process of their self-reflective involvement, the children quite literally and mentally make objects. In some ways, the process of taking account of other children becomes the object. The children are involved in a more general sense, in the process of learning to take account of others and themselves within this particular setting. Making objects and manipulating these objects becomes a vehicle for sustaining this involvement. By recognizing the seriousness of this engagement for the children, the observer is better able to understand this stance of reflection as merely one among other qualitative types in which the child is engaged.

### Stance Two: Interpretive Observation and Display

In contrast to a stance of self-involvement, interpretive observation and display is best conceptualized as children's attempts to learn the ropes. Through various techniques, the children make it evident that they are trying to monitor and follow the ways of others. However, I have called this interpretive observation or involvement 'from afar' since it represents only a peripheral commitment from the observing child. The observer is, in fact, a bystander, a marginal man who hovers on the sideline of involvement eager to take in as much information as he can about children's behaviour and yet not willing to participate with another child.[8]

Marginal involvement often takes place beside other children. How else to learn their ways if you do not follow closely? Interpretive involvement is not a developmental stage in the production of self nor does it characterize only newcomer behaviour. Children move in and out of this involvement stance constantly and use it most fruitfully as a well defined period of quiet observation and reflection. As Mead pointed out in stage one of the act, reflective thinking is only necessary when the act is inhibited or halted. The identifying of objects is a continual problem for children since in the flow of action, new objects constantly arise leading to the reconstruction of past events. Since acts require this continual redefinition and reflection on the emergence of new objects, periods of time required to assess these emergents is continually sought and used by individuals.[9] Marginal involvement is not representative of an underdeveloped self but is an involvement stance central to the continual reassessment which permits the innovation and novelty of human life (Strauss, 1959: 26).

Most characteristic of this stance is that of *staring*.[10] Examples abound of children standing around staring at one child or groups of other children involved in activities. Newcomers are most often seen spending what initially appears as excessively long amounts of time sitting, standing or following the actions of others.

> Jesse wandered in and out of the two (play) rooms watching every-
> one. Then, he stood in the doorway connecting the two rooms. He
> spent approximately the next fifteen to twenty minutes doing this.
> He generally scanned the rooms and then focused on certain children
> for periods of time, often focusing on wherever the greatest noise
> was coming from.

By strategically placing himself in the doorway, this child was able to scan and observe all the activities that were going on in the two rooms.

Clearly, staring is an initial and necessary way of learning what other children are all about.

While staring is the most extreme form of interpretive observation, there are other characteristic stances by which the children begin to make initial indications of their presence to others. Of these, public *announcements* are common.

> Kevin is running back and forth across the gym floor with a hockey stick saying 'Watch me score.'

> Jeremy comes running by, picks up a board and yells 'Superman!'

In all of these examples, an indication is being made to others that their action is a public display. Their action is to be acknowledged by others by staring, commenting on or joining in with. More often than not, the observing children merely watch and resume their own acts. The essential differentiating quality of this stance is its public nature in the form of an announcement or overture. Others are requested to take account.

Similar to these public announcements are *direct invitations* to join in an action. While, in the first case, the overture is decidedly open-ended, in the latter a specific demand is placed on another child. Typically the physical presence of the child is too close to be ignored.

> Norm comes into the lunch room singing 'tea' to himself repeatedly.
> He goes over to the box of felt sticks in the corner, takes one out and brings it over to me saying 'lemon, lemon' and thrusts it in my face.

Or the invitation to join is phrased in the character of a question or an overt demand which is, again, difficult to ignore.

> Kevin approaches me on his bike in the gym and says 'Chase me'.

> Lila looks over and calls out, 'Warren, do you want to be my baby?'

Repeatedly then, the children make obvious their willingness to be joined in action by others. Yet, by virtue of their delivery, these statements and actions are attempts to get others to merely take account of them, recognize their presence and actions. Whether or not the other joins in is superfluous, otherwise more tried and successful joining in tactics would be used. Yet an attempt has been made to become part of the taking account process.

The inner (private) and the outer (public) sides of interaction are not as clearly differentiated in observed action as the concepts suggest. Inner thought expressed outwardly through observable action or language is what Vygotsky (1962) and Markey (1928) and Flavell (1968) call sociocentric declarations of intent. The child is treating other children, or any other child who happens to be present, as an audience for their actions. They are not taking the perspective of the other child, but literally acting at them (Denzin,

1980: 256). The children display this in the form of public monologues, public announcements, and making initial overtures to others. These children's acts are transitional between the hidden covert self-reflection of stance one and the more public other-reflective engagement of stance three. By looking outside his own behaviour and casting others in the stance of audience, the child creates a non-participating, socially distant forum for his acts. While audience members always have the option of commenting directly (Goffman, 1959), the child has the option of not attending to this corrective feedback. Children understand the interactional rule of their mutual obligation to attend to other's views in reciprocal involvements. Children are also notorious rule breakers in that these rules are constantly negotiated. However, the transitional interactional stance of interpretive observation and display allows the child to attend to others to an extent that he alone controls.

In the next type of interaction, which I call *making initial overtures*, the children typically physically join a group without greetings, announcements or any overt displays and, simply, get on with the action.

> Susan arrives in the room that morning, goes over to the mats where some girls are laughing, sits down beside them and starts moving the blocks around, as the others are.

Throughout this kind of episode, the joining child typically remains interactionally aloof, content to be physically present, watching and listening, and yet not directly involved with the others in the creation of an ongoing, meaningful act. There is enough shared understanding in their acceptance into the group and also their knowledge of how to remain anonymous in that situation. By neither disrupting the act nor contributing to its flow, the interested bystander stance is maintained.

A qualitatively distinct yet theoretically similar type of action is found in the form I call *crowding*. Defined as 'invasion of interactional space', it remains analytically distinct from common instances of invasion of property such as grabbing valued possessions. While usually not deliberate, crowding is a frequent form of involvement from afar. There are frequent instances of crowding in which children attempt to join other children who are self-absorbed, an involvement stance in which others are rarely welcome.

Joffe (1973: 107) has observed in her analysis of a pre-school setting how the children engage in territoriality, a tendency to stake out geographical spaces, objects and people as one's own. Territoriality arises over struggles for limited supplies and demands for privacy.

> Angie sat down in the car seat she found lying in the yard. Margo walks over and tries to also sit down beside her. Angie yells 'Get off. Mine.' Angie shoves her on the ground. Margo starts howling.

In this example and others, the child's privacy is being invaded and attempts by others to break into their space are strongly resisted.

In addition to literally crowding a child's interactional turf, often attempts are made to take the trappings of the action. For example,

Brad arrives at the table and grabs Cindy's playdough. Cindy screams, 'That's my birthday.'

It is not the object *per se* which is desirable to the child but rather the action enveloping the object which makes the object become a desirable thing. The crowder correctly takes account of the other child's involvement and wants to join in. What he has yet to learn is that self-involved children rarely want others to join them.

All of these interpretive observations and displays entail a peripheral or marginal involvement with others. Meanings are usually not understood or at best, are shared only minimally with others. In brief, these various stances represent the most initial phases of the taking account process.

### Stance Three: Co-Involvement

The third stance, called co-involvement, is characterized by the attempts of the children to track the public actions of other children and to fit or join their actions with the others. In these involvements, the children have moved into the realm of public interaction. In presenting varied lines of action, the children are attempting to create a situated or focused interaction based on a mutual understanding of social objects. For sustained interaction, there must be sufficient understanding among the children on the common involvement objects in order to continue joint acts. In fact, we rarely do comprehend all aspects of interaction. There simply has to be enough meaning, perhaps roughly understood, for an act to continue. When the children are engaged with others in an attempt to join their lines of action, they are often unsuccessful. A great deal of guess work goes on as the child tentatively puts forth an idea, an action, a physical object, a non-verbal glance or gesture. If these cues are picked up by another child and interpreted accurately, then an initial joint encounter is created. For this exchange to continue, the simultaneous sharing and sending of cues must proceed. However, the characteristic element of this involvement stance is the inability of interaction to proceed in this turn-taking manner.

Problematic activity[11] forces the children to search for alternative lines on which joint acts can be built. Building joint acts is attempted but not accomplished. Enough meaning is not shared. Reciprocal social role taking thus fails. This stance is differentiated from the fourth stance of public action by the child's inability to accurately take into account the feelings, attitudes, and interpretation of the other, and articulate, negotiate and build on these.

There are many tactics which the children use to find these common grounds. When problems halt the flow, if the children are committed to working out tentative agreements to overcome the momentary impasse, they will prod one another, propose alternatives, and doggedly pursue new activities.[12] In short, by continually digging at one another's meaning, the children are engaged in a trial and error process of reaching common understanding.

The degree to which a child is committed (Becker, 1970b) to join an act appears to determine the extent to which the prodding goes on. The key to this concept appears to be that the child sees his searching for alternative lines of mutually agreeable action as consistent with his overall commitment to the involvement object and others. Children spend extended periods of time attempting to adjust their lines of action to the other, sometimes to no avail. The search takes on a protracted negotiated character as the action shifts from one object to another. Co-involved interactive sequences thus strike the observer as disjointed, bumpy, random and rather chaotic occasions. They no doubt strike the children the same way. The children encounter frustration and the fatigue of continual attempts to get another person to understand what they are trying to articulate or perform. For example,

> Lorna says to Jackie, 'You be the baby.' Jackie replies, 'You be the baby, okay Lorna?' Lorna then says, 'No let's cook.' Jackie shakes her head and walks off to the water table. Lorna lies down on the floor beside the piano saying, 'Then I'll be the baby if Jackie won't play.'

In this case, the children never did agree on their involvement objects and the continual switching of themes suggests the dissatisfaction felt.

While these above examples have indicated the verbal element of digging, the search for common ground also goes on non-verbally. In the following example, gestures prevail. After a period of fighting over a train,

> Michael takes Norm's hand and they walk over to the shelf and Michael takes down a train for Norm. Michael then takes his train and runs it along the floor making train noises. Norm starts to tentatively move his train along. When I looked back a minute later, Norm was following Michael around the room as Michael moved his train around. Michael looked up and said, 'Are you walking with me?' Norm nods his head. Michael replies, 'You walk with me and the trains, okay Norm?' Norm smiles and gets down on the floor and starts to push the back of the train with Michael.

Given an openness to joining and being joined, if the children persist, try new lines of action and jointly dig for common ground, they can usually work out a satisfactory agreement. Accomplishing working agreements is a trial and error process in which two or more children continually search for common lines of agreement. The manipulative stage in which something is actually done to the common objects of involvement is rarely smooth. Interpretive problems continually threaten to halt the action unless new areas of understanding are reached.

### Stance Four: Reciprocal Involvement

The final involvement stance is characterized by a smooth, running process in which action is jointly created on shared definitions of the situation.[13] The children stand firmly on the same grounds. While overt digging takes place, it is not the central element in this process. More characteristic is the active, understood, ongoing flow of involvement. It represents a rather finished product of the whole taking account process in which the joint action is not circumvented by the problem of perception, definition or evaluation. The children are adept at reading the cues put forth by their partners and adjusting their responses. They are, as Becker (1970c) has coined the phrase, capable of situational adjustment.[14]

The children can be mutually involved with one another through a complex series of gestures. In fact, studies of infants in cribs done by, among others, Spiro (1965) and Provence *et al.* (1977) attest to this quality of non-verbal shared understanding.

As verbal competency increases, the children combine their gestural skills with their verbal skills in advancing reciprocal involvement. In this example, talking becomes a focus for their involvement.

> Amanda gets out a book and starts to ad-lib the story, holding the book open to the rest of the children as the teachers do and turning the pages as she tells the story. (There is no story line.) Jason, John and Clare sit absolutely quiet as she reads. When Amanda gets silly by turning to a page and saying, 'wee, wee, wee, gee, gee, gee,' the children laugh for four pages of this and then start fidgeting and looking away. Amanda picks up on this cue and starts to 'read' again.

Perhaps of all the incidents of shared involvement, to both the observer and, judging by their engrossment and repetition, also to the children, the most fascinating are those in which the flow of shared understanding runs on and on, shifting themes and physical locations.[15] I have numerous examples of, among others, children 'watching' Sesame Street on broken televisions, rushing friends in and out of 'hospitals', dashing about putting out 'fires', gassing and repairing broken trucks and cars, attacking as, and defending themselves from 'monsters', cooking, eating, drinking sand food and 'painting' porches. Throughout all of these positions of shared involvement, the central thrust is one of moving the action along, sorting out minor problems and getting on with the business of being finely attuned to the others. Sometimes what the children are doing, like riding buses or making muffins, provides an opportunity for focused interaction and the 'bus riding' is an ancillary activity (Denzin, 1977: 152).

While the most interesting and complex of these examples would take a page to quote, short excerpts will perhaps provide the flavour of this process. The action can include the familiar themes of 'playing house'.

> Lorna is in the doll bed lying down as the baby. Jackie is the mother. Lorna cries like a baby saying, 'wa, wa, wa,' Jackie laughs and sticks a small toy in her mouth and says, 'Stop crying baby. Here's your bottle.' Lorna smiles and drinks; Jackie laughs again. Lorna says, 'Pat me.' Jackie leans over and pats her. Lorna says, 'I'm hungry.' Jackie walks over to the doll centre, pretends to take something out of an empty doll cup, returns and says, 'here baby, here's your food.'

In all of the cases, I was struck by the relative speed and ease of the exchange. The children are tuned into each other in the sense that they seem to understand and be able to follow and anticipate changes in the other's line of action. Denzin (1977: 167–168) has commented on the concept of interactional age. As situational awareness increases and incorporates an expanding range of interactional others, the social exchanges of children become more complex. Obviously, what has come before for a child will have some force in the present, as the '. . . presents slip continually one into another' (Mead, 1959: 9). Yet, without a very detailed and lengthy focused observation, it is quite impossible to do more than hypothesize that newcomers to the taking the role of the other toward self process would not initially be participating in these sometimes lengthy and complex exchanges.

## Conclusion

As this involvement continuum suggests, negotiating social meanings is a complex process ranging from private self-reflective activity to publicly shared agreements. The first two stances include the private, covert side of interaction. Self-reflective activity or self-involvement is conceptually similar to what James (1890) called the phenomenological stream of interaction or stream of consciousness. This is the hidden stance in which the child is thinking, planning and wrestling with objects.

Acts characteristic of the second stance, interpretive observation of and display to others, are again essentially private in that distinct others are not invited to join in an activity. However, the involvement is peripheral or marginal to that of others, since it is these others' lines of action which constitute the focus for the observing child. Being essentially private interpretations of others' activities, the extent to which self-object understanding is shared is indicated by both the child's absorption in the activities associated with this stance and by his ability to involve himself in observation of others without shattering the flow. The child as fieldworker is tracking the ways of others. By visually and auditorily monitoring others, he is attempting to grasp the complex cues and construction of fluid rules of interaction for entry into, procedure within and exit from a focused interaction. The child imaginatively and mentally is rehearsing how he would fit into others' lines of activity. If his assessment of their ways is accurate, the child can maintain his marginal stance neither publicly contributing to, nor disrupting the actions of others.

The third and fourth stances involve public attempts to fit lines of action together. The third involvement stance, labeled co-involvement, is characterized by its essential failure to accomplish this mutual joining activity. Children in this stance are constantly negotiating with and prodding at one another's public actions to reach an understanding about shared social activities. However, despite their wrestling with these stubborn and troublesome objects and despite the often tremendous guesswork which takes place, the children are unable to sustain mutual interaction based on sufficient understanding. Meadian problems halt the flow of activity.

Mistakes at work (Hughes, 1958) or failure of interaction (Goffman,

1959) provide us with a taste of the essential negotiative elements of the children's work. Strauss (1959: 61) has noted that it is unusual for anyone to note all aspects of interaction. In many situations, a great many aspects of interaction are taken for granted. By tentatively putting forth public lines of action, the children are engaged in a continual trial and error process which provides them with corrective feedback. Given their limited interactional experience, many situations are not yet conventionalized. Each child enters a focused interaction with a fund of prior knowledge concerning the social production of situational definitions. This prior experience includes repetition with some familiar others and fewer, regular encounters with unfamiliar others. Hence this co-involvement stance of reaching working agreements with other children is characterized by the constant digging for mutual understanding by switching lines of action until a common object can be grasped. Negotiation (Strauss, 1978), as Meadian problem solving, is central to everyday life for the children in day care centres. The children can commit themselves to handing misunderstandings as they arise by situationally adjusting their public behaviour and thus resolving disputes. However, whether for lack of commitment (Becker, 1970c) or lack of conventionalized methods of handling these problems, the joint attempts fail. Over time, observations of stable groups (Fine, 1979; Becker *et al.*, 1961; Denzin, 1977) reveal that individual, corporate histories and traditional patterns of reaching working agreements (co-involvement) will become part of the group's perspective. What has gone before and perhaps become codified in rules, albeit situationally negotiable, will obviously affect what which is ongoing. But, as Mead's concept of novelty suggests, each emergent in new situations is itself unique and neither structurally nor historically determined. Simply spending time in creating mutual interactions with unfamiliar others no doubt provides the child with a wider range of experience with which to participate in the production of emergents. The children evolve a variety of negotiative tactics which they use to prod the other child into accepting their proposed definitions. Through this interplay of suggested lines of action, the children negotiate a situated product.

The fourth involvement stance,[16] called reciprocal (reciprocated) involvement, is based on successful mutual alignment of joint activity. This stance is characterized by a smooth, running process of children creating publicly shared meanings of social objects. They share similar definitions of their mutual activity and hence stand firmly on the same grounds. While problems arise which threaten to disrupt their actions, these are easily manipulated. What differentiates this involvement from the previous stance is not so much their success at mutually sustaining the interaction but rather their active creation of shared meanings sufficiently agreed on to allow joint acts to continue. The result is reciprocated and often instantaneous understanding of others' public displays. This is the stance characteristic of what Strauss (1959: 55) calls a rhythmic ballet, and what Schaffer (1977: 61) calls a harmonious dialogue. In both cases, the participants are attuned to one another, share the same code of signals and send and receive these signals via several channels simultaneously (Schaffer, 1977: 61).

Sociological research into the world of children (Denzin, 1973; Corsaro, 1981; Glassner, 1976; Fine, 1979; Joffe, 1973) has begun to catalogue the range and complexity of situational behaviour within naturalistic settings. Movement in this research direction has the effect of slowing the search for causal connections of appropriate child behaviour. This is accomplished by emphasizing the gradualistic and relational emergence of role-taking and negotiative behaviours.

Documentation of children's interaction with other children and with themselves demonstrates that role-taking is not a unitary concept. It holds a variety of meanings depending on the relation of self-other to social objects. For this reason, the term involvement in negotiating meaning captures the variety of instances in which children engage.

The notion of various stances of interactional awareness contributes to the growing literature on interpretations, understandings and hermeneutics (Scheler, [1913] 1954; Schutz, 1962; Denzin, 1980). How we understand and interpret the other is essential to Mead's philosophy of the act. In this light, children can be viewed as hermeneutic interpretors of one another's actions in schooling settings. As such, this study suggests that the interpretive process in which the children are engaged is more complex than simply imaginatively projecting oneself into another's line of action or thought. Imaginative projection glosses over the actual process by which the children translate and piece together the meanings of another's actions and place these actions within a meaningful totality. These units of action might include what adults call play, routines, rituals or encounters. But basic to each unit is the child's process of interpretation and comprehension of the acts and objects of others. Our task in childhood socialization studies is to analyze these social fields of experience as they are repeatedly generated in collective settings of young children.

Clearly there are a number of more specific questions left unanswered. Much more detail into the interactional careers of specific groups of children is needed to indicate the place of interactional age and histories of role-taking with unfamiliar others. We require more detail on degrees of reflexivity as these relate to the children's interactional position with others. Does the child adopt the standpoint of the other (Turner, 1961) as his own or as a depersonalized norm? Finally, we need to investigate the place of emotions (Denzin, 1980) in the child's adoption of varying interactional stances with other children.

### Notes

1  Other studies of children's play, notably psychological accounts, rely almost exclusively on the child's physical actions as defined by an adult observer, and make no attempt to discern the child's definition of the act, object or situation.
2  The children's objects I deal with belong essentially to stage two of Mead's act. Some of these objects are mentally manipulated and some are concrete and resistant, such as sand which is defined by the children in non-adult ways and used by the children as food. But generally, stage two objects resist in the sense that they may not permit continuing the act especially if others are involved. See Mead (1938: 59, 74) for a discussion of the resistance of objects, and Mead (1938: 32–33) for a discussion of differing objects in each stage of the act.
3  Goffman (1963: 36) defined involvement close to its dictionary meaning. To

'involve' means to occupy oneself absorbingly, to engross oneself fully. To be engaged in an occasional activity means to sustain some kind of cognitive and affective engrossment in it, some mobilization of one's psychological resources; in short, it means to be involved in the activity.

4   Interactional age is a dynamic and relatively unexplored concept in studies of children. In order to fully examine this concept, one would need to follow the careers of children.

5   See Denzin (1980), Hochschild (1975), Scheler ([1913] 1954), and Schutz (1962) for discussion of the emotional content of interactional analysis.

6   The particular problems I encountered in this role with the teachers are dealt with in another article (Mandell, 1983) [and this book, Chapter 4].

7   Self-involvement is conceptually distinct from Goffman's (1963: 69) 'being away'. This will be discussed in Stance Two, Interpretive Observation and Display.

8   See Geer *et al.* (1968: 209–213) for a discussion of 'learning the ropes'.

9   See Mead (1959:9–12) for his discussion of reflection and emergence.

10  In the psychological literature (Weininger, 1979: 34) what I encompass under one technique of interpretive observation, namely staring, psychologists have labelled onlooker play.

11  For Mead, a problem was always an event or an idea in philosophy or science which did not make sense. My idea of 'Meadian problem solving' relates more narrowly to Mead's stages of the act in which misunderstandings halt the flow of the act. My use of problem solving does not appear as such in *The Philosophy of the Act*. See Mead's (1938: 79) discussion of problems.

12  While negotiation goes on throughout many of these involvement stances, it is not defined here as a distinct perspective. It seems that the initial use of the concept negotiation (Strauss, 1963) as a separate category in various socialization studies was in part a way to remind the reader of the interactional nature of the study. Here, I moved beyond that point and suggest that the interactional socialization perspective always assumes a negotiative character.

13  As Polanyi and Prosch (1975: 44) state, our capacity for making sense of, for understanding another person's action emerges by entering into his situation and by judging his actions from within his own point of view.

14  Becker (1970c: 279) defines situational adjustment as the individual's capacity, as he moves in and out of a variety of social situations, to learn the requirements of continuing in each situation and achieving success in it.

15  Much has been written about the role of fantasy in children's play usually with a view to exploiting its functional significance. See Markey (1928), Ellis (1973), and Herron and Sutton-Smith (1971).

16  According to Mead (1938: 77), the relationship between act and object and these two considered as one can be called a situation. Each involvement stance thus represents varying situations.

### Concluding Note

In Chapter 5 I made the claim that taking children seriously as subjects of sociological analysis would have as one consequence the development of ideas that would contribute to an understanding of adults as well as children. This article by Mandell provides evidence for just such a claim. Rather than viewing the four involvement stances Mandell identifies as applicable only to children, we might, by applying them to adult behavior, gain insights into the social worlds of adults.

Take, for example, a party:

1 *self-involvement* could describe the solitary drinkers, solitary dancers, and those engrossed in the hors d'oeuvres.
2 *interpretive observation and display* might characterize those leaning against chairs and door jambs, watching the party.
3 *co-involvement* could be found in preliminary conversations and small talk.
4 *reciprocal involvement* might be seen in total engrossment in conversation, in dancing with others, etc.

A research study of adult parties using such a model might well support the existence of such stances among adults; such a study might also identify other kinds of stances. Again, if we were to forego the temptation to attribute any such newly-discovered stances to adults only but instead return to a study of young children, we might well find those newly discovered stances present there as well. Working *between* adult worlds and children's worlds rather than studying each in isolation holds promise for bringing to light features of each world that might otherwise be missed.

F.C.W.

## Chapter 13

# Children Doing 'Artwork'

*Erica Cavin*

## Commentary

Cavin conducted the study described in her paper after reading an earlier draft of this book. Her work demonstrates clearly the useful guidance that can be provided by works of the kind presented in this volume. Like Mandell, for example, she examines 'children's ways' and, like Mackay, she focuses on children's competencies.

By directing her sociological attention to aspects of children's behavior that are more commonly considered in psychological terms, she is able to display the social dimensions of such behavior. Of particular theoretical importance is Cavin's questioning of the procedures for identifying *solitary* behavior. What in everyday life is taken for granted as solitary activity may, on the basis of careful sociological observation, be found to be social, in the sense that it is oriented to others and takes them into account. Cavin makes clear that, whether or not it is indeed possible to engage in *solitary* behavior when in the presence of others, a gathering of young children, each working on an individual project, can be a *social* event.

Also worth highlighting is Cavin's recognition of the very different standards and attitudes applied to the 'artwork' of children and of adults. Her data suggests that adults view children's artwork as in some sense trivial, perhaps meaningful for what it discloses of a child's personality or motor skills but not worthy of aesthetic consideration. In contrast, Cavin's observations of children's talk about their work (how it is best executed, whether or not it is pretty) and recognition of its audience (someone in particular that it is *for*, display of the finished product) suggest that children may take their 'artwork' indeed to be 'art'.

F.C.W.

## Background

The purpose of this study[1] is to examine sociologically the classroom activity known as doing 'artwork.' Through the use of sociological methodology, I explored aspects of this activity that, as a teacher, I had found intriguing. My

179

focus shifted several times through the course of my investigation, reflecting my changing understanding of what I was observing. Thus what began as a study of drawing as a solitary activity became an investigation of children doing 'artwork' within the context of a classroom and encompasses such topics as what constitutes drawing and what it means to 'finish' a picture.

The data were gathered in observations which took place in 1984 and 1990. In 1984 I spent a day observing children drawing in a nursery school setting as part of a broad interest in children's activities. From 1984 to 1989, working both as a student teacher and teacher in day care and school settings, I had the opportunity to informally observe children drawing. In 1990 I returned to a day care classroom to carry out more systematic observations.

My first observations drew upon ideas from my previous work as an aide in a number of classrooms. I had certain expectations about what sorts of things I might find. I remembered scenes of individual children drawing in shared space. Though within feet of each other, they would be so intent on the process of drawing that they were seemingly oblivious to the presence of others. I also could envision another 'type' of child who drew while staring straight ahead looking at anything but the paper being used. Finally I could imagine the child who concentrated not only on drawing but on doing it 'right'. This child's picture would often end up torn in frustration and thrown away, despite a teacher's protests that it was a very good picture.

These were the kinds of activities I expected to observe at that time. I anticipated seeing children taking different attitudes towards what they were doing but having certain characteristics in common. They would be engaged in drawing as an individual and nonverbal activity. However, from the very begining my observations contradicted these expectations. My 1990 observations reinforced my 1984 discovery that looking as a sociologist rather than as a teacher at children drawing revealed very different aspects of this activity — aspects that have value for both sociologists and teachers.[2]

In my analysis of each set of observations I tried to follow the data wherever they led. Thus in the first setting I focused on drawing and speech and on drawing as a group activity. I continued this focus in my later day care observations, but I noticed that there was less group drawing and the children tended to use drawing materials in combination with other materials, e.g. markers, paper, and scissors, or stamp pads, stamps, crayons and paper. It seemed overly restrictive to limit my observations to those children who only used drawing materials and paper. Insofar as the use of a variety of materials in a variety of ways was part of doing drawings for these children, I widened the scope of my observations to include these activities and my focus shifted to the details of drawing as a practical accomplishment. Thus the topic of this paper, which began as 'children drawing', now could be more accurately described as 'children carrying out procedures with materials from the working category known as "art materials"'. For the sake of simplicity, I have reduced this phrase to 'children doing "artwork"'.

## The Settings

My 1984 observations were carried out at a nursery school in Brookline, Massachusetts. This school is open five mornings a week with an optional extended day program for part of the afternoon. The school accepts children who are between 2½ and 5 years in age. I spent one morning at this school, visiting two of its five classrooms: the 3-year-olds' room and the 2½-year-olds' room. The younger children I observed who were drawing that day were involved in what was referred to as a 'project': They were coloring on large pieces of paper to which string had been attached to form capes. The children were to wear the capes in a parade. This activity was teacher-directed in that the teacher defined the product. The children received no direction in the actual process of drawing while I was in the room. The children were seated at a rectangular table on which both crayons and magic markers had been placed. When I began my observations in that room, the activity was already in progress. The older children were able to choose to draw as one of a number of activities available to them. In that room, teachers had set up activities on the various tables. I sat near a round table on which a teacher had arranged pieces of paper and boxes of crayons.

The time that elapsed between the sets of observations enabled me to reassess the earlier experience and include new criteria in my selection of a next site. In my first observations, I had decided to observe younger children (2 and 3 years old) due to the types of drawings I had seen made by children of this age in the past. My reasoning was that such drawings would be harder for me, as an adult, to interpret and I would be forced to rely on the children's own interpretations. In this I was trying to follow Garfinkel's recommendation to select a subject of investigation that was 'anthropologically strange' (1967: 9). My interest was in uncovering the children's knowledge of drawing, not in studying my own preconceptions.

By the time of my later observations, access to a classroom in which children were able to choose materials freely became an important consideration. Interest in children's knowledge and competence led me to choose a setting in which children potentially would have more freedom of choice and where, accordingly, I would be able to observe the children's rather than the teachers' choices and decisions.

Thus my 1990 observations took place in a classroom at a day care center in Cambridge, Massachusetts. Children between the ages of 15 months and 5 years attend this center, which is open from 8:15 in the morning to 5:30 in the afternoon. I chose to observe the 4 and 5 year old children at this center. I observed in this classroom five times in the morning and once in the afternoon over the course of three weeks. In the mornings, I arrived before the children, while the teachers were setting up morning activities. I stayed through the free play period and helped the group clean up. I generally left after clean up time but occasionally stayed for portions of the other morning activities including snack, group meeting and outdoor play to get more of a sense of the day as a whole. On the afternoon that I observed I arrived while the children were playing outside and stayed through afternoon group meeting and afternoon free play and activity times until the end of the day.

Although this classroom was similar to the nursery school rooms in that children came in to the classroom to find activities that had been set up by teachers, it differed in the manner in which children could use these activities as well as the materials stored on shelves. In the day care classroom, child-selected art supplies could often be incorporated with or substituted for teacher-selected activities.[3]

## Methodology

I engaged in overt observation in both settings. I sat near the tables at which art activities were taking place in each room and took notes openly. In my later observations, in the day care classroom, my notetaking appeared to be of great interest to some of the children. We seemed to be participants in a process of mutual observation. Even as I was trying to make sense of what the children were doing, so were some of the children trying to make sense of me.[4]

My methodology changed somewhat through the course of both sets of observations, in accord with my developing understanding of the phenomenon being studied. In my initial observations at the nursery school, I decided to supplement observational data by conducting informal interviews, asking children questions about those elements of 'drawing' which I could not make sense of. However, I immediately discovered that this approach had a basic flaw; the children would not answer direct questions. I was unsuccessful in my attempts to interview any of the children. Generally they responded to my questions with smiles or silence. The longest verbal response I received was monosyllabic. As an alternative to formal interviewing I recorded the comments the children made as they drew. This proved to be a valuable source of data. The efficacy of this procedure was such that I followed it in both settings.

## Findings

In what follows I combine the data from both sets of observations and provide analysis under the following headings:

> The *solitary* nature of doing artwork
> Doing artwork as a group activity
> The nature of doing artwork
> The particular problem of *finishing*

The first two topics build on concerns that emerged from my intial observations; the latter topics focus on issues that arose in my later observations.

### The 'Solitary' Nature of Doing Artwork

The utterances made by the nursery school children while drawing proved wrong my most basic assumption regarding that activity, i.e. that drawing is a solitary activity even when more than one child is doing it. Psychological conceptions of young children's play as 'solitary' or 'parallel' colored my viewpoint.[5] Though I deliberately chose an observational setting where it would be possible to see more than one child drawing at the same time. I did not, prior to my first observations, expect to see much interaction between the children as they drew. Interestingly, particularly in the nursery school, I saw much interactive drawing, while solitary drawing was not much in evidence.

In the nursery school rooms, one or two of the children did not speak while drawing. These children nonetheless demonstrated awareness of the other children and the interactions taking place around them, for they occasionally looked up from their pictures, gazing directly at some of the speaking children. I noticed that the speaking children generally did not try to talk to the non-speakers. It was as if they distinguished between one category of children who speak and are spoken to and a second category of children who don't speak and are not spoken to. Membership in these two categories seemed to be determined by individuals' behavior (based on whether or not they spoke) and was generally recognized and respected by other members of the group. I will refer to these individuals who did not choose to interact verbally with others as *solitary workers*.

Having observed solitary workers at the nursery school I was interested to see the following incident at the day care center in which a child approached and attempted to speak to a nonspeaking child. Melissa was sitting alone coloring with markers. She was silent as she worked. Abby approached the table with a rolled up crepe streamer on her hand and held it out announcing, 'Lollipops for sale.' Melissa looked up at Abby but made no verbal response. Abby then asked Melissa to repeat some nonsense syllables. Mellissa again made no response. Abby left and Melissa returned to her picture. This episode demonstrated how it is possible to maintain a solitary status, even when that status is threatened.

It seems as though, while in a classroom setting, being solitary in the sense of working alone while focused on a particular project is problematic. Solitary workers appear to be potential interactants; they seem aware of their surroundings and the people nearby. It is by their ongoing choices that they determine the extent of their involvement with others even while carrying out a particular task, such as drawing. To a certain extent it is possible to do solitary artwork while sharing a table with a group. However I suspect that the only way to do true solitary artwork is to work in a place that has no other people in it.

Distractability, though certainly an issue in doing artwork, does not seem to be a deciding factor in distinguishing solitary from group workers in art actitivies. In one example, a group stopped drawing to watch some boys who were playing noisily at a nearby table. The solitary worker (the child who had not been participating in the group conversation) did not look up once though the distraction continued for several minutes. On the other hand I watched another solitary worker who not only seemed to be aware of what was going on in the room but appeared to change his behavior based on what he saw. The teacher made an announcement that it was time to clean up. This child looked at her when she spoke, then looked down at his picture and began to color at a much faster rate than he had done before. He did this for several minutes, looked up again at the teacher, who did not appear to notice that the child was not cleaning up, and colored again at the faster rate.

In the day care classroom I witnessed many additional examples of solitary work. Some of this solitary work took place while others were co-present, other instances occured where individuals were alone at a table. Yet, as with the solitary children observed at the nursery school setting, these children displayed awareness of their surroundings. One child, Mark, had been coloring quietly when a child in a nearby area began to cry. Mark asked the teacher comforting that child, 'Why Abby sad?' In another instance Joshua had been coloring alone at a table when a loud buzzing sound was heard from across the room. He then joined in a discussion of the probable cause of the noise with children from two other areas in the room.

I do not want to suggest that children engaged in art activities operate like jack-in-the-boxes, popping up at every random noise. Instead, they seem to be selective about what they respond to. In one instance, Melissa looked up at the sound of Cathleen's and Abby's conversation but made no visible response to the crying sounds made by Bobby and Joshua pretending to be babies, although the boys were louder and closer to Melissa. Given the particular physical stance required by drawing in particular, which tends to involve leaning forward slightly and focusing down on a piece of paper, it is not surprising to find examples of children noticing sounds.

Having noticed the presence of 'distractions' during my earlier observations, I decided to focus on this phenomenon in my later ones. I found that children did not demonstrate awareness only of random noise; rather it seemed as though there were logical pauses and natural distraction points in the procedures of doing artwork. For example, a child using markers may shift focus from the paper being used to the box of markers and anything beyond that object when stopping work to switch colors. This time seemed to be a natural one for the child to notice something occuring nearby in the room. Although a child might look up at a sudden noise, a child might also stop work while dipping a paintbrush into paints if something catches the child's eye while doing so. By closely investigating specific instances of 'becoming distracted', such occurrences are revealed to be a logical part of the activity in question.

### Doing Artwork as a Group Activity

As mentioned above, as an alternative to unsuccessful attempts to interview the nursery school children I recorded children's utterances and focused on their speech as a source of data. It was as if talking were a part of doing drawing for many of the children I observed. It was this finding that proved wrong my initial expectation of drawing being a solitary experience. By studying the children's speech I was able to see drawing as a group activity for the first time.

As I listened to the children I was struck by certain patterns of statements that consisted of very similar comments made by different children. These comments were unlike 'normal' conversation in that they seemingly were not directed towards one specific person nor did they appear to require an answer. Nancy Mandell, in 'Children's Negotiation of Meaning' [see Chapter 12 in this volume] describes such utterances as *public announcements*.

The variation on public announcements that I witnessed involved sequential statements that seemed to mirror the initial utterance rather than being an 'answer' to that utterance. In one example of this that took place in the 3-year-olds' room, a child, Carol, came to the coloring table saying, 'I want to make a picture for my mommy'. Another girl came with Carol to the table saying, 'I want to make a picture', almost the same statement that Carol had made earlier. The short time involved gives it an echo-like quality. Almost before the second speaker hears the end of the first speaker's sentence, the second comment is made.

After these girls and two others had been coloring for a while this comment was made, 'I made a design. Look, I made a caterpillar.' Immediately Carol came out with, 'I'm making a picture of my mommy and daddy', and Sharon said, 'I'm making twinkle, twinkle little star'. These statements came quickly, one after the other. Again, it seemed to me upon hearing these utterances as if the later speakers could hardly have had time to hear the end of the initial speaker's sentence. However the sentences themselves suggest that this is not the case. The sentences which follow the initial utterance are similar in both form and content to the initial sentence. A typical pattern might be:

Child 1:   I'm making x.
Child 2:   I'm making y.
Child 3:   I'm making z.

Once the focal characteristic is established, it does not change. Based on what I saw, it would be unlikely for the third child, in the above example, to leave the topic of 'making' and discuss some other aspect of the original sentence. (This child would not be likely to say, 'I like x' instead of 'I'm making z.') This is not to say that such a statement could not be made, but I did not observe such an occurrence and thus could not speculate about what such an utterance might mean.

As the utterances are made so quickly it is difficult to see how the focus emerges. It could be that given the activity of drawing, certain types of things are likely to be a focus. It is possible that in a series of public announcements there is someone who decides what the focus will be. Possibly the second speaker determines the focus by his or her very statement. Further study may clarify this point.

A group public announcement contrasted with the other type of verbalization made by the children which might be termed a *conversational statement*. From the examples outlined above a group public announcement can be seen as an utterance directed towards no one in particular. A conversational statement, by contrast, is a statement made with a specific intended audience and with the expectation of a verbal or nonverbal response. Although one cannot observe an intention directly it is possible to distinguish between an announcement and a conversational statement from the responses made to each type of verbalization. For example, Bobby's intended recipient is clear in the following conversational statements: 'Look at my thing. Lookit, Joshua. Joshua, lookit. Lookit my picture.'

In conversations in general there is likely to be eye contact; in conversations between drawing children the eye contact is more likely to be between a child and a piece of paper than between two children. It is the aspect of there being an intended recipient rather than of there being reciprocal statements which is both important and problematic for an observer. When a child's gaze is directed towards the paper it cannot provide any clue about the recipient.

In the both settings, the tools and activities of doing artwork were the main topics of these observed conversations. In the day care room, however, the children referred to other classroom activities and non-school related items as well as subjects connected to the activities at hand. Subjects that were not related to either the classroom or art activities included 'small talk', e.g. in response to a teacher's question of 'How was your weekend?' Frequently, though not always, topics that did not relate to classroom activities had been raised by teachers. On the whole, however, conversations did not seem to be secondary activities to drawing but a part of the activity itself, as can be seen from the following examples.

Nisha:    I'm working on something real well. I have to do this very quick.

Abby:    You're making it shiny.

Crystal:    My cat's almost done. I'm going to make its babies inside its tummy.

Nisha:    Inside its tummy?!

Molly:    That's silly.

Crystal:    But I can only make its [the baby's] head. You know why? Because I'm going to to color its [the cat's] tummy.

Children used both conversations and public announcements to accomplish a number of tasks. Either could be used to seek or provide information. For example, when Abby covered her hands with ink, Nisha announced, 'She's painting her hands'. Melissa asked Abby directly, 'What are you doing?' Similarly, children used both means to provide information and define situations.

At times the information provided in these utterances was not information that anyone had been noticably seeking. One child made several pictures fairly quickly and handed each one to me saying, 'Aren't they pretty?' An additional example of this sort of statement was provided by Andrea. After watching Sharon color lightly for several minutes she said. 'That's not right' and demonstrated another way of coloring. At another time, Andrea told Carol not to talk, saying that if she spoke they would scribble and they (Andrea and Sharon) did not want to do that. In an example from the day care room, Nisha announced, 'I'm making pretty drawings. I'm making it so pretty.'

The following excerpt from a conversation shows how information provided may be problematic. Two children were tracing and coloring using stencils of St. Patrick's day shamrocks and colored pencils that had been set out on a table by a teacher.

| Don: | That's a wonderful old tree, Joshua. |
|---|---|
| Joshua: | That isn't a tree. |
| Don: | That! (pointing at the 'shamrock' on Joshua's picture). |
| Joshua: | That isn't a tree. |
| Don: | What is it? |
| Joshua: | A clover. |
| Don: | The clover does not have a trunk. |
| Joshua: | I know it doesn't have a trunk. |
| Don: | I've seen one. |
| Joshua: | Well I have too. I've picked one. |
| Don: | I've picked three four-leaf clover. I've picked a three-leaf clover. |
| Joshua: | Well snancy [sic] stupid. Isn't that snupid [sic]. |

(Eventually they agree that Joshua's picture is of a clover and Don's picture is of a tree.)

What is most striking about all the types of utterances made while drawing is how closely related they are to this activity and how significant the activity is to the comments. Although some of the children did not speak, for those who did, talking and drawing were so interrelated as to be virtually inseparable. Certain utterances made by children who were sitting alone offer further evidence of the connection between talking and drawing. The following example comes from the day care classroom. While Don was coloring alone he said, looking down at his paper, 'A giant spaceship. There's a big spaceship.' As he continued to color he made what sounded like spaceship noises. Other children hummed and sang while working. From these observations, it seems that making sounds and talking can be a significant component of doing artwork.

### The Nature of Doing Artwork

Evidence suggests that doing artwork can be seen as a series of completed 'tasks'. A child could pause or even stop at any point in this continuum from the initial approach to the art table to putting away the resulting product. I observed what I thought to be 'aborted' approaches in which a child would come near to the work space, look at what was available, perhaps pick up some of the materials and/or look at stored materials on the shelves and then leave. Some children returned later and used the materials, others did not. In a *completed* approach, a child might examine what was available in a similar manner but would then make use of some materials. During these approaches a child might state aloud an intention to use the materials and/or describe how they will be used. For example, Joshua approached a table set up with stencils, pencils and paper saying, 'I'm gonna make one of these'. Another child used an utterance made during an approach to negotiate with a companion. Cathleen came to the art table saying, 'Abby, let's make it over here. There's gold and silver [crayons].'

When a child remained at a table, there were a number of options available. From what I saw it was possible to use the materials which had been pre-selected by teachers earlier and possibly added to or changed by children, or to select something else from the shelves or from another area of the room. It was also possible to bring in something new either from home or carried over from a previous day.

To do artwork, a child might use any of a number of materials but not anything whatsoever. There seemed to be a category of appropriate art materials which was acknowledged by children and teachers. The children in the day care classroom selected materials from either the *art center* or the *writing center*, both of which contained writing and drawing materials such as pencils, markers, crayons, paints, paper, glue, and scrounge materials (cardboard scraps, ribbons, popsicle sticks and straws). Children could also request or remove certain art-related materials from the teacher's storage area, particularly the masking tape. I did not see any child take something, such as a block or a doll, from a non-art area of the room and use it for art purposes. Rather, the distinction between art and non-art items was maintained. When one child brought a non-art construction he had made to an art table and kept it near him while working on an art activity, another child told him not to do this and told the teacher about it. Although the child did not use this construction in any way related to the art activity, it was seen as 'wrong' to mix art and non-art objects in this setting.

When drawing materials were used, a child could use one item, one color, or a variety of materials and colors. Melissa's use of materials when making what she called a mask of a chipmunk can clarify these distinctions. She used first one and then another type of brown magic marker, then said, 'I guess I can get a colored pencil brown' and went to another table to find one. Drawing materials such as markers, pencils and crayons can be used for drawing, for tracing, for coloring in, for scribbling and for writing. These procedures may be used in combination on a single piece of paper. That is, one could draw shapes, color them in and write letters or words as part of making one picture. I saw different ways of carrying out these procedures. Coloring could be accomplished with back and forth motions, circular motions, moving back over previously colored portions and in 'roller' style in which color was applied in single strokes. Drawing materials could be held and used in a number of ways. Different coloring styles seemed to exist also. I saw one child correct another's style, taking a crayon and demonstrating how to do it 'right'. Children may bear down heavily or color lightly. Varying amounts of pressure could be used to hold a drawing item; one child held a crayon so tightly that I could see the pressure marks on the backs of his fingers. Children may speed up the rate of coloring and later go back to their previous 'normal' speed. I saw no other instances of slowing down the rate of coloring except to return to a previously used rate; in other words, I never saw a child go slower than a level that child had previously used. Markings on a paper could cover anywhere from a tiny portion of one side of a page to every inch of available space to both sides of a page.[6] A child might stop at any point in the use of these materials.

A way to conceive of what producing artwork looks like would be first to imagine a child making marks on a paper. At this point, the child could stop or continue work. Deciding to go on, the child could add more marks of the same or another color or introduce a new medium, depending on the available resources and the restrictions in the environment. Abby provides this example of how available resources can be seen to affect a drawing: While making a picture of a polar bear she asked a teacher for a white marker. She was told they did not have one and began using a black one instead. In producing a completed work, a child might trace using a colored pencil, color in the shape with a marker, then cut out the shape. Again, as each new aspect is added, the child might stop, resulting in a finished product, or might continue until the work is completed or abandoned. At the 'end' of the process, the child might clean up materials, show the work to someone or to a number of people, put away the work, give away the work or carry out a combination of these.

### The Particular Problem of Finishing

When asked directly, the nursery school children could not or would not tell me when a picture was finished and how they knew it was done.[7] Thus during the day care observations, rather than questioning the children, I paid special attention to references to finishing and to what happened to completed pictures in the hope of finding the answer to my question through alternative means. While I heard relatively few comments about this subject, the statements that were made indicated that children had some idea of what being 'done' meant. In one sense, this was synonymous with being ready to be viewed by others, as in these examples.

Bobby:    You like it?
Joshua:   Why you have to show me when it's not finished, silly?

Crystal:  But Nisha, look now my other cat looks.
Nisha:    Pretty.
Crystal:  Look how my other cat looks ugly (turning the page over). See, it looks yucky.
Nisha:    It doesn't look yucky.
Crystal:  You should say it looks yucky. It doesn't have a tail. It's not done yet.[8]

As the above examples also suggest, the subject of finishing arose when it became problematic. In another instance this issue occured when a teacher told a group of children using markers that it was time to clean up and Crystal protested, 'But I need to color mine.' She was told to finish quickly and several minutes later said, 'I'm not done. I need to hurry up really quickly.' In another situation, Abby was instructing Nisha on how to make a greeting card. Nisha asked Abby, 'Are we done?' and Abby replied that they were not. When Nisha asked her, 'Then what [should be done next]?' Abby explained, 'We have to write some letters: Happy Shamrock Day'. Finally, being finished was occasionally referred to when a child stopped work, particularly prior to showing the picture or creation to another. For example, Melissa brought a sock puppet that she had been working on to a teacher saying, 'This is all finished,' and then discussed what she had made with the teacher. Observed instances of what children did with completed work as well as examples of stated intentions provide data for what one can see as constituting 'finishing' and 'being finished'.

The recognition of what being finished means is complicated by the time involved. There appear to be stages in the process of completing pictures; these stages can be carried out over days. On the first day of my observations in the day care center, Joshua was reminded by a teacher of the cardboard python that he'd begun on a previous day. He took out this project, worked on it for a period of time, then put it away to complete later. On another day, the same child burst into the room, holding out a partially completed piece of artwork, saying, 'Look at this what I brought into school to color.' He completed this piece in the classroom that morning.

When the children stopped work on a piece there were a variety of 'finishing touches' that could be employed. Some children rolled up or folded a completed picture prior to putting it away in an 'art cubby' (provided by the teachers). Artwork was also given away on completion. The intention to make a gift of the work could be stated before the work was started or after it stopped. For example Cathleen told a teacher before getting materials, 'I'm going to make a picture for you.' By contrast, Charles said nothing of the destination of his picture until he stopped drawing. At this point he said, 'Momma, lookit. It's a picture for you!'

As the previous example also suggests, completed work often seemed to call for acknowledgment or recognition by others. Some children would show their pictures to individuals who were nearby; additionally some might seek out people throughout the room and show them what they had made. There appeared to be expected responses when work was shown which were revealed when a 'mistake' was made, i.e. the expected response was not produced. In an attempt to be unobtrusive as an observer, I made no response when Melissa, smiling, showed me a chipmunk which she had drawn, colored in, then cut out. Her smile faded when I made no comment. Seeing this, I finally responded and she appeared happier; she smiled again and provided further information about her work. This conversation between Bobby and Joshua serves as another example of unfulfilled expectations.

Bobby:  Mine is done. Lookit mine. Lookit. Isn't it pretty?
Joshua:  Poopy.
Bobby:  Don't! Isn't it pretty?

Joshua also provided this final example of finishing which seemed to incorporate a number of finishing procedures. He showed his picture first to me saying, 'Look at this,' then approached the father of another child who was nearby and said, 'Look at this I made.' He moved on to a student teacher saying again, 'Look at this I made' and finally, in another portion of the room, said, 'Martha, Martha, look at this,' to one of the teachers. After receiving a response from each person in turn, he walked across the room saying (to no one in particular) that he would now put the picture in his cubby.

The variety in what constitutes a completed work can also be seen in the amount of time it takes to finish. This was demonstrated dramatically by Melissa and Molly. Melissa had worked for more than twenty minutes on two pictures. A teacher came by and commented on Melissa's work. While Melissa and the teacher were talking, Molly sat down, put four lines on a piece of paper, folded the paper in half and left. Molly's picture took less than two minutes to complete.

The context in which art activities are carried out may influence finishing. This influence can be seen in children's demonstrated awareness of other activities in the room and in their interactions with others. In an example from the day care classroom, Cathleen announced her plan to make a picture for one of the teachers. After working for a few minutes, she got up and watched that teacher demonstrate use of what was called a 'special' type of ribbon at another table. Cathleen returned to her work, finished coloring in the shape she had traced, gave the picture to the teacher and went to use the ribbons. I observed, primarily in the nursery school, how the social component of drawing sometimes seems to influence finishing a picture. Children who drew steadily for twenty minutes would speed up and stop within minutes of hearing another's announcement of having completed a picture. Watching this occur, I suddenly understood the teacher's dilemma, which I had both observed and experienced many times before. At times, a teacher was assailed on all sides by children who had finished pictures and all wanted new pieces of paper and/or their names written on the finished pieces immediately and simultaneously. It is the sort of occurrence which teachers might write off as being a chance event if they consider it at all. It is fascinating to discover it to be a phenomenon that is routinely observable, occurring in many forms at different times, and explicable in social rather than individual terms. It is reminiscent of the children's verbal behavior, for like group public announcements in which one statement is followed by similar comments immediately by the other children, one child's 'finishing' action is quickly followed by the same actions being carried out by several others.

Starting or stopping drawing as an activity, not just of specific pictures, often took place in the same way. An activity which has been totally ignored by the children may suddenly be unable to accomodate all those who want to participate and may just as suddenly be abandoned again. I suspect teachers of young children have seen this take place many times and could describe this, though they might not see it as predictable, patterned, group behavior.

I am not suggesting that children follow blindly after leaders or that individuals have no control over their own behavior. In fact it was not necessarily one person who initiated these actions and made the first public announcement every time. Nor did I see any evidence that any individual was making a conscious effort to influence the behavior of others. However, given that individuals act within a context, when trying to understand their actions, it seems necessary to take account of that context, just as the individuals themselves do.

## Conclusion

Having described the production of artwork as an ongoing accomplishment, it is now possible to approach the data in two ways. One could try to 'explain' the choices and decisions made in terms of the individuals who made them. Alternatively, one could examine what is common to all in this situation. I will use the latter approach and attempt to present what is essential to doing artwork and consider the data in light of the primary characteristics of these activities.

Doing artwork consists of actions which result in a product. At the end of the process there is something that is tangible and that can be seen. It would logically follow, then, that much of the talk associated with these processes concern looking and acknowledgment. Doing artwork results in something that can be viewed and is produced by actions that are recognizable. However, when this process is examined only in terms of the individual, the call to view the work may have a different connatation. It may appear 'demanding' or 'egocentric' when a child asks an adult 'look at what I made' four times in a row. I suggest that when considering repeated requests to view artwork it is not necessary to look for the emotional causes for what an adult might otherwise call 'bids for attention'. Another answer is in what drawing consists of: pictures are for looking at. Art museums provide physical acknowledgment of this use of pictures.

Another essential aspect of artwork is that it changes while in the process of being made. Every added element affects what has gone before and what can come after. When reviewing the observed range of what the children's artwork could consist of, one senses a continuum which reflects this quality of each step affecting others. The processes suggest shifting possibilities. Each mark both limits what can be done and opens up new choices. Seeing the children's work as a series of tasks or stages, after any of which the product may be 'finished', is in keeping with this characteristic of what doing art would consist of. Thus what constitutes finished work is not merely the arbitrary decision of an artist. The progress of the activity is part of the process.

Further, the materials and environment interact and influence the process of doing artwork. Switching pens, dipping a brush in paint, reaching for a scissors and similar actions that are part of these activities allow for a shift in attention. The focus on drawing a picture, for example, is something that must be maintained through these potential distraction points. When there is something interesting to look at, these pauses in the activity allow for the opportunity to capture the child's attention. Furthermore the noise of a busy classroom may intrude at any time, again acting as a potential distraction from whichever task is at hand.

Examination of the shared characteristics of the activities in question reveals the logic of the children's actions. The purpose of shifting the focus from the individual is not to deny the possible role of individual emotions or biographies in what is taking place but rather to credit the individual's choices by examining ongoing actions within their natural context. By doing so, these actions can be seen as making sense within that particular context. The recognition of the elements common to any carrying out of that activity clarifies individual action.

One could easily look at my observations and see chaos. Rather than attributing what is observed to 'drives', 'needs' or the imposed categories of 'child' and 'childish' behavior, an order is revealed by focusing on the actual practices of the children. The children I observed did not necessarily act in accordance with adult expectations of what working at an activity should look like. The children did not always complete a task in an 'orderly' fashion. They looked up from their work and paid attention to other things not related to the activity at hand. Several talked to others across the room. Children left what they were doing then and came back. They talked, sang, hummed, and shifted in their chairs, while working on their projects. Some would 'demand' attention and acknowledgment for their artwork and do so repeatedly. Yet when one takes seriously what the children were doing and examines their actions in context, what appeared as chaos begins to resolve into orderly actions. By shifting the focus from how much adult knowledge children have acquired to what it is that children know, both types of knowledge become available. The benefit of not accepting adult knowledge as the final standard against which all action should be measured is that children's knowledge, competence, and experience can be viewed in their own right.

The question of the value of this investigation for teachers remains to be addressed. By looking at classroom activities from a sociological perspective new aspects of these familar activities were uncovered. This study revealed children's competence in a number of areas. Children were shown to be solving problems that are not customarily recognized. It is generally assumed that maintaining focus while doing artwork is not problematic. Yet the natural pauses in such activities allow for potential distraction throughout the course of the activity. Children routinely carry out these art activities despite challenges in the environment and the activities themselves. In their use of art and non-art materials, children distinguish between complex categories that do not have clear boundaries.

That children's actions may be logical, as the evidence of this study suggests, is contrary to common expectations about what it means to be an adult or a child. Assumptions regarding children's incompetence mask aspects of ordinary classroom activities, particularly those aspects in which children's knowledge and competence may be seen. The recognition of the possible logic of children's actions may be of use to teachers. It was a revelation to me that children's finishing patterns could be seen as orderly. Having recognized this, I could make use of this knowledge in my encounters with children as a teacher. I could prepare myself for waves of finishing and sudden shifts from one activity to another. Seeing the pattern in when children look up from an activity could guide a teacher who wishes to encourage focus in children. Waiting for a natural pause in an activity in speaking to a child would allow a teacher to limit interruptions. Furthermore, an understanding of how distractions occur in a classroom could be of interest to a teacher working with a child who seems easily distracted.

This study demonstrates the value of examining the actions of individuals by looking at what is common to the experience of any individual. To the extent that this perspective illuminated my data, I would recommend such an approach to teachers in their attempts to understand occurences in their own classrooms.

## Notes

1 I would like to thank Fran Waksler and Michael Lynch for their thoughtful criticism of earlier versions of this paper. I would also like to express my appreciation to Fran Waksler for her extremely useful organizational suggestions.

2 This paper is addressed to both sociologists and teachers. Although I have tried to minimize use of the jargon of either field, differences in the theoretical background and experience of the two groups may lead to certain aspects of the paper appearing obvious to one while strange to the other. A teacher is likely to be familiar with what is meant by 'free play' and 'project' but may find the divergence from developmental theory surprising. On the other hand, to a sociologist my contrasting of my theoretical statements with certain psychological standpoints may appear unnecessary. It is beyond the scope of this paper to provide an overview of developmental theory and it is not my purpose to argue with developmental theory as it is presented to teachers. However, its focus on development as an individual process seems to orient theorists toward the individual. In my experience as an educator, it is theories based on the individual which form the basis of educational theory and practice. Thus in my discussion of social context, I contrast my theoretical standpoint to that which focuses on the individual and looks for its explanations within the individual.

3 I do not mean to imply that this difference in the organization of the classrooms between the settings is due to some difference between day care and nursery school. In referring to the 'day care' or 'nursery school' rooms, I am primarily distinguishing between the different sites used for my observations.

4 There was a notable instance of how a child tried to account for my presence and actions. This child paused in her approach to the drawing table and asked me if I was drawing. I told her that I wasn't drawing. She then asked why I was writing. I replied that I wanted to remember what was happening in school. Again she asked why and I said that it was because I was interested. She said, 'Our other teachers aren't interested in us' and sat down to draw.

5 Parten, 1932.

6 Generally, only one side of a page was used. In all my observations I saw a child color on both sides of a page twice.

7 It is possible that this is not a question that is easy to answer by anyone. It might be interesting to question artists to find out whether they would consider such a question answerable.

8 This is not to suggest that children only showed finished pictures to others. My data indicates otherwise; I have numerous examples of children showing others works in progress.

*Chapter 14*

# On the Analysability of Stories by Children

*Harvey Sacks*

## Commentary

This article may well be the most complicated of those included in this book. It certainly requires careful and attentive reading. I provide a rather extended introduction to facilitate understanding of this most valuable article. Futhermore, in the course of the article I add, in brackets, explanatory notes to assist readers in staying on course.

Sacks is in fact only incidentally concerned with children here; his major focus is on how utterances (verbal statements) are understandable. Nonetheless, his article can move the sociological study of children to a new level of complexity and sophistication. Sacks' work reinforces the claims of Mackay and other authors in this volume about children's competence, for the ability to describe with words embodies extensive knowledge about how the world looks from the perspective of the language being used to describe it. In the Concluding Note I present some specific implications of Sacks' ideas for the study of children.

This article displays both the insights and the problems inherent in a detailed and thoroughgoing analysis of that which is taken for granted. It is difficult to write about that which is not customarily written or talked about, and difficult to write about what 'everyone knows,' but it is of great sociological significance to recognize what and how much everyone knows and how much can be heard in the simplest of utterances and seen in the simplest of events. Sacks' repetition may initially seem a stylistic drawback but each time he returns to the utterance under analysis he discovers and presents new aspects of it.

Sacks' particular concern is with what people in everyday life can *hear* or *understand* when an utterance is made. He documents the extensive information that is implicit in even the simplest of utterances. His focus is not on what people *mean* or *intend* by what they say but rather on what can be *inferred* or *gleaned* by others from what is said. Through repeated examination of the same two sentences from a child's 'story', he identifies a wealth of

From *Directions in Sociolinguistics: The Ethnography of Communication*. Edited by John J. Gumperz and Dell Hymes (1972). Reprinted by permission of Basil Blackwell Inc. and Dell Hymes. Originally published by Holt, Rinehart and Winston.

information available, taken-for-granted, used, yet seldom actually recognized. He shows just how much can be gleaned from two short sentences. He does not suggest that children necessarily *intend* all that can be heard in what they say, but implicit in his argument is that children's utterances can be heard as sophisticated formulations of the social world in which they live. To learn to use language is to learn extensive details about the social world. Embedded in language are a multitude of claims about what the world is like. As children learn to talk, their use of the categories of talk (words) structures their view of the world and their category use is heard by others in terms of the assumptions embedded in such categories.

Sacks begins with a consideration of the process of *describing*. Using two sentences uttered by a child, he asks if these sentences can be heard, by anyone who hears them uttered, as a description of an event. To demonstrate that they can be heard as such, he details some of the descriptive information that can be gleaned from the utterance. Sacks is concerned with description because it is an important feature of social life, a common everyday activity, a crucial feature of 'talk', and thus important data for sociologists. Even though it is so fundamental a process, seldom in everyday life is its full complexity recognized. Sacks details this complexity, bringing to light taken-for-granted features of talk that are surprising in their multiplicity.

In the course of his article Sacks offers a number of maxims or rules that ordinary members of society use in making sense out of the world. Since these maxims are somewhat complex and apt to be confusing — for they are rules that members themselves do not articulate — I introduce the major ones here. They may not be immediately understandable but their presentation here provides an initial acquaintance with them. This section can also serve as a useful place to which to refer as a way of maintaining orientation to Sacks' developing argument.

### Sacks' Maxims*

Recognizing a description *as a description* entails understanding what it is about. Sacks' maxims provide rules for just how such understanding is achieved in everyday life. Looking at an utterance, Sacks considers *what a* listener hears — what any listener can hear — and how that can be heard, for what is heard goes well beyond what is said. Similarly, in looking at events, he considers what any observer can see — and how that can be seen. The first section of Sack's article, 'Problems in recognizing possible descriptions', provides an overview of the issues with which he is dealing; in the remainder of the article he elaborates on these ideas.

Sacks here takes as his sociological task the identification of the taken-for-granted rules that underlie everyday talk. He is not claiming that the maxims he identifies are in any absolute sense 'true' or 'correct' but he is

---

* In the remainder of these introductory remarks I draw liberally on Sacks' words as well as formulating his ideas in my own words. The use of quotation marks and page references would only complicate an already complicated undertaking. Those who would cite or quote Sacks should work directly from the text of his article, which follows my commentary.

asserting that members *use* these maxims, and thus they are of interest to sociologists. When he asserts of a particular utterance 'hear it that way' or 'see it that way', he himself is not claiming that is what one should do; rather he is saying that in everday life we are *expected* to hear it or see it that way and that indeed we do so. It may even turn out that we are wrong and confusion develops but even in such a case clarification may entail reference to the maxims that have been violated.

In their everyday lives, people create categories (of people, objects, acts, etc.) and develop rules for assigning members (instances) to categories. Thus the category 'teacher' includes many members, many teachers. How one assigns a person to a category, e.g. how one decides that a person is a teacher, is a complex process. Its complexity may well be obscured because on the surface it looks so common-sensical but consider the following: On the first day of class, how do students 'know' that a particular person is the teacher? Here I simply suggest a few alternatives: that person may be some-one in the wrong room, an impostor, an older student.

Any set of categories that 'goes together' Sacks terms a *membership categorization device*, i.e. a device (method) for categorizing members (instances). A device also includes the actual members as well as rules for how members are assigned to categories. Continuing with the above exam-ple, the categories of teacher, student, and administrator; members of these categories; and the rules for assigning members to these categories constitute a *membership categorization device*. Sacks identifies two rules which people use to fit instances to categories:

1 *the economy (reference satisfactoriness) rule*: assigning a person (or object or thing) to one category can be sufficient to identify that person. For example, for students' purposes it is sufficient to know that I am the teacher of a particular course; it is not *necessary* (though it may be interesting) to know my marital status, recreational preferences, race, etc.

2 *the consistency (relevance) rule*: if a categorization device contains a set of categories (e.g. teachers, students, administrators), if one category is used to identify a person, other categories may be used to cate-gorize other members. For example, if I am talking about teachers, I can move to discussion of students or administrators without 'changing the subject.'

Against the background of rule 2, Sacks provides a subsidiary rule which he calls a 'hearer's maxim' since it is a rule for how utterances can be heard:

the consistency rule corollary: if two categories are presented and can be heard as categories from the same collection (device), then: hear them that way. For example, if someone is talking about teachers and then begins to discuss administrators, I hear them to be talking about *school* administrators, not IBM or government administrators.

Sacks goes to provide another hearer's maxim:

If a number of categories constitute a set or 'team' such that only *some* members from each category constitute each set (in Sacks' terms, if 'devices' are 'duplicatively organized'), and if categories can be heard as a set, then: hear them as such. If, for example, I hear talk by teachers about students, I hear, if I can, that they are talking about *their* students. A teacher and that teacher's students can be seen as constituting a set. Alternatively, I do not hear a sociology teacher's reference to students as to ballet students.

Some activities are bound to categories. Thus those in the category of 'teacher' are expected to engage in the activity of 'teaching', 'students' in the activity of 'studying'. With this ideas in mind, Sacks provides the hearer's maxim:

> If a number of possible categories are available and a category-bound activity is presented, hear *at least* that category to which the activity is bound.

Sacks then elaborates on the idea of category-bound activities in the process of articulating 'viewer's maxims', rules that people follow in making sense of what they see. Thus:

> If one sees a category-bound activity being done and if one can see it as being done by a member of a category to which the activity is bound, then: see it that way. If I walk into a classroom and see someone teaching, I see that person as the teacher. Indeed it may be that students are doing class presentations and the person teaching is in fact a student. If, however, the person teaching looks too young to be a teacher, I may decide that I cannot 'see it [teaching] as being done by a member of a category to which the activity is bound,' in which case I may look elsewhere for the 'real' teacher or simply be puzzled.

> If there is a norm (expectation) that B follows A, then when A and B occur, see them as following the norm. For example, if a student raises a hand and a teacher calls on that student, I see the teacher as calling on the student *because of* the raised hand. (It may have been, however, that the teacher was going to call on the student anyway and/or that the student was not raising a hand but simply stretching.)

> Futhermore, if those who engage in the acts (A and B) are members of categories for whom those actions are proper, see them as such. Thus if a student raises a hand, it makes sense to me. If a teacher raises a hand, I find such an action on the face of it meaningless.

Sacks is not presenting a complete analysis of an utterance; rather he is exploring the available paths of analysis. Furthermore, it should be noted again, he is not offering these rules as how things ought to be, how they must be, or how *he* sees them. He is simply trying to spell out the rules that people use in their everyday lives. His reference (below) to *subjectivism* — a term that refers to talking one's own views as everyone's views — indicates his awareness that readers might, erroneously, say to him: 'That's only the way *you* hear those sentences.' In response he claims that he is not *assuming* that others' views are like his; rather his empirical evidence suggests that in fact others hear things as he does and, furthermore, he asks readers to assess his maxims on the basis of their own experiences. If indeed they hear what he hears, then he cannot be accused of subjectivism.

Sacks invites readers to join him in this exploration as he moves from idea to idea. The best test of his ideas is an examination of their use in one's own everyday life. This article is best read as a joint venture of author and reader.

F.C.W.

## On the Analysability of Stories by Children

In this chapter I intend, first, to present and employ several of the more basic concepts and techniques which I shall be using. Since most of those I shall use at this point may also be found in the paper 'An initial investigation of the usability of conversational data for doing sociology' (Sacks, 1972), the discussion here may be seen as reintroducing and extending the results developed there. Second, I shall focus on the activity 'doing describing' and the correlative activity 'recognizing a description', activities which members may be said to do, and which therefore are phenomena which sociologists and anthropologists must aim to be able to describe. It will initially be by reference to an examination of instances of members' describings that my attempts to show how sociologists might solve their own problem of constructing descriptions will be developed. Proceeding in the fashion I have proposed will permit a focus on several central and neglected issues which social science must face, most particularly, the problem of members' knowledge and the problem of relevance. Let us then begin.

### Problems in Recognizing Possible Descriptions

The initial data are the first two sentences from a 'story' offered by a 2 years and 9 months old girl to the author of the book *Children Tell Stories*. They are, 'The baby cried. The mommy picked it up'. I shall first make several observations about these sentences. Before doing so, however, let me note: if these observations strike you as a ranker sort of subjectivism, then I ask you to read on just far enough to see whether it is or is not the case that the observations are both relevant and defensible. When I hear 'The baby cried. The mommy picked it up', one thing I hear is that the 'mommy' who picks the 'baby' up is the mommy of that baby. [Readers might be tempted to say, 'Of course. That's obvious.' But how does one know that *when the sentence itself does not say so*? How one can hear that the mommy is the mommy of the baby when it is not said is the problem Sacks is addressing and for which he wants to construct an explanatory apparatus.] That is a first observation. (You will, of course, notice that the second sentence does not contain a genitive. It does not read 'its mommy picked it up', or variants thereof.) Now it is not only that *I* hear that the mommy is the mommy of that baby, but I feel rather confident that at least many of the natives among you hear that also. That is a second observation. One of my tasks is going to be to construct an apparatus which will provide for the foregoing facts to have occurred; an apparatus, i.e. which will show how it is that we come to hear the fragment as we do.

Some more: I take it we hear two sentences. Call the first [sentence] $S_1$ and the second $S_2$; the first reports an occurrence [that we can call] $O_1$ and the second reports an occurrence [that we can call] $O_2$. Now, I take it that we hear that as $S_2$ follows $S_1$, so $O_2$ follows $O_1$. This is a third observation. And also, we hear that $O_2$ occurs because of $O_1$, i.e. the explanation for $O_2$ occurring is that $O_1$ did. That is a fourth observation. I want the apparatus to show how we come to hear those facts also. If I asked you to explain the group of observations which I have made, observations which you could have made just as well — and let me note, they are *not* proposed as sociological findings, but rather do they pose some of the problems which social science shall have to resolve — you might say something like the following: we hear that it is the mommy of the baby who picks the baby up because she's the one who ought to pick it up, and (you might eventually add) if she's the one who ought to pick it up, and it was picked up by somebody who could be her, then it was her, or was probably her.

[Again, readers might respond, 'Of course', but, again, none of this information is contained in the sentence itself but is something that is *brought to* the sentence. *That* one hears all this information is obvious; *how* one comes to hear it is quite perplexing.]

You might go on: while it is quite clear that not any two consecutive sentences, not even any consecutive sentences that report occurrences, are heard, and properly heard, as reporting that the occurrences have occurred in the order which the sentences have, if the occurrences ought to occur in that order, and if there if no information to the contrary (such as a phrase at the beginning of the second, like 'before that, however'), then the order of the sentences indicates the order of the occurrences. And these two sentences do present the order of the occurrences they report in the proper order for such occurrences. If the baby cried, it ought to have started crying before the mother picked it up, and not after. Hearing it that way, the second sentence is explained by the first; hearing them as consecutive or with the second preceding the first, some further explanation is needed, and none being present, we may suppose that it is not needed.

Now let me make a fifth observation: all of the foregoing can be done by many or perhaps any of us without knowing what baby or what mommy it is that might be being talked of. With this fifth observation it may now be noticed that what we've essentially been saying so far is that the pair of sentences seems to satisfy what a member might require of some pair of sentences for them to be recognizable as 'a possible description'. They 'sound like a description', and some form of words can, apparently, sound like a description. To recognize that some form of words is a possible description does not require that one must first inspect the circumstances it may be characterizing.

[There is a group game played by adults called 'Dictionary', in which one person selects a word whose definition is unknown to the others. The others each make up a definition and participants vote on which one of the definitions (the unidentified dictionary definiton or one of the made-up definitions) sounds correct. Those making up definitions seek to construct ones that sound right, that sound like a possible dictionary definition. The 'real' meaning of the word is irrelevant to the game. This game is constructed on the very state of affairs that Sacks is describing.

The point Sacks makes in the following paragraph is that members' descriptions of the social world and how it works is useful information for sociologists. Sociologists need not be concerned with 'how it really works' — perhaps an impossible task — but can focus on how members see the situations in which they are acting. The concern throughout this book with how children define situations — rather than what situations are 'really like' — exemplifies Sacks' point here.]

That 'possible' descriptions are recognizable as such is quite an important fact, for members, and for social scientists. The reader ought to be able to think out some of its import for members, e.g. the economies it affords them. It is the latter clause, 'and for social scientists', that I now wish to attend to. Were it not so both that members have an activity they do, 'describing', and that at least some cases of that activity produce, for them, forms of words recognizable as at least possible descriptions without having to do an inspection of the circumstances they might characterize, then it might well be that social science would necessarily be the last of the sciences to be made do-able. For, unless social scientists could study such things as these 'recognizable descriptions', we might only be able to investigate such activities of members as in one or another way turned on 'their knowledge of the world' when social scientists could employ some established, presumptively correct scientific characterizations of the phenomena members were presumably dealing with and knowing about. If, however, members have a phenomenon, 'possible descriptions' which are recognizable *per se*, then one need not in the instance know how it is that babies and mommies do behave to examine the composition of such possible descriptions as members produce and recognize. Sociology and anthropology need not await developments in botany or genetics or analyses of the light spectra to gain a secure position from which members' knowledge, and the activities for which it is relevant, might be investigated. What one ought to seek to build is an apparatus which will provide for how it is that any activities, which members do in such a way as to be recognizable as such to members, are done, and done recognizably. Such an apparatus will, of course, have to generate and provide for the recognizability of more than just possible descriptions, and in later discussions we shall be engaged in providing for such activities as 'inviting', 'warning', and so forth, as the data we consider will permit and require.

My reason for having gone through the observations I have so far made was to give you some sense, right off, of the fine power of a culture. It does not, so to speak, merely fill brains in roughly the same way, it fills them so that they are alike in fine detail. The sentences we are considering are after all rather minor, and yet all of you, or many of you, hear just what I said you heard, and many of us are quite unacquainted with each other. I am, then, dealing with something real and something finely powerful.

## Membership Categorization Devices

We may begin to work at the construction of the apparatus. I'm going to introduce several of the terms we need. The first term is *membership categor-*

*ization device* (or just *categorization device*). [An explanation of this term to supplement Sacks' is available in the introduction to this paper.] By this term I shall intend: any collection of membership categories, containing at least a category, which may be applied to some population containing at least a member, so as to provide, by the use of some rules of application, for the pairing of at least a population member and a categorization device member. A device is then a collection plus rules of application.

An instance of a categorization device is the one called 'sex'; its collection is the two categories (male, female). It is important to observe that a collection consists of categories that 'go together'. For now that may merely be seen as a constraint of the following sort: I could say that some set of categories was a collection, and be wrong. [Sacks is not saying that he does not care about being wrong; he is simply recogizing that at this point his data is incomplete, his conclusions tentative.] I shall present some rules of application very shortly.

Before doing that, however, let me observe that 'baby' and 'mommy' can be seen to be categories from one collection: the collection whose device is called 'family' and which consists of such categories as ('baby', 'mommy', 'daddy' ...) where by '...' we mean that there are others, but not any others, e.g. 'shortstop'.

[In what follows Sacks proceeds to spell out some rules by which categories are applied to particular instances. These are rules that people use in their everyday life, though they seldom articulate them. As he suggests later in this section, these rules govern how one *hears* what people say.]

Let me introduce a few rules of application. It may be observed that if a member uses a single category from any membership categorization device, then they can be recognized to be doing *adequate reference* to a person. We may put the observation in a negative form: it is not necessary that some multiple of categories from categorization devices be employed for recognition that a person is being referred to, to be made; a single category will do. (I do not mean by this that more cannot be used, only that for reference to persons to be recognized more need not be used.) With that observation we can formulate a 'reference satisfactoriness' rule, which we call 'the economy rule'. It holds: a single category from any membership categorization device can be referentially adequate.

A second rule I call 'the consistency rule'. It holds: if some population of persons is being categorized, and if a category from some device's collection has been used to categorize a first member of the population, then that category or other categories of the same collection *may* be used to categorize further members of the population. The former rule was a 'reference satisfactoriness' rule; this latter one is a 'relevance' rule (Sacks, 1972).

The economy rule having provided for the adequate reference of 'baby', the consistency rule tells us that if the first person has been categorized as 'baby', then further persons may be referred to by other categories of a collection of which they are a member, and thus that such other categories as 'mommy' and 'daddy' are relevant given the use of 'baby'.

While in its currently weak form and alone, the consistency rule may exclude no category of any device, even in this weak form (the 'may' forms — I shall eventually introduce a 'must' form), a corollary of it will prove to be useful. The corollary is a 'hearer's maxim'. It holds: if two or more categories are used to categorize two or more members of some population, and those categories can be heard as categories from the same collection, then: hear them that way. Let us call the foregoing 'the consistency rule corollary'. It has the following sort of usefulness. Various membership categorization-device categories can be said to be ambiguous. That is, the same categorial word is a term occurring in several distinct devices, and can in each have a quite different reference; they may or may not be combinably usable in regard to a single person. So, e.g. 'baby' occurs in the device 'family' and also in the device 'stage of life' whose categories are such as 'baby', 'child', ... 'adult'. A hearer who can use the consistency rule corollary will regularly not even notice that there might be an ambiguity in the use of some category among a group which it can be used to hear as produced via the consistency rule.

It is, of course, clear that the two categories 'baby' are sometimes combinably referential and sometimes not. A woman may refer to someone as 'my baby' with no suggestion that she is using the category that occurs in the 'stage of life' device; her baby may be a full-fledged adult. In the case at hand that problem does not occur, and we shall be able to provide the bases for it not occurring, i.e. the bases for the legitimacy of hearing the single term 'baby' as referring to a person located by reference both to the device 'family' and to the device 'stage of life'.

With this, let us modify the observation on the consistency rule as follows: The consistency rule tells us that if a first person has been categorized as 'baby', the further persons may be referred to by categories from either the device 'family' or from the device 'stage of life'. However, if a hearer has a second category which can be heard as consistent with one locus of a first, then the first is to be heard as *at least* consistent with the second.

Given the foregoing, we may proceed to show how the combined reference of 'baby' is heard for our two sentences, and also how 'the mommy' is heard as 'the mommy of the baby'. We shall deal with the latter task first, and we assume from now on that the consistency rule corollary has yielded at least that 'baby' and 'mommy' are heard as from the device 'family'. We assume that without prejudice to the further fact that 'baby' is also heard as 'baby' from the device 'stage of life'.

The device 'family' is one of a series which you may think of by a prototypical name 'team'. One central property of such devices is that they are what I am going to call 'duplicatively organized'. I mean by the use of that term to point out the following: When such a device is used on a population, what is done is to take its categories, treat the set of categories as defining a unit, and place members of the population into cases of the unit. If a population is so treated and is then counted, one counts not numbers of daddies, numbers of mommies, and numbers of babies but numbers of families — numbers of 'whole families', numbers of 'families without fathers', etc. A population so treated is partitioned into cases of the unit, cases for which what properly holds is that the various persons partitioned into any case are 'coincumbents' of that case.

[Not all devices are duplicatively organized. 'Stage of life', for example, is not. The categories 'baby', 'child', ... 'adult' are not the sources of sets;

there is no meaningful unit made up of merely one or more members from each stage of life. Sacks makes this distinction for purposes that are clarified in the next paragraph.]

There are hearer's maxims which correspond to these ways of dealing with populations categorized by way of duplicatively organized devices. One that is relevant to our current task holds: If some population has been categorized by use of categories from some device whose collection has the 'duplicative organization' property, and a member is presented with a categorized population which *can be heard* as coincumbents of a case of that device's unit, then: Hear it that way. (I will consider the underscored phrase shortly.) Now let it be noticed that this rule is of far more general scope than we may seem to need. In focusing on a property like duplicative organization it permits a determination of an expectation (of social scientists) as to how some categorized population will be heard independently of a determination of how it is heard. It is then formal and predictive, as well, of course, as quite general.

Now, by the phrase 'can be heard' we mean to rule out predictions of the following sort. Some duplicatively organized devices have proper numbers of incumbents for certain categories of any unit. (At any given time a nation-state may have but one president, a family but one father, a baseball team but one shortshop on the field, etc.) If more incumbents of a category are proposed as present in the population that a unit's case can properly take, then the 'can be heard' constraint is not satisfied, and a prediction would not be made.

## Category-Bound Activities

The foregoing analysis shows us then how it is that we come to hear, given the fact that the device 'family' is duplicatively organized and the 'can be heard' constraint being satisfied, 'the mommy' to be 'the mommy of the baby'. It does, of course, much more than that. It permits us to predict, and to understand how we can predict, that a statement such as 'The first baseman looked around. The third baseman scratched himself' will be heard as saying 'the first baseman of the team of which the third baseman is also a player' and its converse.

Or, putting the claim more precisely, it shows us how, in part — 'in part' because for the materials at hand it happens that there are other means for providing that the same hearing be made, means which can operate in combination with the foregoing, otherwise sufficient ones, to further assure the hearings we have observed. That will be done in the next section. Let us now undertake our second task, to show how 'the baby' is heard in its combined form, i.e. as the category with that name from both the 'stage of life' device and from the 'family' device.

Let me introduce a term which I am going to call *category-bound activities*. While I shall not now give an intendedly careful definition of the term, I shall indicate what I mean to notice with it and then in a while offer a procedure for determining that some of its proposed cases are indeed cases of it. By the term I intend to notice that many activities are taken by members to be done by some particular or several particular categories of members where the categories are categories from membership categorization devices.

Let me notice then, as is obvious to you, that 'cry' is bound to 'baby', i.e. to the category 'baby' which is a member of the collection from the 'stage of life' device. Again, the fact that members know that this is so only serves, for the social scientist, to pose some problem. What we want is to construct some means by reference to which a class, which proposedly contains at least the activity-category 'cry' and presumably others, may have the inclusion of its candidate-members assessed. We will not be claiming that the procedure is definitive as to exclusion of a candidate-member, but we will claim that it is definitive as to inclusion of a candidate-member.

It may be observed that the members of the 'stage of life' collection are 'positioned' ('baby' ... 'adolescent' ... 'adult' ...), an observation which, for now, we shall leave unexamined. I want to describe a procedure for praising or degrading members, the operation of which consists of the use of the fact that some activities are category bound. If there are such procedures, they will provide one strong sense of the notion 'category-bound activities' and also will provide, for any given candidate activity, a means for warrantably deciding that it is a member of the class of category-bound activities.

For some positioned-category devices it can be said as between any two categories of such a device that A is either higher or lower than B, and if A is higher than B, and B is higher than C, then A is higher than C.

We have some activity which is a candidate-member of the class 'category-bound activities' and which is proposedly bound to some category C. Then, a member of either A or B who does that activity may be seen to be degrading himself, and may be said to be 'acting like a C'. Alternatively, if some candidate activity is proposedly bound to A, a member of C who does it is subject to being said to be acting like an A, where that assertion constitutes 'praising'.

[In this section Sacks is searching for ways in which category-bound activities can be identified. One way (exemplified by note 1) is to see that an activity can be praised when performed by a member of one category and blamed when performed by a member of another. Thus the activity is bound to the category for which it is viewed as routine and not bound to that category for which it is viewed as in some sense unusual. A second way of identifying an activity as category bound (exemplified in note 2) is to see one activity (hair styling) as suggesting or hinting at another (homosexuality). Sacks is in no way reinforcing stereotypes; he is simply recognizing those links that are made by people in everyday life and exploring how those links are in fact made. If on the basis of one activity we predict that someone is a member of a particular category, then there is evidence that that activity is category-bound.]

If, using the 'stage of life' categories, we subject 'crying' to such a test, we do find that its candidacy as a member of the class 'category-bound activities' is warrantable. In the case of 'crying' the results are even stronger. For, it appears, if a 'baby' is subject to some circumstances which would for such a one warrant crying, and he does not, then his 'not crying' is observable, and may be used to propose that 'he is acting like a big boy', where that assertion is taken to be 'praise'.[1]

The foregoing procedure can, obviously enough, be used for other devices and other candidate activities. Other procedures may also be used, e.g. one way to decide that an activity is category bound is to see whether, the fact of membership being unknown, it can be 'hinted at' by naming the activity as something one does.[2]

Having constructed a procedure which can warrant the candidacy of some activity as a member of the class 'category-bound activities', and which warrants the membership of 'cry' and provides for its being bound to 'baby', i.e. that category 'baby' which is a member of the 'stage of life' collection, we move on to see how it is that 'the baby' in our sentence is heard in the combined reference we have proposed.

We need, first, another 'hearer's maxim'. If a category-bound activity is asserted to have been done by a member of some category where, if that category is ambiguous (i.e. is a member of at least two different devices) but where, at least for one of those devices, the asserted activity is category bound to the given category, then hear that *at least* the category from the device to which it is bound is being asserted to hold.

The foregoing maxim will then provide for hearing 'The baby cried', as referring to at least 'baby' from the 'stage of life' device. The results obtained from the use of the consistency rule corollary, being independent of that, are combinable with it. The consistency rule corollary gave us at least that 'the baby' was the category from the device 'family'. The combination gives us both.

If our analysis seems altogether too complicated for the rather simple facts we have been examining, then we invite the reader to consider that our machinery has intendedly been 'overbuilt'. That is to say it may turn out that the elaborateness of our analysis, or its apparent elaborateness, will disappear when one begins to consider the amount of work that the very same machinery can perform.

In the next section I will attempt to show that the two sentences 'The baby cried. The mommy picked it up' constitute a possible description.

## Identifying Possible Descriptions

I shall focus next on the fact that an activity can be category bound and then on the import of there being a norm which provides for some second activity, given the occurrence of a first, considering both of these with regard to the 'correctness', for members, of 'possible description'.

Let me for the moment leave aside our two sentences and consider some observations on how it is that I see, and take it you see, describable occurrences. Suppose you are standing somewhere, and you see a person you don't know. The person cries. Now, if I can, I will see that what has happened is that a baby cried. [Note that Sacks says 'if I can'; clearly there are occasions in which one cannot so see things, and one doesn't.] And I take it that you will, if you can, see that too. That's a first pair of observations. Suppose again you are standing somewhere and you see two people you don't know. Suppose further than one cries, and the other picks up the one who is crying. Now, if I can, I will see that what has happened is that a baby cried and its mother picked it up. And I take it that you will, if you can, see that too. That's a second pair of observations.

Consider the first pair of observations. The modifying phrases, to deal with them first, refer simply to the possibility that the category 'baby' might be obviously inapplicable to the crier. By reference to the 'stage of life' collection the crier may be seen to be an adult. And that being so, the 'if . . . can' constraint wouldn't be satisfied. But there are certainly other possible characterizations of the crying person. For example, without respect to the fact that it is a baby, it could be either 'male' or 'female', and nonetheless I would not, and I take it you would not, seeing the scene, see that 'a male cried' if we could see that 'a baby cried'.

The pair of observations suggest the following 'viewer's maxim': If a member sees a category-bound activity being done, then, if one can see it being done by a member of a category to which the activity is bound, then: See it that way. The viewer's maxim is another relevance rule in that it proposes that for an observer of a category-bound activity the category to which the activity is bound has a special relevance for formulating an identification of its doer.

Consider the second pair of observations. As members you, of course, know that there is a norm which might be written as: A mother ought to try to soothe her crying baby. I, and you, not only know that there is such a norm but, as you may recall, we used it in doing our hearing of 'The baby cried. The mommy picked it up'. In addition to the fact of duplicative organization, the norm was relevant in bringing us to hear that it was the mommy of the baby who did the picking up. While we would have heard that it was the mommy of the baby for other pairs of activities in which the two were involved (but not for any pair), the fact that the pair were relatable via a norm which assigns the mother of the baby that duty may have operated in combination with the duplicative organization to assure our hearing that it was she who did it.

Leaving aside the hearing of the sentence, we are led to construct another viewer's maxim: If one sees a pair of actions which can be related via the operation of a norm that provides for the second given the first, where the doers can be seen as members of the categories the norm provides as proper for that pair of actions, then: (a) See that the doers are such-members and (b) see the second as done in conformity with the norm.

This second viewer's maxim suggests an observation about norms. In the sociological and anthropological literature, the focus on norms is on the conditions under which and the extent to which they govern, or can be seen by social scientists to govern, the relevant actions of those members whose actions they ought to control. While such matters are, of course, important, our viewer's maxim suggests other importances of norms, for members.

Viewers use norms to provide some of the orderliness, and proper orderliness, of the activities they observe. Via some norm two activities may be made observable as a sequentially ordered pair. That is, viewers use norms to explain both the occurrence of some activity given the occurrence of another and also its sequential position with regard to the other, e.g. that it follows the other, or precedes it. That is a first importance. Second, viewers use norms to provide the relevant membership categories in terms of which they formulate identifications of the doers of those activities for which the norms are appropriate.

Now let me observe, viewers may use norms in each of the preceding ways, and feel confident in their usage without engaging in such an investigation as would serve to warrant the correctness of their usages. This last observation is worth some further thought.

We may, at least initially, put the matter thus: For viewers, the usability of the viewer's maxims serves to warrant the correctness of their observations. And that is then to say, the usability of the viewer's maxims provides for the recognizability of the correctness of the observations done via those maxims. And that is then to say, 'correct observations' or, at least, 'possible correct observations' are 'recognizable'.

(Members feel no need in warranting their observation, in recognizing its correctness to do such a thing as to ask the woman whether she is the mother of the baby,[3] or to ask her whether she picked it up because it was crying, i.e. they feel no such need so long as the viewer's maxims are usable.)

[Elsewhere in this book I have suggested using the term 'adult' in place of the terms 'parent', 'mother', and 'father' unless parenthood is both known and at issue. Sacks' point here provides the grounds for such a recommendation: although members may feel that assumptions of parenthood are warranted, sociologists who make such assumptions end up *assuming* that which they are claiming to *investigate*; in Mackay's terms, they are confusing topic and resource.]

In short: 'Correctness' is recognizable, and there are some exceedingly nice ties between recognizably correct description and recognizably correct observations. One such tie which is relevant to the tasks we have undertaken is: A string of sentences which may be heard via the hearer's maxims, as having been produced by use of the viewer's maxims, will be heard as a 'recognizably correct possible description'.

## Sequential Ordering

The rest of this chapter will be devoted to two tasks. I shall try to develop some further rewards of the analysis so far assembled, some consequences it throws off; and to show also how it is that the two sentences ('The baby cried. The mommy picked it up') can warrantably be said to be from 'a story'. I start with the latter task.

[In what follows, Sacks' general concern is with rules that govern talk. He focuses on adult rules for children but provides a valuable framework that could be used to examine the rules that children follow when they are with one another.]

It ought to be apparent that the fact that the children whose talk is reported in *Children Tell Stories* were asked to tell a story is not definitive of their having done so. It is at least possible that the younger ones among them are not capable of building stories, of building talk that is recognizable as a 'story', or, at least, as a 'possible story'.

It happens to be correct, for Western literature, that if some piece of talk is a possible description it is also, and thereby a possible story or story part. It appears, therefore, that having established that the two sentences are a possible description, I have also, and thereby, established that they are possibly (at least part of) a story. To stop now would, however involve ignoring some story-relevant aspects of the given sentences which are both interesting and subjectable to analysis. So I go on.

Certain characteristics are quite distinctive to stories. For example, there are characteristic endings ('And they lived happily ever after') and character-istic beginnings ('once upon a time'). I shall consider whether the possible story, a fragment of which we have been investigating, can be said (and I mean here, as throughout, 'warrantably said') to close with what is recog-nizable as 'an ending' and to start with what is recognizable as 'a beginning'.

In suggesting a difference between 'starts' and proper 'beginnings', and between 'closes' and proper 'endings', I am introducing a distinction which has some importance. The distinction, which is by no means original, may be developed by considering some very simple observation.

1 A piece of talk which regularly is used to do some activity — as 'Hello' is used to do 'greeting' — may not invariably be so used, but may do other activities as well — as 'Hello' is used to check out whether another with whom one is talking on the phone is still there or has been cut off — where it is in part its occurrence in 'the middle' and not 'the start' of a conversation that serves to discriminate the use being made of it.

2 Certain activities not only have regular places in some sequences where they do get done but may, if their means of being done is not found there, be said, by members, to not have occurred, to be absent. For example, the absence of a greeting may be noticed, as the following conversation, from field observation, indicates. The scene involved two adult women, one the mother of two children, ages 6 and 10. The kids enter and the following ensues:

| | |
|---|---|
| Woman | Hi. |
| Boy | Hi. |
| Woman | Hi, Annie. |
| Mother | Annie, don't you hear someone say hello to you? |
| Woman | Oh, that's okay, she smiled hello. |
| Mother | You know you're supposed to greet someone, don't you? |
| Annie | [Hangs head] Hello. |
| | [Note, however, that when children are together in the absence of adults, they may omit 'greetings' *and* their omission may not be noticed by other children.] |

3 Certain activities can only be done at certain places in a sequence. For example, a third strike can only be thrown by a pitcher after he has two strikes on a batter.

Observations such as these lead to a distinction between a 'slot' and the 'items' which fill it, and to proposing that certain activities are accomplished by a combination of some item and some slot.

The notion of slot serves for the social scientist to mark a class of relevance rules. Thus, if it can be said that for some assertable sequence there is a position in which one or more activities properly occur, or occur if they are to get done, then: The observability of either the occurrence or the nonoccurrence of those activities may be claimed by reference to having looked to the position and determined whether what occurs in it is a way of doing the activity.

An instance of the class of relevance rules might run: To see whether a conversation included 'greetings', look to the first utterance of either party and see whether there occurs in it any item which passes as a greeting; items such as ('hello', 'hi', 'hi there', ...). The fact that the list contains the ellipsis might be deeply troublesome were it not the case that while we are unable to list all the members of the class 'greeting items', we can say that the class is bounded, and that there are some utterables which are not members of it, perhaps, for example, the sentence now being completed. If that and only that occurred in a first utterance, we might feel assured in saying that a greeting did not occur.

Consider just one way that this class of relevance rules is important. Roughly, it permits the social scientist to nontrivially assert that something is absent. Nontrivial talk of an absence requires that some means be available for showing both the relevance of occurrence of the activity that is proposed-ly absent and the location where it should be looked for to see that it did not occur. Lacking these, an indefinite set of other activities might equally well be asserted to be absent given some occurrence, and the assertion in question not being discriminable from the (other) members of that indefinite set, it is trivialized.

It does seem that for stories it is correct to say that they can have beginnings, and we can then inspect the items that occur at their start to see whether they can be seen to make a beginning. Given further that stories can have endings, we can inspect the items that occur at their close to see whether they can be seen to make an ending.

While my main interest will be with the story's start as a possible proper beginning, let me briefly consider its close: 'She went to sleep'. With this the speaker would seem to be not merely closing but closing making a proper ending. It so seems by virtue of the fact that such a sentence reports an occurrence, or can be heard as reporting an occurrence, which is a proper ending to something for which endings are relevant and standardized, that very regularly used unit of orientation, the day. A day being recognized as ending for some person when they go to sleep, so a story may be recognized as closing with an ending if at its close there is a report of the protagonist's having gone to sleep. This particular sort of ending is, of course, not at all particular to stories constructed by young children; it, and other endings like it, from 'the last sleep' death unto the shutting down of the world, are regular components of far more sophisticated ventures in Western literature.

[Although in what follows, Sacks' interest in children's talk with adults is as an example of beginnings, the material he presents suggests fruitful lines for further study of children by means of the approach he is developing. His consideration of children's restricted rights to talk, although scant, is sugges-tive as a topic for sociological study. Detailed analysis of the talk of children as young as the child described here is clearly possible, as is the study of how others — both children and adults — 'hear' the talk of children.]

Let me turn then to the start, to consider whether it can be said to be a beginning. I shall attempt to show that starting to talk to adults is for small children a rather special matter. I shall do that by focusing on a most characteristic way that small children, of around the age of the teller of the given story, characteristically open their talk to adults, i.e. the use of such items as 'You know what?' I shall offer an analysis of that mode of starting off, which will characterize the problems such a start can be seen to operate as a methodical solution to.

The promised analysis will warrant my assertion that starting to talk is, for small children, a special matter. That having been established, I shall turn to see whether the particular start we have for this story may be seen as another type of solution to the same problem that I will have shown to be relevant.

If I can then show that another solution is employed in our problematic utterance (the sentence 'The baby cried'), I will have shown that the story starts with something that is properly a beginning, and that therefore, both start and close are 'proper' beginning and end. Such, in any event, are my intentions.

I begin, roughly and only as an assumption (though naively, the matter is obvious), by asserting that kids have restricted rights to talk. That being the case, by assumption, I want to see whether the ways that they go about starting to talk, with adults, can be most adequately seen to be solutions to the problem which focuses on needing to have a good start if one is to get further than that. Starts which have that character can then be called beginnings.

Now, kids around the age of 3 go through a period when some of them have an almost universal way of beginning any piece of talk they make to adults. They use things like: 'You know what, Daddy?' or 'You know something, Mommy?'

I will introduce a few rules of conversational sequencing. I do that without presenting data now, but the facts are so obvious that you can check them out easily for yourself; you know the rules anyway. The sequencing rules are for two-party conversation; and, since two-party conversation is a special phenomenon, what I say is not intended as applying for three- or more party conversation.

One basic rule of two-party conversation concerns a pair of objects, questions and answers. It runs: If one party asks a question, when the question is complete, the other party properly speaks, and properly offers an answer to the question and says no more than that. The rule will need considerable explication, but for now, it will do as it stands.

A second rule, and it's quite a fundamental one, because by reference to it the, in principle, infinite character of a conversation can be seen as: A person who has asked a question can talk again, has as we may put it, 'a reserved right to talk again', after the one to whom he has addressed the question speaks. *And*, in using the reserved right he can ask a question. I call this rule the 'chaining rule', and in combination with the first rule it provides for the occurrence of an indefinitely long conversation of the form Q-A-Q-A-Q-A-. . . .

Now the characteristic opener that we are considering is a question (e.g. 'You know what?'). Having begun in that way, a user who did not have restricted rights to talk would be in a position of generating an indefinite set of further questions as each question was replied to, or as the other otherwise spoke on the completion of some question.

But the question we begin with is a rather curious one in that it is one of those fairly but not exceptionally rare questions which have as their answer another question, in this case the proper and recurrent answer is 'What?' The use of initial questions of this sort has a variety of consequences. First, if a question which has another question as its proper answer is used and is properly replied to, i.e. is replied to with the proper question, then the chaining rule is turned around, i.e. it is the initial answerer and not the initial questioner who now has the reserved right to speak again after the other speaks. The initial questioner has by his question either not assumed that he can use the chaining rule or has chosen not to. (Note that we are not saying that he has not chosen to invoke the chaining rule but rather that he has instead given the choice of invoking it to the initial answerer. There are two different possibilities involved.)

Second, the initial questioner does not only not make his second speech by virtue of the chaining rule but he makes it by virtue of the first sequencing rule, i.e. by reference to the fact that a person who has been asked a question properly speaks and properly replies to it. His second speech is then not merely not made as a matter of either the chaining rule or his choice by some other means of making a second speech but it is something he makes by obligation, given the fact that he has been asked a question and is therefore obliged to answer.

Third, the question he is obliged to answer is, however, 'an open one' in the sense that what it is that an answer would be is something that its asker does not know, and further is one that its answerer by the prior sequence should know. What an answer is then to the second question is whatever it is the kid takes to be an answer, and he is thereby provided with the opportunity to say whatever it is he wanted to say in the first place, not now, however, on his own say-so but as a matter of obligation.

In that case then — and the foregoing being a method whereby the production of the question 'You know what?' may be explicated — we may take it that kids take it that they have restricted rights which consist of a right to begin, to make a first statement and not much more. Thereafter they proceed only if requested to. And if that is their situation as they see it, they surely have evolved a nice solution to it.

[For the most part Sacks has been focusing on what others, presumably though not necessarily adults, *hear* in children's utterances and not on what children *intend*. In the above paragraph, however, he suggests the possibility that children indeed do have the competence not only to use adult rules but to use them in such a way that they, the children, can accomplish their own goals. The subject of children's talk thus becomes available as a topic for detailed sociological research.]

With the foregoing we can say then that a focus on the way kids begin to talk is appropriate, and we can see whether the beginnings of stories, if they are not made of the culturally standardized beginnings (such as 'once upon a time'), might be seen to be beginnings by virtue of the special situation which kids have *vis-à-vis* beginning to talk.

We may arrive at the status of 'The baby cried' as a proper beginning, in particular as a start that is a beginning by virtue of being a proper opener for one who has restricted rights to talk, by proceeding in the following way. Let us consider another solution to the problem of starting talk under restricted rights. I'll begin by introducing a word, 'ticket'. I can show you what I mean to point to with the word by a hypothetical example. Suppose two adults are co-present and lack rights to talk to each other, e.g. they have never been introduced, or whatever. For any such two persons there are conditions under which one can begin to talk to the other. And that those conditions are the conditions used to in fact begin talk is something which can be shown via a first piece of talk. Where that is done we will say that talk is begun with a ticket. That is, the item used to begin talk is an item which, rights not otherwise existing, serves to warrant one having begun to talk. For example, one turns to the other and says, 'Your pants are on fire'. It is not just any opening, but an opening which tells why it is that one has breached the correct silence, which warrants one having spoken. Tickets then are items specially usable as first items in talk by one who has restricted rights to talk to another. And the most prototypical class of tickets are 'announcements of trouble relevant to the other'.

Now it is clear enough (cf. the discussion of norms earlier) that the occurrence of a baby crying is the occurrence of a piece of trouble relevant to some person, e.g. the mother of the baby. One who hears it gains a right to talk, i.e. to announce the fact that it has occurred, and can most efficiently speak via a ticket, i.e. 'The baby cried'. That being so, we can see then that the opener 'The baby cried' is a proper beginning, i.e. it is something which can serve as a beginning for someone whose rights to talk are in the first instance restricted.

With the foregoing we have established that the story we have been examining has both a proper beginning and a proper end, and is thus not only a story by virtue of being a possible description but also by virtue of its employing, as parts, items which occur in positions that permit one to see that the user may know that stories have such positions, and that there are certain items which when used in them are satisfactory incumbents.

### Notes

1   Consider, e.g. the following: 'These children are highly aware that they have graduated from the rank of "baby" and are likely to exhibit considerable scorn of babies, whether a neighbor's child or a younger sibling. This feeling of superiority is the residue of the parents' praise for advance behaviour and their inciting the child by remarks like "only *babies* do that. *You're* not a baby". The frequency of these remarks at this age, however, suggest that in adult minds, at least, there is concern lest the children lapse into babyish ways' (Fischer and Fischer, 1963).

2   The following data is from a telephone call between a staff member (S) and a caller (C) to an emergency psychiatric clinic. Note the juxtapositions of 'hair stylist' in item 4 with suspected homosexuality in the last item.

S:   So, you can't watch television. Is there anything you can stay interested in?

C: No, not really.
S: What interests did you have before?
C: I was a hair stylist at one time. I did some fashions now and then. Things like that.
S: Then why aren't you working?
C: Because I don't want to, I guess. Maybe that's why.
S: But you do find that you just can't get yourself going?
C: No. Well, as far as the job goes?
S: Yes.
C: Well, I'll tell you. I'm afraid. I'm afraid to go out and look for a job. That's what I'm afraid of. But more, I think I'm afraid of myself because I don't know. I'm just terribly mixed up.
S: You haven't had any trouble with anyone close to you?
C: Close to me. Well, I've been married three times and I'm — Close, you mean, as far as arguments or something like that?
S: Yes.
C: No, nobody real close. I'm just a very lonely person. I guess I'm very —
S: Have you been having some sexual problems?
C: All my life.
S: Un huh. Yeah.
C: Naturally. You probably suspect — as far as the hair stylist and — either go one one way or the other. There is a straight or homosexual, something like that. I'm telling you, my whole life is just completely mixed up and turned over and it's just smashed and I'm not kidding.

3 'A late child was at times embarrassing to one woman who, while enjoying him, found that in public places she often overheard people saying, "They must be his grandparents"' (Fischer and Fischer, 1963).

## Concluding Note

Given the complexity of this article, a few additional comments may prove useful in directing attention to the particular fruitfulness of Sacks' ideas for the sociological study of children. If the article is reread — an endeavor I recommend — then the following considerations may serve to guide this second journey.

A major goal of this article is to demonstrate the many meanings embedded in even the simplest of utterances. Sacks himself notes that the edifice (or apparatus, as he also calls it) he constructs to understand the story he presents is indeed elaborate for that task. The edifice, however, is so constructed that it can be used to examine a multiplicity of other topics, some of which are suggested by Sacks. He offers many intriguing ideas about children's worlds in themselves and in relation to adult worlds.

Sacks illustrates, though he does not directly discuss, children's competence to construct descriptions, to create stories, to recognize adults' expectations for children, and to modify rules to meet both their own goals and adult requirements. All these ideas emerge from the study of the utterance of child who is not quite 3 years old. Certainly children may not intend all that adults can 'hear' or 'see', but for that matter adults may not intend all that can be gleaned from adult words and acts. The point here is not *intention* but *formulation* of words and deeds that are viewed as understandable and meaningful. Some of what children say and do indeed does not make sense to others; that some does suggests that even very young children are competent to *make sense* in adult terms at least on some occasions. Adults may engage in some *interpretation* of children's activities but they do not make sense out of non-sense; rather, they interpret behavior that already has at least some meaning.

Another important idea to emerge from this article is that adults in fact do interpret children's activities — 'hear' and 'see' on the basis of adult taken-for-granted rules about 'hearing' and 'seeing'. It is these rules, rather than 'pure' acts in themselves, that give sense to activities. Of particular significance here is the idea that adults draw on norms about children in their interpretation of children's behavior; adults expect children to 'act like children'; if they 'act like adults' they are seen as in some sense violating norms. Sacks might offer a maxim of the sort: *if you can see children as acting like children, then: see them that way.*

The implications of such a maxim for the sociological study of children are profound, for such a rule embodies the adult bias criticized throughout this book. Sociological study of children requires a suspension of this maxim if children's activities in all their variety and sophistication are to be recognized. Otherwise sociology is simply the articulation of common sense, hardly a scientific undertaking.

Sacks also provides a basis for asking 1) do adults use their interpretation of children's utterances as a way of teaching children what their utterances *ought to mean*? thus, 2) is adults' 'understanding' of children's utterances an epistemological (knowledge-related) undertaking or, rather, is it a political or moral one? 3) are children's interpretations of other children's utterances different from the interpretations made by adults?

Yet another idea about children that can be drawn from Sacks' article is the idea that children are able to distinguish between adults' rules for them and their own rules for one another and for adults. In this aspect children are like 'foreigners' — those who participate in two worlds, with all the juggling that such duality entails. In a study of children playing tag (done as an assignment in a course that used an earlier version of this book of readings) Lisa Cutrona found in children's talk about the game of tag that they 1) articulated special rules for adults because 'bigger people can run faster' and, more importantly, 2) made such a rule while recognizing that adults pretend not to be able to run as fast as they really can. The extent of children's understanding of adult *concessions* to them, and children's *concessions* to adults, are fruitful topics for further study. That such knowledge exists at all is significant and yet another indication of children's competence.

Sacks does not ask unexamined acceptance for all his claims; he urges readers to consult their own experiences. As participants in social worlds, we know how to 'do' participation. Such knowledge is valuable data. If some of Sacks' claims seem questionable, test them in the world of everyday life, for that is their source.

F.C.W.

*Chapter 15*

# The Hard Times of Childhood and Children's Strategies for Dealing with Them

*Frances Chaput Waksler*

## Introduction

The purpose of this paper is to provide an overview and some illustrative findings from an ongoing study of 'The hard times of childhood and children's strategies for dealing with them'. Let me make clear at the outset that when I refer to the 'hard times' of childhood, I do not refer to experiences such as malnutrition and starvation, serious illness, deprivation, and the horrors of child abuse. My concern is with identifying and examining some of the ordinary, everyday difficulties of simply 'being a child' in relation to adults, other children, and the broader social world — experiences that children themselves at the time see as hard. Consider the following excerpt from my data:

> In my second year of preschool I had a few problems. I remember drawing a picture of my family. When it came time to draw my father I couldn't remember if a mustache was over or under the nose. I was too embarrassed to ask anyone, so I think I put it over his nose. (Carol)

The kind of experiences I seek are not ones that adults would necessarily characterize as hard for children. As one of my respondents noted:

> The experiences that I have told all seem so trivial now, like it was ridiculous to even have worried about them. But at the time they were so real, so important to me. (Pam)

In the terms in which my informants describe their experiences they constitute a serious challenge to the idealization of childhood as a time of unalloyed innocence and joy.

The study on which I am reporting grows out of phenomenology (Husserl, 1913), symbolic interactionism (Mead, 1964, 1966, 1982), and ethnomethodology (Garfinkel, 1967). Of particular relevance is work in these theoretical areas directed to the study of children as full-fledged social beings

(Mackay, 1973; Sacks, 1974; Goode and Waksler, 1989 and 1990; and papers collected by Adler and Adler, Mandell, and Cahill in *Sociological Studies of Child Development*, Volumes I through IV). The immediate sources of the study are a theoretical piece I wrote entitled 'Studying children: Phenomenological insights' (1986 [Chapter 5]; see also Waksler, 1987 [Chapter 8]); a variety of spirited discussions in college classrooms; and a surprisingly large number of excellent student papers on the topic.

What is the sociological significance of establishing the social facticity of the hard times of childhood? To establish that from their perspective children do indeed have hard times expands our knowledge of the social world, but this finding has further sociological significance. First, it serves to document adults' limited knowledge about children. This limited knowledge does not seem to be accidental. Rather it is politically useful, for it enables adults to act as they routinely do towards children, carrying out adult plans and projects in which children are included, though not necessarily as willing participants. Were adults regularly to take into account children's perspectives, they might continue to act as they would otherwise, but their knowledge might well give lie to the presumed altruism of adults and willing participation of children.

Second, the discovery of the hard times of childhood brings to light the social contexts in which these hard times come about. Children's difficulties emerge in interaction, where children are misunderstood, both intentionally and unintentionally, and where they lack power in relation to others, especially adults. They may be expected to follow rules that they are not taught (see Mackay, 1973 and Waksler, 1987) and have limited resources for changing or bending rules.

Third, if we think of adults as teaching children how to become adults, and if we recognize that children learn from what they see as well as what they are told, then what do children learn from the kinds of experiences described in this paper? In a story about fear written by Rose, she describes her mother's statement, 'Don't worry. There is no such thing as a monster' not as a lesson that monsters don't exist; rather, in Rose's words, 'I would wonder to myself about how she could be so stupid. I knew they were there and she didn't care. I cried myself to sleep for years. This was partly because I was so terrified and partly because mommy didn't care.' Unless Rose's mother was indeed trying to teach Rose that her mother didn't care, her teaching methods both failed to teach what she intended and taught what she didn't intend.

And lastly, the discovery of the hard times of childhood displays the many similarities between children and adults, similarities that cannot be recognized by sociologists who separate the study of children from the broader sociological enterprise. Children's hard times and those of adults are not after all so very different in their basic characteristics.

## Methodology

As a way of exploring this topic, I have solicited stories of children's hard times. I have begun not with children but primarily with college freshmen —

a perhaps exploited category of informants but for this particular study a very knowledgeable one. I did not begin by studying children themselves for a number of reasons, the major one being that the kinds of experiences in which I am interested are those that children may well find politically unwise to disclose to adults. Indeed, to my surprise, these experiences proved somewhat problematic for college students to disclose to their own parents. Such disclosures might be even more troublesome for young children and, until I can more fully explore the political issues involved and responses that might be made to them, I will forgo my study of young children directly.

The primary source of the data with which I am currently working is papers that forty-four students[1] wrote in fulfillment of an assignment for a freshman college course entitled 'Studying the Social Worlds of Children'. Students were asked to write a five-page first person account that focused on memories of their own childhood, with particular emphasis on the difficulties of being a child. They were to consider the questions: What was hard? unfair? unable to be done? and to pay particular attention to the difficulties presented by adults. Additional data comes from papers written for the course the previous year, when I was less systematic about collecting data, from class discussions, and from stories I continue to collect, both formally and informally.

Students' writing of this assignment followed a class discussion on the topic. In initiating these discussions, I began by simply asking students to reflect upon hard times of childhood, giving as an example 'being kissed by adults when you didn't want to be'. Classroom response has customarily been knowing smiles followed by a flood of anecdotes. It is my impression that my topic was not one about which students had already formulated ideas, except of the quite different kind that adults routinely have about childhood.

My initial concern was simply with identifying 'hard times'; it soon became clear, however, that equally significant were strategies for dealing with these experiences. Unsolicited student reports of such strategies were accompanied by a seeming certain pride expressed in describing the effective use of such strategies. I therefore expanded my topic accordingly. In this paper I focus on 'hard times' but provide a note and some illustrative examples of the kinds of strategies children may develop to offset, forestall, and endure their hard times.

The stories included in this paper may appear to have been selected with a bias towards those that provide a negative view of childhood. To the contrary, the ones I have selected for inclusion are representative of the stories I have collected. From the texts that I received from informants I have deleted only some of the general commentary. I have also made some minor editorial changes, mostly to correct grammar, give anonymity, and provide clarification. Otherwise the data I present is in the words of the respondents.

## A Note on Memories as a Source of Data

Events from their childhood routinely invoked in everyday life by adults seem to be those that are memorably good or bad. When publicly presented as recollections, the good experiences tend to be very good; the bad, very bad. My method of data gathering has been to ask respondents to select from their memories according to different criteria, focusing on aspects of childhood that in everyday adult life are seldom chosen for presentation.

Certainly it is naive to take memories as literal accounts of past events, and I have no intention of so doing. Thus throughout this paper I refer to data I have collected as *stories*, *tales*, and *anecdotes*. Whether or not the stories I have heard and read are literally faithful to lived experience, they nonetheless display a range of possible children's feelings and actions that, to the best of my knowledge, are not widely attended to or even suspected. To what extent children do endure hard times awaits further empirical study but the data I have gathered provides evidence for the social facticity of children's hard times.

To know what children are experiencing, it is certainly necessary, as far as I am concerned, to ask them at the time of the experiences. To know what to ask, however, and to know what experiences might be occurring, seems to be aided by the kinds of data I have gathered.

## The Hard Times of Childhood

I am not claiming that childhood is a time of unmitigated hard times; I am claiming that children, from their perspective, do endure hard times. I have not been concerned with frequency but have simply gathered examples to demonstrate that, contrary to everyday adult views, children, even the very young, are capable of a wide range of thoughts, plans, tastes, moral views, emotions, and, as well, actions directed to furthering their own goals, within which framework they encounter hard times. (For further testimony to children's competence, see Mackay, 1973.)

I begin with a somewhat lengthy example that in its detail testifies eloquently to the 'hard times' of childhood.

> *A Prototypical Case of the Hard Times of Childhood:*
> *The Swimming Lessons* by Veronica

Do not bite your nails. Do not crack your knuckles. Do not slouch in your chair. Do not spill your milk. Do not mash your peas. Do not wear through the knees of your good pants. These are a few of the commands that I remember hearing as a child. I also recall wondering if there was anything that I could do. In the following paragraphs, I have recorded some of my childhood memories as I recollect them.

My first and most vivid memory is of swimming lessons. I was 4 years old at the time, It was a humid day in June and I was anxious to go to see Janet and her pool. My mother parked the station wagon on the road and quicly undid my seatbelt. As we started our journey up the path that was covered with rocks and moss, I could smell chlorine in the air. My mother swung open the gate and I was suddenly blinded by the reflection of the sun in the pool. I readjusted my Minnie Mouse sunglasses to shield my eyes. The next thing I remember is my mother leaving and Janet, the teacher, telling the seven of us to grab one flutter board each and to get in the pool. The thought of getting in the pool sent me into a panic. I sat there, glued to a plastic lounge chair. Janet was talking to me sweetly and, at the same time, handing me a flutter board. I felt that I was being singled out not only because it was a red flutter board and I disliked that color but also because it was the only red flutter board. I hated Janet at that moment.

After minutes of debating over how I could escape, I finally gave in and took the horrid piece of red plastic. I walked to the steps of the pool and stood there. The rest of my peers were in the water waiting for me. I felt that they were staring at me and my stomach that was protruding from my orange and yellow checked bikini. Janet sauntered into the pool and glanced back over her shoulder at me. I dipped a toe in the pool and suddenly realized why the rest of the children looked slightly blue. I cleared my throat and asked, 'Can your turn up the heater in there?' She laughed and told me that there was no heater in the pool. I had never heard of a pool without a heater. The instructor kept urging me to get in the water and it looked to me as if the class was getting a bit restless too. I put my left foot on the first step and quickly pulled it out. 'It's too cold. I just can't do it,' I said, as I felt tears coming to my eyes. Janet told me to sit on the edge of the pool for a while until I was used to it. I remember thinking that maybe she was not as bad as I had thought.

Some time passed and I was completely content sitting there with my feet dangling in the water. Then Janet told me that it was time to get in. 'The water is still too cold,' I told her. She did not look as though she believed me. 'I feel like an ice cube,' I explained. I sat on the steps of the pool for the rest of the lesson. The only good part of the whole hour was when we got to have cookies and juice.

The next week I had to sit on the steps in the pool, so I at least got wet up to my shoulders. After the lesson, I got cookies and juice again. The week after that, Janet told me that I had to participate. My worst fear was happening. I tried to get out of it by sitting on the steps but it did not work. It appeared to me that she was that mean lady I had thought she was that first day we met. She made me put my face in the water and blow bubbles, a task that I found totally pointless. After I had accomplished that, I was allowed to get out of the pool. I say on a lounge chair, wrapped in a towel. My mother arrived early that day to pick me up. She was full of questions as to why I was not in the pool like all the other children. When I would not supply the answers that she wanted, she went and talked to Janet. I remember them standing there talking about me while I was sitting right there. What an awful, humiliating feeling that was. Janet said that if I did not participate in the whole exercise the next week, my mother should consider removing me from the class. On the way home in the car, I burst into tears and sobbed about what a mean person the instructor was and about how I never wanted to go back. My mother ended my tantrum with a short, 'You must learn to swim.'

On the day of my fourth lesson, I tried every illness that I could think of. My mother did not believe me. The path that had seemed so pretty the first day now seemed long, slippery and windy. The smell of the chlorine was making me sick. My mother pushed me inside the gate and left. I was left alone to face Janet and the pool. I had been deserted. The lesson started and I was told, not asked, to get in the pool. It felt colder that day than any other day before it. I remember thinking that I would get everyone back for making me do this. After I was submerged in water up to my shoulders, Janet pulled me across the pool to the side opposite the steps. I was left with no escape route. I clung to the side of the pool for the entire hour. I thought that my fingers would never uncurl again. That awful, horrible woman had left me there, clinging to the side of the pool. I recall thinking that no one would ever come and rescue me. I would die grasping on to the concrete. I did not dare let go because I thought that I might sink. I could not even use my evil red flutter board to float on because when Janet had dragged me across the pool, it had been left over near the steps. Finally, my mother came over and pulled me out. I thought it was, by far, the least she could do. I swore that I would never go near that pool again.

Moreover, I managed to get out of the next two lessons. This seemed perfect at the time but it was not until my seventh class that I realized I was in trouble. They were diving and I was expected to do the same. I cried and cried but it appeared that nothing was going to work. I announced that the water was too cold but Janet told me that it was not. She finally agreed to letting me sit on the side of the pool. I thought that I was safe for another hour until I comprehended what she was doing. She had the entire class sit on the edge of the pool next to me and do sitting dives into the water. One by one my classmates dove into the pool until it was my turn. I sat there shaking. I tried to retreat to a lounge chair but Janet caught me. She made me point my hands above my head while she pushed me into the pool. I had not taken a breath until I was under the water. I became disoriented and began paddling towards the bottom of the pool. That was when she ended up dragging me out of the coldness. I cried hysterically until my mother arrived. My mother sided with Janet and left me to tell my story to my dog.

When it was the day of our last meeting, I did not put up such a fight to go. It was family day which meant that my mother would be there the whole time while we dove for pennies. We also got to eat more cookies than usual. Janet had promised me that she would put my pennies on the steps. I found this only reasonable since she had tried to drown me the week before. She threw nine pennies on the first and second steps and one on the third. I quickly stooped down and picked up the first nine pennies and handed them to my mother. I looked at the tenth penny gleaming on the third step. I wanted that penny so badly. I thought that Janet had put it down there because she thought that I would have to go under to get it. I shimmied up next to the penny and looked at it. I made it look like I was pondering over it. I tried to reach it a few times with my hands. I looked up at everyone who was watching me and smiled. I took a deep breath and grasped the penny with my toes. I dropped it in my hand and then climbed out of the pool. I was so proud of myself.

What constitute the 'hard times' of childhood? My data indicates that children's lack of control over many and important aspects of their lives serves as the grounds of their hard times. One respondent, Holly, for example, speaks of 'all the numerous times adults made my decisions for me'. I have been able to categorize my data into stories chronicling lack of control over the physical world, the world of emotions, and the moral world. In what follows I suggest the nature of these different kinds of hard times.

### Lack of Control Over the Physical World

Children's lack of control in the physical sphere is evident in stories where children are denied control of:

a. their bodies, such that others deal with their bodies against their will or without their permission
b. of the activities in which they engage, i.e. others determine where they go, how they conduct themselves, what they do, and what they cannot do
c. appearance, and thus their presentation of self
d. relations with others, including friends and enemies
e. additionally, children may be frustrated by inabilities or inadequacies, much as adults may be, but may also lack control over resources to cope with, minimize, or change their deficits

The lack of control over the physical world described by informants indicates a wide range of areas of limitation. The sources of these limitations include adults (especially parents), other children, and the child's own physical abilities. Adults may well argue that adult limitations are necessary in order to protect children physically, to guarantee their health, and to turn them into responsible adults, but adults may not realize that the costs of implementing such goals may be very high. Two obvious questions to ask are: Are the costs too high, given the goals? and, Could the costs be reduced? A more fundamental issue, however, arises by questioning adult claims, routinely taken for granted, that such limitations placed on children indeed do accomplish what they claim to and that taking children's views into account more fully would impede the accomplishment of those goals.

*a. Bodies*  Consider the following two stories:

*Naps*
Nap time was an adult imposed rule that I found especially hard to do. When I was 3 I was forced to take a nap during the day. Being a very active child, I could never sleep at nap time. It was so hard to lie still on my mat when I had so much energy inside of me. The toys around me always seemed to be calling my name to come over and play, and consequently I had the reputation of being a hard-to-control napper. My mother even used to make me take naps on Christmas day after dinner, but before we opened our presents from Grandma and Grandpa. I remember thinking 'How do they expect me to sleep with all of these unopened presents?' (Irene)

*A Tale of Food*
We always had to finish everything on our plates. If we did not finish we were sent to our rooms for the night. My mother always used to make tuna fish casserole. All of us kids hated it. It was always such a hassle when it was made. My brother John was always sent to his room. Everyone, even adults, have foods that they do not enjoy the taste of. It just did not seem fair that we had to finish everything on the plate. (Inez)

With respect to lack of control in the physical sphere, why indeed do adults bathe children, put them to bed and send them for naps, feed them according to adult standards set for children, control their access to bathroom facilities, and so on? Running through the stories I have collected are tales of adult convenience, taste, and standards. Adults differ from one another in the standards they set for themselves; children, on the other hand, seem to be held to whatever standards are set by those who care for them. How frequent must bathing be to produce cleanliness? How clean is clean enough? Who decides? Do adults put children to bed because children need their sleep or because adults need time without children? That children can, through a variety of strategies, not get the amount of sleep they are said to need and still function suggests that their 'need' for specific amounts of sleep may be more an adult than a biological need. That adults fail to observe children's strategies for avoiding sleep — strategies that nonetheless keep children as quiet as if they were asleep — suggests either that adults are not particularly vigilant or that it is in their interest to have children act as if they were asleep rather than necessarily being asleep.

*b. Activities*   Children's lack of control over their activities are clearly exemplified in the following pair of stories:

*Too Many Lessons*
The year I was 10 I might as well have had a job because I was always being driven to some other activity. Didn't my parents know kids just like to sit around and do nothing some of the time? On Mondays it was gymnastics lessons, on Tuesdays it was guitar lessons, Wednesdays were swim day, Thursdays were Girl Scouts, Friday was art class, and Saturday mornings I played basketball. All I wanted to do was play the piano. I don't want to do all these things, I am not a superkid, I am just a kid who wants to play the piano. (Mary)

*Lessons Denied*
When I was 12 years old, I wanted to sign up for cheerleading, but my parents said they did not have the extra money. They did have the money to sign my brother, Tom, up for football, though. I wanted to take flute lessons. My mother said 'What do you want to do that for?' Tom later took drum lessons and Phil now takes guitar and piano. My father did find the money to sign me up, without my consent, for basketball and soccer. Sports were important to him. I

wasn't aggressive, hated competition. He would say 'If you'd only try harder. You have the potential.' I tried to tell him how much I hated sports, especially when I was the only girl on the team. He just didn't listen. (Linda)

*c. Appearance* Adults routinely take clothing, hair style and length, and a host of other appearance-related phenomena to be important aspects of their own presentation of self, over which they maintain considerable control. Children may share this sense of importance without so routinely being able to exert significant control. One issue here may be that the appearance of a child may have implications for how others will view the adult with that child. Since at least some of the 'work' involved in the child's appearance may devolve upon an adult, issues of time, cost, etc. also may affect the adult's decisions.

Clothing and hairstyle can clearly have important implications for a child's journeys into the world outside home. Informal surveying of informants indicates that those who had long hair wanted short, those with short, long, those with curly hair wanted straight, etc. Children's concern may be with appearance and adults' with care as well, though children may also weigh the bother involved and adults may be particularly concerned with appearance. The key issue here, however, is children's experiences of not looking the way they want to and being troubled by it, both for reasons of aesthetics and for its implications in presenting one's self to others.

### The Problem of Short Hair
I always wanted to have long, straight hair like most of my friends did. However, my mother insisted on keeping my hair short, because she said it would be too much trouble to take care of. I also wanted to have my hair straightened, but my mother laughed every time I mentioned this suggestion. At the time, I was very frustrated by the situation. Not only did I want to be like my friends, but several times people who didn't know me referred to me as a boy. When I was at home, I would take a pink blanket that I used for my dolls, and tie it around my head, so I could pretend I had long hair. I also used to take my mother's old wigs that were stored in the attic and wear them when I was in the house. (Sally)

Why are adults concerned about the appearance of their children in such a way that they override children's notions of appearance? Why would one deny children permission to have their ears pierced or to wear clothes of a particular kind? Perhaps adults don't want to be seen as the kind of person who would 'allow' a child to look like 'that', but such concerns seem to be for the benefit of adults, not children. Throughout these stories are many claims about adult preferences and making things easier for adults — not negligible claims but nonetheless less for the good of the child than for the good of the adult.

*d. Relations with others* Relations with others — siblings, friends, enemies — emerge as an issue over which children lack control. Stories tell of being separated from siblings and friends and of being teamed up with undesired others. Complaints about adult choreography of children's relationships are described as having been routinely dismissed as illegitimate by adults.

A consideration of children's relationships with others displays clearly adult concerns for their own well-being. Children's concerns about relationships can routinely be superseded by adults' concerns with those relationships or with other issues. Thus siblings and friends can be separated 'for their own good' and children can be forced into associating with others for adults' 'own good'.

### Separation from Siblings

When my sister Pat and I were younger we did everything together from sharing a crib, clothes and toys to making diagrams on the walls with toothpaste, cakes on the floor of the kitchen, and writing with markers on our parents' bedspread. We were like twins. We were only a year and three days apart and we were inseparable. But when it was time for nursery school, we were not allowed to go together. My mom wanted me to experience school alone and be recognized as an individual being. She wanted me to have friends and not have to be home all day with just Pat and her. I thought she was so unfair to send me to school without Pat. How could she think I would be able to survive without her? I didn't want to go to school. I was scared of being alone and having no friends. I cried all the way to school every day for two weeks, but once I got there I was fine. Pat, on the other hand, resented the fact that I was leaving her to go to school and have fun. It was very hard on me because I wanted her to be there too and she was, the next year. We spent a year of nursery school together because I was too young to go into kindergarten. So for a year we got our own way and spent every day together in school and made our parents' lives a living hell with our schemes. (Diane)

Children's likes and dislikes may be routinely overridden, perhaps because they go unrecognized. The following tale describes a situation where the adult's reasoning may seem quite understandable, but it becomes less so in the face of the degradation described.

### Forced Association with Children

My earliest memory of myself is when I was 5 years old. The year was 1974. I was 5 and my brother was 3. My mother was into a 'diet mode,' a mode that made her want to lose weight and exercise, so she enrolled herself into the Gloria Stevens' program. This program would allow her to work out with a class and an instructor. The place was fully equipped with rowing machines, exercise bikes, exercise mats, and weights. That was only part of the reason she enrolled. The other part was that she could bring us and put us in a playroom. This is where I had a problem. I dreaded the day each week when my mom would put us in the car and we would head to Gloria Stevens. The playroom was about the size of a bathroom. The doorway was blocked with one of those gates that are used to prevent a baby from crawling down stairs. I was furious to be confined to such an area where most of the kids were younger than I was and the toys were geared for toddlers. There I was, confined to a room where I was unable to get out because the gate was too high for me to get my leg over. I never threw a temper tantrum because I knew that would aggravate my mom. So I would just stand by the gate waiting for the hour to go by. I would be in a bad mood the whole time I was there. It was no fun for me. I was too old to be in that small room with toddlers! All I wanted was to be on the other side of the gate but because I was a 'child' I was confined.

I saw that I was different from the toddlers and could distinguish between the labels. I saw that I was not a toddler because I wasn't in diapers and I didn't talk in broken sentences. I knew that 5-year-olds don't throw temper tantrums to get something or at least it didn't work in my house with my parents. (Judy)

Being put into situations with those one would rather avoid is captured again in the following tale:

*Forced Association with Relatives*
Ever since I can remember, my family has been trying to put me and my cousin Jake together. My family would take pictures of us holding hands or him kissing me on the cheek. Every time this occurred I felt like I was going to be sick. I could not stand Jake and always refused to go to visit him.

One particular incident occurred when I was about 6 or 7 years old. My grandmother and grandfather were taking me to visit the cousins, including Jake. I begged and pleaded to stay home, but they would not listen to me. I even told them that I hated Jake and that he was always trying to touch and kiss me. They just laughed and said, 'Isn't that cute.' I felt frustrated because nobody would pay attention to my feelings.

When we arrived at my cousins', I sat very close to my grandmother. I was hoping I would not be bothered. But, sure enough, Jake came over to me and I was forced to play with him. I was so angry and upset at this point that I threw a temper tantrum and we left.

I am usually a very quiet, well behaved child, so for me to resort to a temper tantrum must have been the ultimate. But it worked. I have not seen my cousin Jake since this incident. (Ellie)

*e. Inabilities and inadequacies* Regarding the limits of one's physical being, informants spoke of being unable to do things because of size or abilities. Being 'too young' was not cited by informants as in itself a physical problem but rather as a claim used by others as a rationale for restricting children, as in the following:

### Being 'Too Young'

One of my sisters was nine years older that I was, and my other was thirteen years older than I was. The age difference was so great that I was always too young to do something or go somewhere. I can remember my sisters going out at the same time that I was supposed to go to bed. I always wanted to go with them to a basketball game or to a movie, and it was always past my bedtime, and I was too young. (Irene)

Some sources of frustration for children may be irremediable. Whoopie Goldberg's comic skit on a black child wanting long blonde hair is one such instance. Interestingly, white informants have spoken of using the same pretense Goldberg describes — putting a shirt on one's head as a facsimile of long hair (see above, p. 224).

The following two tales speak of other 'irremediable' characteristics.

### Freckles

Not everything was my parents' fault. I had freckles — and lots of them. Other children teased me and called me freckle-face. Younger children asked me what was wrong with my face and why it was dirty. My mother told me they were a sign of beauty. They did not look beautiful to me. (Linda)

Although adults and children may experience a similar lack of control over the physical world, they also may have access to different resources. Thus children might remedy short hair or the wrong color hair by wearing shirts on their heads; adults might simply let their hair grow or dye it. Adults may disguise freckles with makeup, an option not routinely available to children.

### Physical Size

Physical differences were a big part of the pain childhood at times gave me. I was always very tiny and small. I was several inches shorter than my peers and it made me feel very self-conscious. This was especially true in my pre-school and elementary years. I remember everyone saying I was so 'cute'. That wasn't the bad part, however. What hurt the most was when people would think I was younger than I actually was because of my short height. Two examples come to mind:

The first example relates directly to Mary Joyce's article, Watching People Watching Babies [see Chapter 9]. Even when I was 6 and 7 years old, adults would crouch down to my level and treat me as if I were years younger. The 'Look' Joyce talks about was usually absent, but her findings on how adults talk to babies was certainly present. Relatives that I had not seen in years would pinch my cheeks and say 'Look at Yooooou! Aren't yooooou a cuteeeeee!' (Gini)

Clearly children can be said to lack control in many aspects of the physical world. To note this lack is certainly not to recommend that children

227

be given everything they want. It does, however, suggest that what children want, what adults think children want, what adults want children to want, what adults want, etc. are very different from one another. These distinctions become readily blurred when one speaks in terms of children's 'needs' and when one defines all adult behavior towards children as altruistically motivated. One way to read the foregoing stories and the ones to follow is to look for instances where it appears to be to adults' advantage to not notice that children are perceiving their experiences as hard times and where adult decisions seem to be motivated at least in part by adults' own welfare, even when they may claim otherwise.

### A Caveat

I want to emphasize that I am not attributing the hard times described herein to *bad* parents or other *bad* adults. Indeed, as one of the respondents noted:

> As I reread my paper it occurred to me that I did not make my parents look very good. I realize that this was part of the assignment but I feel that it would be wrong if I left a bad impression on anyone about my parents. I must give them credit for being such good parents because if they had not been I would not have had so much trouble trying to think of things to write about for this paper. (Gina)

Trouble or not, this respondent was nonetheless able to recount experiences in no way significantly different from those of others. My data includes other such disclaimers. An important finding that emerges from my data is the very fact that these kinds of children's experiences can occur with what might even be viewed as 'ideal' parents; the experiences seem to be an outcome of simply *being a child*.

### Lack of Control Over the World of Emotions

In examining claims made by informants about emotions experienced in childhood, it appears that children may experience a wide range of emotions of which adults may not think them capable. My data includes descriptions of embarrassment, anger, vindictiveness, fear, and feelings of inadequacy.

One might speak of adults possessing taken-for-granted 'rules' for children's feelings — rules that children themselves may neither follow nor indeed recognize. Adult rules may encompass both the emotions that children can and cannot feel and the objects towards which they can feel them.

#### Inadequacy
I was one of those children that dreaded gym class because I was so clumsy and uncoordinated. I remember fearing the time that it would be my turn in kickball or volleyball because I was never any good at sports and I was afraid that everybody would laugh at me. I tried everything but I wasn't much of an athlete. It wasn't that I was discriminated against by my teachers because I was clumsy; it was

more like I was discriminated against by the other kids. After all, if all I can remember about gym class when I was in elementary school was being picked next to last for kickball, then the kids must not have liked my athletic ability too much. (Pam)

In his article 'Embarrassment and Social Organization' (1967), Goffman offers insights that seem applicable to children, even though he refers entirely to adult situations, in line with what he sees as the 'non-person' status of children in everyday life. Consider this tale of embarrassment:

*Embarrassment: Behavior of adults in public*
Once, at an amusement park, my parents got into a huge fight. We were sitting in the parking lot of the park when they started to fight. My father didn't want to stay because he hates amusement parks. My mother said 'Fine, let's go!' Then she asked how he could do that to us (take us to an amusement park and not let us go on the rides). My mother got out of the car, took my sister's hand and started walking into the park. My father was walking about a block behind, and I was in between the two of them, crying hysterically. It was so embarrassing, because all of the people were watching me cry and telling each other to look at me and saying how sorry they felt for me. Some of the people even wanted to help me. I was so humiliated. I hated my mother for doing this to me. (Sara)

Children may respond to objects and events with emotions that adults deem inappropriate. Thus, for example, in the stories I collected about divorce, divorce itself did not emerge as a hard time from the children's point of view as respondents described it, despite the fact that adults routinely so characterize it both for themselves and for children.

*Divorce*
The strongest memory I have is one involving my parents' divorce. When I was really young, I didn't pay much attention to the fact that I didn't have my father around. Nobody made a big deal about it. I wasn't sad, I didn't feel as though I was missing out, and I felt content. As I got older and started school, however, all that changed.

'All right, class, today we are going to make Father's Day cards,' my first grade teacher announced. I felt my stomach tighten and silently I raised my hand.

'Mrs. Fields, I . . . I don't have a father who lives with me.'

'Oh! Oh, you poor child. Well, I guess you can just draw a picture then,' she told me. I nodded, but I was shaking inside. Was I different? Did I fit in anymore? Why didn't the other kids just draw pictures? Why couldn't I have a father too. These were only a few of the feelings and questions I had.

'Tammy, I'm so, so sorry that your dad isn't living with you. That must be awfully hard for you to deal with.' After these words were spoken to me, I wanted to tell the adult that it was no big deal. It really didn't affect me. After hearing the two comments just mentioned, I began to think more about not how I really felt but rather how everyone else thought I should feel. I started missing a man I didn't even know, I started to cry about not having a dad, and I also developed feelings of jealousy. I hated hearing about what my friends did with their fathers because it made me feel empty and sad. (Tammy)

Clearly neither adults nor children possess limitless control over the world of emotions, but adults seem to be able to help one another out in ways that they may not routinely employ in their interactions with children. Adults' power over children enables them to overlook children's feelings without such consequences as destruction of the social encounter that would be likely in adult-adult interactions.

### Lack of Control Over the Moral World

A number of aspects of truth emerged in my data as moral concerns: telling the truth and lying; discrepancies between what adults said and what they did; believing that adults routinely spoke the truth; learning, perhaps with dismay or disappointment, that adults do lie, both to others in general and to oneself (the child) in particular; and the difficulties in having one's word as a child taken as truth, especially if it conflicts with the claims of an adult or if it conflicts with 'reason' (i.e. as defined by adults). Not being believed was identified as an instance of hard times and the stories describing the experience make clear the particular frustration one can feel as a child at having one's word questioned or rejected.

#### Not Being Believed
When I was 5 years old my sister and I were playing in the sandbox and my sister poured sand all over her head and told my grandmother that I did it and I got in trouble and I didn't do it and she did it again and each time I got in worse trouble. When I told my grandmother that I didn't do it, she said that my sister wouldn't pour sand on her own hair on purpose. I felt so powerless — I couldn't prove I was right. So I had to take the punishment and my sister kept on playing in the sand and laughed at me because I couldn't play. (Anonymous notes from class discussion)

The following story deals with deception, demonstrating how adults' practical concerns may be at odds with children's sense of morality, as well as with their presentation of self.

#### Passing as Younger
Once a year my family and I would go on a vacation. Ever since I remember (approximately 4 or 5 years of age) up until the present we have gone away. We went to places like Florida, California, Canada, Mexico, Washington D.C., and more. We would plan (my brother and I) where we wanted to go one year in advance. We had so much fun on these trips. I did, however, encounter some difficulties.

One difficulty which I would get steamed about had to do with the age situation. Every time we went on a vacation, my dad would pass me off for a younger age to get the cheaper rates. I remember his saying 'two adults, one junior, and one child.' My brother at the time was 12 and I was 9. 'Child,' however, was anybody under 8. I always wanted to yell out my real age because I wanted to be myself, not a 'little kid' .... (Fern)

### Excursus: 'You'll understand when you grow up' or 'Looking back, I can see that my parents were right'

One way that adults, looking back on their childhoods, seem to resolve the contradiction between their feelings at the time and their view of their parents as basically honorable is by adopting an adult point of view on childhood experiences — that childhood experiences that seemed difficult at the time were 'really' trivial and that adults routinely acted on the basis of children's best interests, even if as children such did not seem to be the case.

In class discussions about the hard times of childhood, participants regularly end stories with a tag line of the 'Looking back, I can see that my parents were right' variety. What strikes me as noteworthy is that when I ask that such an idea be seriously evaluated rather than automatically appended, it seems to disappear. The tag displays the quality of a 'self-evident' view that any ordinary adult is expected to hold. The ready disappearance of the tag suggests that its use is based more on custom that on commitment to its message.

The uncritical adoption of the views that children's experiences can be judged trivial and that adults' actions can be judged altruistic, especially in the face of memories to the contrary, suggests that such adult views are socially useful to adults. One such use is to 'make sense' of one's experiences as a child in ways that do not challenge adults. Another use is to enable adults to continue their ways of acting with children. And thus the change in practices that might result from adults' remembering and taking seriously their childhood experiences is weakened or destroyed.

After a lengthy and somewhat outraged description of adults telling lies to children in order to get them to behave, one anonymous respondent concluded with the statement, 'It is funny, because I now find myself telling my 8 year old sister or any child the same stories.' In order to use with children the techniques one learned from adults when one was a child, it is necessary to set aside one's childhood memories of those experiences as bad. To be able to say 'Now that I'm an adult, I can understand' enables one to use the techniques with which one is familiar and, at the same time, establish oneself as a member of the category 'adult' and no longer of the inferior category of 'child'.

### A Note on Strategies for Dealing with The Hard Times of Childhood

Embarking on this study I never considered the idea that children might develop systematic strategies to cope with what they perceived as hard times.

My informants, however, provided abundant examples of myriad methods for exerting some degree of control over their circumstances. I have begun analyzing this data by using categories comparable to those used to examine children's lack of control, demonstrating how children can exert control over physical, emotional, and moral worlds to further their own ends. Here I simply introduce a bit of the data to give a sense of its character.

### Control Over the Physical World: Faking Illness

Faking illness, especially as a way of avoiding going to school, emerged as a workable method for gaining control. The following story demonstrates particular care, attention to detail, and complexity in working out a suitable method for achieving a goal.

#### Faking Illness

The relevant background features to this incident are: 1) It was a weekday night and I did not want to go to school the next day. 2) My mother, a nurse, was working at a nearby hospital from 3:00 p.m. until 11:00 p.m. 3) I had discovered previously (in the process of trying to create Orangeade) that if I mixed Coca-Cola and orange juice, a peculiar substance emerged. It looked a lot like vomit.

After my mother left for work, I climbed up on the counter and found one of the big coffee mugs that my father used only on Sundays. He would not be looking for it until then, which left me plenty of time to wash it and get it back up there. I then made my creation out of Coca-Cola and orange juice. I carried the cup up to my room and hid it in the drawer next to my bed. That night, I purposely drank orange juice with dinner. An hour later, I complained to my sister that I felt sick. I did not tell my father because I thought that he would tell me to go to bed and then he would check on me. I also thought that he was really smart and might figure out my plan. I went to bed at my usual time but I did not go to sleep. I watched my clock. At 11:05 p.m., I got up and went to the bathroom. I rinsed my mouth out with warm water for about ten minutes. When I heard the garage door go up, I took out the mug. I poured the vomit-look-alike on the floor next to my bed. I put the mug in the drawer and pushed it way in the back. When I heard my mother coming up the basement stairs, I began to whine and call to her. She came upstairs and saw the mess. She asked me what I had eaten and I made a point to tell her that I had orange juice with dinner. Then she took my temperature. It was up a bit. She cleaned up the mess and told me not to worry about getting up in the morning. My plan had worked. (Veronica)

### Control Over the World of Emotions: Temper Tantrums

Some of my data suggests that temper tantrums were viewed as hard times, events over which children felt they had little control. Other data suggests that children could use temper tantrums intentionally, manipulating their emotions as a method for achieving their ends. Although the following story documents failure rather than success, nonetheless it displays a temper tantrum as a strategy for dealing with hard times.

> Talking about temper tantrums is a very easy topic for me. As a child they happened all of the time.
>
> I remember one tantrum in particular. My mother, my sister, and I were on our way to watch the fireworks show in my town on the fourth of July. I was around 3 years old at the time. I was getting tired of walking so I wanted my mother to carry me. I kept bothering her to pick me up, but she refused to do so. I began to cry and jump up and down but she still kept walking. I stopped where I was and held my breath until I turned blue and passed out. Of course after falling face first into the dirt I became conscious again but my mother would still not pick me up. I was furious! (Dawn)

### Control Over the Moral World: Lying and Subterfuge

Despite children's expressed distress at lying and subterfuge, they appear to be capable of using such strategies to their own benefit.

#### Subterfuge for Disliked Clothing

I had a blue polyester, zip-up-the-front outfit. It was short sleeved without a collar, attached to shorts, and on the front pocket was a sea horse. I would've loved to have burnt it, but instead I would always try to lose it. My mom would always manage to find it.... It was easy for her to dress me in and she thought it looked cute — YUCK! I eventually learned to rip the clothes I didn't like because my mom didn't sew so they would end up in the mending hamper for years. (Holly)

#### Subterfuge for Avoiding Disliked Food

At the age of maybe 5 or 6, I started to overcome this difficulty of dinnertime. The rules remained the same but the end solution changed a little. I would still sit there until the meal got cold but when it came to three big mouthfuls I got a little smart. I would take the three mouthfuls and excuse myself from the table. I would then go into the bathroom and spit those three mouthfuls into the toilet. I don't think my mother ever knew, mainly because I used to wiggle around while giving my dog the rest of my dinner. This added to the idea that I had to go to the bathroom....

That was dinner, the same thing every night. (Fern)

### The Special Resource of 'Being Cute'

One resource that children can learn to employ at a very young age is their 'cuteness'.

As a small child, I knew how to get adults to 'approve' of me. It was quite simple ... be cute, do what you're told, and don't question authority. My third grade teacher was a firm believer in my theory — and she loved me! If that old woman only knew how I felt about her, it would break her mean heart. (Amy)

You can't be mad at me. I'm too cute. (anonymous 3-year-old)[2]

Exactly how children learn this strategy and the specifics of how they go about employing it is an intriguing topic for future research.

## Conclusion

The purpose of this paper has been to provide an overview and illustrative findings from a study of 'The hard times of childhood and children's strategies for dealing with them'. Whether or not the stories I have heard and read accurately reflect actual lived experiences, they nonetheless display a wide range of possible children's feelings and actions that are not regularly investigated, taken into account, or even identified in the sociological literature.

Certainly the relation between memories and literal accounts of past events is problematic. To what extent children do endure hard times awaits further empirical study. Findings of the sort described in this paper should, however, facilitate such study. I do want to caution researchers that disclosures of hard times may be problematic for those who disclose them and may involve political issues and serious adult responses, even retaliation.

The discovery of the hard times of childhood brings forward for attention knowledge that is obscured when sociologists separate the study of children from the broader sociological enterprise. I have gathered abundant examples of hard times and, serendipitously, of myriad methods children might use to exert some degree of control over physical, emotional, and moral worlds. The data I have gathered displays children as far more than mere objects in the social world of adults; they emerge as full-fledged social actors in their own right, possessed of a range of pleasures and pains, knowledge and strategies.

A shorter paper, drawn from these materials was presented at the meetings of the Eastern Sociological Society, Boston, MA, March 1990.

## Notes

1  Most of those from whom I have collected data are female. The small number of male respondents have not provided data that differs in any significant way and males who have read versions of this paper have offered not objections but rather examples of the same sort, drawn from their own experiences. Certainly the inclusion of more males is a necessary next research step but it is my suspicion that their inclusion will not significantly alter the findings.
2  Example provided by Erica Cavin.

# Conclusion

*Frances Chaput Waksler*

In the early days of sociology (and of anthropology as well), it was common to view tribal groups (in Africa, Australia, and South America and, in the US, Native Americans) as 'primitive' and 'child-like'. Comparisons of and analogies between children and 'primitives' were common. Nowadays it is recognized that such comparisons minimize the complexity of tribal life. Although tribal social arrangements indeed differ from those of modern-day Western societies, both involve assumptions, beliefs, knowledge, science, and practical action *as those are defined by participants*. Differences can be recognized without necessitating a judgment that one way is in any absolute sense better or truer than another.

Just as it has turned out that tribal societies are not 'child-like', it may be that children themselves are not either. Rather, the idea may be an adult stereotype of children, a stereotype that facilitates adult control and an adult assumption of superiority. In many respects the children encountered in the foregoing pages have not been 'child-like' but, rather, competent actors in the social world, creating and transmitting lore (Opies); telling stories (Sacks); displaying aesthetic concerns and creating art (Cavin); even participating in drug-taking (Adlers); encountering 'hard times' and developing ways of dealing with them (Waksler); and possessing a variety of ways of 'being in the world' (Mandell, Goode). Indeed, when children appear child-like it may be that they are playing a role expected by adults rather than displaying some necessary, age-related characteristics.

The readings and my commentary on them that constitute this book offer a variety of ways to approach the understanding of children's experiences in and of the social world. Fundamental to this understanding is the recognition of the many ways that adult biases impede such understanding — biases that are often hard to avoid because in everyday life adults regularly take them for granted and use them unreflectively. These assumptions that adults make about children are crucially important to bring forward and identify if adult behavior towards children and children's behavior towards adults is to be understood. Only by articulating such assumptions and setting them as topics of empirical research, and as potentially falsifiable, is it possible to understand the varieties of children's possible behavior and the alternative adult stances that can be taken. Such assumptions are not sociological *knowledge*; they *are* topics for sociological research.

I have sought to present children as *actors* in social worlds, in many ways faced with the same kinds of issues and concerns that adult actors face. If the adult view of children as immature and but partially developed is set aside, children emerge as full-fledged actors in the social world, drawing on the resources they possess to make sense out of and act in the worlds that confront them and to create social worlds of their own.

Against the background of the range and depth of children's competence, the idea of socialization as a process of creating group members emerges as a process that would seem to *require* children's participation, whether that participation is actually recognized or not. Children's views of this process might fruitfully be studied. Socialization as a process of creating a self also requires re-examination. If children are active participants in the creation of their own selves, then the nature of that participation becomes available for detailed examination. Sociological focus on adults as determinative of this process seems questionable in the light of Mackay's explicit and Sacks' implicit recognition of the competence which children must have *in order to understand the very things they are being taught and in order to do the very things they do.*

Given children's competence, socialization also emerges as but one aspect of children's experiences. By dividing the sociological understanding of children into two spheres, 1) children in adult worlds and 2) children in child's worlds, it becomes possible to move beyond socialization. The former sphere embodies an adult perspective towards children, with socialization as one such adult perspective; the latter adopts children's perspectives. Both are important, for children inhabit both worlds, but they are not the same. Sociological study has focused primarily on the former, taking it to be the only possible view of children rather than merely one view. I have sought to preserve the insights of studies that adopt an adult perspective (as exemplified by those presented in Part II) while noting the value of studies of children in their own worlds (as exemplified by the articles in Part III). The description of children from an adult perspective is clearly important sociological data, but just as clearly it is partial, not complete. Recognition of its partiality allows for the consideration of children in their own worlds and opens up other possibilities, such as children's views of adults' worlds (the converse of adults' views of children's worlds).

Studying children against the background of the ideas presented in this book promises to contribute to the refinement of sociological knowledge about the social world in general. Both the approaches suggested and the findings presented here also have a variety of implications for adults who interact with children, either professionally (as teachers, babysitters, doctors, social workers, etc.) or socially (parents, friends, etc.). Here I simply allude to some such implications.

Insights into adult assumptions about children may prove valuable for those who want to alter their own behavior in relation to children, children's behavior, or both. Bringing assumptions to light allows them to be considered and to be dismissed or adopted as results or judgment recommend.

There are, however, both practical dangers and moral considerations in either denying or recognizing children's experiences.

If children were to be treated like any other person, adults in general and those who spend extensive time with children in particular might find it exceedingly difficult to operate. Adult power would be undermined. Indeed, adults customarily have physical power available as a ready option to convincing children to follow adult rules; foregoing such power would require time and skills that many might find an imposition (were they not simply to see such efforts as ridiculous). Would doctors find their time well spent in obtaining informed consent from a 3-year-old? Such an example may seem silly, but the option currently and routinely selected is to force the child *in spite of* the child's view of the situation. Even where explanations are offered, they are commonly offered as a kindness or a lure, not as a moral obligation, and thus can be overridden if adults deem the situation urgent. Thousands of ways that adults coerce children — many deemed by adults as 'for children's own good' — occur routinely. Taking children seriously as actors in the world suggests that such coercion be reconsidered, with implications that adults may find problematic. Many taken-for-granted assumptions are used to justify adult actions towards children. Perhaps some of the problems that adults experience with adolescents have their source in the increasing inapplicability of adults' assumptions to those who have increasing power to reject being treated like children.

I am not here arguing for granting children adult status, nor am I arguing for the preservation of assumptions about children in order to facilitate adult action. I am suggesting that sociologically fruitful knowledge may present practical problems and am urging that sociological knowlege not be denied but at the same time be adopted with caution as a guide to practical action.

The distinctions I am making here may be clarified by two experiences I had with children while I was in the midst of preparing this book and thus especially sensitive to issues it raises. In the first instance, I walked by a 3-year-old. As I passed his chair, I patted him on the head. Then I stopped and asked, 'Do you mind if I pat you on the head like that?' He considered a moment and then said 'No'. 'Do you like it?' 'Yes'. 'So it's okay if I do it when I walk by?' 'Yes'. My recognition of the presumptuousness of my initial act came from the kind of considerations presented throughout this book.

In the second instance, a 4–year-old was carrying around baby kittens in ways that seemed to me clearly perilous to them. I was not convinced by her claim that 'They like it,' and I attempted, unsuccessfully, to take them away from her and divert her to other activities. She was not about to be convinced of the legitimacy of my argument, nor was I by hers, so in effect I 'pulled rank' and, as an adult and 'bigger', I acted as I saw fit and moved the kittens beyond her reach. Here too I would say I acted against the background of what has been presented in this book, for I *acknowledged* the situation as one in which I could and did use my power. I certainly cannot claim that I did what I did for the child's good or to teach her. I did it for what I saw as the kittens' 'good'.

I have chosen these two incidents with which to conclude in order to make the point that the goal of this book is not to show how children 'ought to be treated' but to suggest the implications of however they are treated. Children are customarily treated simply 'as children'. In the first incident described above, I defined the child as a person; in the second, I defined the child as one with less power, a decision I saw as justified by the kittens' welfare. Whatever the practical advantages and disadvantages of treating children 'like children,' sociological undestanding requires moving beyond such a view to a consideration of children in their own right.

# Appendix I: Rules for Reading and Writing Sociology

*Frances Chaput Waksler*

## Introduction

I wrote a version of 'Rules for reading and writing sociology' some years ago in order to provide a common body of knowledge for students who had varying backgrounds in sociology. Students have found it useful in directing both their reading and writing. I have included it here to serve the same function, as well as to provide one theoretical and methodological framework within which to consider the materials in this book and to give guidance to those unfamiliar with sociology. Readers will find that the rules I set forth are followed more closely by the authors whose works comprise this book than they are by sociologists in general.

Although certain fundamental ideas are shared by many sociologists, any presention of sociology as a unitary and unified discipline contributes to what Mitroff (1974) has called the 'storybook image of science'. Different sociologists indeed 'do' sociology differently and a number of theoretical and methodological frameworks exist. Certainly my own views draw heavily on the works of many other sociologists, but what I present here reflects what I actually do and think when I am doing sociology. Those new to sociology are advised to keep in mind that other sociologists would present somewhat different ideas and give somewhat different emphases. (Indeed teachers using this book as a textbook might want to write and substitute their own 'Rules for reading and writing sociology'.)

The perspective on sociology that I take draws heavily on phenomenology, the philosophical method developed by Edmund Husserl (1913; see also Kohak, 1978). Phenomenology emphasizes the importance of conducting studies from the point of view of those being studied and encourages researchers to suspend judgments about those studied. Husserl urges respect for 'the originary right of all data', i.e. its existence in its own terms prior to its formulation by investigators.

I define sociology as *that science that systematically studies the social, i.e. the interactions of two or more individuals and the many products of those interactions.* It is a science in the sense that its goal is understanding in and of itself. Towards this end it provides specified procedures that others can reproduce and it develops theories that can be tested by data gathered from the world of everyday life. Other social sciences — psychology, anthropology, history, political science, economics — are concerned with the social, but only for sociology is it the subject matter, the central topic of investigation.

Sociology is concerned with individuals as *vehicles of social behavior*. In contrast, individuals *as* individuals are the subject matter of psychology. Sociology studies interactions that take place between and among individuals — in face-to-face situations, over the telephone, through the mail, etc. and in the myriad circumstances in which individuals exchange ideas. It also examines the social arrangements and institutions that individuals together create, sustain, and destroy — everything from parties to international governments.

## The Rules

Different views of sociology produce different rules for how sociology is to be done, how the works of others are to be read and understood, and how one's own work is to be written. Often such rules are implicit in the work of sociologists. I seek here to articulate the rules I use and that emerge from my view of sociology. They are designed to provide a perspective from which to read critically the works of others and to assess one's own sociological writings.

I have identified eight rules:

Rule 1:  Be constantly alert for taken-for-granted assumptions both of sociologists and of those being studied.
Rule 2:  Draw inferences carefully.
Rule 3:  Beware of the magical use of variables.
Rule 4:  Suspend both belief and doubt about everything that can be seen/heard/read.
Rule 5:  Make sociological claims that are falsifiable.
Rule 6:  Distinguish between what is and what ought to be.
Rule 7:  Distinguish between what people say and what they do.
Rule 8.  Respect the originary right of all data.

For purposes of clarity, these rules are stated here in formal and absolute terms, but any of these rules is open to revision if it is found to distort the data that it is designed to explain. Some of the rules may initially appear problematic, but readers are urged to try using them before assessing their usefulness. When, in reading or writing, one finds any of these rules to have been violated, one can reasonably ask two questions: 1) has the writer in some way distorted the data and thus broken the rule? or 2) does the rule need revision?

> *Rule 1: Be constantly alert for taken-for-granted assumptions both of sociologists and of those being studied*

Identification of taken-for-granted assumptions is a part of both the goal and the method of sociology as I conceive of it. As a goal of sociology, it provides sociologists with data that would otherwise be missed, enabling them to unearth a wide range of new topics for study. As a method, identification of such assumptions enables sociologists to recognize possible sources of bias and overcome them.

Our everyday lives take place against the background of a host of assumptions that we take for granted. A number of different strategies can be used to bring them into our awareness. One involves transforming statements of fact into questions for *empirical* investigation. (*Empirical* refers to those features of the world that can be observed and documented.) A common, but to my mind inappropriate, place for research to begin — a place that embodies a host of taken-for-granted assumptions — is with an unexamined claim that something exists. Consider, for example, the following four questions that might serve as topics for research:

Why do women have more trouble with math than men?
Why do people look like their dogs?
Why is divorce on the increase?
Why do children have difficulty understanding death?

Starting research without examining taken-for-granted assumptions on which research questions are based, and thus without examining the legitimacy of the initial questions, can lead researchers off on false trails. Although the above four questions may appear reasonable, and can perhaps be supported by a host of common-sense explanations, in the absence of actual empirical investigation we cannot, as sociologists, claim that the assumptions they embody are indeed accurate. Those embarking on a study based on any of these four questions might profitably begin by rephrasing as follows:

Do women have more trouble with math than men?
Do people look like their dogs?
Is divorce on the increase?
Do children have difficulty understanding death?

Such rephrasing makes empirical investigation possible. And if, for example, study demonstrates that divorce is not on the increase or that children do not have particular difficulty in understanding death, one is saved from having looked for reasons to explain something that doesn't exist.

Anyone who has begun writing a paper to prove a point and then found that one's initial ideas were in error knows the frustration and the sense of having wasted time. Neither distorting the data nor giving up is a fully satisfactory solution. The way to avoid such a problem is to phrase one's initial topic in such terms that any data gathered, whether supportive or destructive of one's initial ideas, can be used as new information about how the social world works. Even the most obvious of statements, those assumed to be unquestionably true in everyday life according to the canons of common sense, may, under empirical investigation, turn out to be false or to require modification.

One of my students carried out a modest study designed initially to explain why people look like their dogs. At my suggestion, she reformulated her topic and pursued the question: Do people look like their dogs? She took separate pictures of people and their dogs and asked respondents to match up the correct pairs. Preliminary results suggested that the task was far more difficult than everyday common-sense theories would predict. It seems that if one sees people and dogs together, one can find common features that support the view that they look alike, but when people and their dogs are separated, those common features are not obvious enough to allow for ready reuniting. Had the study pursued the question of *why* people look like their dogs, the findings would have been meaningless.

Another approach for increasing awareness of the sphere of the taken-for-granted involves the constant repetition of the question: *How do I know that?* This question directs one again and again to the evidence, or lack of evidence, for claims being made. Unsupported statements emerge as assumptions rather than as facts and thus become available for empirical testing.

Another useful technique is to adopt a 'Martian perspective', to pretend that one is an absolute stranger to any situation one is studying and that one must question everything that happens. Questioning can produce abundant and detailed information that would remain concealed if one were simply to assume that one 'knows' what is going on. A Martian perspective is a way of pretending that one doesn't know anything; a surprising result of such a stance is that one learns that one indeed didn't know a great deal.

What initially seems obvious can, with questioning, turn out to be far from obvious. For example, in our everyday lives we know what people mean when they say 'Hello. How are you?' and we know that the correct response in general is 'Fine, thank you. How are you?' To direct questions to this pair of utterances, however, is to embark on a study of a complex set of taken-for-granted assumptions and interrelated meanings. Consider how one might teach a Martian to use this greeting pattern. Under what circumstances is it appropriate? inappropriate? How does one decide? If one goes to a doctor because one is ill and the doctor asks 'How are you?' the response 'Fine, thank you. How are you?' might seem distinctly odd. A close examination of greetings would disclose many rules that are far from obvious.

Researchers can also gain insights into that which is taken for granted by studying instances of rule-breaking. Rules that are taken for granted when all is running smoothly come into view when they are broken. Embarrassment, anger, outrage, insult, or a diffuse sense that 'something is wrong' suggest that rules of some kind are being broken or challenged. When embarrassment, anger, etc. appear, it is sociologically useful to inquire into the source of such responses. One strategy researchers use to establish the existence of a social rule is to engage in behavior that would be a violation of that rule if indeed it existed and then chronicle the responses. Harold Garfinkel (1967) suggested that there were social rules for how close people could stand to one another when talking. To test this claim, he asked students to talk to people and at the same time to move closer and closer to them. The responses of those others suggested that indeed there are social rules for 'talking distance'.

Humor is another invaluable aid in bringing to light the taken-for-granted. A fundamental element in humor is the violation of assumptions. The surprise of humor is the surprise of the unexpected. Humor can bring to light assumptions and problems that are obscured by a more serious interpretation. When I am constructing a questionnaire and want to assess elements in it that might embody taken-for-granted assumptions, I administer the questionnaire to people I know who have senses of humor and are willing to bring them to bear on my task. Their humorous interpretations make clear to me alternative understandings of which I was previously unaware.

Identification of taken-for-granted assumptions seems to be of necessity a never-ending task. Nonetheless, every assumption that is identified contributes to our understanding of the social world.

### Rule 2: Draw inferences carefully

Little that goes on in the social world is directly observable. Routinely there is a gap between what is seen and what it is taken to mean, a gap that is filled by inferences. I can see a baby crying but I can only infer the reason or meaning. Our everyday conversations are filled with talk of inferences, of drawing the link between what was done and what it meant. Gossip, for example, can be seen as a quest for meaning in the face of a variety of possible inferences.

The same behavior can have a variety of meanings; selecting one meaning over another in any particular situation involves inferences. In everyday life, inferences are made on the basis of our past experiences and knowledge, our 'common sense', our hopes and fears and beliefs, and anything else we can bring to bear on our search for understanding. What does a baby's first smile mean? Pleasure? Gas? Both are inferences, based on behavior *and an interpretation of that behavior*. Given the essential ambiguity of all behavior and the tentativeness of all inferences, it is particularly important for sociological knowledge that researchers display great care in drawing inferences if they are to 'do science' rather than simply rephrase common sense.

Inferences are embodied in our everyday language in such a way that they may be obscured: I frown and you see my frown as a 'response' to something you did. You yell and I 'react' by crying. Built into, though obscured, by such terms is an inference: that the behavior of one person *caused* the action of the other. But do we know this? Perhaps I was frowning at something I was thinking. Perhaps I was crying because I was unhappy even before you started yelling. Sociological knowledge requires pursuing issues beyond common-sense inferences. One way to minimize the inferences in descriptions of observations is to refuse to use words that embody inferences — words like 'response' and 'reaction' and 'cause' — and to struggle with and gain insight from the resolution of the problems that thus arise.

Another way to be cautious in the use of inferences is to seek out multiple inferences to explain any given behavior rather than stopping with the first explanation that comes to hand. The baby is crying. How many factors might be identified as *possible* reasons? The first reason or the obvious reason is not necessarily the 'real' reason. Identification of a variety of possible explanations provides a broader base for further investigation. It also recognizes that humans act on the basis of a wide variety of motives, that more than one motive can be involved in any given act, that the motives that one person can attribute to others are not necessarily the motives that those people attribute to their own acts, and that motives can be applied to actions both before and after the acts themselves. The answer to the question: Why did you do that? can, and does, change over time. When, for example, students are asked at the time they begin college and again after graduation why they chose the college they did, their answers are likely to be quite different.

In studying inferences, it is important for sociologists to recognize both the inferences made by those they are studying and the inferences they as sociologists are making. Those made by people in their everyday lives are one of the fundamental topics of sociological study; those made by sociologists, on the other hand, can distort data unless unnecessary inferences are eliminated and necessary ones articulated so that their use is open to scrutiny.

### Rule 3: Beware of the magical use of variables

Sociologists, along with all other scientists, regularly employ variables in their analysis. A *variable* is any characteristic that can have two or more values, e.g. gender (male/female), barometric pressure (rising/falling/steady), age, religion. The values of a variable may be quantitative (expressed in numbers, e.g. height, years of school completed) or qualitative (expressed in words, e.g. season of the year, country of birth). As sociological studies have cumulated, a number of variables that seem particularly important in explaining social behavior have been identified. Such variables include age, sex, race, ethnicity, religion, social class, marital status, and education. People who share one value of one of these characteristics (e.g. a particular religion) may share a host of other social characteristics as well. Note, however, that they *may* share these characteristics; in no sense do they *have to*. In sociological phrasing one would say that people who are members of the same religion are *likely* to possess certain other attributes. The famous nineteenth century sociologist Emile Durkheim found, for example, that Protestants were more likely to commit suicide than were Catholics and that married women and single men were more likely to commit suicide than single women and married men.

The frequent importance of a certain variable or cluster of variables in understanding certain kinds of social behavior has, however, often led to their being invoked in a somewhat magical way as a source of explanation. Slight differences between males and females, blacks and whites, upper and lower class members, etc. have at times been given inordinate significance. Some sociologists routinely collect information about a whole set of rather standard variables and upon occasion try to use them to explain behavior that might well be more satisfactorily understood in terms of less common or more subtle kinds of variables.

Caution in the use of variables begins with a renunciation of the practice of gathering data on a programmatic set of variables just because other sociologists do so. Certainly there are times when it is reasonable to suspect that the most commonly used variables will be useful in analyzing a particular topic, but equally certain is that there are times when such variables have no apparent significance. It is in these latter instances that I speak of variables being used in a magical way, for they are being treated as having some special explanatory power over and above what reason would suggest.

Any variable, but particularly those variables most commonly used by sociologists, can embody common-sense, everyday assumptions about what aspects of the social world are of greatest importance. To use such variables may be to perpetuate rather than study common-sense ideas. Thus common sense tells us that men and women will differ in spheres where sociological study might demonstrate they do not differ, but unless room is made for this latter finding to emerge, it will not. Thus men and women do indeed differ in some characteristics but the routine use of gender as a variable in sociological studies suggests, quite inaccurately, that they differ in all characteristics. Reports of opinion polls, for example, may state that men approve of one political candidate while women do not. Such a claim may be heard as suggesting that 100 per cent of the men and 0 per cent of the women expressed approval. When one examines the percentages on which such a claim is based, however, it may turn out that 60 per cent of the men but only 40 per cent of the women expressed approval. What is ignored is that 40 per cent of the women and men gave the same response and only 20 per cent did not.

If some variables have come to be used in a magical fashion by sociologists, those variables that are quantifiable (i.e. able to be expressed in numbers) have come to be used as if they had especially magical features, as if in some sense being quantifiable is better than being unquantifiable. Certainly quantifiable variables possess advantages for analysis: numbers are a convenient form for presenting findings, they make the collation of data a relatively easy task, and they can be manipulated statistically. Anyone faced with sociological results in quantitative form (e.g. those derived from a questionnaire where all the responses are given in numbers) and pages and pages of descriptive field notes will, for ease of the task, choose the former to work with, but ease does not necessarily mean good. Nonetheless, a common-sense assumption exists that numerical or quantitative distinctions are scientific and descriptive or qualitative ones are not.

Indeed it is useful at times to be able to give numbers to variables but in no sense is such a practice necessarily scientific. Qualitative information, presented in qualitative form, can be equally scientific. Quantitative data can, for example, allow a sample to be drawn from a population in such a way that it is possible to make statistical claims about the frequency with which something will occur in that population. Quantitative data, however, cannot provide the kind of information on what, how, or why something occurs that qualitative data can provide.

So strong is the bias in favor of quantitative findings that qualitative findings may be expressed in terms that suggest a quantitative basis to claims that in fact is absent. To argue on the basis of qualitative, descriptive studies where sampling or the study of an entire population has not been done that something has occurred 'usually', 'often', etc. or that something is true of 'most', 'many', 'the majority', or 'few' of those studied is meaningless. For example, if I find in my college class of twenty students that ten ask questions in class and ten do not, to say that 'half' of the students ask/do not ask questions does not tell me anything additional. If eleven bring coffee to class and nine do not, to say that 'the majority' does so is, although true, actually a distortion of the data, for 'the majority' sounds like more. Furthermore, formulation in terms of 'most', 'the majority', etc. seems to lend itself to generalization to the college as a whole or even to college students as a whole. On the basis of the example just presented, there is some tendency to understand that data as meaning that the majority of college students bring coffee to class. Clearly such a claim could only be made reliably by studying the entire population of college students or a sample drawn from that population.

When qualitative studies focus on intensive investigation of small numbers of people, the dangers of using variables magically become particularly acute. In a small study it is impossible to determine which activities and ideas are influenced by age, sex, race, etc., which by personality, and which by the particular social context being studied. An intensive study of a small number of mothers and their children, for example, cannot establish which findings are related to the roles of mother and child and which to a host of other variables. That the research is focused on mothers does not mean that the observed behavior of the mothers is caused by or even influenced by their 'motherness', rather than by their age, their 'womanness', or social expectations.

What one can say on the basis of studies of small numbers of people is that the observed activities indeed took place in the ways in which they were observed to take place. Things happened that would not have been seen and thus known about if such observations hadn't been done. Sociologists thus can learn what actions are *possible* in specific contexts — not necessary or likely but simply possible. To discover what people do is an important outcome of sociological study. The findings may not provide information about frequency, but in sacrificing such knowledge one can gain detailed understanding about how particular activities can be engaged in. Such knowledge is necessarily prior to quantification, for it is impossible to know *how many* until one knows how many *whats*. Ultimately the question of 'how many' may turn out to be far less important than questions related to alternative possibilities that exist in the social world.

Sociologists are equally concerned with those things that are true of many people and those that are true of a few. Common features and alternative, less common ones are equally important socially and sociologically. Qualitative data that provides information not about how many people act in certain ways but about the alternative ways in which people act can be both scientific and useful for understanding the social world. To learn *what* happens and *how* is as valuable, as difficult, as scientific, and as sociological as to learn how frequently it happens. Qualitative studies are particularly valuable in providing information about the many *different* ways that people act.

*Rule 4: Suspend both belief and doubt about everything that can be seen/heard/read*

This rule advocates a critical stance. To be critical is not, however, to find fault with everything. Neither gullibility nor cynicism alone is as fruitful a sociological approach as is the suspension of both belief and doubt. Such suspension is particularly important in conducting sociological studies, for it makes it possible to take seriously the views of those being studied without necessarily either accepting or rejecting those views. Judgment is suspended in the service of understanding.

Such suspension is not necessarily useful in the conduct of our everyday lives, for everyday actions are routinely based on judgments and choices, on ideas, beliefs, values, and desires. Without judgment, choice is meaningless if not impossible. In everyday life, for example, one might quite reasonably be a follower of one religion and find another religion strange or wrong or even dangerous. For a sociologist to take such a stance, however, would be to distort data gathered on either of those religions. In sociology, judgment on the part of the sociologist interferes with understanding data in its own terms. When sociologists suspend their own judgments, those being studied can be viewed in their own terms and in light of their own values. The goal of sociology as a science is to understand social behavior, not to catalogue sociologists' different judgments about that data.

A critical stance involves a weighing of all evidence. It also involves a recognition that others may come to different conclusions, not because others are wrong but simply because they are different. If one finds another's ideas strange, unbelievable, or unimaginable, such does not mean that the other finds them so. Others may hold their ideas just as seriously and sincerely as one holds one's own. Or they may not. Either is possible.

There is a particular temptation to believe the printed word: 'Of course it's true. I read it in a book.' A particularly extreme instance of the power of the written word can be seen in the following interchange between a doctor and patient, presented by Oakley in her sociological study of childbirth:

> Doctor [reading case notes]:   Ah, I see you've got a boy and a girl.
> Patient:   No, two girls.
> Doctor:   Really, are you sure? I thought it said ... [checks in case notes] oh no, you're quite right, two girls.
>
> (Oakley, 1980: 41)

Truth is not a necessary outcome of the process of writing something down. Printed ideas can be wrong. They can even be a product of deceit. In critically assessing sociological material it is appropriate to base decisions on evidence that can be documented and can be reproduced by others. Although this task is by no means easy and perhaps never entirely successful, it serves as a goal that is at least partially realizable and fruitful even in approximation.

There can also be a temptation to believe and accept the point of view of those people and groups one is studying and about whom one is gathering data. Clearly subjects of a study have specialized knowledge about their own beliefs and activities, but their knowledge is not the only knowledge available. It is one thing to believe that one's subjects of study are sincere and quite another to believe that they are correct. Indeed sociologists studying categories and groups with perspectives that differ from one another may find themselves agreeing with whatever group they are currently studying. As a temporary strategy, belief in one's subjects' perspectives is useful, but in sociological analysis it is important to distinguish between participants' views and other views and to refrain from arranging them hierarchically, from better to worse. The knowledge of sociologists and that of group members being studied is likely to be different — neither knowledge has privileged status for sociologists, for each makes sense in its own sphere. Sociologists' knowledge works for sociology; members' knowledge works for members.

Suspension of belief and doubt, and thus of judgment, although difficult, can provide useful sociological insights. It allows an appreciation of varied points of view and activities and a consequent understanding. It allows the many and contradictory things that people do and say and believe to come into view. It encourages constant questioning of what people do and say and write and read. It brings forward the richness, complexity, and ambiguity of social life as it is lived. It avoids the pitfalls of both gullibility and cynicism while preserving the virtues of both.

### Rule 5: Make sociological claims that are falsifiable

A relatively simple but often violated rule, this one advises the statement of sociological claims, questions, and hypotheses in terms that allow for either yes or no answers, either positive or negative findings, either proof or refutation. Such a rule might at first appear strange. One is tempted to say, 'Of course. Why conduct a study if you already know the answer?' In practice, however, one may find oneself hoping that findings turn out one way rather than another. The hope in itself is not a problem, but designing a study to fulfill rather than to test a hope violates the spirit and method of science.

Studies of highly emotional topics are particularly likely to be constructed in ways that make one kind of finding more likely than another. For example, those who study child abuse may expect 'abusers' to possess a set of 'bad' qualities and may look harder for those qualities than for 'good' ones. Studies of any kind of abuse — whether child, spouse, or drug abuse — are so formulated that the notion of abuse itself is not falsifiable and not a topic of study. The very use of the term 'abuser' stands in the way of understanding the perspective of those so labeled. To study abusers suggests from the outset that such people are 'bad' and can obscure the fact that they may have their own perspectives from which what they do is not abuse but something else, e.g. discipline.

In Rule 1 it was noted that unexamined statements may embody assumptions that, when subjected to critical study, cannot be empirically validated or can indeed be proved erroneous. Unexamined statements may also establish certain claims as unfalsifiable, for one cannot prove false that which remains in the taken-for-granted sphere. Reconsider the question: Why do people look like their dogs? Such a formulation makes it very difficult to find that people do not look like their dogs. Rephrasing the research question in the terms: Do people look like their dogs? makes the claim falsifiable and makes possible the marshalling of data both in support and refutation of the claim.

Statement of topics for study in falsifiable terms is quite easy *once the need for such a form is recognized.* The need, however, although quite apparent in retrospect, is not always so obvious at the start of a study. It is possible for one to begin a study with such a strong taken-for-granted assumption that something is true that the possibility of questioning that beginning point never arises. The advice to state claims in falsifiable terms — even when those claims appear, in common-sense terms, 'obviously' true — directs one to examine statements that otherwise might go unexamined and that may indeed turn out to be false.

### Rule 6: Distinguish between what is and what ought to be

Sociology can be a rich source of surprises about how the social world works, but not all such surprises are pleasant ones. The social world does not always turn out to be the way one hopes it will be. Two different kinds of problems can arise when a discrepancy exists between what is and what either readers of sociology or sociologists themselves think ought to be.

First, when readers are negatively affected by sociologists' findings — shocked, disappointed, saddened — they may direct their negative feelings towards sociologists, somehow holding them responsible for the beliefs and/or actions of those studied. For sociologists to present the views of those studied is not, however, a necessary indication that sociologists do (or, for that matter, do not) hold those views. Sociologists' views of the matter are not at issue, for they are not the subject of study. 'Good' sociologists can study 'bad' things. Sociologists have been criticized for agreeing with those they studied when those sociologists have only reported the views of those studied; sociologists have also been criticized for not speaking out against those they have studied. The Adlers' study of marijuana smoking by children under the age of eight (1978), Humphreys' study of impersonal sex in public restrooms (1970), Letkemann's study of *Crime as Work* (1973), and Roth's study of alternative medicine (1977) are but a few of the studies that have come in for one or both of these kinds of criticism, and in each instance it is clear to me that the authors did no more nor less than simply let the data speak for itself. In reading the works of others, it is helpful to recognize that the relationship between the views of those studied and those of the author are not identical. To present a view is not necessarily to espouse it. In the absence of any explicit statement by the author, inferences about the author's views are risky at best.

Second, in the face of unpleasant findings, one can claim that they must be erroneous because people 'ought not to do that' or 'ought not to be like that'. Although it may be true in some spheres that 'wishing can make it so', such a stance does not advance sociological inquiry. For example, studies that present data about adults who are aroused by and enjoy child pornography may be rejected by some simply because they think that adults ought not to be aroused in such a way. Similarly, studies that suggest that young children who engage in sexual relations with adults may find pleasurable elements in such encounters may be dismissed automatically because of a view that 'children couldn't feel that way' and that since such encounters are judged 'bad', all aspects of them must be bad. A moral view that something ought not to be is not, however, evidence against existence. Scientific refutation requires more than a claim of immorality.

When encountering findings that contradict one's view of what ought to be, one need not accept such findings without question. Studies can be wrong. A common-sense intuition of such wrongness can serve as a useful beginning point in the search for *evidence* to refute claims. Intuition is however a useful beginning point, not a conclusion. I remember hearing a paper presented at the meetings of a sociological association where the presenter was arguing, on the basis of a study conducted, that white men use that part of the brain associated with logic and reason and that black men and women of both races use that part associated with emotion and artistic ability. My own values were severely assaulted by such a finding and I dearly *wanted* it to be wrong. For me, however, the most significant response to the study was an audience member's perceptive and incisive critique of the methodology of the study, a critique that made clear the fallacy of the findings. Although I admit to being relieved by this outcome, I also feel that if the study had been methodologically sound and the findings scientifically justified, I as a sociologist would be compelled to take them into account, like them or not.

What is and what ought to be are both possible topics for sociological analysis. Studies of 'what is' can be conducted through a variety of methods, including direct observation. Studies of 'what ought to be' require somewhat different approaches and are necessarily centered on notions held by members of the social world. As such they cannot be directly observed but require analysis of the talk of those being studied or other such indirect methods. The views of sociologists on 'what ought to be' have no place in their findings even though, as members of society, sociologists may be vitally interested in working towards social change.

One of sociology's strengths is its ability to describe the social world as it is experienced by social members. Members' notions of 'what ought to be' certainly influence actions and thus are legitimate topics of sociological study in their own right. Knowledge of 'what is' also provides a firm foundation for bringing about social change, for it is this dimension of 'what is' that is the very focus of change. The confounding of 'what is' and 'what ought to be' leads to confused findings and impedes both understanding and social change. The clearer the view of 'what is', the more adequately can one work towards bringing about 'what ought to be'.

*Rule 7: Distinguish between what people say and what they do*

In everyday life, we perceive the relationship between talk and action quite differently from the way that sociologists view that relationship. In everyday life, we commonly take what people say as an indicator of what they do or will do or have done. We recognize lying and delusion and changed plans and so forth, so what people say is not *necessarily* what they do, but 'all other things being equal', we expect a strong relationship between reports of action and the action itself.

Given sociologists' concern with identifying taken-for-granted assumptions, it is not surprising that they question the relationship between talk and action as it is characterized in everyday life. Two major reasons for question-ing this relationship can be identified. First, studies that compare what people say with what sociologists can observe them doing demonstrate discrepancies that are far more complex and subtle than what can be attributed to lying or mistakes. The following example, drawn from a study of schizophrenia by Meynell, although extreme, displays with clarity the complexity of the matter:

> Maya said her parents constantly put difficulties in the way of her reading what she wanted, which they denied with laughter. When Maya mentioned her Bible reading as an example, her father, still laughing, asked why she wanted to read the Bible anyway when she could find out about that kind of thing better from other books. Again, the father and mother constantly winked at one another when the whole family was interviewed together. The interviewer com-mented on this after twenty minutes of the interview; *and the parents denied they were doing it, went on doing it, and continued to deny that they were doing it* (Meynell, 1971: 22, emphasis added).

Certainly it is not clear what was going on here — and the author does not explain further — but what *is* clear is that what people say and what they do is not the same.

Second, since there are social rules for talk, and since one of those rules is that concealing or distorting the truth is permissible or even mandated in certain situations, it is evident that talk about what one does will not always or necessarily reflect what one can be observed to do. For example, if I ask students in large sociology class to raise their hands if they have ever snorted cocaine, or if they have engaged in sexual relations in the past twenty-four hours, I would be considered naive if I took the show of hands (or absence thereof) as evidence of those students' behavior. Indeed, 'simply' answering the question truthfully might seem quite strange in such a setting, and even hand-raisers might not be believed.

A useful sociological dictum is: *If you want to know what people do, watch them. If you want to know what they say, ask them.* A common but, to my mind, risky practice is to ask people, e.g. through interviews or question-naires, what they do and then present the findings as if they documented actions rather than talk. Equally risky is the practice of observing what people do and then, on the basis of those observations, presenting as data speculations on people's reasons for their actions. Reasons cannot be observed and claims about one's actions cannot be sociologically substituted for observations of those actions.

Talk and action are both social behavior but in some respects they are different kinds of social behavior. They do different things. In my own work I have recently begun exploring the notion that one function of talk may be to make the social world look more structured and planful and predictable than it can be observed to be, but at this point I mention this idea without documentation simply as one way in which talk and action might differ. Whatever the differences and similarities between talk and action as social behavior, what is clear that they are not the same thing, cannot stand in place of one another, and that neither is reducible to the other. Each is a legitimate topic of sociological study but studying one is not studying the other.

### Rule 8: Respect the originary right of all data

This rule is drawn directly from Husserl's phenomenology. For sociologists it is an affirmation that the data — what one studies — is primary. Data may be complex, ambiguous, strange, apparently irrational, even unbelievable, but even so, the task of sociology is to present the data with those qualities, not to revise and 'clean-up' findings so that they appear 'normal'. Data that in its very nature is ambiguous is distorted if it is presented as if it were unambiguous. Take for example the notion of 'right to life'. It is not uncommon for those who espouse such a position to reject abortion and support capital punishment, thereby not supporting everyone's 'right to life' but only those of the unborn. The very notion of 'right to life' is ambiguous; any study that neglects or defines away or 'corrects' this ambiguity also distorts the data.

This rule also cautions against overgeneralizing or going beyond the data. Even one case or instance can be sociologically significant as one social possibility but one case does not provide any empirical evidence that other cases can be found. Only the actual finding of them can serve as empirical evidence. Generalization is a fundamental aspect of any science but only if it is faithful to the data — all the data but not more than the data — can it be taken as scientifically valid.

The originary right of all data can emerge through a variety of methods. Limiting methods to those that 'look' scientific, e.g. those that produce quantitative results, restricts the full display of data. Any promising method — old or new — directed towards gaining understanding would seem worth a try, success being judged by outcomes, not by appearances or expectations.

### Conclusion

The rules detailed in the foregoing can be used as guides both in conducting studies and in assessing the work of others. In all probability, however, it will be easier to apply these rules to others, for others' failings have a tendency to be clearer than one's own. One's own work can take on the quality of something special to which such criteria do not apply. Nonetheless, applying these rules to others' and one's own work can serve as a critical framework for assessment and revision of ideas. Different readers and writers may well interpret and use these rules in somewhat different ways, so a final caution may serve as a useful guide. In the words of Swami Rama (quoted in Boyd, 1974: 271):

Every person can have his own hypothesis, but one still has to account for the facts.

# Appendix II: Exercises

*Frances Chaput Waksler*

Through the years I have developed a variety of different exercises to accompany the chapters of this book. They can serve as the basis for papers, class presentations, or simply informal discussions and can be carried out at various levels of expertise. Below are listed exercises that have proved useful, instructive, and enjoyable. Further ideas are provided in the index entry 'sociological study, suggestions for'.

### Chapter 1: Becoming a Member of Society — Socialization and Chapter 2: Beyond Socialization

Examine one's own childhood in terms of those things that were taught by agents of socialization. Distinguish between those that were/were not accepted and that do/do not constitute a part of one's present day life. Direct attention to the following questions: Do you do everything you were taught to do, be, think, etc.? How do you choose which teachings to accept and which to reject?

### Chapter 3: Conceptions of Children and Models of Socialization

Gather historical and/or current information on children engaged in productive economic work. (The illegality of child labor in many countries should not obscure the fact that children nonetheless engage in a wide range of productive work activities.) Seek specific details of the work that children can do and use that data as a basis for examining some of the many competencies of children. Child labor laws are one useful source of data.

### Chapter 4: The Least-Adult Role in Studying Children and Chapter 5: Studying Children: Phenomenological Insights

Use these chapters as methodological and theoretical guides in conducting studies of children.

### Chapter 6: Once Upon a Time

Observe the interactions between adult animals and young animals of the same species. Data sources include zoos, pet stores, and the homes of those whose pets have new offspring. Such observations are particularly effective when one is not familiar with the species and thus must determine which are the adults and which the children, which the mothers and which the fathers, e.g. snakes, turtles.

### Chapter 7: Tinydopers: A Case Study of Deviant Socialization

Observe children in an 'adult' setting and identify adults' rules for children in that setting. Justify the choice of setting as 'adult', e.g. children are not 'supposed' to be there (a bar/pub), children are a disturbance (an exclusive expensive restaurant). Consider both adults' rules for children's behavior in such a setting and children's options and resources. Address the questions: Where do children fit in an adult world? What roles are they expected to play?

### Chapter 8: Dancing When the Music is Over: A Study of Deviance in a Kindergarten Classroom

Those who work with children might find it especially helpful, though also difficult, to have their activities studied in the way described in this paper.

### Chapter 9: Watching People Watching Babies

Continue gathering the kind of data described in this study.

### Chapter 10: The Culture of Children

With a group of people, ask participants simply to begin quoting rhymes and demonstrating games remembered from childhood. Urge participants to join in with rhymes and games they know. Those from very different parts of a country or even different countries are able to display shared knowledge.

### Chapter 11: Kids, Culture and Innocents

Provide data to support the claim that some children are not considered children or childlike.

### Chapter 12: Children's Negotiation of Meaning

Following the guidelines set forth in the Concluding Note to this article, examine adults' use of different involvement stances.

### Chapter 13: Children Doing 'Artwork'

Observe children playing a game or engaging in an activity of their own making and describe the rules they use. Such rules can be inferred from behavior or articulated by children in response to questioning. Use of both observations and questioning, although likely to provide discrepant answers, can be especially interesting. Asking children to teach one a game is a particularly useful strategy for data-gathering. If the game under investigation has written rules (often referred to in adult-centric terms as 'real' rules, e.g. board games), such rules can serve as a basis of comparison but should not be used as determinative of correct or incorrect play. Card games played by children who cannot yet read can be especially instructive.

### Chapter 14: On the Analysability of Stories by Children

Listen to adults talking to children who are just learning to talk, focusing on the attributions adults make to children in terms of what they mean. Make detailed transcripts of such conversations and use them to exemplify Sacks' maxims.

### Chapter 15: The Hard Times of Childhood and Children's Strategies for Dealing with Them

Describe memories of one's childhood, with particular emphasis on the 'difficulties' of being a child. What was hard? unfair? unable to be done? Describe any strategies developed to cope with one's 'hard times'. Draw examples from as young an age as possible.

# References

By combining all the bibliographic references cited by all of the authors in this book, it has been possible to prepare an extensive listing of books and articles on children. Although other theoretical and substantive topics are also included, the primary emphasis is on the sociological study of children. Those books from which selections have been made and those articles that appear in this book are indicated by an asterisk (*).

*ADLER, P.A. and ADLER, P. (1978) 'Tinydopers: A case study of deviant socialization', *Symbolic Interaction*, **1**, 2, Spring, pp. 90–104.

ADLER, P.A. and ADLER, P. (1979) 'Symbolic interactionism', in ADLER, P.A., ADLER, P., DOUGLAS, J.D., FONTANA, A., FREEMAN, C.R. and KOTARBA, J., *An Introduction to the Sociologies of Everyday Life*, Boston, Allyn and Bacon.

ADLER, P.A. and ADLER, P. (eds) (1986, 1987a) *Sociological Studies of Child Development*, Vols 1 and 2, Greenwich CT, JAI Press.

ADLER, P.A. and ADLER, P. (1987b) *Membership Roles in Field Research*, Newbury Park, CA, Sage.

ADLER, P.A., ADLER, P. and DOUGLAS, J.D. (forthcoming) 'Organized crime: Drug dealing for pleasure and profit', in DOUGLAS, J.D. (ed.) *Deviant Scenes*.

ARDENER, S. (ed.) (1977) *Perceiving Women*, London, J.M. Dent; New York, Wiley.

ARIES, P. (1962) *Centuries of Childhood: A Social History of Family Life*, New York, Knopf; (1965) Random House; (1969) New York, Vintage; (1973) Penguin.

BATESON, M.C. (1975) 'Mother-infant exchanges: The epigenesis of conversational interaction', in AARONSON, D. and RIEBER, R.W. (eds) *Developmental Psycholinguistics and Communication Disorders*. New York: New York Academy of Science, pp. 101–113.

BAUMRIND, D. (1980) 'New directions in socialization research', *American Psychologist*, **35**, 7, pp. 639–52.

BECKER, H.S.L. (1953) 'Becoming a marijuana user', *American Journal of Sociology*, **59**, November.

BECKER, H.S.L. (1970b) 'Problems of inference and proof in participant observation', *of Sociology*, **66**, pp. 32–40.

BECKER, H.S.L. (1963) *The Outsiders: Studies in the Sociology of Deviance*, New York, Free Press.

BECKER, H.S.L. (1970) *Sociological Work*, New Brunswick, NJ, Transaction Books.

BECKER, H.S.L. (1970a) 'Field work evidence', in *Sociological Work*, New Brunswick, NJ, Transaction Books. pp. 39–62.

BECKR, H.S.L. (1970b) 'Problems of inference and proof in participant observation', in *Sociological Work*, New Brunswick, NJ, Transaction Books, pp. 25–38.

BECKER, H.S.L. (1970c) 'Personal chance in adult life', in *Sociological Work*, New Brunswick, NJ, Transaction Books, pp. 275–88.

BECKER, H.S.L., GEER, B., HUGHES, E.C. and STRAUSS, A.L. (1961) *Boys in White: Student Culture in Medical School*, Chicago, University of Chicago Press.

BEM, D.J. and FUNDER, D.C. (1978) 'Predicting more of the people more of the time: assessing the personality of situations', *Psychological Review*, **85**, pp. 485–501.

*BERGER, P.L. and BERGER, B. (1972, 1975) *Sociology: A Biographical Approach*, 2nd expanded edn, New York, Basic Books.

BERGER, P.L. and LUCKMANN, T. (1966) *The Social Construction of Reality*, Garden City, NY, Doubleday Anchor.

BETTELHEIM, B. (1959) 'Feral and autistic children', *The American Journal of Sociology*, **64**, 5, pp. 455–67.

BJELIĆ, D. (1987) 'On hanging up in telephone conversation', *Semiotica*, **67**, 3/4, pp. 195–210.

BLUM, A. (1970) 'Theorizing', in DOUGLAS, J. (ed.) *Understanding Everyday Life*, Chicago, Aldine.

BLUMER, H. (1969) *Symbolic Interactionism*, Englewood Cliffs, NJ, Prentice-Hall.

BOWER, T.G.R. (1977) *The Perceptual World of the Child*, Cambridge, MA, Harvard University Press.

BOWERS, K. (1973) 'Situations in psychology: an analysis and a critique', *Psychological Review*, **80**, 5, pp. 307–36.

BOYD, D. (1974) *Rolling Thunder*, New York, Dell.

BRAINERD, C. (1977) 'Cognitive development and concept learning: An interpretive review', *Psychological Bulletin*, **84**, pp. 919–39.

BREDEMEIER, M.E. and BREDEMEIER, H.C. (1978) *Social Forces in Education*, Sherman Oaks, CA, Alfred.

BRIDGES, K.M.B. (1931) *Social and Emotional Development of the Preschool Child*, London, Routledge.

BRIM, O.G. (1968) 'Adult socialization', in CLAUSEN, J. (ed.) *Socialization and Society*, Little, Brown.

BROOM, L. and SELZNICK, P. (1968) *Sociology*, 4th edn, McGraw-Hill.

BRUYN, S. (1966) *Human Perspective in Sociology: The Methodology of Participant Observation*, Englewood Cliffs, NJ, Prentice-Hall.

BURNS, N. and CAVEY, L. (1957) 'Age differences in empathic ability among children', *Canadian Journal of Psychology*, **11**, pp. 227–30.

CAHILL, S. (forthcoming) *Sociological Studies of Child Development*, Vol. 4, CT, JAI Press.

CAREY, J.T. (1968) *The College Drug Scene*, Englewood Cliffs, NJ, Prentice-Hall.

CASTANEDA, C. (1971) *A Separate Reality*, Simon and Schuster.

CAVIN, E. (1990) 'Using picture books', in MANDELL, N. (ed.) *Sociological Studies of Child Development*, Vol. 3, Greenwich CT, JAI Press.

CICOUREL, A.V. (1970a) 'Basic and normative rules', in DREITZEL, H.P. (ed.), *Recent Sociology No. 2*, Macmillan.

CICOUREL, A.V. (1970b) 'The acquisition of social structure', in DOUGLAS, J. (ed.), *Understanding Everyday Life*, Chicago, Aldine.

CICOUREL, A.V. (1972) 'Ethnomethodology', in SEBEOK, T.S. *et al.*, (eds) *Current Trends in Linguistics*, **12**, Mouton de Gruyter.

CICOUREL, A.V., JENNINGS, K.H., JENNINGS, S.H., LEITER, C.C.W., MACKAY, R., MEHAN, H. and ROTH, D.R. (1974), *Language Use and School Performance*, New York, Academic Press.

CLAUSEN, J. (1968) 'Introduction', in CLAUSEN, J. (ed.) *Socialization and Society*, Little, Brown.

COENEN, H. (1986) 'A silent world of movements: Interactional processes among deaf children', in COOK-GUMPERZ, J., CORSARO, W.A. and STREECK, J. (eds) *Children's Worlds and Children's Language*, Berlin, Mouton de Gruyter, pp. 253–87.

COOK-GUMPERZ, J. and CORSARO, W. (1977) 'Social-ecological constraints on children's communicative strategies', *Sociology*, **11**, 3, pp. 411–34.

COOLEY, C.H. (1922) *Human Nature and the Social Order*, New York, Charles Scribner's Sons.

CORSARO, W. (1979a) 'We're friends right: Children's use of access rituals in a nursery school', *Language in Society,* **8**, pp. 315–36.

CORSARO, W. (1979b) 'Young children's conceptions of status and role', *Sociology of Education*, **52**, pp. 46–59.

CORSARO, W. (1981) 'Entering the child's world: Research strategies for field entry and data collection in a preschool setting', in GREEN, J. and WALLAT, C. (eds) *Ethnography and Language in Educational Settings*, Norwood, NJ, Ablex, pp. 117–46.

CORSARO, W. (1985) *Friendship and Peer Culture in the Early Years*, Norwood, NJ, Ablex.

COTTRELL, L. and DYMOND, R. (1949) 'The empathetic responses: A neglected field for research', *Psychiatry*, **13**, pp. 355–9.

COUCH, C. (1970) 'Dimensions of association in collective behaviour episodes', *Sociometry*, **33**, 4, pp. 457–71.

COUTU, W. (1951) 'Role-playing vs. role-taking: An appeal for clarification', *American Sociological Review*, **16**, pp. 180–7.

DAMON, W. (1977) *The Social World of the Child*, San Francisco, Jossey-Bass.

DENZIN, N. (1970a) *The Research Act*, Chicago, Aldine.

DENZIN, N. (1970b) *Sociological Methods: A Sourcebook*, Chicago, Aldine.

DENZIN, N.K. (1972) 'The genesis of self in early childhood', *The Sociological Quarterly,* **13**, Summer, pp. 291–314.

DENZIN, N.K. (1973) *Children and Their Caretakers*, New Brunswick, NJ, Transaction Books.

DENZIN, N.K. (1975) 'Play, games and interaction: The contexts of childhood socialization', *The Sociological Quarterly,* **16**, pp. 458–78.

DENZIN, N.K. (1977, 1979) *Childhood Socialization*, San Francisco, Jossey-Bass.

DENZIN, N.K. (1980) 'A phenomenology of emotion and deviance', *Zeitschrift fur Sociologie*, **9**, 3, pp. 25–261.

DEVILLIERS, P.A. and DEVILLIERS, G.J. (1977) *Early Language*, Cambridge, MA, Harvard University Press.

DEVRIES, R. (1970) 'The development of role-taking as reflected by the behavior of bright, average and retarded children in a social guessing game', *Child Development*, **41**, September, pp. 759–70.

DOUGLAS, J.D. (1970) 'Deviance and respectability: The social construction of moral meanings', in DOUGLAS, J.D. (ed.), *Deviance and Respectability*, New York, Basic Books.

DOUGLAS, J.D. (1976) *Investigative Social Research*, Beverly Hills, Sage.

DOUGLAS, J.D. and WAKSLER, F.C. (1982) *The Sociology of Deviance: An Introduction*, Boston, Little, Brown.

ELKIN, F. and HANDEL, G. (1960) *The Child and Society: The Process of Socialization*, New York, Random House.

ELLIS, M.J. (1973) *Why People Play*, Englewood Cliffs, NJ, Prentice-Hall.

ERIKSON, E. (1950) *Childhood and Society*, New York, Norton.

ERIKSON, E. (1968) *Identity, Youth and Crisis*, New York, Norton.

EMERSON, R.M. (1981) 'Observational field work', *Annual Review of Sociology*, **7**, pp. 351–78.

FEFFER, M.H. and GOUREVITCH, V. (1960) 'Cognitive aspects of role-taking in children', *Journal of Personality*, **28**, pp. 383–96.

FEIN, G.G. and CLARKE-STEWART, A. (1973) *Day Care in Context*, New York, Wiley.

FELDMAN, D.H. (1980) *Beyond Universals in Cognitive Development*, Norwood, NJ, Ablex.

FINE, G.A. (1979) 'Small groups and the creation of culture: determinants of the development of idio culture', *American Sociological Review*, **44**, October, pp. 733–45.

FINE, G.A. (1987) *With the Boys*, Chicago, University of Chicago Press.

FINE, G.A. and GLASSNER, B. (1979) 'Participant observation with children: Promise and problems', *Urban Life*, **8**, pp. 153–74.

FISCHER, J. and FISCHER, A (1963) 'The New Englanders of Orchard Town, USA', in WHITING, B. (ed.) *Six Cultures: Studies in Child Rearing*, New York, Wiley.

FLAVELL, J.H. (1968) *The Development of Role-Taking and Communication Skills in Children*, New York, Wiley.

FLETCHER, R. (1971) *The Making of Sociology: A Study of Sociological Theory, Vol. 2: Developments*, London, Michael Joseph.

FREUD, S. (n.d.; first published in German in 1930) *Civilization and its Discontents*, Garden City, NY, Doubleday Anchor.

GANS, H.J. (1968) 'The participant observer as a human being: Observations on the personal aspects of field work', in BECKER, H.S. *et al.* (eds) *Institutions and the Person*, Chicago, Aldine, pp. 300–17.

GARFINKEL, H. (1967) *Studies in Ethnomethodology*, Englewood Cliffs, NJ, Prentice-Hall; Cambridge, UK, Polity Press.

GARFINKEL, H. (1976) Personal communication. Department of Sociology, U.C.L.A.

GARVEY, C. (1977) *Play*, Cambridge, MA, Harvard University Press.

GARVEY, C. and BERNDT, R. (1975) 'The organization of pretend play', paper presented at the annual meeting of the American Psychological Association, Chicago.

GEER, B. (1967) 'First days in the field', in HAMMOND, P. (ed.) *Sociologists at Work*, New York, Basic Books, pp. 370–98.

GEER, B., HAAS, J., VIVONA, C., MILLER, S.J., WOODS, C. and BECKER, H.S. (1968) 'Learning the ropes: Situational learning in four occupational training programs', in DEUTSCHER, I. and THOMPSON, E. (eds), *Among the People: Encounters with the Poor*, New York, Basic, pp. 209–13.

GEER, B. (1970) 'Studying a college', in HABENSTEIN, R.W. (ed.) *Pathways to Data*, Chicago, Aldine, pp. 81–89.

GLASER, B.G. and STRAUSS, A.R. (1967) *The Discovery of Grounded Theory*, Chicago, Aldine.

GLASSNER, B. (1976) 'Kid Society', *Urban Education*, **11**, 1, pp. 5–21.

GOFFMAN, E. (1959) *Presentation of Self in Everyday Life*, New York, Doubleday.

GOFFMAN, E. (1961) *Asylums*, New York, Anchor.

GOFFMAN, E. (1963) *Behavior in Public Places*, New York, Free Press.

GOFFMAN, E. (1967) 'Embarrassment and social organization', in his *Interaction Ritual: Essays on Face-to-Face Behavior*, Garden City, NY, Doubleday and Co., pp. 97–112.

GOFFMAN, E. (1971) *Relations in Public*, New York, Harper Colophon.

GOLD, R. (1969) 'Roles in sociological field observations', in MCCALL, G. and SIMMONS, J.L. (eds) *Issues in Participant Observation*, Reading, MA, Addison-Wesley, pp. 30–38.

GOLDING, W. (1955; 1959) *Lord of the Flies*, Coward-McCann; New York, Putnam's.

GOLDMAN, B.D. and ROSS, H.S. (1978) 'Social skills in action: An analysis of early peer games', in GLICK, J. and CLARKE-STEWART, K.A. (eds), *The Development of Social Understanding*, New York, Gardner, pp. 177–212.

GOODE, D.A. (1979) 'The world of the congenitally deaf-blind', in SCHWARTZ, H. and

JACOBS, J. (eds) *Qualitative Sociology: A Method to the Madness*, New York, Free Press.

GOODE, D.A. (1983) 'Who is Bobby? Ideology and method in the discovery of a Downs' syndrome person's competence', in KIELHOFNER, G. (ed.), *Health through Occupation*, Philadelphia, F.A. Davis.

GOODE, D.A. (1984) 'Socially produced identities, intimacy and the problem of competence among the retarded', in TOMLINSON, S. and BARTON, L. (eds) *Special Education and Interests*, London, Croom-Helm.

*GOODE, D.A. (1986) 'Kids, culture, and innocents', *Human Studies*, **9**, 1, pp. 83–106.

GOODE, D.A. and GADDY, M.P. (1976) 'Ascertaining client choice in alingual, deaf-blind retarded', *Mental Retardation*, December.

GOODE, D.A. and WAKSLER, F.C. (1989) 'A case of profound ambivalence', unpublished manuscript.

GOODE, D.A. with WAKSLER, F.C. (1990) 'The missing "who": Situational identity and fault-finding with an alingual blind-deaf child', in MANDELL, N. (ed.) *Sociological Studies of Child Development*, Vol. 3, Greenwich CT, JAI Press.

GOODE, E. (1969) *Marijuana*, New York, Atherton.

GOODE, E. (1970) *The Marijuana Smokers*, New York, Basic Books.

GOTTLIEB, D. (1973) *Children's Liberation*, Englewood Cliffs, NJ, Prentice-Hall.

GOUGH, H.G. (1948) 'A sociological theory of psychopathy', *American Journal of Sociology*, March, pp. 359–366.

GRINSPOON, L. (1971) *Marihuana Reconsidered*, Cambridge, MA, Harvard University Press.

GRUPP, S.E. (ed.) (1971) *Marihuana*, Columbus, OH, Charles E. Merrill.

GRUPP, S.E. (1973) *The Marihuana Muddle*, Lexington, MA, Lexington Books.

GUSFIELD, J.R. (1967) 'Moral passage: The symbolic process in public designations of deviance', *Social Problems*, **15**, II, Fall.

HALL, E.T. (1959) *The Silent Language*, Greenwich, CT, Fawcett Publications.

HENRY, J. (1964) *Culture Against Man*, New York, Random House.

HERRON, R.E. and SUTTON-SMITH, B. (eds) (1971) *Child's Play*, New York, Wiley.

HOCHMAN, J.S. (1972) *Marijuana and Social Evolution*, Englewood Cliffs, NJ, Prentice-Hall.

HOCHSCHILD, A. (1975) 'The sociology of feeling and emotion: Selected possibilities', in MILLMAN, M. and KANTER, R.M., *Another Voice*, Garden City, NY, Doubleday, pp. 280–307.

HOFFMAN, M. (1976) 'Empathy, role-taking, guilt and development of altruistic motives', in LICKONA, T. (ed.) *Moral Development and Behavior*, New York, Holt, Rinehart and Winston.

HOLT, J. (1969) *The Underachieving School*, Dell Publishing; Penguin, 1971.

HORTON, P.B. and HUNT, C.L. (1968) *Sociology*, 2nd edn, McGraw-Hill.

HUGHES, E.C. (1945) 'Dilemmas and contradictions of status', *American Journal of Sociology*, **L** (March) pp. 353–59 and cited in BECKER, H.S. (1963), *Outsiders: Studies in the Sociology of Deviance*, New York, Free Press, p. 32.

HUGHES, E.C. (1958) *Men and Their Work*, Glencoe, IL, Free Press.

HUGHES, E.C. (1960) 'Introduction', in JUNKER, B. *Field Work*, Chicago, University of Chicago Press.

HUGHES, R. (1928; 1929) *A High Wind in Jamaica*, New York, Harper and Row.

HUMPHREYS, L. (1970; 1975) *Tearoom Trade: Impersonal Sex in Public Places*, Chicago, Aldine.

HUSSERL, E. (1913, 1962) *Ideas: General Introduction to Pure Phenomenology*, New York, Collier Books. (First published in German, 1913.)

INKELES, A. (1966) 'Social structure and the socialization of competence', *Harvard Educational Review*, **36**, 3.

INKELES, A. (1968) 'Society, social structure and child socialization', in CLAUSEN, J. (ed.) *Socialization and Society*, Boston, MA, Little, Brown.

ISAACS, S. (1952) *Social Development in Young Children*, Routledge and Kegan Paul.

ITARD, J.-M.G. (1801; 1972) *Of the First Developments of the Young Savage of Aveyron*, as produced in MALSON, L. (ed.) *Wolf Children and the Problem of Human Nature*, New York, New Left Books.

JAMES, W. (1890) *The Principles of Psychology in Two Volumes*, New York, Holt.

JOFFE, C. (1973) 'Taking young children seriously', in DENZIN, N. (ed.) *Children and Their Caretakers*, NJ, Transaction Books, pp. 101–16.

JOHNSON, J.M. (1975) *Doing Field Research*, New York, Free Press.

KAGAN, J., KEARSHLEY, R. and ZELAZO, P. (1978) *Infancy: Its Place in Human Development*, Cambridge, MA, Harvard University Press.

KAPLAN, J. (1971) *Marihuana: The New Prohibition*, New York, Pocket.

KELLY-BYRNE, D. (1989) *A Child's Play Life: An Ethnographic Study*, New York and London, Teacher's College Press.

KIELHOFNER, G. (1983) 'Rose-colored lenses for clinical practice', in KIELHOFNER, G. (ed.) *Health Through Occupation: Theory and Practice in Occupational Therapy*, Philadelphia, F.A. Davis.

KITSUSE, J.I. (1962) 'Societal reactions to deviant behavior', *Social Problems*, **9**, 3, Winter.

KOHAK, E. (1978) '*Idea and Experience: Edmund's Husserl's Project of Phenomenology*' in Ideas I, Chicago, University of Chicago.

KOHLBERG, L. (1969) 'Stage and sequence: The cognitive developmental approach to socialization', in GOSLIN, D.A. (ed.) *Handbook of Socialization Theory and Research*, Chicago, Rand McNally, pp. 347–480.

KONRAD, G. (1974) *The Caseworker*, New York, Harcourt, Brace, Janovich.

KUPFERBERG, T. (1983) 'Kiddie porn', *High Times*, January.

LABOV, W. (1969) 'The logic of nonstandard English', *Georgetown Monographs on Language and Linguistics*, **22**.

LABOV, W. (1972) 'The logic of nonstandard English', in GIGLIOLI, P.P. (ed.) *Language and Social Context*, Harmondsworth, Penguin.

LAING, R.D. and ESTERSON, A. (1964) *Sanity, Madness and the Family*, New York, Basic Books.

LETKEMANN, P. (1973) *Crime as Work*, Englewood Cliffs, NJ, Prentice-Hall.

LEWIS, M., MACLEAN, W.E., BRYSON-BROCKMANN, W., ARENDT, R., BECK, B., FIDLER, P.S. and BAUMEISTER, A.A. (1984) 'Time series analysis of stereotyped movements: Relationships of body-rocking to cardiac activity', *American Journal of Mental Deficiency*, **89**, 3, pp. 287–94.

LEWIS, M. and ROSENBLUM, R.A. (1975) *Friendship and Peer Relations*, New York, Wiley.

LICKONA, T. (ed.) (1976) *Moral Development and Behavior*, New York, Holt, Rinehart and Winston.

LIEBOW, E. (1967) *Tally's Corner*, Boston, MA, Little, Brown.

LOVELL, K.A. (1959) 'A follow up of some aspects of the work of Piaget and Inhelder on the child's conception of space', *British Journal of Educational Psychology*, **29**, pp. 107–17.

LYMAN, S. and SCOTT, M.B. (1968) 'Accounts', *American Sociological Review*, **33**, 1.

LYMAN, S. and SCOTT, M.B. (1970) *A Sociology of the Absurd*, New York, Appleton-Century-Crofts.

*MACKAY, R.W. (1973) 'Conceptions of children and models of socialization', in DREITZEL, H.P. (ed.) *Recent Sociology No. 5*, New York, Macmillan, pp. 27–43; and revised by the author for Turner, R. (ed.) (1974) *Ethnomethodology*, Harmondsworth, Penguin, pp. 180–93.

MACKAY, R.W. (1974) 'Standardized tests: Objective and objectified measures of "competence"', in CICOUREL, A.V. *et al.* (eds) *Language Use and School Performance*, New York Academic Press.

MALSON, L. (1972) *Wolf Children and the Problem of Human Nature*, New York, New Left Books.

MANDELL, N. (1983) 'Studying children: The field worker's challenge', Unpublished manuscript, Department of Sociology, York University, Toronto [and published as 'The Least-Adult Role in Studying Children', 1988a.]

MANDELL, N. (1984a) 'The research role in observational field work with pre-school children', Paper presented at the meetings of the Eastern Sociological Society, March.

*MANDELL, N. (1984b) 'Children's negotiation of meaning', *Symbolic Interaction*, **7**, Fall, pp. 191–211.

MANDELL, N. (1986) 'Peer interaction in day care settings: Implications for social cognition', in ADLER, P.A. and ADLER, P. (eds) *Sociological Studies of Child Development*, Vol. 1, Greenwich, CT, JAI Press, pp. 55–79.

*Mandell, N. (1988a) 'The least-adult role in studying children', *Journal of Contemporary Ethnography*, **16**, 4, January, pp. 433–67.

MANDELL, N. (1988b) (ed.) *Sociological Studies of Child Development*, Vol. 3, Greenwich CT, JAI Press.

MANDELL, N. (ed.) (1990) *Sociological Studies of Child Development*, Vol. 3, Greenwich CT, JAI Press.

MANIS, J.G. and MELTZER, B.N. (1978) *Symbolic Interaction: A Reader in Social Psychology*, Boston, Allyn and Bacon.

MANNONI, O. (1972) 'Itard and his savage', *New Left Review*, **74**, July/August.

MARKEY, F. (1976) *Imaginative Behavior of Preschool Children*. New York, Arno.

MARKEY, J. (1928) *The Symbolic Process and Its Integration With Children*, New York, Harcourt, Brace.

MARTIN, W. (1976) *The Negotiated Character of the School*, Toronto, MacMillan.

MATZA, D. (1969) *Becoming Deviant*, Englewood Cliffs, NJ, Prentice-Hall.

MAYER, C.L. (1967) 'Relationships of self-concepts and social variables in retarded children', *American Journal of Mental Deficiency*, **72**.

McDERMOTT, J. (ed.) (1973) *The Philosophy of John Dewey, Vol. 2: The Lived Experience*, New York, Putman.

McNEILL, M.C., POLLOWAY, E.A. and SMITH, J.D. (1984) 'Feral and isolated children: Historical review and analysis, *Education and Training of the Mentally Retarded*, **XIX**.

MEAD, G.H. (1959) *The Philosophy of the Present*, MURPHY, A. (ed.) La Salle, Open Court. [First published in 1932.]

MEAD, G.H. (1934) *Mind, Self and Society*, MORRIS, C. (ed.) Chicago, University of Chicago Press.

MEAD, G.H. (1938) *The Philosophy of the Act*, MORRIS, C. (ed.) Chicago, University of Chicago Press.

MEAD, G.H. (1964a) *Selected Writings*, RECK, A. (ed.) Indianapolis, IN, Bobbs-Merrill.

MEAD, G.H. (1964b) *On Social Psychology*, STRAUSS, A. (ed.) Chicago, University of Chicago.

MEAD, G.H. (1982) *The Individual and the Social Self: Unpublished Work of George Herbert Mead*, MILLER, D.L. (ed.) Chicago, University of Chicago.

MEHAN, H. (1971) 'Understanding in educational settings', Unpublished PhD dissertation, University of California, Santa Barbara.

MERLEAU-PONTY, M. (1962) *The Phenomenology of Perception*, (trans. Colin Smith), New York, Humanities Press.

MERLEAU-PONTY, M. (1964) *The Primacy of Perception*, Evanston, IL, Northwestern University Press.

MEYNELL, H. (1971) 'Philosophy and schizophrenia', in *The Journal of the British Society for Phenomenology*, **II**, 2, May, pp. 17–30.

MITROFF, I. (1974) *The Subjective Side of Science*, New York, Elsevier.

MURPHY, L.B. (1937) *Social Behavior and Child Personality*, New York, Columbia University Press.

NEILL, A.S. (1960) *Summerhill*, Hart Publishing; Harmondsworth, Penguin, 1962.

OAKLEY, A. (1980) *Women Confined: Towards a Sociology of Childbirth*, New York, Schocken Books.

*OPIE, I. and OPIE, P. (1959) *The Lore and Language of Schoolchildren*, London, Oxford University Press.

OVERTON, W.F. and REESE, H.N. (1973) 'Models of development: Methodological implications', in NESSELROADE, J.R. and REESE, H.W. (eds) *Life-Span Developmental Psychology: Methodological Issues*, New York, Academic Press.

PAPERT, S. (1980) *Mindstorms*, New York, Basic Books.

PARSONS, T., and BALES, R.F. (1955) *Socialization and Interaction Process*, Free Press.

PARTEN, M.B. (1932) 'Social participation among preschool children', *Journal of Abnormal and Social Psychology*, **27**, pp. 243–69.

PIAGET, J. (1948) *The Moral Judgement of the Child*, NY: Free Press.

PIAGET, J. (1952) *The Origins of Intelligence in the Child*, New York, International Universities Press.

PIAGET, J. (1962) *Play, Dreams and Imitation in Childhood*, New York, Norton.

PIAGET, J. and INHELDER, B. (1969) *The Psychology of the Child*, (trans. H. Weaver), New York, Basic.

PINES, M. (1966) *Revolution in Learning*, Harper and Row.

PITCHER, E.G., and PRELINGER, E. (1963) *Children Tell Stories: An Analysis of Fantasy*, International Universities Press.

PLATO (399 B.C.) (1951) *Phaedo*, (trans. F.J. Church), Indianapolis, Bobbs-Merrill.

PLATO (1956), *Great Dialogues of Plato: The Meno*, (trans. Rouse, W.H.D.) New American Library.

PLUMP, J.H. (1971) 'The great change in children', *Horizon*, **8**, 1.

POLANYI, M. and PROSCH, H. (1975) *Meaning*, Chicago, University of Chicago Press.

PROVENCE, S., NAYLOR, A. and PATTERSON, J. (1977) *The Challenge of Day Care*, New Haven, CT, Yale University Press.

PSATHAS, G. (1976) 'The structure of directions', *Semiotica*, **17**, 2, pp. 111–30.

RECK, A. (1963) *Recent Philosophy: Studies of Ten Representative Thinkers*, New York, Pantheon.

ROBERTSON, I. (1989) *Society: a Brief Introduction*, New York, Worth.

ROSEN, C. (1974) 'The effects of sociodramatic play on problem-solving behavior among culturally disadvantaged preschool children', *Child Development*, **45**, pp. 920–7.

ROTH, D. (1972) 'Children's linguistic performance as a factor in school achievement', Unpublished PhD dissertation, University of California, Santa Barbara.

ROTH, J.A. (1957) 'Ritual and magic in the control of contagion', *American Sociological Review*, **22**, 3, June, pp. 310–4.

ROTH, J.A. (1977) *Health Purifiers and their Enemies*, New York, Prodist.

RUBIN, K.H., MAIONI, T.L. and HORNUNG, M. (1976) 'Free play behaviors in middle and lower class preschoolers: Parten and Piaget revisited', *Child Development*, **47**, pp. 414–9.

SACKS, H. (1972) 'An initial investigation of the usability of conversational data for doing sociology', in SUDNOW, D.N. (ed.) *Studies in Social Interaction*, Free Press.

*SACKS, H. (1972) 'On the analysability of stories by children', in *Directions in Sociol-*

inguistics: *The Ethnography of Commounication*, GUMPERZ, J.J. and HYMES, D. (eds) Basil Blackwell. Originally published by Holt, Rinehart and Winston. Reprinted in TURNER, R. (ed.) *Ethnomethodology*, Middlesex, England, Penguin.

SAMPSON, E.E. (1978) 'Scientific paradigms and social values: Wanted: A scientific revolution', *Journal of Personality and Social Psychology*, **36**, pp. 1332–43.

SCHAFFER, R. (1977) *Mothering*, Cambridge, MA, Harvard University Press.

SCHELER, M. ([1913], 1954) *The Nature of Sympathy*, (trans. Peter Heath), Stark, W. (Introduction), Hamden, CT, Archon Books.

SCHUTZ, A. (1962) 'The problem of social reality', in NATANSON, M. (ed.) *Collected Papers, Vol. 1: The Problem of Social Reality*, The Hague, Martinus Nijhoff.

SCHWARTZMAN, H. (1976) 'The anthropological study of children's play', *Annual Review of Anthropology*, **5**, pp. 289–328.

SCOTT, M.B. and LYMAN, S.M. (1968) 'Account', *American Sociological Review*, **33**, 1, pp. 46–62. Reprinted in LYMAN, S.M. and SCOTT, M.B., *A Sociology of the Absurd*, 1970, Pacific Palisades, CA: Goodyear Publishing Co.

SELMAN, R. (1971) 'Taking another's perspective: Role-taking development in early childhood', *Child Development*, **42**, pp. 1721–34.

SELMAN, R. and BYRNE, D. (1974) 'A structural–developmental analysis of levels of role-taking in middle childhood', *Child Development*, **45**, pp. 803–6.

SIMON, W. and GAGNON, J.H. (1968) 'Children of the drug age', *Saturday Review*, September 21.

SKOLNICK, A. (ed.) (1976) *Rethinking Childhood: Perspectives on Development and Society*, Boston, Little Brown.

SMILANSKY, S. (1968) *The Effects of Sociodramatic Play on Disadvantaged Children*, New York, Wiley.

SPIER, M. (n.d.) 'The child as conversationalist: Some culture contact features of conversational interactions between adults and children', Unpublished.

SPEIER, M. (1976) 'The adult ideological viewpoint in studies of childhood', in SKOLNICK, A. (ed.) *Rethinking Childhood*, Boston, Little Brown, pp. 168–86.

SPIRO, M. (1965) *Children of the Kibbutz*, New York, Schocken.

STERN, D. (1977) *The First Relationship*, Cambridge, MA, Harvard University Press.

STONE, G. (1970) 'The play of little children', in STONE, G. and FARBERMAN, H. (eds), *Social Psychology Through Symbolic Interaction*, Waltham, MA, Ginn, pp. 545–53.

STONE, G. and FARBERMAN, H. (1981) *Social Psychology Through Symbolic Interaction*, 2nd ed., New York, Wiley.

STRAUSS, A.L. (1959) *Mirrors and Masks*, Glencoe, Free Press.

STRAUSS, A.L. (1963) 'The negotiated order', in FRIEDSON, E. (ed.) *The Hospital in Modern Society*, Glencoe, Free Press, pp. 147–69.

STRAUSS, A. (1978) *Negotiations: Varieties, Contexts, Processes and Social Order*, San Francisco, Jossey-Bass.

SYKES, G. and MATZA, D. (1957) 'Techniques of neutralization', *American Sociological Review* **22**, December.

THOMAS, W.I. (1931) *The Unadjusted Girl*, Boston, Little, Brown.

THORNE, B. (1986) 'Girls and boys together but mostly apart: Gender arrangements in elementary schools', in HARTUP, W.W. and RUBIN, Z. (eds) *Relationships and Development*, Hillsdale, NJ, Lawrence Erlbaum, pp. 161–84.

TURIEL, E. (1975) 'The development of social concepts', in DEPALMA, D.J. and FOLEY, J.M. (eds) *Moral Development: Current Theory and Research*, Hillsdale, NJ, Lawrence Erlbaum.

TURNBULL, C.M. (1972) *The Mountain People*, New York, Simon and Schuster.

TURNER, R. (1956) 'Role-taking, role standpoint and reference group behaviour', *American Journal of Sociology*, **61**, January, pp. 316–28.

TURNER, R. (1961) 'Role-taking process versus conformity', *American Journal of Sociology*, January, pp. 316–28.

TURNER, R. (ed.) (1974) *Ethnomethodology*, Harmondsworth, Middlesex, England, Penguin.

VANDER ZANDEN, J.W. (1990) *The Social Experience: An Introduction to Sociology*, 2nd ed., New York, McGraw-Hill.

VON UEXKULL, J. (1934) 'A stroll through the worlds of animals and men' in SCHILLER, C. and LASHLEY, K. (eds), *Instinctive Behavior*, New York, International University.

VYGOTSKY, L.S. ([1927], 1962) *Thought and Language*, Cambridge, MA, MIT Press.

VYGOTSKY, L.S. (1965) *Mind in Society*, Cambridge, MA, MIT Press.

*Waksler, F.C. (1986) 'Studying children: Phenomenological insights', *Human Studies*, Dordrecht, The Netherlands, Martinus Nijhoff, **9**, 1, pp. 71–82.

*WAKSLER, F.C. (1987) 'Dancing when the music is over: A study of deviance in a kindergarten classroom', in ADLER, P.A. and ADLER, P. (eds) *Sociological Studies of Child Development*, Vol. 2, Greenwich, CT, JAI Press, pp. 139–58.

WAX, R. (1979) 'Gender and age in fieldwork and fieldwork education', *Social Problems*, **26**, pp. 509–22.

WAX, M. (1980) 'Paradoxes of "consent" in the practice of field work', *Social Problems*, **27**, pp. 272–83.

WAX, R. (1971) *Doing Field Work: Warnings and Advice*, Chicago, University of Chicago Press.

WEININGER, O. (1979) *Play and Education*, Springfield, IL, Charles C. Thomas.

WILSON, T.P. (1970) 'Normative and interpretative paradigms in sociology', in DOUGLAS, J. (ed.) *Understanding Everyday Life*, Chicago, Aldine.

WOLFENBERGER, W. (1981), 'The extermination of handicapped persons in World War II Germany', *Mental Retardation*, **19**, 1, pp. 1–7.

WRONG, D.H. (1961) 'The oversocialized conception of man in modern society', *American Sociological Review*, **26**, April pp. 183–93.

ZIMMERMAN, D.H. and POLLNER, M. 'The everyday world as a phenomenon', in DOUGLAS, J. (ed.) *Understanding Everyday Life*, Aldine Press (1970).

# Notes on Contributors

*Patricia A. Adler* received her Ph.D. from the University of California, San Diego. An Assistant Professor of Sociology at the University of Colorado, she has written and taught in the areas of deviance, social theory, and the sociology of children. Her publications include *Wheeling and Dealing*, *The Sociology of Financial Markets*, and 'Intense loyalty in organizations'.

*Peter Adler* received his Ph.D. from the University of California, San Diego. He is Associate Professor and Chair of Sociology at the University of Denver. His research interests include social psychology, qualitative methods, and the sociology of sport and leisure. Recent publications include *Membership Roles in Field Research*, 'Everyday life sociology', and 'The glorified self'.

The Adlers edit the *Journal of Contemporary Ethnography* and *Sociological Studies of Child Development*. Their most recent book, *Backboards and Blackboards*, based on a five-year participant observation study of college athletes, will be published in 1991.

*Brigitte Berger* received her Ph.D. from the New School for Social Research, New York. She is Professor of Sociology at Boston University. Her works include *The War of the Family: Capturing the Middle Ground* and *Child Care and Mediating Structure*.

*Peter L. Berger* received his Ph.D. from the New School for Social Research, New York. He is University Professor, Professor of Sociology and of Religion, and Head of The Institute for the Study of Economic Culture at Boston University. His books include *Invitation to Sociology*, *A Rumor of Angels*, and, with Thomas Luckmann, *The Social Construction of Reality*.

*Erica Cavin* received her Bachelor of Science degree in Education from Wheelock College. She has taught in nursery schools and day care centers, has published an article entitled 'Children drawing', and is currently a doctoral candidate in the Department of Sociology at Boston University.

*Mary Constantine Joyce* received her Bachelor of Science degree in Education from Wheelock College. She has taught in a preschool program and is currently the director of a kindergarten and extended day program. She lives in Brookline, Massachusetts with her husband Jay and new baby, Jayson.

*David A. Goode* received his Ph.D. from the University of California at Los Angeles. An Associate Professor of Sociology at the College of Staten Island, New York, he has published numerous phenomenological studies of persons with severe disabilities. He lectures nationally and internationally about social and research policy relating to people with disabilities, specializing in studies of quality of life.

*Robert W. Mackay* received his Ph.D. from the University of California, Santa Barbara. His publications include 'How teachers know: A case of epistemological conflict', 'Children's intellectual rights', and Rebecca Hagey and Robert Mackay, *Signs of Sickness: Sickness of Signs*. His current research interests are in film and the state.

*Nancy Mandell* received her Ph.D. from Northeastern University, Boston, Massachusetts. She is Associate Professor in Sociology at York University, Toronto and Coordinator of the Women's Studies Programme. She is the guest editor of Volume 3 of *Sociological Studies of Child Development*. In addition to her sociological studies of children, she has recently published two books with Ann Duffy, *Few Choices: Women, Work and Family* and *Reconstructing the Canadian Family: Feminist Perspectives*.

*Iona Opie*, folklorist, was the author, with her late husband Peter, of a number of admired works on the folklore of children, including *The Oxford Dictionary of Nursery Rhymes*, *The Oxford Book of Children's Verse*, and *Children's Games in Street and Playground*. With Moira Tatem she has written *A Dictionary of Superstitions*.

*Peter Opie* was engaged in research and authorship with his wife from 1944 until his death in 1982. He was president of the Folklore Society from 1963–64, received the RSA Silver Medal in 1953, the Coote-Lake Medal in 1960 (jointly with Iona Opie), and, like his wife, was awarded an Honorary M.A. from Oxford University in 1962.

*Harvey Sacks* received his LL.B. from Yale Law School in 1959. His association with Harold Garfinkel led him to the University of California, Los Angeles, where he was Acting Assistant Professor of Sociology. He also taught at the University of California at Irvine. His pioneering work in the development of conversational analysis and ethnomethodology was cut short in 1975 by his death in a tragic accident. His published works have recently been supplemented by the publication of his lecture notes.

*Frances Chaput Waksler* received her Ph.D. from Boston University. She is Associate Professor of Sociology at Wheelock College, Boston, Massachusetts. Her publications include Jack D. Douglas and Frances C. Waksler, *The Sociology of Deviance: An Introduction* and a special issue of *Human Studies* devoted to the work of Erving Goffman. Her substantive interests, in addition to the sociology of children, include the sociology of deviance and the sociology of everyday life.

*Norman Waksler* is a freelance author whose work has appeared in various literary magazines and in *Best Short Stories of 1980*. He lives in Cambridge, Massachusetts, with the editor.

# Index

NOTE:
Many entries include information on both children and adults without distinguishing between them.

Attention is called to the entry 'sociological study, suggestions for' as a guide to research projects.